Digital Youth, Innovation, and the Unexpected

This book was made possible by grants from the John D. and Catherine T. MacArthur Foundation in connection with its grant making initiative on Digital Media and Learning. For more information on the initiative visit www.macfound.org.

The John D. and Catherine T. MacArthur Foundation Series on Digital Media and Learning

Digital Youth, Innovation, and the Unexpected

Edited by Tara McPherson

The MIT Press
Cambridge, Massachusetts
London, England

For information about special quantity discounts, please email special_sales@mitpress.mit.edu.

This book was set in Stone sans and Stone serif by Aptara, Inc.

Printed and bound in the United States of America.

Library of Congress Cataloging-in-Publication Data

Digital youth, innovation, and the unexpected / edited by Tara McPherson.
 p. cm.—(The John D. and Catherine T. MacArthur Foundation series on digital media and learning)
 Includes bibliographical references.
 ISBN 978-0-262-13495-8 (hardcover : alk. paper)—ISBN 978-0-262-63359-8 (pbk. : alk. paper)
 1. Technology—Social aspects. 2. Technological innovations. 3. Digital media. 4. Internet and teenagers. I. McPherson, Tara.
T14.5.I5645 2008
600—dc22 2007029786

10 9 8 7 6 5 4 3 2 1

CONTENTS

Foreword

In recent years, digital media and networks have become embedded in our everyday lives, and are part of broad-based changes to how we engage in knowledge production, communication, and creative expression. Unlike the early years in the development of computers and computer-based media, digital media are now *commonplace* and *pervasive*, having been taken up by a wide range of individuals and institutions in all walks of life. Digital media have escaped the boundaries of professional and formal practice, and the academic, governmental, and industry homes that initially fostered their development. Now they have been taken up by diverse populations and non-institutionalized practices, including the peer activities of youth. Although specific forms of technology uptake are highly diverse, a generation is growing up in an era where digital media are part of the taken-for-granted social and cultural fabric of learning, play, and social communication.

In 2005, The John D. and Catherine T. MacArthur Foundation began a new grant-making initiative in the area of digital media and learning. An initial set of exploratory grants in the study of youth practices and the development of digital literacy programs has expanded into a major initiative spanning research, educational reform, and technology development. One component of this effort is the support of this book series. As part of the broader MacArthur Foundation initiative, this series is aimed at timely dissemination of new scholarship, fostering an interdisciplinary conversation, and archiving the best research in this emerging field. Through the course of producing the six initial volumes, the foundation convened a set of meetings to discuss the framing issues for this book series. As a result of these discussions we identified a set of shared commitments and areas of focus. Although we recognize that the terrain is being reshaped even as we seek to identify it, we see these as initial frames for the ongoing work to be put forward by this series.

This book series is founded upon the working hypothesis that those immersed in new digital tools and networks are engaged in an unprecedented exploration of language, games, social interaction, problem solving, and self-directed activity that leads to diverse forms of learning. These diverse forms of learning are reflected in expressions of identity, how individuals express independence and creativity, and in their ability to learn, exercise judgment, and think systematically.

The defining frame for this series is not a particular theoretical or disciplinary approach, nor is it a fixed set of topics. Rather, the series revolves around a constellation of topics investigated from multiple disciplinary and practical frames. The series as a whole looks at the relation between youth, learning, and digital media, but each book or essay might deal with only a subset of this constellation. Erecting strict topical boundaries can exclude some of the most important work in the field. For example, restricting the content of the series only to people of a certain age means artificially reifying an age boundary when the phenomenon demands otherwise. This becomes particularly problematic with new forms of online participation where one important outcome is the mixing of participants of different ages. The same goes for digital media, which are increasingly inseparable from analog and earlier media forms.

In the case of learning, digital media are part of the redefinition and broadening of existing boundaries of practice and our understanding of what learning means. The term *learning* was chosen rather than *education* in order to flag an interest in settings both within and outside the classroom. Many of the more radical challenges to existing learning agendas are happening in domains such as gaming, online networks, and amateur production that usually occur in informal and non-institutional settings. This does not mean we are prejudiced against learning as it happens in the classroom or other formal educational settings. Rather, we hope to initiate a dialog about learning as it spans settings that are more explicitly educational and those that are not.

The series and the MacArthur Foundation initiative respond to certain changes in our media ecology that have important implications for learning. Specifically, these are new forms of media *literacy* and changes in the modes of media *participation*. Digital media are part of a convergence between interactive media (most notably gaming), online networks, and existing media forms. Navigating this media ecology involves a palette of literacies that are being defined through practice but require more scholarly scrutiny before they can be fully incorporated pervasively into educational initiatives. Media literacy involves not only ways of understanding, interpreting, and critiquing media, but also the means for creative and social expression, online search and navigation, and a host of new technical skills. The potential gap in literacies and participation skills creates new challenges for educators who struggle to bridge media engagement inside and outside the classroom.

The shift toward interactive media, peer-to-peer forms of media communication, and many-to-many forms of distribution relate to types of participation that are more bottom-up and driven by the "user" or "consumer" of media. Audiences have always had the opportunity to "talk back" to corporate media or to create their own local media forms. However, the growing dominance of gaming as a media format, the advent of low-cost digital production tools, and online distribution means a much more dynamic range in who participates and how they participate in the production and distribution of media. Gamers expect that media are subject to player control. Add to this the fact that all forms of media are increasingly being contextualized in an online communication ecology where creative production and expression is inseparable from social communication. Finally, new low-cost digital production tools mean that amateur and casual media creators can author, edit, and distribute video and other rich media forms that were once prohibitively expensive to produce and share with others.

We value the term *participation* for the ways in which it draws attention to situated learning theory, social media literacies, and mobilized forms of media engagement. Digital media networks support existing forms of mass media distribution as well as smaller publics and collectivities that might center on peer groups or specialized niche interests. The presence of social communication, professional media, and amateur niche media in shared online spaces introduces a kind of leveling effect, where small media players gain new visibility and the position of previously authoritative media is challenged. The clash between more socially driven or niche publics and the publics defined by professional forms of media is playing out in high-profile battles in domains such as intellectual property law, journalism, entertainment, and government. For our purposes, the questions surrounding knowledge and credibility and young people's use of digital media to circumvent adult authority are particularly salient.

The emerging power shift, where smaller and edge players are gaining more visibility and voice, is particularly important to children and youth. If we look at children and youth through the lens of digital media, we have a population that has been historically subject to a high degree of systematic and institutional control in the kinds of information and social communication to which they have access. This is one reason why the alchemy between youth and digital media has been distinctive; it disrupts the existing set of power relations between adult authority and youth voice. While many studies of children, youth, and media have for decades stressed the status of young people as competent and full social subjects, digital media increasingly insist that we acknowledge this viewpoint. Not only must we see youth as legitimate social and political actors, but we must also recognize them as potential innovators and drivers of new media change.

This does not mean that we are uncritical of youth practices or that we believe that digital media necessarily hold the key to empowerment. Rather, we argue against technological determinism, stressing the need for balanced scholarship that recognizes the importance of our current moment within the context of existing structures and unfolding histories. This means placing contemporary changes within a historical context as well as working to highlight the diversity in the landscape of media and media uptake. Neither youth nor digital media are monolithic categories; documenting how specific youth take up particular forms of media with diverse learning outcomes is critical to this series as a whole. Digital media take the form they do because they are created by existing social and cultural contexts, contexts that are diverse and stratified.

As with earlier shifts in media environments, this current turn toward digital media and networks has been accompanied by fear and panic as well as elevated hopes. This is particularly true of adult perception of children and youth who are at the forefront of experimentation with new media forms, and who mobilize digital media to push back at existing structures of power and authority. While some see "digital kids" as our best hope for the future, others worry that new media are part of a generational rift and a dangerous turn away from existing standards for knowledge, literacy, and civic engagement. Careful, socially engaged, and accessible scholarship is crucial to informing this public debate and related policy decisions. Our need to understand the relation between digital media and learning is urgent because of the scale and the speed of the changes that are afoot. The shape and uses of digital media are still very much in flux, and this book series seeks to be part of the definition of our sociotechnical future.

Mizuko Ito
Cathy Davidson
Henry Jenkins
Carol Lee
Michael Eisenberg
Joanne Weiss
Series Advisors

A Rule Set for the Future

Tara McPherson

University of Southern California School of Cinematic Arts, Division of Critical Studies

[T]hanks to science, the whole world is now aflame. Time and space are practically annihilated: night is turned into day; social life is almost revolutionized, and scores of things which only a few years ago would have been . . . impossible are being accomplished daily.

The stage is being set for a communications revolution . . . there can come into homes and business places audio, video and [other] transmissions that will provide newspapers, mail service, banking and shopping facilities, data from libraries, . . . school curricula and other forms of information too numerous to specify. In short, every home and office will contain a communications center of a breadth and flexibility to influence every aspect of private and community life.

Today in our cities, most learning occurs outside the classroom. The sheer quantity of information conveyed by [the new media] far exceeds the quantity of information conveyed by school instruction and texts. This challenge has destroyed the monopoly of the book as a teaching aid and cracked the very walls of the classroom so suddenly, we're confused, baffled. . . . [M]any teachers naturally view the offerings of the new media as entertainment, rather than education. But this carries no conviction to the student.

Quotes such as these have become quite familiar today. They are so ubiquitous that their sources hardly matter (although we will return to them). We are continually reminded that new digital technologies are transforming the flow of information, our experiences of geography, temporality and sociality, and even the individual's sense of self or identity. If, as adults, we feel anxious about the digital revolution or our own technological prowess, we have also learned that youth will lead the way. Numerous popular books have explored the emergence of the "Net" or "Digital" generation, describing in great detail the media-saturated environments that these young people inhabit.[1]

If such reports sometimes can seem overly optimistic, others assess the rise of the digital native with blanket condemnation, asserting, as Andrew Keen (2006) has, that new forms of youth-based social networking like YouTube or MySpace "are inherently dangerous for the vitality of culture and the arts."[2] All of these popular accounts tend toward hyperbole, making it harder to understand the complexity of the moment we are in. This volume identifies core issues concerning how young people's use of digital media may lead to various innovations and unexpected outcomes, including a range of unintended learning experiences and unanticipated social situations. While such outcomes might typically be seen as "positive" or "negative," our investigations push beyond simple accounts of digital media and learning as either utopian or dystopian in order to explore specific digital practices with an eye attuned to larger issues of history, policy, and possibility.

The essays collected here also examine how youth can function as drivers for technological change while simultaneously recognizing that technologies are embedded in larger social systems, including the family, schools, commercial culture, and peer groups. A broad range of topics are taken up, including issues of access and equity; of media panics and cultural anxieties; of citizenship, consumerism, and labor; of policy, privacy and IP; of new modes of media literacy and learning; and of shifting notions of the public/private divide.

The authors brought together in this volume have worked together over the last year under the auspices of the MacArthur Initiative in Digital Media and Learning, but they come from a variety of academic backgrounds, methodologies, and institutional settings. Early in the process of creating this book and as a way of bridging different scholarly approaches and interests, the authors and I mapped out a series of questions that we would collectively explore:

- What's new about "new" technologies? What's not? What is specific to these emergent media? What continuities and discontinuities are there, and why do they matter?

- What cultural fears, hopes, or anxieties do emergent technologies animate, provoke, or otherwise call into being? How do these emotional valences link up with (or not) earlier moments of rapid technological change? In other words, how might we historicize our contemporary moment of technological development?

- How does technological change happen? That is, how do users innovate in unexpected ways that reconfigure technologies to act as drivers for change, and create informal modes of learning? How are youth functioning as early adopters? How do larger cultural, economic, historical, and social forces shape or curtail innovation and impede or facilitate learning?

- How can we best discern and even foster what is liberating, empowering, or enlivening about today's forms of participatory networked culture? Are there recommendations we might make for policy, curriculum, or infrastructure? How do we balance overviews and systemic analyses with textured readings of specific examples?

These are big questions, and, not surprisingly, in investigating them, we haven't as a group reached a neat and tidy conclusion. This volume does not offer a unified perspective on the possible stakes, outcomes, and innovations we might expect of the digital era, nor does it offer a single image or description of the "digital native," although several fine-grained portraits do emerge. Nonetheless, each author agrees that we inhabit a moment of both technological risk and possibility, especially vis-à-vis young people and modes of learning. Drawing from these ten essays, related research, and the questions outlined above, I here offer six maxims to guide future research and inquiry into the questions motivating this study. They form a kind of flexible rule set for investigations into the innovative uses and unexpected outcomes now emerging or soon anticipated from young people's engagements with digital media.

Before delineating this rule set and charting its relationship to the essays in this volume, I first reflect on the title *Digital Youth, Innovation, and the Unexpected*. Other books in this series are organized around ongoing research topics in digital media ("Credibility," "Civic Engagement," even "Games"), or, around larger, interdisciplinary themes of academic inquiry ("Identity," "Race"), all with their own supporting bodies of literature. *Digital Youth, Innovation, and the Unexpected* seems much more diffuse. Indeed, taken together, the several essays included here touch upon all of the topics explored in the other five MacArthur volumes. While what is meant by "the unexpected" may seem fairly obvious, the word "innovation" is perhaps less clear. It is worth taking some time to unpack this term in relation to this volume's motivating questions and larger goals.

Understanding Innovation: Some Academic Precedents

Innovation is very much a buzzword in contemporary U.S. culture. National and corporate leaders worry that without innovation, we will lose our national "edge" and be ill prepared to participate in (if not lead) emergent knowledge economies. Many look to new technologies and digital media as platforms for learning vital skill sets for success in this challenging new environment. A quick Google search for the words "corporate" and "innovation" returns over 118 million results. Some of these sites lead to blogs that survey trends and best practices. Many others lead to a growing category of businesses that perform as a kind of "innovation service industry" for corporations, deploying various "cutting-edge" technologies and tools to spur innovation (and, thus, financial success and competitiveness) in business settings. Such tools include "InnovationStyles," "a web-based assessment, feedback, and coaching system . . . a practical, proven resource to help you generate innovative solutions to work challenges, foster high levels of innovative teamwork, and develop an organization-wide culture for innovation."[3] The product Web site affirms that the application has been adopted by a wide variety of large corporations, including ATT, IBM, Kraft, P&G, DuPont, Motorola, and Schwab.

These approaches and products often figure innovation in fairly functionalist ways, imagining technology as a quick fix that will fuel creativity, learning, and imagination. Such functionalist conceptions of innovation are, of course, tightly bound up with various historical discourses about America's uniqueness or ingenuity, that is, with the popular founding myths of the United States as a special hotbed of pioneering and inventive individuals. They bring together a sense of American exceptionalism with a belief that simply using the right tools will get the job done. Such attitudes also extend to the "business" of education, where firms like Pearson reap tidy profits by selling large and expensive software systems to cash-strapped school districts. For instance, their "SuccessMaker® Enterprise" is described as "a learning environment that offers a powerful combination of management system, assessment, and curriculum resources," while "KnowledgeBox seamlessly delivers a wealth of instructional media designed specifically to help meet the varied needs of learners in 21st Century classrooms."[4]

Scholars have questioned the value of such large technology systems for true innovation in the classroom, observing that they often function as little more than glorified workbooks and promote "unimaginative and deeply traditional methods of learning."[5] Likewise, at the university level, some professors have challenged the functionalist ideas at the core of many technology-driven distance-learning initiatives.[6] These critiques dispute the assertion that innovation (or valuable learning) is a simple consequence or function of particular technologies. They also highlight an important observation about innovation: it is unlikely to be easily standardized and packaged. Apart from these functionalist approaches, how else might we understand innovation?

During the past three to four decades, other perspectives on innovation have emerged from within the university. For instance, the field loosely known as Science and Technology Studies (STS) has investigated both technology and innovation in terms of complex social dynamics, moving away from notions of invention or discovery toward explorations of negotiation and process. Early STS researchers applied sociological methods to studying science and argued that scientific ideas should be seen as socially constructed forms of knowledge (rather than as objective facts that are simply "discovered"). Put differently, science came to be understood as an interpretative process that was similar to other everyday modes of thinking and analysis. Scientific knowledge could not be separated from larger social and cultural systems; thus, science was (at least partially) constructed by culture and history. By the early 1980s, these new methodologies were also being used to study technology and to understand innovation.[7] Rather than defining a technology strictly by its function and form, that is, as a closed system, those in the emerging field of STS focused on technologies as being socially and culturally constructed.

Today, there are several STS departments or programs that are well established in universities. STS was in its origins an interdisciplinary field, and, like other such disciplines, there are many variations and debates within it. It is also a discipline that emerged in parallel with other changes in the university in the 1960s and 1970s as various political and social movements led scholars to question modernist or universal claims to knowledge. While STS research sometimes seemed stuck in simply proving that technology or science was socially constructed, some STS researchers instead focused on particular examples of the process of innovation or design while also teasing out larger, more general principles.[8] Such insights often zeroed in on the *use* of technology as much as on its development, pushing beyond the functionalist understandings of technology and innovation that still drive research in many engineering schools (and in many corporate products aimed at packaging and selling "innovation" and "learning" via the right tool or software program).

If STS investigates technology by keeping the focus squarely on social and cultural systems, Actor-Network Theory (ANT) proposes a simultaneous analysis of the material (i.e., of things) as well as the social. It can be seen as a "material-semiotic" approach that looks at the relationship between things and concepts, examining networks and processes. Bruno Latour formulated some of the central principles of ANT as a way of avoiding dualisms which tended to privilege either nature (scientific realism) or culture (some variations of STS). The larger intent of ANT is to understand humans and nonhumans as equal actors situated within networks that are formed and sustained in order to achieve particular goals, including technology design (e.g., building a car) and information management (e.g., running a stock brokerage or a school). ANT can be located as an offshoot of theories of the social construction of knowledge and clearly relates to several approaches in poststructural theory, including the work of French philosophers Gilles Deleuze and Michel Foucault.[9] STS and ANT are often framed as competing paradigms, but they converge in their critique of notions of scientific realism or objectivity.[10]

While these various methodologies have been in use for decades and might thus be seen as "old news," the recent surge of interest in forms of networked computing (an interest evidenced by the very series in which this book is located) also points toward a new relevance for these methodologies, particularly in an era in which public conversations about technology tend to shuttle back and forth between wildly utopian and deeply pessimistic strands that each view technology as the direct cause of societal changes, be they good or bad. Methods of scholarship developed in the past few decades afford us vibrant models for thinking about technology *in context* and for understanding innovative or unexpected uses of digital media. If STS can be accused of a certain social determinism and a narrow focus on the micro, and ANT can be guilty of a kind of technological determinism, each offers valuable insights into how people make meaning from (and are also remade by) their multiple engagements with diverse digital technologies.

Not all authors in this volume explicitly situate themselves vis-à-vis these disciplinary traditions, although Christian Sandvig, Henry Lowood, and Steve Anderson and Anne Balsamo do to differing degrees. Still, you might say that this approach influences all the work in this volume, particularly in a shared rejection of functionalist approaches and in a sustained focus on the multiple contexts in which technologies are always embedded. This turn to context reflects these disciplines' own histories as part of a broader intellectual movement that tested universal claims to knowledge across the fields of the humanities, education, media studies, and the qualitative social sciences. I will return to the question of methodology at this essay's close, but, for now, suffice it to say that grand, one-size-fits-all theories are probably of little use in helping us assess the potential outcomes and affordances of the digital era. Rather than attempting to produce a kind of universal manual for innovation, the authors brought together here seek to understand in some detail several examples of innovation and learning that are now unfolding in the digital era. Such finely grained detail may indeed help us to understand ways to foster innovation and design new technologies for learning. Collectively, they encourage us to recognize that innovation as a cultural phenomenon often happens in unexpected places (as does learning) and produces unanticipated outcomes. They remind us to ask who innovation serves and how we might best reap its benefits for broader visions of social equity and justice. And, finally, they underscore that the term "innovation" is value laden and historically complex.

In what follows, I weave together many of the insights offered across the individual essays at hand in order to produce a kind of conceptual rule set for future investigations into the consequences and possibilities of learning in the era of digital media. This rule set is composed of six rules or maxims that dovetail with the sociocultural approaches favored by STS researchers, while also stressing certain larger frameworks that should guide our examinations of digital technologies and learning.

Rule One: Remember History

Undoubtedly there are "origin stories" other than STS or ANT from which we might have begun an investigation of the innovative uses of digital technologies, but these methodologies usefully underscore that innovation and its outcomes are not unique properties born of the digital era. Many of the richest studies emerging from these and related traditions cast an eye to history in order to better understand the present. Such an attitude is in woefully short supply in much of the contemporary rhetoric about digital technologies. This "present-ism" equally inflects commercial and academic settings and lends itself to grand proclamations about how children, learning, and society are all "new" or "different" today because of the rapid uptake of technology. Such language is very much in evidence in the quotes that opened this essay. Each draws upon the language of revolution and rapid, fundamental change to propose that we inhabit a new era like none we have previously experienced: "social life is almost revolutionized," "the whole world is aflame," "the stage is . . . set for a communications revolution," "most learning occurs outside the classroom . . . . this challenge has destroyed the monopoly of the book." Claims like these make it difficult to draw connections across different moments of technological change.

The limits of such language (and the obfuscating work it does) become more easily apparent when the sources of these quotations are revealed. The first is from a speech to the American Association for the Advancement of Science by retiring president T. C. Mendenhall. The year is 1890, and he celebrates the advances wrought by electricity. The second excerpt derives from the article, "The Wired Nation," published not in 1995 but in 1970 in *Nation*.

The technology it rhapsodizes is cable television. The final excerpt comes from Marshall McLuhan's 1957 essay "Classroom without Walls,"[11] a reflection on learning in the (early) age of television. Well known as a kind of "futurist" in his own era (one resuscitated by *Wired* magazine in the 1990s as their patron saint), McLuhan's views have been frequently criticized for a determinist or functionalist stance toward technology that paid scant attention to social or historical context.[12]

Recent historians of technology, many working explicitly or implicitly within STS traditions, have illustrated the uncanny similarities across various moments of technological "progress." Drawing on a rich array of primary materials (including President Mendenhall's speech), Carolyn Marvin's *When Old Technologies Were New* tracks the disruptions to social order that both electricity and the telephone unfurled while also paying careful attention to the many ways through which existing cultural forces, including class, gender, and nationalism, simultaneously impacted what these once-new technologies might become.[13] In *Selling the Air*, Tom Streeter reminds us that the largest, most active groups of innovators in technological communications weren't scientists or corporations, but everyday citizens and amateur system operators.[14] He examines a world of network enthusiasts who imagined an essentially free and democratic system of bottom-up, participatory culture and two-way exchange. While this might sound like a tale lifted from the hacker boys of the 1990s or from the creators of YouTube, Streeter is actually describing early ham radio enthusiasts almost 100 years ago. He argues that such hobbyists helped create modern broadcasting but also observes that the one-to-many world of commercial radio and TV that developed in their wake bore little resemblance to the open, plural networks imagined by these youthful innovators. His research again illustrates that "new" technologies always enter into powerful, preexisting social systems, networks of meaning and privilege that can serve to circumscribe how technologies develop and delimit whom they best serve. It also highlights that youth are often early adopters of new technologies, deploying emerging devices and platforms in ways that can outstrip the expectations of engineers and parents. More recently, David Edgerton's *The Shock of the Old: Technology and Global History Since 1900* shifts our attention to "a whole invisible world of technologies," arguing for the study of use and maintenance rather than of invention and creation and for an examination of everyday technologies, from the condom to corrugated metal.[15] He convincingly illustrates that old technologies don't just simply disappear: rather, they are adapted and continue, often in the service of warfare and narrow nationalisms. It is crucial that we study such remediations if we are to understand how technologies morph and change.[16]

To underscore the importance of locating through-lines and feedback loops between the present and the past, this volume begins with a section explicitly focused on historical processes of technological development and innovation. Ellen Seiter strikes a productive historical analogy, comparing earlier attitudes about musical education and piano playing with our contemporary focus on computers and learning. Drawing on French sociologist Pierre Bourdieu's categories of economic, cultural, and social capital, she details the various ways in which both musical education and computer education implicitly favor the middle and upper classes.[17] Both musical and computer literacy are more easily achieved when youth have the ability to practice informally at home on new or well-tuned equipment and have social networks in place to support their learning. She convincingly argues that such opportunities will be hard to come by for poor youth in crowded schools and dense urban neighborhoods, illustrating the complex issues at play in a notion like "access."

Justine Cassell and Meg Cramer turn to history to nuance present-day fears that the internet is a welcoming playground for sexual predators and pedophiles. The authors first note that single-offender crimes against girls have actually dropped since 1994, concurrent with the rise of the internet, and then question why popular discourse suggests otherwise. By looking at similar scares during earlier moments of emerging technologies, Cassell and Cramer frame today's fears as a widespread moral panic that covers over social anxieties about "girls as power users of technology." As they argue, such moral panics obscure the positive benefits to girls of internet use and repress the reality that acquaintances and relatives pose a much greater assault risk to youth than do strangers. We might additionally see such panics as convenient smoke screens that blind parents and society to larger systemic issues that oppress youth: increasing poverty, declining public infrastructures, and rampant commercialism (see also Frechette[18]). Christian Sandvig's essay also takes a comparative historical approach, mapping the histories of wireless technology and youthful innovation in both the digital and the analog eras. Through a sustained investigation of both "wardrivers" (young people who charted early Wi-Fi signals around 2005) and youthful adopters of analog wireless circa 1920, Sandvig maintains that happy tales of youthful play and innovation occurred regularly throughout the past 100 years. Such stories paint encouraging portraits of participatory culture and youth-driven change that neatly line up with traditional attitudes about American ingenuity. They can blind us to other hard realities such as this: most technology innovators come from very privileged worlds.

Each of these three essays engages the hopes and anxieties specific technologies animate with regard to youth, from dreams of high-tech jobs to anxieties about outside influences entering the home. Having noted several parallels across earlier moments of technological change and the present, the temptation might be to rest smug in the knowledge that "we've seen this all before," but that is not my point in focusing on these historical examples. If we have seen tales of the youthful inventor more than once in the past and grow suspicious of them, we are also tired of old tales of moral panic, particularly when they work to demonize girls or underprivileged youth. Obviously, we cannot discern every unintended consequence, risk, or possibility from the outset or through recourse to the past. We can, however, turn to history to better detect our own blind spots, to predict stumbling blocks, or to look for patterns of lost or realized opportunity. This embrace of the historical extends beyond these opening essays through other sections of the volume. Historical methods are not engaged via a spirit of negativity but, rather, as a ground for learning and for calculating best guesses for the future.

Rule Two: Consider Context

If history can also help us discern the continuities that persist across time, we need also be mindful of the differences a technology might make. While we've seen the limits of generalized proclamations about the newness of "new" technologies, a careful attention to context can help us better assess what social practices and technological forms *are* changing. Across the essays in this book, a doubled stance emerges in relation to technology: technology is understood to be socially constitutive and simultaneously to be socially constitutive, that is, technology is both shaped by history and sociocultural realities, and is also a shaper of those realities and of possible futures. Such a doubled understanding of technology is consistent with STS methodologies and also calls to mind one of the founding works of the cultural studies of media, Raymond Williams' *Television: Technology and Cultural Form*.[19]

Williams rejected "technological determinism" as an attitude that depends "on the isolation of technology" from history, social forces, and use, in short, from any context. He dismisses the popular notion that "new technologies are discovered . . . which then sets the course for social change and progress" (13–14). Williams' book astutely figures television as a complex nexus of cultural, technological, and historical processes, at once an intention and an effect of a particular social order, and it has been extremely influential in cultural and media studies. It argues against positivist studies in the social sciences and sets aside simplistic ideas of media "effects." The work also famously decries Marshall McLuhan's theories of electronic media, lambasting his formalist methods in which "the media are never really seen as practices" and "are in effect desocialized."[20] Williams' criticisms further suggest that McLuhan's writing is giving the commercial industries just what they want.

Such critiques of McLuhan are fairly easily raised, particularly given his movement toward increasingly "non-academic styles" of writing, his proclamation that the medium is the message/massage, and his tendency to slide into formalist assessments of different types of "hot" and "cold" media. These criticisms shift our focus away from the giddier aspects of McLuhan's prose (statements like "electric technology is reshaping and restructuring . . . every aspect of our personal life" or "minority groups can no longer be contained-ignored") toward concrete material realities. The debate between McLuhan and Williams is frequently framed as a debate between determinism and formalism on the one hand and more culturally situated forms of analysis on the other. The former privileges medium and form, while the latter privileges content and context. However, in the past decade, concurrent with *Wired* magazine's reclaiming of McLuhan, some scholars have begun to parse this debate a bit differently and to argue that McLuhan's perspective is "intersubjective" rather than simply determinist.[21] One strength of McLuhan's writing, beyond its precise attention to the specific properties of a given medium, is its focus on the role of various media in shaping our senses and on the perceptual qualities of media. In *Understanding Media*, he sees media forms as an extension of both the psychic and social complex.[22]

There are interesting parallels in the debates between Williams and McLuhan and those between STS and ANT noted above. Williams and many STS traditions can be seen to foreground the social at the expense of an appreciation of the cognitive or esthetic, while McLuhan and some variations of ANT tend to privilege networks and specific media to the exclusion of social and economic structures. There are useful elements to be gleaned from both sides in these debates. In understanding emergent forms of networked media, we need specific formal, esthetic, and material investigations of individual devices, platforms, and practices that simultaneously engage with social contexts. Put differently, we need to understand the specific mechanisms deployed by and the affective or emotional registers activated by our embodied engagements with digital technologies, while also being mindful of cultural context. Simply to argue that technology is, of course, not determinate and is always situated (as STS and cultural studies have taught many of us to do) is also to sometimes miss an opportunity to explore the many ways in which our devices *do* construct us. In an age of "intelligent agents" and everyday engagements with various machine-based intelligences, we should take seriously the notion that our perceptual and cognitive facilities may be shifting, even as we understand that these shifts are part and parcel of larger cultural forces.

From different disciplinary traditions, various essays in this volume grapple with such debates, offering precise case studies that link investigations of particular computing technologies to larger social contexts. For instance, Paula Hooper examines both the technological affordances of programmable media for learning as well as the important role played by cultural context when such media are introduced into the classroom. Her examination of projects created in the *Turtle* programming language by young girls in an African-centric charter school brings together constructionist ideas (i.e., Seymour Papert's work on the computer as an object to think with[23]) and educational theories on the cultural nature of learning. Her work resonates with the work of Ron Eglash,[24] who has designed several "culturally situated design tools" to teach STEM concepts.[25] Such tools interlace technology and cultural relevance. Instead of imagining that teaching tools are neutral and can be easily adapted to "culturally aware" content, Eglash favors an "ethnocomputing" approach that stresses interconnections between the "universal" and the "local," and between technology and context. Culture becomes part of design, rather than something that gets tacked on after a tool is "finished." Henry Lowood's detailed consideration of machinima—an unexpected development in which video game players use game technologies to make movies—likewise weaves together considerations of what a particular technology makes possible with a spirited examination of specific communities of practice and performance. He argues that machinima developed from a collision of player practices and certain technological features of the game engines built for first person shooter games like *Doom*.

Lowood and Hooper are exploring the use of technology in vastly different communities. A focus on *technology in context* helps each to detail very precise technological affordances. Taken together, their essays remind us, first, that many differences exist *among* young people in terms of technological fluency and access and, second, that youth and adults within a community (like the machinima culture) may share certain dispositions or cultural signposts. While middle-class U.S. parents and youth may experience the internet and digital technologies in very different ways, reinforcing the idea of a digital generation gap, these splits or fissures seem less severe when differences between children across economic, racial, or national lines are explored (see also Buckingham). Finally, in both Lowood and Hooper's work, users merge digital technologies together with commercial media narratives in the context of specific communities, in effect fusing and remaking both the narrative and the tool. From early scrap-booking practices in Studio-era Hollywood to the audio mix tapes of the 1970s to the fan fiction and textual poaching explored by cultural studies researchers, we know that viewers and readers have long "re-mixed" or poached commercial culture.[26] But the practices and engagements that Lowood and Hooper are describing might signal more than just a difference in scale or quantity (i.e., more people are now re-mixing.) It is possible that deep interaction with digital forms encourages new flexible models of thinking and doing that in turn facilitate emergent ways of being and learning.

Rule Three: Make the Future (Hands-On)

I recently spent several hours trapped in an airport after bad weather grounded outgoing planes. As I waited in line to schedule a new flight, I overheard a young boy in front of me ask his mother, "Mom, why can't we just do this trip over." When she asked him what he meant, he replied, "You know, like when I play Mario on my Nintendo. I'd like to play this part of our trip over again." While we could write off such a comment as wishful or magical thinking or as indicative of the cognitive development of a five-year-old, we might also read it as illustrative of the ways in which sustained engagements with digital technologies might generate new dispositions toward process and agency. After all, one of the key affordances of digital technologies is the capacity to iterate and revise, an aspect of the mutability and variability many have noted as core aspects of computing technology.[27] Throughout this volume and in earlier research, scholars have delineated some of the particular pleasures and possibilities of experimenting with digital media technologies. These include a privileging of process over product, a sensation of mobility and control, a feeling of networked sociality, a heightened awareness of audience, learning by doing or tinkering, and an impression of mutability and transformation.[28] While each of these affordances might be found in earlier technological forms (and some might be more imagined than real), scholars from diverse disciplines maintain that computational media engage users in qualitatively different ways, even as they refract and reflect earlier technologies and media forms. Katherine Hayles and others have suggested that we now understand our very selves to be posthuman—interwoven with information or data.[29]

To focus on just one of the properties outlined above, we might discuss the transformative potential digital media tend to signal. There's a heady feeling of possibility laced through our engagements with computing technology: digital code is malleable and subject to manipulation, at levels both accessible and inaccessible to the average user. In a language as simple as HTML, changing the descriptor "FFFFFF" to "FF6600" on a lengthy block of code seemingly transforms the page from a predictable white to a bold orange. A comment posted by a student to a blog seems to appear almost instantly in a public forum. Objects a teen builds on his or her home computer change the landscape of a dynamic virtual community shared by thousands of users. Thus, digital technologies in their very form seem to offer up valuable possibilities for learning by doing, and numerous educators have related success stories and positive outcomes from engaging students with rich, digital media, particularly when these technologies are designed and deployed with a well-honed respect for context. Others have commented on different types of informal learning that seem to very much characterize youth's engagement with digital media.[30] In this volume, both Sandvig and Lowood illustrate various kinds of learning that youth undertake outside of formal educational settings as they actively engage with *making* digital objects, processes of learning that are often supported by peer-to-peer communities.

In her contribution to our project, Sarita Yardi offers a case study that examines the potential for youthful innovations with technology to foster both informal and formal modes of learning. The work draws from a larger investigation of a student-designed Internet Relay Chat (IRC) that was quickly taken up by graduate students in an information school at a prestigious public university. Yardi probes the ways in which this forum functioned as a kind of hybrid "third space" for student community and as an active "backchannel" within many classrooms, as students chatted together during class meetings. Based on this example, she hypothesizes that backchannels can be designed that support "active, collaborative, and engaged knowledge production" within educational environments, while also offering users the opportunity to form friendships and to experiment with identities. Much like Paula Hooper, she ends her essay by offering a series of possible protocols that might be considered when designing such forums; these include the need to "teach the teachers" and to create developmentally appropriate environments. While we want to avoid a tendency to fetishize the latest technological trend (after all, we've cycled rapidly from VR to MUDs to Web sites to games to blogs to cell phones and back to virtual worlds in just the last decade!), studies like these highlight the affordances of situated technologies for learning.

Of course, "learning by doing" or "project-based pedagogy" are not unique to the era of networked computing. Such approaches share common terrain with various inflections of constructivism, a theory of learning and childhood development emerging from Jean Piaget's and Jerome Bruner's work.[31] These theories were taken in more social directions by

Lev Vygotsky,[32] concurrent with broader movements to foreground the social construction of knowledge during the second half of the twentieth century, including cultural studies and STS. As Paula Hooper notes, Seymour Papert applied constructivist paradigms to learning with and through computing, inventing the Logo programming language in 1967 as a way to support active learning.[33] Digitally based approaches to "learning by doing" both resonate with other constructivist ideas and also suggest that computational media afford different and unique experiences to learners (such as visualization, complex simulation, and algorithmic thinking), differences that matter. In a project I am currently undertaking with local charter elementary schools in Los Angeles, many of the older staff have been engaged with constructivist pedagogy for decades. They are often amused by the lack of historical perspective of many of the "new" theories of digitally enhanced learning, but they are simultaneously excited by the possibility of renewing broad interest in project- or problem-based learning through digital media. In particular, they hope that an intertwined focus on experiential learning and digital media will offer a viable alternative to today's rigid focus on standardized testing and to inflexible curricula in American public schools.

Even as they attempt to build new schools and new paradigms at the edges of mainstream education, they are realistic and practical, worrying about many of the issues Ellen Seiter has identified as obstacles to technology-mediated learning.[34] These obstacles include lack of access to technologies, issues of maintenance and teacher training, and the very fact that such experimental campuses drain resources from other mainstream public schools. As Seiter and Sandvig suggest, the richest hands-on opportunities for making and doing are most easily available to the richest in society. Histories of earlier media technologies should also give us pause, for, as we have seen, many of these technologies began as open or many-to-many networks. Furthermore, while much hype surrounds Web 2.0 and its capacity to turn consumers into producers, some recent studies suggest that very few visitors to these sites are actually creating media. As of April 2007, only 0.16 percent of visitors to YouTube are uploading media (down from 0.5 percent in July, 2006); the rest are just watching.[35] Similar low rates of participation occur on other sites like Flickr. While details of this study might be called into question (for instance, how would one categorize viewers who tag content rather than create it?), the larger concern remains, as do worries that interaction with templated formats like blogs might achieve few of the cognitive benefits derived from working with rich computational media.[36]

Finally, should we worry that the most engaging forms of self-expression for youth—forms that animate their creative expression much more than the things they are learning at school—are often tightly wedded to commercial enterprises and consumer products? One response would simply be to hope that the skill sets and dispositions born of interacting in ✓ and with these multimodal environments will translate into other realms. Certainly, several scholars have made such arguments.[37] But others (including many in this volume) have alternately argued that, left solely to commercial forces, such gains will be very uneven in their distribution, likely broadening the "participation gap" and skilling children in forms of consumption rather than in forms of citizenship.[38] If, as claimed above, digital media inspire possibility at least partially through their ability to model transformation, transformation has long been promised by earlier forms of consumer culture. Both Marsha Kinder and Susan Willis have alerted us to the often-illusory status of promises of transformation in children's media products.[39] As Willis notes in relation to transforming toys, there is always the risk "that everything transforms but nothing changes." She describes toys that "weld transformation to consumption" and ascribes the fascination with transforming toys to a "utopian yearning for change, which the toys themselves then manage and control."[40] In a recent article in *Games and Culture* that resonates with Lowood's examination of the performative aspects of machinima communities in this volume, Mike Molesworth and Janice Denegri-Kent strike an optimistic note about the near-constant modes of consumption encouraged in many digital worlds (from games to *Second Life*). They argue that the fantasy shopping that so many digital products promote might lead to a "renegotiation, subtle, or dramatic, of consumption itself."[41] Whether or not this will prove true, we also need to entertain the risks inherent in what appears to be an increasing commercialization of digital media aimed at youth. Given the mergers of media and technology corporations and the increasing commercialization of even bottom-up participatory Web sites, there is no guarantee that all children and young people will get to be media makers in any sustained sense. Many of us who work with children and digital media across a range of environments have seen youthful imaginations fired by engagements with the digital (see Evans, Kafai, Hartley),[42] but we would be negligent to rest content that these sparks will themselves ignite deep social changes or sustain open democratic culture. Those outcomes will require a bigger vision and ongoing efforts to create a broader participatory culture.

Rule Four: Broaden Participation

In his study of wireless hobbyists, Christian Sandvig points out that, rather than "renegotiating consumption" or corporate practices, these youthful early adopters aspired instead to become industry insiders. Several achieved this goal, largely because they already inhabited "an overwhelmingly privileged world." His accounts of the controversy that erupted when two "wardrivers" sold datasets created by a broad peer-to-peer community to Microsoft call to mind recent controversies about the purchase of YouTube by Google and MySpace by News Corp. These and similar sites have been heralded as triumphs of participatory computing and the ascendancy of the "prosumer" by a wide variety of commentators from both corporate and academic worlds. Although countless users helped to create these sites, filling them with content, their efforts were later sold without their consent to the highest bidder. Following Michael Hardt, Trevor Scholz has described these efforts as a "new kind of 'immaterial labor'" whose products are not material goods, but rather feelings of ease and community.[43] Users generate content and reap such feelings, while "sites like YouTube drive more and more people to [a] very small number of sites."[44] For Scholz and others, networked sociality has become a product, and the labor of the many (particularly of youth) fuels the wealth of the few. Nicholas Carr has labeled this practice "sharecropping the long tail," and calls it "the most interesting, *and unsettling*, economic phenomenon the Internet has produced" (emphasis added).[45] Others have succinctly outlined the specific economies of Web 2.0 sites:

Web 2.0 is Internet Investment Boom 2.0. Web 2.0 is a business model; it means private capture of community-created value. No one denies that the technology of sites like YouTube, for instance, is trivial. . . . The real value of YouTube is not created by the developers of the site, but rather it is created by the people who upload videos to the site. . . . Private appropriation of community-created value is a betrayal of the promise of sharing technology and free cooperation.[46]

We might extend these examples beyond "community-created" Web sites. In the new networked economy, "regular" readers help fill the databases of Amazon.com by freely posting their book or movie reviews, and avid video game players help fuel corporate capital by posting homegrown game add-ons to corporate sites without compensation. One could argue that such participation largely works in the service of corporations, seamlessly incorporating users into the forces of commercialization.[47] Thus, those writing free code for game companies are so effectively invested that they don't even mind that they won't get paid. If these consumer-fans are now participating more fully in media culture and have more bargaining power, what *exactly* are they participating in and bargaining for? This is not simply to revert to familiar arguments that commercial culture dupes its viewers, making them complicit in their oppression. Rather, it is meant to suggest that the transformative potentials of digital media do not just figure either the self or the world as malleable and open to (potentially positive) change: they also figure the self and the world as commodities for sale. This is an emergent digital outcome that deserves more attention.

In acquiring the skills of multimodal production youth may, on the one hand, be equipping themselves to better function in the emerging networked economies (although Seiter reminds us that access to these skill sets is very uneven: low-income youth are more likely to be "trained" than "empowered"). But shouldn't we also consider, on the other hand, that these market economies may not, in and of their own accord, promote or sustain the most compelling aspects of these environments? And, further, might these very skill sets increasingly lead youth to think of community and social space as spaces that are inherently commercialized and part of the market, as Sandvig and Scholz suggest? How might we hold on to a sense of the public (and the public good) when networks are exclusively routed through market spaces and the most engaging forms of identity making are those offered up in commercial venues? What role might libraries, schools, electronic commons, and other places have in creating public environments where youth might create, explore, and connect in ways that don't always circulate back into markets? What spaces and experiences might we provide that allow youth to think of themselves as citizens as much as consumers?

These are pressing ethical and social questions: we need to create structures and supports—from hands-on tools to open peer-to-peer systems to curricula—that mobilize the gains in imagination, creativity, and hope that our interactions with mutable, variable technologies animate. We need to study and foster the excitement and engagement we palpably note when children engage digital media, but we need to do more than that. We also need to "cultivate" and "grow" this excitement in very particular directions with a mind to ethical and socially just outcomes, lest it only be harvested for corporate profit. In the context of the larger assaults on civil liberties and rights that unfold around us daily or in the shadow of the pressing health and hunger crises affecting the world at large, tinkering with technology may seem very much a privilege of the few, a glossy 3D and escapist fantasy through which to avoid the messier, physical world around us. Is there a way to maximize the transfer value of the participation skills convergence culture appears to be inculcating?

It is possible that this participatory mode of popular culture will organically spawn a greater push for participation in democracy and public life, but, as we've often been reminded, earlier moments of open, democratic media have been shut down through commercial centralization. From a very different disciplinary base the Italian theorist, Paolo Virno, sees two possibilities inherent in the present moment of digital production.[48] First, a new form of public sphere might emerge, one dedicated to "the good life," which, for Virno, means an ethical and just life based on principles such as freedom of language, knowledge as a shared, common good, and so forth. Or, alternately, we might be left with a kind of artificial publicness that fosters none of these traits. (Think of the difference implied in "having a public" versus "having a public culture.") In all likelihood, some members of society will have greater access to "the good life" than others. The conditions of participation in support of such a life and the oppressive possibilities of the newly networked economies (the 24/7 blur of work and leisure, increased surveillance, decreased privacy, exploited labor) are two sides of the same networked technological environment. For instance, in this volume, Robert Heverly warns that the same impulse to archive the self that fuels many Web 2.0 sites may also pose risks to long-term privacy, particularly given the persistence and reproducibility of digital media. It is much easier to celebrate the pleasures and possibilities of participatory culture than it is to guard against the risks that very culture may mask or pose, but we must try.

The realms of law and policy offer one site for intervention. Heverly surveys a number of legal possibilities that might mitigate potential privacy concerns vis-à-vis children. Joining and amending the activist and intellectual work of Larry Lessig, James Boyle, and David Bollier, Siva Vaidhyanathan has persuasively outlined the need to pursue issues of copyright law.[49] As he eloquently argues, "it is our duty" to translate the intricacies of copyright law into a public and activist agenda.[50] We need to drive home the relevance of fair use to everyone "who reads, writes, watches, photographs, listens, sings and remixes."[51] Both Sandvig and Streeter illustrate that a lack of sustained engagement with policy issues by youthful early adopters was a major factor in the shutting down of the democratic potential of earlier media.[52] Such policy efforts should also focus on telecommunications policy, aiming for a cyber-infrastructure for the public good that also addresses "last mile" issues. This would necessarily link together nonprofits, schools, foundations, activist groups, and "everyday" technology users (who, of course, are often already situated within these other groups as well).[53] Despite the nonregulatory fantasies of the cyber-libertarians, we will also require informed governance and a renewal of the social contract.[54] Open, peer-to-peer platforms should be encouraged and funded by both foundations and the government, perhaps through partnerships with or a levy on corporations, reworking the idea of "public broadcasting" into forms of public participatory culture for the twenty-first century. As Kleiner and Wyrick observe, "any real hope for a genuine, community enriching, next generation of internet-based services is not rooted in creating privately owned, centralized resources, but rather in creating cooperative, P2P, and commons-based systems, owned by everybody and nobody." We need to cultivate technological innovations that serve democracy and civil society.

Such legal, technological, and political issues are complex, and much of this may also feel far afield from the MacArthur initiative's focus on "youth, digital media, and learning." One outcome of the ongoing conversations this volume's authors undertook is a realization that many of the issues we need to take most seriously in relation to our digital future are not particularly "youth-specific." Child-centered policies in the past have often devolved from protectionist attitudes. We might rethink "child-friendly" policies as addressing many of the same issues that affect us all: copyright, privacy, surveillance, access, equity, and social justice. Today's young digital natives will be the beneficiaries of such policies and efforts over the long term.

Rule Five: Foster Literacies

If legal and policy arenas are important terrains for struggle, we must also foster new critical literacies and support these through education policies, extending and intertwining our current focus on media literacy and information literacy. Various forms of information and media literacy are very much on the national agenda today. All fifty U.S. states include media literacy requirements of some form in their educational standards. Yet the recommendations vary wildly from state to state and are often buried in the obscure language of standards, with no curriculum in place to achieve these goals. In a climate relentlessly focused on "accountability" and testing, teachers feel pressured to cover "the basics," leaving scant time to innovate new modes of learning or new models of literacy.

To further complicate matters, the best models of media literacy pedagogy tend to build on students' own interests, skill sets often honed outside of formal education and through a variety of media platforms from game consoles to web sites to mobile phones. Introducing these modes of learning into the classroom dissolves easy boundaries between "inside and outside," moves away from textbook-centric toward project-based education, and threatens to destabilize traditional notions of the teacher/student relationship. Small wonder that change has been slow within school systems.

Still, if we hope to realize the promises of participatory media and if public education is to remain relevant to students, we need to develop innovative models of multimedia pedagogy for K-12 and postsecondary learning *in and out of* the classroom, closing the loop between what students do for "fun" and how and what they learn in school. This means that we need to advocate for systemic changes in how we think about education, learning from grassroots practices that are already having success and fostering literacies that will better equip young people for various aspects of the digital future.

Literacy is a recurring theme throughout this volume, one that takes on several different forms and directions. Some authors zero in on what we might discern about literacy by investigating practices that aren't always seen as explicitly about learning (Cassell and Cramer, Livingstone, Lowood, Samuels, Yardi). Some focus on creating education environments that might enhance critical literacies vis-à-vis digital learning (Anderson and Balsamo, Heverly, Hooper). Others remind us that limitations on access and widespread social inequity are likely to impede literacy for many (Seiter, Sandvig).

Two essays, in particular, take literacy as a central theme. First, Sonia Livingstone offers a nice overview of the origins of literacy as a social force for scrutiny and governance, situating the term within larger cultural and historical contexts. For her (and echoing our earlier discussions of cultural studies and STS traditions), literacy is "a situated form of knowing that bridges individual skill and social practices." She then details how literacy in the digital age poses particular challenges and urges the combination of two schools of thought on literacy: information literacy and media literacy. Information literacy is often concerned with accessing and evaluating Web content, while media literacy often focuses on various elements of critical understanding and on esthetics and design. Livingstone notes that these two traditions rarely converge and argues for a model of "Internet literacy" that brings the two together. Her conception of literacy dovetails with concerns expressed by Seiter, as she argues for a definition of literacy that doesn't just aspire to vocational training and individual skill, but, instead, aims at fostering democratic participation and civic culture.

Anne Balsamo and Steve Anderson shift our attention to the university and sketch a vision of literacy that draws insights from the informal learning currently emerging in remix and game cultures. They focus our view on a hypothetical Class of 2020 and argue that these students of the future will need multiple layers of literacy encompassing cultural, technological, economic, social, and epistemological dimensions. They also advocate for "retooling our sense of students not as younger versions of ourselves, but as members of a generation with its own unique disposition" and urge "the creation of pedagogical protocols that acknowledge and embrace their essential mutability." Such protocols will demand and encourage critical synthesis. They will embrace open, hybrid, and media-rich knowledge and include the ability to "read and write" in the languages of multimedia. This means teaching students to use *and critique* software (and even code) while also recognizing that low-tech, open, or alternative tools can help decenter the dominant force of commercialization in students' lives.

There are useful parallels between these two essays. Unlike SuccessMaker, both are interested in a social rather than an individualist or functionalist conception of literacy. Both imagine students as active producers and interpreters of diverse media forms. Each also highlights something that is often lost in popular journalistic accounts of digital natives and the net generation: children's and young people's internet skills are often limited in very real ways. For Livingstone, this became apparent through detailed empirical observation within domestic settings. Parents as well as children tend to exaggerate the digital competencies that youth possess. Skills are uneven and often don't extend to *making* digital objects. Furthermore, students rarely understand the economic structures behind the internet, so encouraging a kind of "market literacy" will be crucial. Likewise, Balsamo and Anderson stress that we cannot take for granted "what kids know" about digital media. They note that even with respect to a popular form of entertainment like video games, "familiarity and access to gaming platforms and gaming literacy remain stubbornly uneven, with disparities that articulate along predictable axes of racial, economic, and geographic differences." In sketching a new paradigm for twenty-first century education, they also redefine the role of teachers as "*educational designers*, whose expertise may include deep disciplinary knowledge, but whose practice involves mobilizing the efforts of communities and individuals in relation to institutional resources." Taken together, these two essays suggest that we need to teach the teachers and also the parents, encouraging adults to cocreate literacy practices with youth when appropriate. We will also need to cultivate thought leaders in the community of teachers, in higher education, and in policy venues in order to revitalize the classroom, and we need to make sure that these communities are speaking to each other.

Thus, fostering literacy is much more complex than the ambitious yet simple definitions endorsed in many state standards might at first suggest. All too often, the political and cultural stakes of literacy are suppressed. We should insist that emergent digital literacies (and the learning environments that support them) need to work in the service of democratic engagement and empowered citizenship, which includes an ability to reflect on corporate culture and not simply to aspire to be part of it.

Rule Six: Learn to Toggle

From its outset, this project has tried to avoid the kind of binary thinking that frames digital media as either revolutionary or disastrous. Nonetheless, the contributing authors might be seen to occupy a sort of sliding scale or continuum of relative optimism or pessimism. We have struck a balance across the volume between a careful hope for possible progressive futures and cautionary and more negative tales. As you move from essay to essay, it's sometimes as if you are pulling focus, zooming in or out in various ways. For instance, Seiter and Heverly zoom out in a manner that allows large social and historical forces to come into play, powerful networks that underwrite and often delimit what the digital can or will be, particularly for those with less social or economic capital. Yardi, Hooper, and Lowood zoom in to the level of the case study, examining detailed instances of agency and possibility. Optimism seems easiest at the microlevel, the terrain of the case study; such optimism often recedes as the analysis ascends to the macro or systemic. The essays by Sandvig, Livingstone, and Balsamo and Anderson attempt to move between macro and micro, system and subject. If we are to fully understand the innovative uses and unexpected outcomes of digital media and learning, both modes of analysis are crucial. While not every study or research project need encompass both, we do need to learn to toggle fluidly back and forth across scales.

If we need be flexible in terms of the scope and location of our objects of study, we also must develop hybrid methodologies. These ten essays each deploy different methodologies, including ethnography, critical theory, empirical analyses, educational theory, design studies, and media studies. The authors are based in departments of film and critical theory, English, communication, law, sociology, interactive media, information studies, and in educational nonprofits. Some lean toward work that is data driven, while others skew toward the abstract or interpretative; different things "count" as evidence from project to project. This introduction has attempted to frame several lines of thought and analysis that crisscross and reverberate throughout the book, highlighting useful points of contact. This overview involves acts of translation, particularly since our group came to this project with differing vocabularies, even as we shared interests in certain objects of study.

One of the more theoretical essays in this volume is by Robert Samuels. Drawing from and critiquing traditions in both poststructuralism and theories of composition, he argues that we are witnessing a new cultural and social moment that he calls "automodernity." Automodernity interlaces technological automation and a sensation of human autonomy. He examines several of the symptoms of this new way of being, ranging from emergent forms of collaboration to the shifting boundaries between the public and the private to a tendency to create echo chambers that shut out cultural difference. Though his rhetorical style and interpretative stance hew closely to those of literary and critical theory, his analysis might also be understood as running parallel to debates in other fields. In fact, one might argue that his central thesis navigates a middle ground in the debates between STS and ANT, while deploying very different vocabularies and methodologies. That is, he simultaneously recognizes the agency of nonhuman and human agents (the power of automation) and also zooms out to larger sociohistoric forces. While he recognizes the value of ethnographic or sociological analyses, he also insists that "traditions in critical theory, rhetoric, and philosophy offer other modes of thinking about the age we inhabit."

Many authors in this volume recognize the need to articulate a hybrid methodology or theory: Hooper brings together cognitive and cultural analyses, Sandvig melds the traditions of media history, STS, and policy studies, and Balsamo and Anderson bring together science fiction and media and technology studies. Some might view their futuristic tale of the Class of 2020 as more "literary" than scholarly, but I'd argue that we should retain a place for speculative fiction in our methodological approaches. Such tales can harness the power of the imagination to help dream up (and, hopefully, realize) more just futures. If students' "future" literacy requires critical synthesis and code switching, so do our own scholarly methods. The need to toggle applies across multiple realms: from the individual to the systemic, but also from the niche methodology to more transdisciplinary approaches. We will also need to switch between and connect to different sites of investigation: homes, libraries, leisure spaces, virtual worlds, schools, and so on. Different sites or objects of study and different intellectual approaches should function as nodes within a broader network of analysis.

This volume reaches no easy consensus about the likely outcomes of digital media use and innovation, underscoring the very early stage at which we find ourselves in imagining the transdisciplinary teams that will be needed to realize the potential promises of participatory culture. Bringing together diverse skill sets and approaches risks boring the experts. For instance, my quick earlier glosses of STS and ANT or of constructivism will likely bore or frustrate experts who have spent a lifetime parsing the nuanced debates within these fields. The university rewards and encourages very narrow niche knowledges, but such modes of thinking reveal substantial shortcomings when faced with complex social problems that need refracting from multiple points of view. This is not to say that we should jettison the specialized knowledge that emerges from the academy, but we do need to learn to translate niche knowledge concepts into broader frameworks and also to test claims made in one field through engagements with another. This might mean bringing relatively abstract claims into productive collision with "hands-on" work with learning, but it could also mean pressuring "practical" concepts for less-than-apparent meanings or consequences (i.e., challenging the notion that "tools" are somehow neutral.) And, while policy is an important terrain for research and action, our efforts in this area should not only be based on the insights of those who study policy and political economy. Informed policy and economic analyses will crucially depend upon those who work "closer to the ground": ethnographers and educators, but also specialists in media and cultural studies. Too often these disparate disciplines work in isolation from one another.

Of course, rich collaboration is hard; various languages and vocational biases are always in play, if often unrecognized. For example, the research team in the charter schools I work with spent months in ongoing conversation in order to develop a shared vocabulary. From my training as a humanities and media scholar of a particular era, I tend toward interpretative methods that take for granted the social construction of knowledge, gender, and technology. I have a seemingly innate suspicion of certain empirical or cognitive traditions, but I need to overcome this. I also like details and examples (even if I mostly "analyze" or "interpret" them) and tend to glaze over a bit when faced with universal theories or large policy issues. I need to get over that too. Others might have reached a point of absolute frustration with educational bureaucracy and find themselves largely drawn to subcultural or edge practices. None of these biases is inherently wrong (or more wrong than another), but our dispositions as academics or cultural workers of particular types often make it hard to build bridges or to connect with those whose training or interests reside elsewhere. Often, we seem more willing to learn from youth than from scholars outside of our own narrow fields. We might here take a lesson from communities like Wikipedia and try to build research environments that foster a respect for the varied strengths a team of participants might bring to a problem. Some, like Diana Rhoten, have even suggested that virtual networks have the potential to reduce some barriers to robust collaboration, at least within scientific research communities.[55]

Alternately, the very binary forms and partitioned logics that underwrite digital media may make it that much harder to draw connections and to toggle back and forth from the node to the network. We require both fine-grained detail and also systemic or structural analyses. Individual projects might primarily focus at one level or scale, but they should connect up with larger initiatives that deploy hybrid methodologies and understand the mesh-like affordances of networked social systems. Nodes are often easier to see for those doing empirical work, but these approaches can also miss larger systemic issues. We describe the internet through words like "networks" and "webs," as some thing or some place that is knitted together. We imagine it as richly linked and as about connections, but we must also take seriously the possibility that digital forms privilege fragmentation and, in an era of rapid commercialization, walled silos that rarely interconnect. Here we see a tendency toward homogenization where we only connect to those who are pretty much like us to begin with.

Some have described these differences as the difference between the open architecture of Usenet and the self-referential world of blogs. Neither of these realities is yet fully dominant or inevitable, but we need be mindful of them both.

A Final Note on Rule Sets

The six rules or maxims outlined here form a conceptual rule set for an emergent field, highlighting key issues and concerns. While the idea of a rule set may sound prescriptive, in computing usage rule sets are often highly flexible and contingent. They are meant to be tailored and adjusted for concrete applications and to mutate over time. New rules will likely be added. Old rules may be overwritten or reconfigured. The end goal of this rule set is to help us identify and build supports in and around digital culture that might tip the odds in favor of open systems and foreground larger questions of democracy and justice. This can happen across many levels and through many tactics, many of which are discussed in this volume. We can foster the production of socially relevant and culturally diverse games, software, and computational objects through partnerships between educational sites (both universities and K-12), nonprofits, foundations, and private companies. We can develop curricular supports and modifications that allow the use of existing products and virtual worlds in classrooms and after-school programs. We must also advocate for access to and various forms of public space in the digital realm, from commons to open-source platforms to generous understandings of copyright and licensing. While setting up easy dichotomies between "the market" and some imagined "we" that exists outside of commercial pressures (and pleasures) probably won't get us very far, it is still important to hold on to an idea of public life that exceeds things that can be monetized. We can't leave this to the market unless a market is the only form of civil society we can envision. The market has little at stake in certain forms of speech, broad inclusion, and an expansive sense of the public good. If we believe there are certain foundational aspects of a democratic and just society and continue to believe in something that we might call the public good, we must also actively advocate and struggle for bringing these forms into being. The more optimistic authors in this volume believe that, in their engagements with the digital, youth are already beginning to imagine themselves as empowered to create new worlds. Other authors worry that we've heard all this before and that our enthusiasms for emergent technologies often make it hard to see (and thus organize against) the larger social and political forces that limit the beneficial outcomes we see bubbling up in moments of technological change. As Anderson and Balsamo note, "The production of unintended consequences is inevitable; accommodating them is not. Anticipating them is an act of conscious engagement; designing against them is an ethical investment in the future." Consider this rule set a first installment toward that goal.

Notes

1. Marc Prensky, *Don't Bother Me Mom—I'm Learning* (Minneapolis, MN: Paragon House Publishers, 1999); Don Tapscott, *Growing up Digital: The Rise of the Net Generation* (New York: McGraw-Hill, 1998); Neil Howe and William Strauss, *Millennials Rising: The Next Great Generation* (New York: Vintage Books, 2000).

2. Andrew Keen, Web 2.0: The second generation of the internet has arrived. It's worse than you think, *The Weekly Standard*, February 2, 2006, http://www.weeklystandard.com/Content/Public/Articles/000/000/006/714fjczq.asp.

3. See http://innovationstyles.com/isinc/default.aspx. Also see the following sites: Innovation Tools: http://www.innovationtools.com; Business Innovation Insider http://www.businessinnovationinsider. com/; Innovation.net: http://venture2.typepad.com/; Permanent Innovation Blog: http://www. permanentinnovation.com/blog/; and InnovateAmerica: http://innovateamerica.org/index.asp. While there are both subtle and substantial differences across these various blogs, products, and businesses, all can be said to partake of an attitude of cyber-libertarianism.

4. See http://www.pearsondigital.com/successmaker/ and http://www.pearsondigital.com/ knowledgebox/. Langdon Winner has highlighted the impacts of neoliberal economies on education, noting that "Financial analysts at firms such as Lehman Brothers and Montgomery Securities now track education as an emerging profit sector" valued at over $600 billion a year.

5. Ellen Seiter, *The Internet Playground: Children's Access, Entertainment, and Mis-Education* (New York: Peter Lang, 2005).

6. For one version of this critique, see Langdon Winner's "The Handwriting on the Wall: Resisting Technoglobalism's Assault on Education." He argues that "the 'business' of education now looms as a potentially enormous profit center of great interest to corporations" and that buzzwords like "innovation," "leadership," and "creativity" are often deployed to mask the increasing corporatization of the university.

7. The "turn to technology" within STS is often said to have been spurred by the publication of MacKenzie and Wajcman's *Social Shaping of Technology* and of *The Social Construction of Technological Systems* by Bijker, Hughes, et al.

8. See Michael Guggenheim and Helga Nowotny, Joy in Repetition Makes the Future Disappear. A Critical Assessment of the Present State of STS, in *Social Studies of Science & Technology: Looking Back, Ahead,* ed. Bernward Joerges and Helga Nowotny (Dordrecht: Kluwer, 2003), 229–260. For a critique of certain similar tendencies within the field of cultural studies, see Meaghan Morris, Banality in Cultural Studies, in *Logics of Television: Essays in Cultural Criticism,* ed. Patricia Mellencamp (Bloomington: Indiana University Press, 1990), 14–43.

9. Gilles Deleuze and Felix Guattari *A Thousand Plateaus: Capitalism and Schizophrenia* (Minneapolis: The University of Minnesota Press, 1987); Michel Foucault, *The Order of Things: An Archaeology of the Human Sciences* (London: Routledge, 1992); Bruno Latour, *Science in Action: How to Follow Scientists and Engineers Through Society* (Milton Keynes, UK: Open University Press, 1987).

10. This discussion of STS and ANT is, of course, reductive and cursory. It sidesteps many of the debates within and between the fields but does, I hope, illustrate the relevance of these recent traditions of thought to the larger questions that this volume pursues.

11. Marshall McLuhan, Classrooms Without Walls, *Explorations* 7 (1957).

12. The sources of the quotes are as follows Carolyn Marvin, 242; Tom Streeter, 309; Marshall McLuhan, "Classroom Without Walls."

13. Carolyn Marvin, *When Old Technologies Were New: Thinking About Electric Communication in the Late Nineteenth Century* (New York: Oxford University Press, 1990).

14. Tom Streeter, *Selling the Air: A Critique of the Policy of Commercial Broadcasting in the United States* (Chicago: University of Chicago Press).

15. David Edgerton, *The Shock of the Old*: *Technology and Global History Since 1900* (Oxford, UK: Oxford University Press, 2006).

16. Jay Bolter and Richard Grusin, *Remediation: Understanding New Media* (Cambridge, MA: MIT Press, 1999).

17. Pierre Bourdieu, *Distinction: A Social Critique of the Judgement of Taste* (London: Routledge & Kegan Paul, 1984).

18. Julie Frechette, Cyber-Censorship or Cyber-Literacy? Envisioning Cyber-Learning Through Media Education, in *Digital Generations: Children, Young People, and New Media*, eds. David Buckingham and Rebekah Willet (London: Lawrence Erlbaum Associates, 2006), 149–171.

19. Raymond Williams, *Television: Technology and Cultural Form* (Glasgow, UK: Fontana, 1974).

20. McLuhan, Classrooms Without Walls, 127.

21. Paul Grosswiler, *Method is the Message: Rethinking McLuhan Through Critical Theory* (Toronto: Black Rose Books, 1997); Glenn Willmott, *McLuhan, or Modernism in Reverse* (Toronto: University of Toronto Press, 1996).

22. Marshall McLuhan, *Understanding Media: The Extension of Man* (New York: New American Library, 1964), 19.

23. Seymour Papert, *The Children's Machine: Rethinking School in the Age of the Computer* (New York: Basic Books, 1993).

24. Ron Eglash, Culturally Situated Design Tools: Ethnocomputing from Field Site to Classroom, *American Anthropologist* 108, no. 2 (2006): 347–362.

25. See http://www.rpi.edu/~eglash/csdt.html. These tools include the "Virtual Bead Loom: Cartesian Coordinates" and "Cornrow Curves: Transformational Geometry," learning objects created to illustrate that many cultural design traditions are based on mathematical principles.

26. Henry Jenkins, *Convergence Culture: Where Old and New Media Collide.* (New York: Routledge, 2006); Henry Jenkins, *Textual Poachers: Television Fans and Participatory Culture*, (New York: Routledge, 1998); Mimi Ito, Japanese Media Mixes and Amateur Cultural Exchange, in *Digital Generations: Children, Young People, and New Media*, eds. David Buckingham and Rebekah Willet (London: Lawrence Erlbaum Associates, 2006), 149–171.

27. Lev Manovich, *The Language of New Media* (Cambridge, MA: MIT Press, 2001); Jay Bolter and Richard Grusin, *Remediation: Understanding New Media,* 1999.

28. James Gee, *What Video Games Have to Teach Us About Learning and Literacy* (New York: Palgrave, 2003); Jenkins, *Convergence Culture*; Jenkins, *Textual Poachers*; John Seely Brown, Growing Up Digital, *Change* 32, no. 2 (2000): 10–11, http://www.aahe.org/change/digital.pdf; Tara McPherson, Reload: Liveness, Mobility, and the Web, in *New Media, Old Media: A History and Theory Reader*, eds. Wendy Hui Kyong Chun and Thomas Keenan (New York: Routledge), 199–209.

29. N. Katherine Hayles, *How We Became Post-Human: Virtual Bodies in Cybernetics, Literature and Informatics* (Chicago: University of Chicago Press, 1999).

30. Douglas Thomas and John Seely Brown, The Play of Imagination: Extending the Literary Mind, *Games and Culture* 2, no. 2 (2007): 149–172.

31. Jean Piaget, *The Psychology of the Child* (New York: Basic Books, 1972); Jerome Bruner, *Acts of Meaning* (Cambridge, MA: Harvard University Press, 1990).

32. Lev Vygotsky, *Mind in Society* (Cambridge, MA: Harvard University Press, 1978).

33. Papert, *The Children's Machine.*

34. Seiter, *The Internet Playground*; see also Mark Warschauer, *Technology and Social Inclusion: Rethinking the Digital Divide* (Cambridge, MA: MIT Press, 2003).

35. This study was undertaken by Bill Tancer, an analyst with the Web audience measurement firm Hitwise. For a gloss on the report, see http://news.com.com/Study+finds+weak+participation+on+Web+2.0+sites/2100-1032_3-6177059.html.

36. For instance, Dmitri Siegel introduces the notion of the "templated mind" in the online blog/magazine, *Design Observer*. While the article focuses on the effect of DIY aesthetics on the profession of design (with elitist overtones), I find the idea of the "templated mind" fascinating, as it suggests an ongoing standardization of the forms of the Web that could derail the more transformative potential of the medium.

37. Jenkins, *Convergence Culture*; Jenkins, *Textual Poachers*; Ito, Japanese Media Mixes, 149–171.

38. Frechette argues that there are tight feedback loops between advertisers like Disney and the many commercial products designed to filter or screen children's Web access. Pybus has noted that popular children's sites like NeoPets deploy an immersive advertising strategy that seamlessly blends advertising into networked spaces of play, creating emotional ties between participation in social, virtual worlds and consumer products; Jennifer Pybus, Affect and Subjectivity: A Case Study of Neopets.com. In *Politics and Culture* 2, no. 2 (2007). http://aspen.conncoll.edu/politicsandculture/page.cfm?key=557.

39. Marsha Kinder, *Playing with Power in Movies, Television, and Video Games: From Muppet Babies to Teenage Mutant Ninja Turtles* (Berkeley: University of California Press, 1991).

40. Cited in Kinder, *Playing with Power*, 136.

41. Michael Molesworth and Janice Denegri-Kent, Digital Play and the Actualization of the Consumer Imagination, in *Games and Culture* 2, no. 2 (2007): 131.

42. Janet Evans, *Literacy Moves On: Popular Culture, New Technologies, and Critical Literacy in the Classroom* (Portsmouth, NH: Heinemann, 2005); Yasmin Kafai et al., Forthcoming. *Beyond Barbie and Mortal Kombat: New Perspectives on Gender and Computer Games* (Cambridge, MA: MIT Press); John Hartley and Kelly McWilliam, *Story Circle: Digital Storytelling Around the World* (Malden, MA: Blackwell, Forthcoming).

43. Trevor Scholz, What the MySpace Generation Should Know About Working for Free, in *Re-public*, 2007, http://www.re-public.gr/en/?p=138.

44. Scholz here cites Nicholas Carr and observes that "user-generated content was the main reason that the top ten websites in the world accounted for 40 percent of total page views." He describes this as "mind-boggling" evidence of "monocultures."

45. Nicholas Carr, "Sharecropping the Long Tail," online blog, entry posted December 19, 2006, http://www.roughtype.com/archives/2006/12/sharecropping_t.php.

46. Dmytri Kleiner and Brain Wyrick, "InfoEnclosure 2.0," *Metamute*, http://www.metamute.org/en/InfoEnclosure-2.0.

47. For a detailed reading the economic structures of our networked, post-Fordist economies in relation to the feelings of control, transformation and mobility proffered by digital technologies, see McPherson.

48. Paolo Virno, "Interview with Paolo Virno by Branden Joseph," *InternetActivist.com* January 17, 2006, http://info.interactivist.net/article.pl?sid=06/01/17/2225239&mode=nested&tid=9.

49. Lawrence Lessig, *Code and Other Laws of Cyberspace* (New York: Basic Books, 1999); Lawrence Lessig, *The Future of Ideas: The Fate of the Commons in a Connected World*, Reprint ed. (New York: Vintage, 2002); James Boyle, "A Politics of Intellectual Property: Environmentalism for the Net?" 1997, www.law.duke.edu/boylesite/Intprop.htm; David Bollier, *Silent Theft: The Private Plunder of Our Common Wealth* (New York: Routledge, 2003); Siva Vaidhyanathan, *Copyrights and Copywrongs: The Rise of Intellectual Property and How It Threatens Creativity* (New York: New York University Press, 2001).

50. Vaidhyanathan, *Copyrights and Copywrongs*, 254.

51. Ibid., 253.

52. Jeanne Allen makes a similar argument regarding early "ham TV" operators. Many are surprised to learn that early innovations in television technology included two-way multicast potential, a use promoted by amateur hobbyists. Allen details this history and argues that corporate interests were able to end run user aspirations because amateurs did not press for "a widely diffused grass-roots egalitarian form of communication" (116); Jeanne Allen, The Social Matrix of Television: Invention in the United States, in *Regarding Television*, ed. A. Kaplan (Los Angeles: AFI, 1983).

53. On the important role to be played by nonprofits, see Kathryn Montgomery and Barbara Gottlieb-Robles, Youth as e-Citizens: The Internet's Contribution to Civic Engagment. In *Digital Generations: Children, Young People, and New Media*, eds. David Buckingham, and Rebekah Willet (London: Lawrence Erlbaum Associates, 2006), 131–147.

54. Langdon Winner, The Handwriting on the Wall: Resisting Technoglobalism's Assault on Education, in *Tech High: Globalization and the Future of Canadian Education*, ed. Marita Moll (Ottawa: Fernwood Publishers, 1997); Tom Streeter, The Romantic Self and the Politics of Internet Commercialization, *Cultural Studies* 17, no. 5 (2003): 648–668.

55. Diana Rhoten, "Final Report, National Science Foundation. BCS-0129573: A Multi-Method Analysis of the Social and Technical Conditions for Interdisciplinary Collaboration," 2003, http://www.hybridvigor.net/publications.pl?s=interdis.

PART I: REVISITING "OLD" MEDIA: LEARNING FROM MEDIA HISTORIES

Practicing at Home: Computers, Pianos, and Cultural Capital

Ellen Seiter

University of Southern California School of Cinematic Arts, Division of Critical Studies

Last week, Time Warner sent an installer to my home to set up the digital cable boxes and my DSL line. I've moved often in the last three years, so I have been in this situation a lot. First, a young man of about twenty arrived and got to work on the cable lines under the house. Then, he called his friend, because he was having trouble with the DSL line setup. This young man, Marco, could handle three different kinds of TV remotes and their interaction with each other in seconds. When we turned to the DSL box, it took him only a moment to find the system preferences and get the Mac laptop set up. He looked around the room, where three other Macintosh laptops were visible. "Man, I don't even have one yet," Marco tells me. "Wow. You've got Bluetooth on this. Do you download songs to your phone from this?"

The expert on DSL lines of the Time Warner installers working in my area does not own a computer, and my family (one parent, three kids) has six of them and that's not counting the old ones in the garage. Why does Marco have no computer and I have six? Because I am better with technology? Obviously not, for I could never begin to set up my own DSL connection, much less go from house to house troubleshooting computer connections all day. Because I recognize the importance of digital media and he doesn't? Wrong again, because Marco works for Time Warner and witnesses the proliferation of DSL and computers, as well as the links between these and all forms of home entertainment on a daily basis. He probably recognizes the significance of these shifts in technology usage better than many of my colleagues who are university professors. Do I have so many computers because I am an excessive consumer typical of white-collar Anglos? Some of this could be true, but I didn't buy most of my computers, my employers did—in my sphere of work, computers are handed out like candy, updated constantly, and everyone is expected to transport and use them 24/7. At Time Warner, Marco is not getting the same benefits. Because Marco's job requires a narrower skill set, and that skill set as defined by Time Warner is kept at its lowest possible level to hold down costs, no matter how much Marco knows, he is paid by the hour or by the installation.

When Marco looks at my computer and its Bluetooth capability, he sees a music machine, and a piece of technology he cannot afford despite the fact that his capacity to use it may well be superior to mine. When I look at my computer, I see endless files to read, endless files I am under deadline to write, and a means for my workplace to send me more work. This is the privilege of a Ph.D.

How is knowledge of digital media converted into educational or occupational advantage? There has been surprisingly little attention to substantive content in digital pedagogy. In far too many school settings, students' multimedia presentations of very traditional content that is restricted to fit curricular standards (book reports, science projects, autobiographical essays) has substituted for more imaginative and more critical pedagogy. Along with standardized testing and back-to-basics reforms, computers have contributed to the trivializing of the content of the curriculum and the work of teachers in ensuring the quality of the substance of schooling. We need to examine current digital pedagogy in terms of unarticulated and implicit models of labor and the job prospects that students, parents, and teachers imagine computer skills will lead them to. There are clear benefits that access to technology can bring to disheartened and disenfranchised student populations. Computers can be a hook to do more sustained academic work for working-class students of color. Yet, the process of education cannot be made more cost effective through technology, and computers cannot teacher-proof the classroom. The enthusiasm among school board members and local business communities for high technology in public education was based on a desire to teacher-proof the classroom.

Teaching with computers requires a smaller teacher-to-student ratio than conventional classrooms. The legacy of the last decade of technology implementation in public schools in the United States has firmly established new markets for hardware and educational software makers, and entrenched a new tier of digital pedagogy consultants and experts in using computers for teacher and student management. How much it has improved learning and the quality of relationships between teachers and students remains to be seen. Students and parents are strongly attracted to schools with better technology, and now that the grant money of the dot-com boom has dried up, school districts are left with prohibitive costs to maintain and upgrade existing systems. These costs are impossible to cover in working-class urban school districts. These same students are on the losing end of the home technology divide.

Yet parents and students tend to rate schools in terms of technology, and magnet or charter schools that offer high technology can be a powerful draw. What types of employment does high technology prepare students for? How have corporate needs rather than pedagogical goals gained a foothold in our discourse around public education? In what ways have we set up unrealistic expectations for digital pedagogy as a magic bullet to solve the complex and historically rooted challenges facing public education today. By employing sociologist Pierre Bourdieu's categories of economic, cultural, and social capital to digital literacy, I wish to describe the barriers that make the dream of winning something like a "cool job" in new media a very distant one for working-class students. These include a reliance on public computers rather than domestic ones, a lack of access to prestigious educational credentials, and an exclusion from the social networks crucial to employment in the "new" economy.

Bourdieu focused attention on the role of education and the influence of "status distinctions" on the selection and valorization of certain cultural forms. He described the purpose of his project as being "to grasp capital...in all of its different forms, and to uncover the laws that regulate their conversion from one into another."[1] Although Bourdieu did not write about digital media per se before his death in 2002, he often referred to distinctions regarding musical taste, aptitude, and talent. He was also a keen observer of status distinctions in education and how these translate into job markets. Through an extended analogy between the piano and learning to use computers, I demonstrate Bourdieu's relevance for an expanded vision of digital literacy—one that would be at the forefront of the material and social inequalities that define children's lives in the United States in the twenty-first century. In what follows, I draw out the similarities between learning to play the piano and learning to use computers. The analogy helps to emphasize the privileged role of early domestic learning in gaining the "right" skills, the kind of competence that seems to come naturally and is therefore of higher status than what is learned at an institution such as a public school.

Musical education has a longer history, and the work on music education is less surrounded by hyperbole at the moment than work on digital media learning. During the heyday of piano marketing, however, as a necessary piece of bourgeois furniture, there was considerably more hyperbole about the wonderful effects on a child's life of the mere copresence of the instrument in the home.[2] Today, new research on early cognitive development is rekindling the interest in early music training and its power to enhance mental capacity. While advocacy (and Steinway advertisements) for musical training commonly took the form of a cultural uplift argument in mid-twentieth century American culture, today the argument is made in terms of brain science and the urgency of early cognitive development. Pregnant mothers are urged to play classical music to reach their child in utero, and Baby Mozart has made a handy profit exploiting brain science claims of the injection of higher intelligence through exposure to classical music. Traditionally, elite private schools (and some parochial schools) have offered excellent music education. Public schools in the United States added more music education in the 1960s, to appeal to baby boom parents and in response to demands for pedagogical liberalization and even democratization. However, music has been taught unevenly in public schools, and today, resources for music education in pubic schools are almost entirely dependent on massive parent-run fundraising efforts. No one expects a concert pianist to emerge from the casual training of the public elementary school.

While public schools are brimming with musical talent in other genres—hip hop, pop, Latina, and so forth, most of it is taking place outside the classroom, and much of it involving the impressive manipulation of electronic and digital technologies. The status of the classical music canon—what music historians define as European art music from the eighteenth and nineteenth centuries—and its preferred association with intelligence remains the most prestigious and the most difficult to master without access to expensive instruments and formal training.

In many ways, digital learning resembles classical music in that it has "barriers to entry," to borrow a term from free-market economics, that are primarily financial. The cash outlays involved in providing computers for children have been overlooked in the burst of enthusiasm for how mere association with computers will lift children intellectually and magically increase their potential value as adults. There is an overestimation of access to computers in terms of economic class, and an underestimation of specific forms of cultural capital required to maintain the systems themselves and move beyond the casual, recreational uses of computers to those that might lead directly to well-paid employment.

The miraculous benefits of digital learning are now expected to overcome entrenched educational inequalities that result from decades of class- and race-based resourcing to public schools—what Jean Anyon has called the pauperization of urban school districts.[3] In states such as California and Texas, the high-technology focus of the economy placed a new and Sisyphean burden on the public school system.[4] Added to the expectations for schools were the demands of a corporate elite, as in the case of San Diego's High Tech High, supported by the founders of Qualcomm and Microsoft. These philanthropic efforts disguise, in many ways, the ratcheting-up of blame on public school systems, and the top–down imposition of controls and penalties that ignore the expertise of teachers in terms of pedagogy and understanding children's development. The demand for a revision of the school curriculum based on corporate management philosophies and an emphasis on technology training for

Figure 1
In this advertisement for Steinway pianos from the 1940s, celebrated pianist Josef Hofman gives a tip on technique to the young boy practicing at home on his baby grand piano.

the shift to a knowledge economy has resulted in the installation of a new set of experts—many of whom have little understanding of the history and economics of the U.S. public school system, and no experience in the local community context in which teachers, parents, and students struggle.

Pierre Bourdieu's work on the ways that status systems are reproduced in education and the labor market highlights the decisive role that social networks play in providing encouragement, assistance, and recognition to learners, and in conferring legitimacy on what has been learned, including helping students to perceive its value and status. This analogy of the piano and the computer helps to pinpoint some of the buried assumptions in the most optimistic projections of digital literacy among youth, as well as focusing on the daunting material and pedagogical issues involved when schools prioritize the digital over more traditional materials, such as books.

Economic Capital

The provision of the musical instrument involves much more than the basic cost of purchase or rental. Is there room at home to play? Is the dwelling spacious enough to provide sufficient separation from other family members, and from neighbors who might be bothered by the noise? The bigger the family, the cheaper and denser the housing, the more difficult it becomes to keep a piano at home. The piano movers will cost more if the piano is to go upstairs or through the narrow doorways of multiple-family housing units. The piano tuner is an additional expense: the older and cheaper the piano, the more it has been transported and used by multiple musicians, the more piano tuning and repair are required to play in key. One student I interviewed explained how her parents, Taiwanese immigrants working double shifts and extra jobs to make it in the Californian economy of the 1980s and 1990s, moved to a different metropolitan area just so that they could afford the more spacious housing where her grand piano—which the family had invested in at the advice of a teacher, and which represented the focus of the family's educational aspirations—could be accommodated.

Of course, there are easier, cheaper ways to get access to a piano. There are pianos parked in the corners of gymnasiums or community centers that a highly motivated or disciplined kid could gain permission to use after school to practice on. Usually, in the highly disciplinary environment of today's public schools, such access would be hard to gain, and janitors would chase out any child caught playing a school piano after hours. Home computers are smaller and more portable than pianos, but present similar obstacles to ownership based on family income. Procuring the device itself is the smallest—and in many ways the easiest—part of access provision, keeping up with the accelerating rate of planned obsolescence of computer products has nearly eradicated the benefit gained from falling hard-drive prices. In order for internet access to succeed, the device must be purchased in conjunction with a host of other peripherals, software, and a DSL line (currently making the total for basic cable or phone service plus high speed internet around $90 per month). Finally, there are ways that computers are difficult to maintain in the physical domestic space, despite their greater portability. Larger families result in more demand and therefore more fighting over the machine. The privacy on which much youth-oriented play with computers relies is harder to come by when there are fewer rooms and more people in them. Even the number of electrical outlets available in an apartment becomes an issue, as priority is usually given to media that is more easily shared—like television sets, game consoles, and DVD players.

Old pianos play much better than most hand-me-down computers function, and the job of setting up and maintaining outdated software can be truly daunting: "When old computers come without documentation, missing crucial cords to connect monitors to hard drives and hard drives to printers or keyboards, when the software is no longer available for sale, and no telephone assistance or other technical expert is available, attempting to make them work is often a pointless waste of dozens of hours of work."[5] While a used piano can still be a source of excitement for kids—a fun novelty—old computers are simply frustrating. Kids of all classes recognize an old computer when they see one. Surrounded by secondhand things in their daily lives, working-class children are experts at recognizing hand-me-downs, and resist using cast-off machines.[6] Planned obsolescence is the guiding principle of the new technology industries, and families are poorly situated to bear the costs of constant replacement and upgrading. Families who have not yet purchased a new computer with an internet connection do not appear likely to take on the added expense now, when over one third of families in Southern California must spend *more than half* of their income just to pay the rent.[7] The last census report underlines that gross disparities in income and home ownership follow racial lines. White incomes are two-thirds higher than blacks, and 40 percent higher than Hispanics. Seventy-five percent of whites own their homes, compared with only 46 percent of blacks and 48 percent of Hispanics.[8] New media was introduced into a world where the gap between the middle-class and poor families was very wide in terms of income and access to educational opportunity, and sadly, new technology has exacerbated these gaps in the everyday lives of children. Huge numbers of kids go to class in schools that cannot afford new technology, and then come home to apartments where keeping the utilities turned on and possibly the TV uses up the budget long before the family could get around to saving for expensive computers, software, and DSL lines.

Being unable to afford the latest computer and fastest internet connection is especially hard on kids, because the very activities that inspire peer learning—teaching oneself HTML to put up a Web page or playing the latest computer games—are the ones that require the newest machines, the latest chip, and the fastest connections. If you want to develop digital literacy skills that are robust and confident, continually updated equipment is required. The largest gaps between rich and poor children are apparent in the arena of multimedia authorship: the very video, audio, and gaming applications that are most popular with children. "The economics of the information technology industry, together with the social stratification of educational systems, means that multimedia creation is highly *inaccessible* to the masses. On the one hand, while the cost of computers and Internet access continues to fall, the cost of the hardware, software, and bandwidth necessary to create the newest forms of multimedia will always be more expensive."[9] In other words, working-class children have little chance of enjoying the kind of computer and internet access that is residential and high speed, the kind that facilitates music downloading, online gaming, and instant messaging. And while these activities seem like nothing more than play, we know that they are vital to social inclusion. As education researcher Mark Warschauer points out: "What is at stake is not access to ICT [information and communication technologies] in the narrow sense of having a computer on the premises, but rather in a much wider sense of being able to use ICT for personally or socially meaningful ends."[10] For youth especially, because they are heavily targeted by marketers and are dependent on sites like MySpace or iTunes, the restrictions of the public lab or the outdated PC especially interfere with their desired uses for peer communication.

Some argue that the necessity for children to have a PC—and the costs for families—will soon be obviated by new technologies of ubiquitous computing. Will the obstacles based on lack of access to economic capital disappear with ubiquitous computing? In his book *Everyware*, Adam Greenfield posits the "vision of processing power so distributed through-out the environment that computers per se effectively disappear."[11] The promise is that household objects and things in the environment will allow "ordinary people finally get to benefit from the full power of information technology, without having to acquire the eso-teric bodies of knowledge on which it depends." The question of sufficient economic capital to provide equitable access to all would surely disappear when "information dissolves into behavior."

Greenfield's book is a thoughtful inventory of the potential problems: especially regard-ing design, the time required for use—the "hassle" factor, problems relating to opting out, and privacy, that ubiquitous computing represents. It is not until his concluding chapter, however, that he considers the potential for ubiquitous computing to exacerbate class dif-ferences: "I see how readily the infrastructure that gets us these amenities also lends itself to repression, exclusion and the reinscription of class and other sorts of privilege." The issue that Greenfield does not enumerate is that the classes of "smart" goods that will hold the chips to deliver seamless computing will themselves be based on cost. Those that are hassle-free, durable, and fast will be the most expensive—whatever they are—and the cheap, the free, and the hand-me-downs will be more difficult to use and more time consuming in every way. Ubiquitous computing will function best in spaces never frequented by working-class families like hotel rooms, airplanes, stock brokerages, and so on.

This is the irony of media culture in all its forms: being the target upscale market can lead to the invasion of privacy, "the colonization of everyday life, and marketers [who] use children to cull valuable marketing information about parents from the children's Web activities." If you belong to the downscale market, you barely exist for the developers of cutting-edge technologies, whether you reside in New Delhi or Los Angeles. Children in the downscale market are subjected to a barrage of advertising for small ticket items on free Web sites. Kids gain free access to gaming or music sites by renting out their eyeballs for the viewing of ads, just like television viewing for those who cannot afford TiVo and premium channels. Smart technologies will not be targeted at households where English is not the first language, those with parents who do not qualify for major credit cards, or where the family does not reside in a prime zip code area equipped with digital cable lines. These are the same households where the largest concentrations of U.S. youth reside, as well as the most African-American and Latino children.

These downscale markets are left to the mass marketers of toys and junk food and popular music—firms that go after the kids' pocket money rather than their parents'. The growing importance of the internet has created a new disparity across class lines in the quality and quantity of access. While the mass market is targeted as consumers of junk food, publicity and promotional materials, and potential consumers of music and movies, the affluent children are targeted for "premium" content, cutting-edge hardware, subscription-based Web content and digital cable, educational software, and online courses.

Cultural Capital

Cultural capital consists of knowledge, tastes, and preferences: it is the totality of an individual's learning, both formal and informal. Bourdieu stressed that the means of acquisition of cultural capital can be as important as what is acquired, thus stressing the way that learning in all forms is tightly intertwined with the social circumstances in which it takes place, and the value of various knowledges, as accorded within and between specific social divisions. Bourdieu proposed the term "cultural capital," "to account for the fact that, after controlling for economic position and social origin, students from more cultured families not only have higher rates of academic success but exhibit different modes and patterns of cultural consumption and expression in a wide gamut of domains."[12]

There are similarities in the array of processes and literacies—the specific forms of cultural capital—involved in playing the piano and using a computer.

1 Learning is time consuming, with time spent practicing rewarded by qualitatively different levels of mastery. When large amounts of time "practicing" are invested, the computer user is rewarded by the achievement of a kind of automaticity of many levels of competence. This is similar to the way music learning requires a level of rote learning, practicing scales, and physical routinization—the pianist cannot read notes one at a time or visually search to finger each note on the piano. Similarly, if software programs (and games) are not mastered to a level where the interface, the shortcuts, and the keystrokes become second nature, the process is too cumbersome and tedious to expect children to even desire to use. There are striking similarities between the ability to waste time on computers and on music—learning early and having the free time to fool around are big advantages. Arriving at a deeper understanding of how hardware and software work—strong digital literacy skills—requires dozens of hours of trial and error. Video game play is just the most obvious example of this.

2   Practicing for large blocks of time results in a physical orientation to the piano or PC, so
     that the relationship of the body to the object becomes automatic rather than conscious.
     This is what Bourdieu would call "embodied" cultural capital. Music teachers obsessively
     teach, experiment with, and improve the student's posture, fingering, and stance. The
     greater physical ease with which users approach computers when they have their own
     machine, and have had hundreds of hours of practice, is obvious. For a child to sit at
     a computer or a piano for the requisite number of hours to achieve mastery requires
     an adaptation to the sedentary (and the solitary, when children use computers alone)
     behavior that can be very difficult for children who have been socialized to a more active,
     outdoor orientation of the physical (just as the piano or computer prodigy usually is not
     competitive in soccer, for example). In the middle-class home, parents nagging children
     to spend more time practicing the piano is commonplace; children need no nagging
     to spend time at the computer keyboard and parents may alternately worry about the
     unhealthiness of too much screen time, or conversely admire their children's cleverness
     in mastering digital technology.

3   Because of the requirement of free time and the desirability of achieving this physical
     ease, there is an advantage to learning at an early age. No one expects a person who
     began playing at the age of eighteen to become a professional classical musician. Many
     researchers have noted how quickly children can catch up on new technologies to their
     better equipped peers.[13] This catching up, however, requires unfettered access, and takes
     place more easily at home. Similarly, new research shows a correlation between early
     exposure to digital technologies at home and the widest array of technology use as
     adults—there is no correlation between exposure to digital technologies at school and
     later use.[14]

4   Mastery requires learning a symbolic language, with conventional patterns of logic and
     sequencing and some mathematical skills. A small percentage of musicians master these
     intuitively (playing by ear) and innovate in profound ways that later may be conferred
     with status—I'm thinking of jazz. Most fans of music do not understand music theory or
     composition, just as most computer users do not understand programming. But knowl-
     edge at this advanced level is required for paid work, that is, to convert what might have
     been learned in one's spare time, partially through leisure pursuits, such as gaming.

Beyond these requirements, there is uncertainty about what is deemed worthwhile—and
in which social realms that judgment holds—in the musical and the digital realms. There
is some instability in the system of distinctions, a problem exacerbated by the association
of both music and digital media with youth. Certain musical tastes (pop) are much less
distinguished than others (baroque music), but the system of distinctions is situated within
a field, so that a knowledge of pop music might be valuable in film or television editing, for
example, although not helpful for getting into Julliard. Bourdieu analyzed the complicated
situation of risk when investing in cultural forms—what he termed "middle ground" arts—
that are newer, and less legitimate:

Arts such as cinema, jazz and even more, strip cartoons, science fiction or detective stories are predisposed
to attract the investments either of those who have entirely succeeded in converting their cultural capital
into educational capital or those who, not having acquired legitimate culture in the legitimate manner
(i.e., through early familiarization), maintain an uneasy relationship with it. . . . These arts, not yet fully
legitimate, which are disdained or neglected by the big holders of educational capital, offer a refuge
and a revenge to those who, by appropriating them, secure the best return on their cultural capital

(especially if it is not fully recognized scholastically) while at the same time taking credit for contesting the established hierarchy of legitimacies and profits.[15]

Digital media culture is associated with many of these middle-ground arts, from video gaming, to popular music, to advertising. They appeal to kids as new and cutting-edge, and promise an appealing shortcut to success that bypasses traditional academic and cultural hierarchies. This lack of certainty over what is worthwhile is endemic in the digital realm because of its relative newness. Nowhere is this more apparent than in the field of gaming, where skill at gaming is common and admired within fields of both a digital elite and a working-class youth culture. Gaming employs a wide variety of skills, most of which, when seen objectively, seem to be at least as good for children's cognitive development as music lessons. Consider David Buckingham's description of the variety of skills involved in playing a computer game.

. . . an extensive series of cognitive processes: remembering, hypothesis testing, predicting and strategic planning. Game playing is a "multiliterate" activity: it involves interpreting complex three-dimensional visual environments, reading both on-screen and off screen texts (such as games magazines) and processing auditory information. In the world of computer games, success ultimately derives from the disciplined and committed acquisition of skills and knowledge.[16]

Researchers have noted a wide array of cognitive abilities that are facilitated by video and computer game playing, and anecdotal evidence suggests that high achievers in computer science and programming are also often avid gamers.[17] As I will discuss below, through an example of two students at High Tech High, their interest in gaming is not sufficient to either enable broader academic success or learn how to program. Bourdieu's value in thinking about digital literacy skills comes from the recognition of the arbitrariness of systems of distinction, and the ways that some skills—however indicative of intelligence and mastery— never convert into economic gain at a predictable rate. The PlayStation 3 may be equipped with Linux, but this does not mean that owning and playing one grants any advantage in the educational system of distinctions, or that the capacity to program will be used by avid players. Being one of the first to own the latest PlayStation platform might make one highly recognized within a subculture of one's peers, or being an early innovator using Linux on the PlayStation 3 might grant one acclaim in the online communities devoted to discussing video game hardware and software, and user-generated content. However, converting these into a form of cultural capital with sufficient value to get one a job is an uncertain endeavor. Even the newest forms of cultural capital may require other kinds of material support— economic and social capital, as Bourdieu calls them—to convert them into a paying job. Cultural capital works best when it is tied to the kinds of social networks provided through family members who are themselves employed in the culture industries, or the mentoring or cohort groups that prestigious universities provide.

One of the biggest differences between music and computers as they are used for the internet, social networking, and word processing, is that computer learning—even in its more casual forms that do not involve programming, for example—requires a high level of verbal literacy. In many ways, computers have made literacy and the ability to manipulate linguistic codes more important than ever before. The use of the internet, for example, requires a higher level of reading skill than textbooks, and children need a great deal of explicit instruction in how to evaluate information. Schofield and Davidson's five-year research project on the introduction of the internet into elementary, middle-school, and high-school classrooms in a large urban school district elucidates the many complexities of introducing new media in a school setting: educational benefits do not flow automatically from internet access. Attitudes and expectations, technical knowledge, classroom culture and internet culture, and curriculum design, implementation, and follow-through all affect what teachers and students can accomplish with the internet. When students often possess quite different levels of literacy—technical and language-based—the downside of opening up access to the internet was that students easily wandered off-topic to entertainment sites, and that in the context of a busy computer lab it is impossible for teachers to monitor Web browsing.[18] In many ways, the better your reading skills, the less likely you are to be distracted by ads, games, and multimedia pyrotechnics. While the internet offers a vast resource for student research, it has disadvantages over the traditional children's library:

Information overload may be the biggest problem for younger students. Unlike library resources, the material found on the Web has not been prepared with students' level of background knowledge and reading ability in mind. . . . Even students with advanced reading skills sometimes found it difficult to sift through the masses of information they acquired about a topic of interest to select accurate and pertinent information. This in turn meant that teachers often needed to work very closely with students as they used the Internet, particularly at the earlier grade levels.[19]

Most schools have separated computer lab time to highly regulated, disciplined, project-based work. Better suited to digital learning than traditional classrooms are situations that rely on peer learning, scaffolding, and unrestricted time. However, these classroom practices are at odds with the school reform emphasis on increased discipline, narrow focus on curricular standards, and "accountability" through standardized testing measures. This is one reason why after-school programs have been more successful in teaching digital media than regular classrooms.[20] The hours of trial-and-error that many digital skills require and the freedom to develop a deep understanding of software that includes programming are nearly impossible to practice in a public school computer lab. This fact is what gives young people with high-end connections and the newest computers at home a massive advantage over those limited to school or public lab use.

Thus, we return to the advantage of domestic access. Students with this advantage become bored and restless in classrooms where their peers are behind and their skills may even exceed those of the teacher. Classroom instruction is poorly suited to bridging that gap. In Bourdieu's formulation, the means of acquisition of cultural capital are significant and have lasting effects. Early learning, especially learning "that takes place without any express intention to teach" as happens with children whose parents already work on computers, is the most effective and the most distinctive form of cultural capital. The cultural capital of digital literacy reflects its origin in the middle-class home, taking its place alongside other forms of cultural capital, such as knowledge of music and art:

The "inimitable character" of the bourgeois relation to culture derives from the fact that they are acquired, pre-verbally, by early immersion in a world of cultivated people, practices, and objects. When the child grows up in a household in which music is not only listened to but also performed, and a fortiori when the child is introduced at an early age to a "noble" instrument—especially the piano— the effect is at least to produce a more familiar relationship to music, which differs from the always somewhat distant, contemplative and often verbose relation of those who have come to music through concerts or even only through records . . . (the system of distinction) only recognizes as legitimate the relation to culture (or language) which least bears the visible marks of its genesis, which has nothing "academic, scholastic bookish, affected or studied about it, but manifests by its ease and naturalness that true culture is nature—a new mystery of immaculate conception."[21]

There is a presumption that youth now have universal access to computers—even if they do not own one, they can use one at school or at the library. But the likelihood of gaining strong digital literacy skills on this type of machine is much slimmer than on a home computer. In other words, learning to use computers at school is like the music education class in which you have forty minutes to hold an instrument in your hands once a week, along with thirty other kids. The chances of success are not even remotely comparable to the experience of a kid who learns to play on his or her own instrument, at home, with lessons from a private instructor. Just as the music education teacher traveling from one public school to the next has probably pared down his or her skills to the minimum requirements of knowing what each instrument looks like, how it works, and which group of orchestral instruments it belongs to, the student at the public computer lab is at best likely to come away with only the most basic—the weakest version—of digital literacy skills: an ability to manipulate the keyboard, the mouse, Web browsers, graphics programs, and word processing programs. Learning programming, and how to write software as opposed to just using it, is much more difficult at the public computer lab.

The recognition of these distinctions among forms of digital literacy determines the convertibility of digital skills into social prestige or earning capacity. The speed of acquisition is an aspect of cultural capital that is blatantly more prominent in digital literacy than in musical literacy. The canon of classical music is relatively unchanging (although composers and styles of performance go in and out of fashion)—piano training has a longer market value than digital skills. In the digital realm "early adoption" is key: getting there first, learning to use a new piece of software or equipment is extremely important for its relative value.

Andrew Ross notes the way that the youngest job candidates replace more mature workers in the new media firms he studied:

For those who had spent years in the trenches learning Web skills, it was a ceaseless struggle to stay ahead of software upgrades that threatened to render these skills obsolete. The Web developer's trade was increasingly standardized, as the industry developed programs and idioms to accomplish Internet work with the same degree of efficiency as in the software development sector. Throughout history, elder artisans had possessed the fullest knowledge of the trade, and they passed it on to youthful apprentices. In the modern technology industries, this order no longer applied. The newest recruits were often the most skilled because they were up to date on the latest technologies.[22]

The treadmill of computer upgrades and self-learning has increased rapidly, as some skills have been more widely disseminated.

For those playing catch-up in digital media skills, the outlook is discouraging. In a correlation of home computing with employment, gender, and education, a recent study found that:

Women or the poorly educated have increased their computer and Internet access. However, in many cases, men, the well-educated labor force participants, have increased access and use even more; thus many digital gaps remain or grow.[23]

The 2006 Pew Internet and American Life study reported on the closure of the digital divide based on the survey data that the numbers of blacks and Latinos who use the internet have steadily risen. The numbers who have a home computer still show a large disparity, however, with less than 50 percent of blacks and Latinos having internet access at home. Spanish speakers are excluded from the study, a group that comprises over 40 percent of the U.S. Latino population. For households earning less than $30,000 annually, only 21 percent are online. According to a 2006 Pew study, high-speed internet connections—which strongly correlate with users who ever post material in the internet—are found in only 31 percent of African-American households. Broadband access is strongly correlated with education: 62 percent of households where an adult has completed college have access as opposed to 17 percent of those without high-school diplomas.[24] Andy Carvin warns that while progress is being made in terms of the racial digital divide, income and education remain enormous roadblocks.[25] As Stanley Aronowitz warns, "Despite the well-publicized claim that anyone can escape their condition of social and economic birth—a claim reproduced by schools and the media with numbing regularity—most working-class students, many of whom have some college credits but do not graduate—end up in low- and middle-level service jobs that do not pay a decent working-class wage."[26] A lack of economic capital reinforces the lack of higher status cultural capital. The determining role of social networks in digital communications exacerbates these divisions even further.

Social Capital

Social capital consists of networks, connections, group memberships, and familial relationships: Bourdieu defined social capital as "the sum of the resources, actual or virtual, that accrue to an individual or a group by virtue of possessing a durable network of more or less institutionalized relationships of mutual acquaintance and recognition."[27] One of the most significant aspects of digital communication has been its provision of new forms of social networking—a democratization of access to social capital, unfettered by the restrictions of physical space and geography. Although technological determinists championed these networks as more open than previous forms of networking, such as church membership, school attendance, or country clubs, there are ways that digital networks might increase both class cohesion and the exclusion of those poorer or less educated.

To return briefly to the example of music: How does social capital increase the chances of becoming a concert pianist or securing a job on a symphony orchestra? Musical talent does not lead directly to recognition, awards, or employment. The private music teacher, one who is also a distinguished performer, is required for success. Usually, a student moves up a network of progressively more expensive and prestigious teachers, each with a wider set of professional connections. Social capital is gained by circulating through a series of teachers, and these teachers lead to other coaches, knowledge of summer institutes or prestigious camps, competitions, and so on. A hierarchical system of connections is required in order for the musician to display what has been learned and cash in on it, as it were. To be a child prodigy—or rather to be recognized as a child prodigy—for example, means proceeding through an elaborate institution for recognizing and credentialing musical talent. Social capital and the networks it makes available are the keys to accessing this system. Attendance at one of a handful of elite conservatories in the United States is another.

The digital realm appears to be more open to larger numbers of participants than the field of classical music. However, the maintenance of strong digital literacy skills relies upon social networks of people who have knowledge of computers and can provide assistance, and a level of literacy that will provide the ability to type, read manuals, use e-mail fluently and benefit from written exchanges online. There is a "multiplying factor for social inclusion" of the groups who successfully gain access. Warschauer has emphasized that the necessary resources—physical (the box), digital (the connection), human (literacy), and social (friends and family members who are also online)—for Internet access are "iterative," mutually reinforcing. Networking online requires as a basis the capacity to know others with at least the minimal amounts of economic and cultural capital necessary to participate in digital communications.[28]

Yet the internet, once thought to hugely facilitate social networks, is rapidly becoming more exclusive. Consider the trend toward exclusivity represented by the progression from AOL chat rooms to password-protected Web sites, from the first online computer games to the elite World of Warcraft guild. As Geert Lovink comments:

The response to massification and regulation is the creation of an invisible cyber elite. . . . As a response, business and developer groups, as well as activists and researchers, have started mailing lists and discussion forums within password protected sites. Who wants to discuss sophisticated concepts with all the booboos and weirdos who are surfing the Web, looking for places to make trouble? Are you able to keep up with hundreds of e-mail messages in your inbox every day? I do not like you, and your silly opinions, so why waste precious time on opinions and attitudes one detests?[29]

One crucial flaw in the claims about the greater democracy of online communications is that it ignores the operation of social distinctions. One of Bourdieu's important contributions was to conceive that participation in culture is a dynamic system in which jockeying for position was always at play. One of the most important forms of distancing applies to digital culture: "The higher classes . . . observing the cultural style of the classes below them, engage in reflexive role distancing, once again re-establishing their superiority to those who have a less sophisticated view of cultural symbols."[30] Youth are not impervious to status distinctions—in fact, adolescents may be more status conscious than other age groups—hence the movement from Xanga to Live Journal to MySpace to Facebook.

Young people famously use digital communications—instant messaging, cell phone texting, and social networking Web sites—to maintain their social capital, at least with those peers who can afford to keep up with the costly requirements of these technologies. However, there is nothing inherently democratic about the young and the wired. Facebook illustrates the ways that youth can be strongly invested in keeping social networks exclusive. Facebook also exemplifies the continued importance of socioeconomic and geographic location as determinants of access to social networks. In its initial version, Facebook allowed students enrolled at Harvard to participate in a network of online communications. Soon it expanded to other major universities: participants could gain access to all other members at their university by providing proof of enrollment in the form of a registered e-mail account at their university. Facebook has been wildly successful and its use among students is rapidly expanding beyond dating, parties, clubs, and classmates to launching small businesses, advertising one's career, and networking with other alumni. According to the founder, the success of Facebook is based on the fact that people are willing to divulge more and more personal and interesting information about themselves when they are certain that it will be viewed by only a limited network of people.[31] From a commercial point of view, the greater valuation of Facebook than MySpace derives from the greater exclusivity of its network, the frequency of log-ins and time spent on the site, and the potential to gain access to the especially desirable market of young people attending college. Users started to complain when Facebook expanded to state colleges, community colleges, and high schools. The dilution of the site's exclusivity threatens the value of the social network.

Social capital is crucial to the convertibility of cultural capital into employment—for youth with digital skills, the school-to-work transition is as much about connections as it is about talent or ability. The lack of social capital screens out working-class youth from employment in the highest income and most challenging jobs in the digital realm. Their lack of economic capital bars them from the assumption of risk that the new media industries have foisted on employees by promising stock options and the hope of vast financial rewards. Yet these are the kinds of jobs youth dream of—and are encouraged to dream of—at every charter school across the country that specializes in digital media. Good jobs in new media are jobs for the young, the well connected, and those with enough family capital to float them through lengthy education, and long periods of employment-seeking in expensive housing markets. At the trendy new media firm Razorfish that Andrew Ross studied, a personnel officer explained that "diversity usually means race and gender, it rarely means age, background or class. Everyone here has a similar educational background."[32]

New media jobs are prime examples of the ways that the intersection of economic, cultural, and social capital function according to some new rules and demands in the new economy. Gina Neff defines this work as entrepreneurial labor in her study of workers in Silicon Alley in New York: these cool jobs are especially attractive to the young. What is required to pursue "entrepreneurial labor" is an acceptance of much higher risk than other industries and a greater personal responsibility for one's career through constant self-training and social networking. In his interviews with hundreds of workers in the new media industries, Andrew Ross noted that even in the progressive, humane workplaces "advances in corporate democracy could turn into trapdoors that opened onto bottomless seventy-hour-plus workweeks."[33] Besides extended periods of unemployment, this also entails the acceptance of jobs with no benefits, long hours, part-time work, and short-term contracts. As educators, it is important to think through and to talk about with young people the realities of these forms of creative work.

Because cultural work is prominently featured in popular discourse, especially in visual images, and associated with trendsetters, beautiful people, hipness and cool, this problematic normalization of risk serves as a model for how workers in other industries should also behave under flexible employment conditions...without strong stabilizing norms and regulations of workplace behavior and rewards, media workers develop entrepreneurial labor in the dual hope that they will be better able to navigate uncertainty and maintain their association with a "hot" industry—even when that industry is marked by a "winner take all" inequity in both income and status.[34]

The significance of social capital exhibits itself in the tendency of new media workers to incessantly network. Entry into the profession is often based on implicit rules of the culture— norms that are imparted through the experience of attending elite universities, and often mirror the kinds of social relations of the Ivy League students on Facebook. Thus, a new industry and a new form of social networking reproduce the old class advantages of a predigital generation.

Digital media teachers and policy makers must recognize how the dream of success in industries of gaming, design, and digital media production is often unrealistic. In fact, the rapid spread of digital media as communication technologies and a source of leisure among youth has encouraged legions of students (and often their parents) to dream of escaping the dull grind for a cool job. The dream of working in music, advertising, design, or gaming of all kinds has now been disseminated on a vast scale. As Aneesh reminds us:

The idea of treating computer-mediated labor as mostly design-oriented work also suffers from the problem of exaggerating what is still a tiny part of IT work.... The majority of IT labor still consists of some sort of data entry and data manipulation work, including the work performed by bank tellers, accountants, secretaries, and all others who serve at the front and back ends of state and corporate bureaucracies.[35]

The type of employment using a computer that is likely to be familiar to the vast majority of people, then, is a kind of work where keystrokes might be counted, where supervisors may listen in on phone calls uninterrupted, where productivity is scrutinized on a daily and hourly basis, and where conversation with coworkers is forbidden.[36] The stressful and unpleasant circumstances under which this kind of work is performed helps explain why blue- and pink-collar adults might feel more alienated from computer technology and tend to stay away from it during their leisure time.

Working-class students are more likely to have parents employed in jobs that do not use a computer, or in jobs requiring the more alienating forms of computer work, or they are likely to perceive the impossibility of succeeding in the field of computers. This is related to the fact that there can be penalties—in the form of a loss of social capital—when working-class students devote effort to acquiring cultural capital related to computers. It is the penalty of being a nerd, a geek, a kid too identified with school and teachers. Social class, ethnicity, and language interact with gender expectations in determining who likes to use computers. Computer affinity develops out of one's school experience, access to computers, and social networks of friends and kin. John Hall reminds us that cultural capital does not have the same currency everywhere it circulates:

. . . cultural distinctions do not represent some generalized currency of "legal tender" among all individuals and status groups. . . . Cultural capital, after all, is good only (if at all) in social worlds where a person lives and acts, and the value that it has depends on sometimes ephemeral distinctions of currency in those particular social worlds.[37]

Urban working-class children and children of color may reject computers for the values they represent (such as dehumanization) and denigrate digital media for its emphasis on written rather than oral culture, their associations with white male culture (hackers and hobbyists), and their solitary, antisocial nature.

Failure to recognize the way social networks are defined and constituted through relations of economic and cultural capital is the logical flaw in the work of many new media theorists. Benkler's *The Wealth of Networks* is a recent example of this blind spot. In the following passage, Benkler moves rapidly from an acknowledgment that digital networks reproduce older social determinants, to an invocation of the fabulous potential for these networks to create new forms of capital:

We merely need to see that the material conditions of production in the networked information economy have changed in ways that increase the relative salience of social sharing and exchange as a modality of economic production. That is, behaviors and motivation patterns familiar to us from social relations generally continue to cohere in their own patterns. What has changed is that now these patterns of behavior have become effective beyond the domains of building social relations of mutual interest and fulfilling our emotional and psychological needs of companionship and mutual recognition. They have come to play a substantial role as modes of motivating, informing, and organizing productive behavior at the very core of the information economy.[38]

Benkler allows that internet tools "are skewed in favor of those who are already well-off in society," but skips over the digital divide because public access is increasing, and because computer skills are far and away more widely distributed than the tools of mass-media production. Instead of the thorny problem of inequality and entrenched disparities in wealth and access, Benkler turns to psychological terms and a discussion of the extrinsic and intrinsic motivations of individual behavior. The focus on motivation erases the social and material constraints that cause inequality, reducing them instead to personality and individual choice. For Benkler, the problems of inequity have been magically solved by the limitless opportunities offered by technology: "The majority of individuals in these societies have the threshold level of material capacity required to explore the information environment they occupy, to take from it, and to make their own contributions to it."[39] This divides society into good productive people, on the one hand, and those who "choose" not to engage, on the other. In the happy world of networks, all that remains is different tastes for types of rewards.

Clearly, some people are more focused on making money, and others are more generous; some more driven by social standing and esteem, others by a psychological sense of well being. The for-profit and nonprofit systems probably draw people with different tastes for these desiderata. Academic science and commercial science also probably draw scientists with similar training but different tastes for types of rewards. . . . We spend some of our time making money, some of our time enjoying it hedonically; some of our time being with and helping family friends, and neighbors; some of our time creatively expressing ourselves, exploring who we are and what we would like to become. Some of us, because of economic conditions we occupy, or because of our tastes, spend very large amounts of time trying to make money—whether to become rich or, more commonly, just to make ends meet. Others spend more time volunteering, chatting, or writing.

Social differences, then, have dissolved, substituted by the great "we" who engage in digital networks. We need Bourdieu to correct the idea that digital networks are free and unfettered, that everyone has already reached the threshold of participation that, as Benkler idealistically puts it, "Information is nonrivalrous (we can both use it at the same time)." Benkler's model only works in a world where the playing field is level for participation in digital networks. The latest Pew study showed that only 31 percent of internet users posted material on the internet (from home or work)—presumably the first step in the kind of participation that Benkler is talking about. Users are strongly determined by whether they can afford the most expensive kinds of access: of those who post online content (blogs, Web pages, etc.), 71 percent have a domestic broadband connection.[40]

When these barriers are ignored, new media theory simply reiterates ideology and reifies social inequity, turning gross discrepancies in access to economic, cultural, and social capital into differences of proclivity, as Benkler does. Some of us just happen to "spend more time volunteering, chatting, or writing." It is just a question of motivation, of psychology, of human nature, as Bourdieu explains: like all the ideological strategies generated in the everyday class struggle it *naturalizes* real differences, converting differences in the mode of acquisition of culture into differences of nature.[41] Rather than interrogating the persistence of the technology divide—especially the home technology divide—Benkler counts on digital technology itself to solve the problem: "While the digital divide critique can therefore temper our enthusiasm for how radical the change represented by the networked information economy may be in terms of democracy, the networked information economy is itself an avenue for alleviating maldistribution."[42] Benkler's model considers the difference as a matter of individual will and attributes to technology itself the agency for change. The example of High Tech High demonstrates some of the pitfalls of this model when applied to education.

High Tech High

San Diego's High Tech High opened in 2000, graduating its first four-year class of 105 students in 2004, with Larry Rosenstock, a former attorney, as its CEO and principal. The school is equipped with a great deal of expensive technology, donated by its founders, and in some ways tested for future school markets. The curriculum is project based, with students enrolling in fewer courses, dedicating a substantial portion of the school day to teamwork on these projects. Coursework is typically conceptualized in terms of multimedia projects. Final examinations focused on the review of the students' digital portfolios. Student work is available in a digital portfolio accessible to the public through their Web site. As one journalist enthusiastically described the school: "High Tech High students learn through a hands-on approach that encourages them to pursue projects of interest to them. Classrooms look like high-tech workplaces, and students have frequent interactions with career professionals through internships, projects, and other activities."[43]

The charge for High Tech High was to supply for Irwin Jacobs the 800 engineers he needed for the annual expansion of the wireless company Qualcomm. Jacobs frequently complained that students were lacking in math and science training, and that they had poor communication skills—he needed engineers who could read and write. His charge to Rosenstock for High Tech High was for small enrollments and school size, and an emphasis on technology. Forbes magazine's admiring portrait of Rosensock describes him in terms like, a "frustrated soul" who "outsmarted the bureaucrats," by getting around the teachers' union and school district regulations. Rosenstock's philosophy is that "if you treat kids like adults, even the most bruised and battered will play up to the role." High Tech High School provides an important case study of corporate and business interests influencing education, and how a lack of social capital can prevent students from cashing in on the skills and training they have.[44]

Kenny and Lucas are two boys who joined the freshman class of 2004 at High Tech High. Kenny is the only son of parents who both held Masters' degrees from the University of California. They could not afford to own their own home, but they had white-collar jobs and used computers at home and at work. Kenny was extremely keen on video games, but also ambitious enough to want a job in game design. Kenny was a childhood and family friend of Lucas. Lucas's parents had BA degrees, but they were divorced and their attention was divided among multiple kids. Lucas went to High Tech High as his last hope of fitting in at school, as he had a history of dyslexia and a flagging interest in formal education.

How did these two boys fare at High Tech High? Both boys were excited by the laptop computers, the multimedia access, and the curricular style of unstructured afternoons and group projects, but Lucas accomplished little on his digital portfolio projects, which comprised the majority of his grade, and nearly failed. He dreamed throughout high school of being a video game tester. This was his number one ambition in the world of technology, and his interests never expanded beyond forms of gaming (including card-based role playing games). He never learned programming at HTH, and the unconventional structure meant that he learned little math or English, either. With no family members using computers at work or employed in traditional white-collar jobs, the project-based curriculum left Lucas far behind. His parents, who were not computer literate themselves, were less able than they had been when Lucas attended a traditional school to monitor his progress on the digital portfolios, and mistook his long hours spent "practicing" on the computer in the afternoons as a sign of his success. They were repeatedly surprised by Lucas's failing midterm and final progress reports.

After barely gaining the units to graduate, Lucas took a job as a magician for conventions and parties. Nothing he learned at High Tech High was put to use here. Lucas had no interest in attending any college. His experience at High Tech High never extended his ambitions beyond being a video game tester, and when the access to technology was restricted, Lucas turned to playing the role playing card game Dungeons and Dragons. For Lucas, the High Tech High pedagogy, with its long-term deadlines, free afternoons for project work, and fewer classes, allowed him to optimize his play with new technologies and his interest in gaming, but Lucas was not an outstandingly clever or quick gamer (not that the career plan of being a game tester was realistic for any of the High Tech High students), nor was he curious enough to explore the programming behind the games. The curriculum's value of technical skills over traditional English skills did little for Lucas's lagging verbal communication skills—he did not learn to type or spell, and avoided written communication—preferring to remain in the live, peer-driven Dungeons and Dragons group.

Kenny found the opportunity to fuel his interest in gaming a temptation at High Tech High, but earned good grades and kept up with his work. Kenny was interested in manipulating technology and found the school to be a place where he could experiment with good technology. Kenny's driving interest was in video gaming, however, and it often distracted him from his schoolwork. When it came time to apply for college, however, he was rejected from all the University of California campuses—he was not competitive in standardized testing with students from a traditional curriculum. Kenny attended the local community college and would transfer later to a four-year college. His parents were monitoring the situation carefully, having been dismayed by his college rejections. Both Kenny and Lucas enjoyed the privilege of going to a high school they liked, even if the results were less than encouraging. The access to high technology did not prove to be the magic bullet for learning and motivation—in some ways it was a distraction for both Kenny and Lucas, who were unable to convert their Web site making skills, honed through all those digital portfolios, into a job or a premium college admission. High Tech High has since moved to more structured coursework and abandoned the free afternoons for project work. While the school regularly and enthusiastically offers tours, it does not open its doors to outside researchers. Rosenstock keeps a very tight rein on the kind of information about the school that becomes publicly available, and its image in the press is carefully crafted, from vivid portraits of kids lifted from dysfunctional homes to MIT admissions. All press coverage of the school quotes the statistics that all of its graduates attend college—a carefully spun piece of public relations.

Expensive charter schools on the model of High Tech High increase equity problems in a school district. While the initial emphasis was on working-class and minority youth in admissions, by 2006, only 15 percent of the students enrolled in High Tech High qualified for federal free lunches. Admissions are reportedly based on proportional rates based on county zip code—if this were restricted to city zip codes, the student body would undoubtedly be of a lower income, given the predominance of wealthy suburbs and sky-high real estate prices in San Diego County. This higher rate of middle-class children attending the charter suggests several things about schools and family social networks. They also attract those parents with the most cultural capital, who are likely to be the most active participants in fundraising, and volunteer time, thus depleting the support resources for traditional schools. The application process for charters like High Tech High constitutes an enormous barrier for working-class families. The amount of writing places most non-English speaking families beyond the applicant pool already. Knowing how and when a child needs to get on the waiting list alone requires diligent research and a strong social network. It takes parents with a certain level and kind of cultural capital to worry enough to put an infant on a waiting list for a charter high school. It also takes a rare kind of job stability to predict the family's whereabouts a dozen years ahead. A charter like High Tech High is difficult to reach by public transportation, offers no bus service, requires waking early, and returning home late (thus precluding the student from caring for siblings or helping with dinner or housework after school). Social capital in the form of networks, reinforced by de facto income segregation in housing markets, become urgently important for carpooling to school. Charter schools thus attract and concentrate those parents with the most cultural capital at the smallest schools. These parents are the most active participants in fundraising, and volunteer work ranging from the administrative (school site councils, budgetary oversight panels, and school boards) to the educational (computer help, reading, and math tutoring), thus depleting the support resources for traditional schools. While parents can hardly be blamed for deserting traditional schools—especially when their worst fears about drugs, violence, and educational achievement are continually reinforced in the press—the effect has been to create, within publicly funded schools, an elite stratum that resembles the privileges formerly reserved for those who can afford the (now exorbitant) tuitions of elite private schools.

Educational inequality in a state or school district worsens when high profile, well-publicized, and expensive experiments in education like High Tech High attract vast amounts of grant money, reducing the pool for neighborhood schools and school districts. High Tech High was rewarded in 2003 with enormous grants from the Gates Foundation that were designed to enable Rosenstock himself to choose ten schools to recreate the High Tech High paradigm. A commitment of $7 million has been made by the Gates Foundation and other corporate philanthropies to extend the High Tech High model to other U.S. cities.

What dangers does the High Tech High model, where large investments from high tech firms commit start-up money to charters, pose for students and local schools? The High Tech High model suggests that the solution to school problems will be corporate driven, and that the solution will be turning out students with skills and work habits suitable to the new digital economies. This reinforces the notion that the appropriate work of schools and teachers is to focus on fixing problems with the economy and the labor market, and to facilitate the transition to digital–knowledge-based forms of production. Biddle and Berliner trace these ideas to the nineteenth century, while usefully reminding us of their popularization in the 1950s with the "Human Capital" trend in educational reform, which emphasized thinking about students as human resources, and investing in education to the extent that it would "benefit industry and fuel the national economy. In early years this argument had been seized by canny industrialists, who realized they could reduce costs if the public schools could only be persuaded to provide the specialized training their firms would otherwise have to fund in apprenticeship programs."[45] Worries about the ability of the United States to compete in the global economy, and calls to prepare students for work in some kind of new—and typically vague—forms of employment were not born with the internet. Before the Gates Foundation got into the business of reforming U.S. public schools, Ross Perot, having made a fortune in computers, did the same in the state of Texas, with a host of negative, unintended consequences.[46] The idea that having made a fortune in high technology is the right credential for dictating educational policy, or that highly successful entrepreneurs are more thoughtful and perspicacious about schools than other leaders in society, needs to be rigorously challenged. Indeed, one of the modifications to Bourdieu's theories that must be made when using his work in the United States regarding cultural legitimacy, as sociologists Michele Lamont and Annette Lareau (1988) have explained, is that purchasable, rather than culturally acquired, symbols of legitimate culture have been more acceptable than in Western Europe and granted more weight.[47] There has also been a deeply held regard for technically oriented knowledge and for material accumulation, allowing those with less command of Western humanism, for example, to be held in the highest esteem.

Charter schools, especially those with the kind of profile of High Tech High, are less accountable to their local communities than neighborhood schools. This is true of all magnet schools to some extent, but it is especially true of high-profile schools driven by corporate philanthropists. Such schools depend on successful public relations efforts to make their achievements seem vastly superior to the efforts of teachers in traditional public schools. A constant stream of celebrities and politicians visit High Tech High, while serious researchers are kept out; instead, private educational consulting firms do the work of evaluation. Under these circumstances, it is easy to hide the failure of High Tech High for a student such as Lucas. How is a neighborhood school to compete with these combined advantages? Dozens of newspaper and magazine articles each year—written by journalists directly from press releases—parrot the successes of Gates Foundation educational experiments. Yet some evidence is accumulating (more systematic than my anecdotal cases of Lucas and Kenny, and their invisibility in the statistics about college success churned out by High Tech High) that challenges the wisdom of the Gates Foundation pedagogical strategies. In 2005, a study by SRI International and the American Institutes for Research (commissioned by the head of the Gates Foundation) found that, compared to traditional schools in the same school district, the Gates-funded schools had better attendance, more "welcoming" atmospheres, and harder reading and writing assignments than traditional schools. It is test scores on which traditional schools are crucified, however, and on these measures they did no better or even worse than traditional schools:

English and reading were only slightly improved, with 35% of the small schools' students doing moderate-quality work or better, compared with 33% at large high schools. The small-school goal of engaging students in projects that combined math with other subjects produced poor results because rigorous math instruction often got short shrift. Only 16% of students at Gates schools made the grade in math, vs. 27% at traditional schools.[48]

If these high profile philanthropic experiments in public education fail, the new breed of educational "CEOs" (as the principals of such endeavors are called) do not hesitate to close down the operation. The head of the New Visions project in New York—a Gates Foundation project—is described admiringly by Business Week. Yet the power of Gates Foundation money paved the way for an extraordinary new state law, enabling key charter school corporations, like Rosenstock's High, to completely bypass local school board approval for building ten more charter high schools in the state. The state law, Assembly Bill 1994, created an "alternative authorizer" process allowing the State Board to directly approve and oversee charters without intervention of the local school district.[49] A new San Diego venture capital firm, Revolution Community Ventures, is working on a for-profit basis to secure tax credits for the new charter schools.[50] The founder is working closely with Rosenstock, having moved from the high tech venture capital business to the charter school tax credit business. The granting of this exceptional opportunity to Rosenstock's chain of charter schools widens the San Diego precedent of hiring nonunion teachers and forgoing union rules for teacher training to the state as a whole. It removes the thorny issue of local accountability and local politics from the educational equation. Qualcomm and Microsoft, as represented by the philanthropies of Irwin Jacobs and Bill Gates, have bought their way into unprecedented, direct influence on matters of public schooling that have historically been the province of teachers, local communities, local elected officials, and families. They have paved the way for the deregulation of public schools and for public funding of what would have formerly been considered the kind of exceptions only available in private schools. They have rewritten the curriculum to place technology and the favored management techniques of their own firms at the center. They have installed their own school administrators and teachers, and they have done so without any long-term commitment of funds to sustain these very expensive—and untested—experiments in education.

Private philanthropy is obviously no substitute for public funding and support for schools. After these multimillion dollar grants have expired, the school is charged with the task of finding some other means of support. Foundations give the money and run. In their wake, they leave a precedent for subverting teacher union rules and lowering job security for teachers.[51] The erosion of teachers' rights threatens the very demographic group the Gates Foundation claims to serve, because public school teaching has historically been one of the primary avenues for working-class, African-American, and Latino students to gain a living wage, benefits, and a foothold in the middle class. Historically, employment as a unionized schoolteacher is a far more likely point of entry to the middle class than employment in high tech industries. Devaluing the work of teachers, by conferring on outside experts the right to decide what is best for specific communities of students, and favoring technological solutions to pedagogy, fundamentally marginalizes women, who have been and continue to be the majority of public school teachers.

Philanthropies are ruthless and fickle as funders of public schools. The results are always disappointing compared to the corporate world. After the money is gone, the tab must be picked up by local and state institutions, or by federal grants. After the funding is gone, the damage in public support for traditional schools remains: High Tech High stacks the deck for better outcomes on measures such as college attendance against neighborhood high schools and then blames the school district. Every exaggerated press release about the handful of success stories (such as MIT admission) from High Tech High, at the same time constitute a condemnation of the local schools that do not benefit from the extravagant budgets the philanthropists provide, and further evidence for technology as a cure-all for educational problems.

To return to the piano analogy, we might consider the spread of the piano in eighteenth century Europe when there was a widespread, rapid adoption of the instrument and a consequent growth in the production of pianos and the writing of piano music. In sociologist Max Weber's 1921 essay, "The History of the Piano," he traces the development of the piano from other keyboard instruments, and its relationship to artists and participants in Europe in the seventeenth and eighteenth centuries. "Because the instrument's free touch favored its use in rendering popular airs and dances, however, its specific public consisted essentially of amateurs, in the first instance, naturally enough those belonging to sections of society which were confined to their homes—monks . . . and then, in modern times, women. . . . "[52] His description of the ubiquity and universality of the piano as an instrument of modern education parallels contemporary accounts of desktop computers and Internet access:

The piano's present unshakeable position rests on its universal usefulness as a means of becoming acquainted at home with almost all the treasures of musical literature, on the immeasurable riches of its own literature and finally on its character as the universal instrument for the accompanist and the learners.[53]

Weber's account of the spread of the piano carefully notes, however, the specific requirements for early piano participants: bourgeois background, Northern European climate (due to the greater time spent indoors and more developed domestic culture of Northern as opposed to Southern Europe), and the capacity for enormous amounts of free time required to master the instrument.

To return to computers, the domestic PC is taking on a kind of universal status—certainly, it has attained profound impact as a "learning machine" and as a universal object of the bourgeois domestic sphere both for educational and leisure purposes. However, recognizing these features should not preclude scholars from attending to the large-scale geopolitical, social class, gender, and political economic dimensions of its presence in schools, homes, and workplaces. School credentials have become more necessary on the job market, even as the public school system has failed. Decisive choices about schooling are made earlier in children's lives. Demands originating in the corporate world for skilled, technically competent workers constantly necessitate discussions of youth and digital learning, and influence our descriptions of best practices. Yet, high tech jobs on the whole have experienced far less growth than predicted, as compared to service jobs and skilled trades.[54] When students do find a "high tech" job, it is more likely to be the kind described at the beginning of this essay: Marco's work installing DSL lines in upscale neighborhoods for Time Warner. The High Tech High credo is "Technology is not a subject, it is the primary mode of learning." Yet, this is a formalist view of pedagogy; technological determinism conveniently erases the struggle over curricular content, and how that content should concern historical, ethical, social, and esthetic concerns that are necessary for democracy.

We need efforts to invigorate the experience of school because it consists, for so many students, of a grinding repetition of failure—and is, in Bourdieu's words "rooted in absolute uncertainty about the future and in the conflicting aspirations that school opens and closes at one and the same time."[55] Student enthusiasm for computers and the internet has been embraced in many settings as a means of trading access for a stronger investment in learning and the life of the classroom. Yet, we must also ask deeper questions about digital learning that encompass the undesirable consequences—the ways learning through technology favors higher income and better equipped students, and the forms of knowledge that tend to be excluded in the digital environment. Pedagogical strategies must be framed in the specifics of local, diverse groups of learners. As Peters warns:

When we talk of the knowledge economy, we must realize that knowledge has a strong cultural and local dimension as well as a universalistic dimension . . . the other half of the equation that often gets forgotten in development talk. We should speak, then, of knowledge cultures (in the plural) and cultural knowledges, just as we should acknowledge alongside the knowledge economy, the economy of knowledges.[56]

School reform efforts of the last decades have tended to devalue local knowledge, fluency in Spanish and languages other than English, and to discredit the perspective and understanding gained from the immigration experience, and the "culture of caring," as Angela Valenzuela has documented in her study of Texas high schools.[57] This complete discreditation of the forms of cultural capital that students already possess is summed up by one of Rosenstock's often-repeated statements: "You want to transform where kids are going, not replicate where they've come from."[58]

Weber's account of piano history takes care to note the instruments and musical systems that were lost or discounted by the rise of the piano—as well as the amateur musical culture of users, artists, and performers whose culture diminished. We need to bring into our account of digital learning the same keen attention to the forms of cultural knowledge—cultural and social capital—that are underrepresented on the internet and marginalized by new technologies.

Conclusion

In the field of cyber education, it pays to be optimistic. The government and the private corporations whose interests it guards like to hear that the use of digital media is a superior "delivery system" for learning. In other words, there are powerful economic interests behind the promotion of hardware and software in educational institutions at all levels. As D. A. Menchnik has noted, this has made "the line that separates benevolent, authentic concern for student learning enrichment from self-interested entrepreneurship difficult to ascertain."[59] This is a pessimistic essay. I earned my pessimism the hard way—by teaching computers and the internet in an after-school elementary program for four years. The children in that program astonished me with their resilience and their deep experience of the complexities of the global. I am not pessimistic about the ability of children to learn rapidly about technology when provided with good opportunities, and to think critically about the new media environment. I am pessimistic about the long-term effects on public education of the vast concentration of wealth at the top that has accompanied the digital revolution, the unprecedented concentration of media ownership, and the shift of power from the public realm to that of private corporations. I am pessimistic about the home technology divide in a society where income inequality is so immense, and profit imperatives prevail over the social good. I am even more pessimistic about the future of public schools, especially if they are to be entrusted to the Gates Foundation.

The rise of digital technologies coincided with the blockage of opportunity in affordable, public higher education, intensified antiimmigrant policies, and a disturbing increase in the numbers of children living below the poverty line. When corporations set the goals for classroom technology use, the goal of strong digital literacy falls far short of its potential to foster critical thinking.[60] As Raymond Williams reminds us, about literacy in nineteenth century England: "the acquisition of literacy, then as now, almost always involved submission to a lengthy period of social training—education—in which quite other things than literacy or similar skills were taught; in which, in fact values and norms were taught which became, very often, inextricable from the literacy."[61] We need to develop an ideal of strong digital literacy that would encompass both the capacity to author in ways that might impact civil society and an understanding of the political economy of new media that includes not only challenges to intellectual property and copyright, but also an analysis of wealth distribution and the potential for exploitation in labor involving computers.

The analogy of the piano and the computer, in light of Bourdieu's model of social, economic, and cultural capital, has demonstrated some of the fallacies of logic behind digital technology as a cure-all for education. Steinway has always made exaggerated, optimistic predictions in its marketing campaigns: vastly overestimating the statistical occurrence of musical genius in the general population, as well as the chances for success as a musical impresario. Yet, no school board would decide to purchase a Steinway for every student as a means of enriching the overall achievement of students or their motivation to learn. No educator would accept the elimination of curricular content that would be necessary in order for children to learn the piano during normal school hours. It would be preposterous to imagine that a child could master the piano at school without having access to one at home. Laptops might seem cheaper than baby grand pianos, but with the planned obsolescence of hardware and software, they are more costly over the long run, in terms of the continual need to replace and upgrade them. There are pressing questions about the sustainability of a technology emphasis in K-12 education, how long the generosity of even the wealthiest parties, such as the Gates Foundation, will last, and what will have been lost when his educational interventions are done. Computers might seem more necessary to modern life than the piano, but the costs of rewriting the curriculum to accommodate them are as yet uncalculated. The time for technological utopianism is past: we need to be clear and precise about the goals and the feasibility of technology learning, in the context of a realistic assessment of the labor market and widening class divides, struggles for fair employment in both technology industries and other job sectors, and the pressing need to empower students as citizens who can participate actively in a democracy.

Notes

1. Pierre Bourdieu and Loic Wacquant, *An Invitation to Reflexive Sociology* (Chicago: University of Chicago Press, 1992), 118.

2. Max Weber, The History of the Piano, *Selections in Translation*, ed. W. G. Runciman, trans. E. Matthews (Cambridge, UK: Cambridge University Press, 1977), 378–83.

3. Jean Anyon, *Ghetto Schooling: A Political Economy of Urban Educational Reform* (New York and London: Teachers College Press, 1997).

4. David Berliner and Bruce Biddle, *The Manufactured Crisis: Myths, Fraud, and the Attack on America's Public Schools* (Reading, MA: Addison-Wesley, 1995); Linda McNeil, *Contradictions of School Reform: Educational Costs of Standardized Testing* (New York and London: Routledge, 2000).

5. Clifford Stoll, *High-Tech Heretic: Reflections of a Computer Contrarian* (New York: Anchor, 2000).

6. Ellen Seiter, *The Internet Playground: Children's Access, Entertainment and Mis-Education* (New York: Peter Lang, 2005).

7. Lori Weisberg, Local Housing Costs Drain Family Budget, *San Diego Union Tribune*, 27 August 2002,1.

8. Boring but Important, *The Week*, November 24, 2006, 22.

9. Mark Warschauer, *Technology and Social Inclusion: Rethinking the Digital Divide* (Cambridge, MA: MIT Press, 2003), 202.

10. Warschauer, 2003, 12.

11. Adam Greenfield. *Everyware: The Dawning of the Age of Ubiquitous Computing* (Berkeley, CA: New Riders, 2006), 1.

12. Bourdieu and Wacquant, *An Invitation to Reflexive Sociology*.

13. Seiter, *The Internet Playground*.

14. Urbana/Dearborn study; Gaskins.

15. Pierre Bourdieu, *Dinstinction: A Social Critique of the Judgment of Taste,* trans. Richard Nice (Cambridge, MA: Harvard University Press, 1984), 87.

16. David Buckingham, *Media Education: Literacy, Learning and Contemporary Culture* (London: Polity, 2003), 175.

17. Jane Margolis and Allan Fisher, *Unlocking the Clubhouse: Women in Computing* (Cambridge, MA: MIT Press, 2002); Sandra Calvert, *Children's Journeys Through the Information Age* (New York: McGraw-Hill, 1999).

18. Ellen Seiter, *The Internet Playground*, 2005; Marcia C. Linn, Elizabeth Davis, and Phillip Bell, *Internet Environments for Science Education* (Mahwah, NJ: Lawrence Erlbaum, 2006).

19. Janet Ward Schofield and Ann Locke Davidson, *Bringing the Internet to School: Lessons from an Urban District* (San Francisco: Jossey-Bass, 2002), 202.

20. Michael Cole, *The Fifth Dimension: An After-school Program Built on Diversity* (New York: Russell Sage Foundation, 2006); Olga Vasquez, *La Clase Magica: Imagining Optimal Possibilities in a Bilingual Community of Learners* (Mahwah, NJ: Lawrence Erlbaum, 2002).

21. Pierre Bourdieu, *Pascalian Meditations* (Palo Alto, CA: Stanford University Press, 2000); Pierre Bourdieu, *Distinction: A Social Critique of the Judgment of Taste,*1984; Pierre Bourdieu et al. *The Weight of the World: Social Suffering in Contemporary Society* (Cambridge, UK: Polity Press, 1999).

22. Andrew Ross, *No Collar: The Humane Workplace and its Hidden Costs* (Philadelphia: Temple University Press, 2003), 263.

23. Susan C. Losh, Gender, Educational and Occupational Digital Gaps 1983–2002, *Social Science Computer Review* 22, no. 2 (2004): 165.

24. John B. Horrigan, Home Broadband Adoption 2006 Report. Pew Internet and American Life Project, http://www.pewinternet.org/PPF/r/184/report_display.asp.

25. Andy Carvin, Race and the Digital Divide: A Current Snapshot, March 31, 2006. http://www.andycarvin.com.

26. Stanley Aronowitz, Against Schooling: Education and Social Class, Social Text 22, no. 2 (2004): 30.

27. Bourdieu and Wacquant, *An Invitation to Reflexive Sociology*, 119.

28. Warschauer, *Technology and Social Inclusion*, 201.

29. Geert Lovink, Strategies for Media Activism, Presented at Code Red event, The Performance Space, Sydney, 23 November 1997.

30. Pierre Bourdieu, *Dinstinction: A Social Critique of the Judgment of Taste*, 217.

31. John Cassidy, Me Media, *The New Yorker,* 15 May 2006, 50.

32. Ross, *The Humane Workplace*, 30.

33. Ibid. 18.

34. Gina Neff, Elizabeth Wissinger, and Sharon Sukin, Entrepreneurial Labor among Cultural Producers: "Cool" Jobs in "Hot" Industries, *Social Semiotics* 15, no. 3 (2005): 308.

35. Anand Aneesh, Skill Saturation: Rationalization and Post-industrial Work, *Theory and Society* 30, no. 3 (2001): 387.

36. Rob Kling, *Computerization and Controversy: Value Conflicts and Social Choices* (San Diego, CA: Academic Press, 1996).

37. John R. Hall, The Capital(s) of Cultures: A Nonholistic Approach to Status Situations, Class, Gender, and Ethnicity, in *Cultivating Differences: Symbolic Boundaries and the Making of Inequality,* eds. Michele Lamont and M. Fournier (Chicago: University of Chicago Press, 1992).

38. Benkler, 2006.

39. Ibid.

40. Horrigan, "Home Broadband Adoption 2006 Report."

41. Pierre Bourdieu, *Pascalian Meditations*, 2000; Pierre Bourdieu, *Dinstinction: A Social Critique of the Judgment of Taste,* 1984; Pierre Bourdieu et al. *The Weight of the World: Social Suffering in Contemporary Society,* 1999.

42. Benkler, 2006.

43. Helen Gao, State OKs 10 charter High Tech schools; S.D. chain needs no local approval, *San Diego Union Tribune B-1,* January 13, 2006a; Helen Gao, "Venture capitalist seeks education revolution; Investment focus is charter schools," *San Diego Union Tribune B-1,* July 11, 2006b.

44. Victoria Murphy, Where Everyone Can Overachieve, *Forbes,* October 11, 2004, http://www.forbes.com/free_forbes/2004/1011/080.html?rl04.

45. Berliner and Biddle, *The Manufactured Crisis,* 141.

46. McNeil, *Contradictions of School Reform.*

47. Michele Lamont and Annette Lareau. 1988.

48. Jay Green and William C. Symonds, "Bill Gates gets schooled: Why he and other execs have struggled in their school reform efforts, and why they keep trying," *Business Week,* June 26, 2006.

49. Business Wire, 2006.

50. Helen Gao, "State OKs 10 charter High Tech schools; S.D. chain needs no local approval," *San Diego Union Tribune B-1,* January 13, 2006a; Helen Gao, *San Diego Union Tribune B-1* (July 11, 2006b).

51. McNeil, *Contradictions of School Reform.*

52. Weber, "The History of the piano," 379.

53. Ibid., 381.

54. Berliner and Biddle, *The Manufactured Crisis,* 142; Dan Schiller, *Digital Capitalism: Networking the Global Market System* (Cambridge, MA: MIT Press, 1999); Kenneth Saltman, Junk-king education, *Cultural Studies* 16 no. 2 (2002): 253; Ross, *The Humane Workplace.*

55. Pierre Bourdieu et al. *The Weight of the World: Social Suffering in Contemporary Society,*185.

56. Michael A. Peters. *Building Knowledge Cultures: Education and Development in the Age of Knowledge Capitalism* (Lanham, MA: Rowman and Littlefield, 2006), 158.

57. Angela Valenzuela, *Subtractive Schooling: US Mexican Youth and the Politics of Caring* (Albany: State University of New York Press, 1999).

58. Victoria Murphy, Where Everyone Can Overachieve, *Forbes,* (October 11, 2004), http://www.forbes.com/free_forbes/2004/1011/080.html?rl04.

59. D.A. Menchik, Placing Cybereducation in the UK Classroom, *British Journal of Sociology of Education* 25, no. 2 (2004): 193.

60. T. Vaden and Juha Suoranta, Breaking Radical Monopolies: Towards Political Economy of Digital Literacy, *E-Learning* 1, no. 2 (2004).

61. Raymond Williams, *Television, Technology and Cultural Form* (New York: Anchor Books, 1974), 131.

High Tech or High Risk: Moral Panics about Girls Online

Justine Cassell and Meg Cramer

Northwestern University, Center for Technology and Social Behavior

Imagine a suburban neighborhood at sunset. A police car drives past a quaint one-story home. The children inside are so precious; their parents would do anything to protect them. When children are at home, they should be safe. But what about the internet?

A man at the end of the information super-highway sits in a dark room and with glazed eyes, he sits typing this to someone's blond daughter:

Scott16:   When can we meet 4 real?

LizJones13:   Tomorrow after soccer?

LizJones13:   Let's meet at 4

Scott16:   I'll be there.

Sincere thanks to Brooke Foucault, Susan Herring, Henry Jenkins, Jane Margolis, Tara McPherson, Ellen Seiter, and the members of the ArticuLab for comments and discussion that vastly improved this manuscript. All remaining inconsistencies are certainly not their fault.

The images and dialogue above come from a public service announcement (PSA) from NetSmartz Workshop, an online interactive educational safety resource. Like many internet safety campaigns and news reports, the PSA warns parents of terrible danger: "When your children are at home you think they are safe. But are they? What about the internet? Have you taught them how to protect themselves online?,"[1] and parents are indeed afraid. According to a recent CTIA Wireless Survey cited in PC Magazine, 85 percent of U.S. parents believe that the internet is the medium that poses the most risk for teens.[2]

According to the oft-cited Youth Internet Safety Survey from 2001, whose respondents consisted of 1,500 teenagers, approximately one in five American teenagers have been sexually solicited online.[3] Dateline NBC's "To Catch a Predator" quotes law enforcement officials as estimating that "50,000 predators are online at any given moment."[4] Based on these warnings and these statistics, it's not surprising that parents are scared, and that government officials are feeling pushed to act, as witnessed by President Bush's July 27, 2006 signature of the Sex Offender Bill which, among other programs, will fight online porn with twenty-year minimum prison terms for participation in "child exploitation enterprises" and criminal prosecution for "deceiving children into viewing obscene material."[5]

But, does the internet pose as much of a constant—and unusual—danger to online teens as these descriptions suggest? If so, what is the actual nature of the danger—is it exposure to inappropriate images, such as pornography, or is it also the risk of kidnapping, rape, or murder? Are the eleven million American teenagers who use the internet daily unknowingly subjecting themselves to certain danger? Are the 87 percent of teens who are online more at risk of victimization than the 13 percent of teens who are not online? In this chapter we argue that there is much more to the story than teens, computers, and criminals. It is not by chance that the viewer of the Netsmartz PSA sees a nice suburban house, a cop car, a fence, a window with a security system logo, two white parents, a large screen television, and a clean, average living room. If there is panic surrounding the dangers of the internet, it is also a moral panic. However, the panic over young girls at risk from communication technologies is not new rhetoric in America. There has been a recurring moral panic throughout history, not just over real threats of technological danger, but also over the compromised virtue of young girls, parental loss of control in the face of a seductive machine, and the debate over whether women can ever be high tech without being in jeopardy.

In what follows, we first look to the facts—the crime statistics that diverge in a number of important respects from the way in which many people seem to believe that child victimization takes place on the internet. In fact, contrary to popular belief, the percentage of single offender crimes against girls where the offender is an adult and a stranger has *declined*, not increased, since 1994—concurrent with the rise of internet use. And, even online, the number of stranger offenders is declining. Given this good news, why do we hear only bad news about the internet in the media? In order to explain this widespread fear on the part of parents, educators, and politicians, we will look at the point-to-point communications technologies of the past, and the parallels between public responses to their use with today's moral panic. Then, we will address the perspective of the users themselves, the young women who have been the object of so much concern. Like the representation of Liz Jones, who literally has no face in the Netsmartz PSA, the female users have virtually no agency in the media responses to crimes. While they are ascribed roles of naiveté, innocence, or delinquency in the media, in actuality, they turn out to be active and informed consumers and producers of mediated conversations and texts. The important identity construction, self-efficacy, and social network production work that they do online is not only largely ignored, but too often condemned. In sum, in this chapter we argue that the dangers to girls online are not as severe as they have been portrayed, and that the reason for this exaggeration of danger arises from adult fears about girls' agency (particularly sexual agency) and societal discomfort around girls as power users of technology.

One in Five

It is common to hear, on the news or at the water cooler, that parents and schools must regain control and oversee their children on the internet, for the risk to unsupervised children is extremely high. And the reality, of course, is that there does exist a risk for teens on the internet. In the same ways that teens have used the internet to network, construct more robust identities, and gain feedback on their transgressive activities, so too pedophiles have used the internet for much the same purposes.[6]

Yet, teens are also at risk in the mall, walking home from school, and spending a vacation with distant relatives, and, as we will discuss further below, family members and friends, rather than strangers, are still the most frequent perpetrators of child sexual abuse. Why, therefore, do the media and many parents seem so obsessed with the dangers of the internet, why are they so unbridled in their condemnation, so overstated in their description of the risk? The following snippet of an interview with internet activist Perry Aftab illustrates well the tendency to exaggeration:

Aftab told co-anchor Julie Chen: Sadly, (those stories don't) surprise me. We're having a huge growth of anybody who's ever thought about molesting children getting online and talking to anyone they think is a young teen. . . . Anybody who's ever thought about it can do it quite easily, they think, anonymously.[7]

MSNBC similarly stirs up fear without a source:

Experts interviewed for this article could not cite a single case of a child predator hunting for and finding a child through a blog. But there are cases of children being lured through other Internet services, such as chat rooms.

"I don't see why pedophiles wouldn't use this tool, if this is where kids are," said Ann Coulier of Net Family News.[8]

So what are the facts? In fact, the bottom line is that sexual exploitation and other offenses against children remain tragic, whatever their numbers, but those numbers have been diminishing, not increasing, since the advent of the internet. That is, in looking across the board, aggregating internet-initiated and real world crimes, according to the Juvenile Offenders and Victims 2006 National Report, the nonfatal violent victimization rate of youth ages 12–17 was half the rate in 2003 than it was ten years earlier.[9]

Overall, the rate of serious violent crimes, including aggravated assault, rape, robbery, and homicide, is on the decline for ages 12–17 for both boys and girls, as can be seen in the following two graphs, and summary.[10]

The serious violent victimization decline in the graphs below combines the rates of aggravated assault, rape, robbery, and homicide. However, the crimes most feared by parents, and most cited by those in favor of restricting girls' access to social networking sites, are rape and sexual assault; therefore, we assembled statistics on these crimes by compiling data from eleven years of National Crime Victimization Survey data, as published by the U.S. Department of Justice/Office of Justice Programs Bureau of Justice Statistics. These statistics

Figure 1a Serious violent victimizations per 1,000 juveniles in age group.   Figure 1b Serious violent victimizations per 1,000 juveniles ages 12–17.

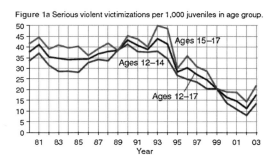

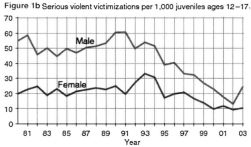

Table 1

Percent change in victimization rates—1993–1995 to 2003–2005[11]

Type of Crime	Ages 12–14	Ages 15–17
Nonfatal violence	−59%	−50%
Robbery	−66	−53
Aggravated assault	−69	−61
Simple assault	−57	−46

show a clear decrease between 1992 and 2004 (the most recent date for which statistics are available). The decline has been so well documented by different types of evidence, and involves so many different kinds of children, offenders, types of abuse, and areas of the United States, that Finkelhor and Jones believe the decrease to be due at least in part to a true decline in instances of sexual abuse (as opposed, for example, to a decrease due to diminished reporting of sexual abuse).[12] In fact, as Finkelhor and Janes report, diminished instances of sexual abuse appear to account for a large part of the 15 percent decline in child maltreatment in general.[13] Additionally, in the years when young people would have begun using social networking sites (Friendster in 2002, MySpace in 2003), the rape and sexual assault crime rate has been lower than in the 1990s.

Given these statistics, it is difficult to believe, as Aftab claimed above, that anybody who has ever considered child molestation is getting online and talking to teens, for if that were the case, we would expect the overall statistics to rise and not decrease. However, perhaps it is the case that the bad guys are migrating from the physical world online, and so, whereas the overall statistics are decreasing, perhaps there is a leap in child sexual solicitation and victimization by adults online.

In order to examine that question, we are lucky to have the brand new Youth Internet Safety Survey (YISS) statistics, released on August 9, 2006. The YISS survey was first administered to 1,501 young people between August 1999 and February 2000,[14] and was administered a second time to a different sample of 1,500 young people, between March and June 2005.[15] The earlier survey, the YISS-1, has often been quoted in the media as a proof of the risk of child predators on the internet, since the data showed that one in five youth online had been sexually solicited. In fact, a closer look revealed that the majority of these sexual solicitations in 2001 were not from adult predators, but instead came from other youth. The questions posed to the youths in the current study concerned experiences of sexual solicitation, unwanted exposure to sexual material, and harassment via the internet in the past year. The results of YISS-2 do show increased exposure to unwanted sexual material (for example, through obscene spam) and increased nonsexual harassment (for example,

Table 2
YISS-2 Internet sexual solicitation of youth

Age of youth	All incidents	Aggressive incidents	Distressing incidents
10	0	0	0
11	3%	1%	5%
12	7%	5%	10%
13	9%	14%	10%
14	15%	14%	18%
15	23%	27%	15%
16	24%	16%	25%
17	19%	22%	16%
Gender of youth			
Girl	70%	79%	81%
Boy	30%	21%	19%
Gender of solicitor			
Male	73%	84%	86%
Female	16%	16%	7%
Don't know	11%	0%	7%
Age of solicitor			
Younger Than 18 Years	43%	44%	40%
18 to 25 Years	30%	34%	31%
Older Than 25 Years	9%	15%	15%
Don't Know	18%	7%	14%

through cyber bullying from peers). However, the category of actions that is most often held up as a danger—solicitation to meet offline from a stranger adult—is smaller today than it was five years ago—one out of every seven youths online reports being solicited in 2005 (table 2). And, once again, the data show that the majority of these solicitations come from family, family friends, and peers, rather than strangers. In fact, the ratio of acquaintances to strangers is growing. In YISS-2, 14 percent of solicitations were from offline friends and acquaintances compared to only 3 percent in YISS-1. As the authors of the study state, "as in YISS-1 many of the YISS-2 solicitors did not match the stereotype of the older male 'Internet predator.'"[16]

While solicitors often do not match the stereotypical offender that is so often feared, it is also the case that the victim is not the stereotypical teen girl. Of the youth in the study, girls aged 14–17 have the highest rate of online solicitation. This is not surprising, as most juvenile victims of violent crimes are female.[17] Online, however, these girls are experiencing a change of solicitation rates in the past five years that is larger than that of boys of the same age, and boys and girls, aged 10–13. Where solicitations for boys aged 14–17 only dropped 5 percent, solicitations for girls of the same age dropped 11 percent. As for the increased exposure to unwanted sexual material since 2000, the rate of increase was the least for girls aged 14–17, at plus 7 percent. In 2005, boys surpassed girls in their rate of exposure to unwanted sexual material.[18]

In addition, interactions between a teen and a person soliciting sexual behavior are not always carried out in the relative privacy of the online interaction. Forty-one percent of youth who received online solicitations in 2005 were with a friend or a group of friends at the time of the incident. The authors of the YISS-2 hypothesize that "it may be that some youth tend to ignore Internet safety guidelines when they are in groups. They may be more likely to do things such as going to questionable chat rooms or engaging in risqué conversations with people they know only online, situations in which solicitations may be more likely to occur."[19] As youth negotiate group structures and their own behavior according to the social conditions, they are likely to explore and test out adult scenarios. Youth may be more daring in groups and they also may be more self-regulated.

Despite the clarity of the data reported here, strikingly, the Center for Missing and Exploited Children, which funded the report, buries the good news about reduced stranger solicitation and trumpets on the front page of their Web site "new study shows youth online subject to more sexual material and harassment."

A final interesting statistic concerns the 4 percent of online youth who experienced an aggressive solicitation in 2005. Aggressive solicitation involves offline contact with the perpetrator through regular mail, by telephone, or in person, or attempts or requests for offline contact, and this percentage has remained constant since 2001. The statistic is small; however, it is still interesting to investigate how teens dealt with these solicitations. In fact, 66 percent of those solicited removed themselves from the situation by blocking or leaving the computer; 16 percent told the solicitor to stop, confronted, or warned the solicitor; and 11 percent ignored the solicitor. Social networking site users themselves tell us that they interact primarily with their peers online, and eschew stranger adults, so these results should not come as a surprise. As Henry Jenkins and danah boyd have argued:

The fear of predators has regularly been touted as a reason to restrict youth from both physical and digital publics. Yet, as Barry Glassner notes in *The Culture of Fear*, predators help distract us from more statistically significant molesters. Youth are at far greater risk of abuse in their homes and in the homes of their friends than they ever are in digital or physical publics.[20]

Sadly, Jenkins and boyd's statement is true. The offenders of youth violent crime are not likely to be adult strangers, unless the crime is robbery. The most common offender in juvenile victim crimes is a family member or an acquaintance. Only 8 percent of violent crimes committed against female juveniles (ages 0–17) are carried out by strangers. As juveniles age, offenders are less likely to be family members and more likely to be acquaintances, but the number of offenders in sexual assault that are related to the victim remains high. Around one out of every five sex offenders is a relative for victims aged 12–17, and an additional third of juvenile sexual assaults are perpetrated not by adult strangers, but by juvenile offenders. As we have seen above in the YISS-2 study, teens are ignoring predators and solicitations online. The majority are not inviting the potential molester into their homes or meeting up with them. Often, children who do begin online relationships with an abuser fit a particular profile—the profile fit by Justin Berry, the young man who operated a teenage pornography internet site featuring his own erotic performances beginning at the age of thirteen. "Children in contact with online molesters may have a greater tendency for conflict or lack of communication with their parents; high levels of delinquency, including committing assault, vandalism, or theft; or have a troubled personality due to depression, peer victimization, or a distressing life event."[21] However, it must be remembered that, sadly, many children are more at risk in their homes, with their families and friends, and during times of the day when children are often not alone. These statistics are horrifying, and it would be terrible if panic over the use of the internet came to obscure the real danger posed to young people by those close to them, and if legislation came to ignore this familiar danger, in favor of the often mythic online predator.

What is behind the fear of predators, if not a rise in the number of predators? What is the fear of going online, when the risks it poses are trumped by the actual statistics about victimization? What function does the fear serve, and who is its object? In order to answer this question, we look at a number of parallels from the past.

Panic at the Keyboard ... the Dial ... and the Transmitter ...

The telegraph network crisscrossed the world. As Tom Standage has shown in *The Victorian Internet,* although the equipment was different, the responses to the telegraph and the modern internet are strikingly similar.[22] The telegraph provided users with faster responses to their communication with others, more frequent interactions, and more access to others around the world. It improved access to goods and services, and to knowledge of all sorts. And yet, even while the telegraph (and the internet) led to a revolution in business practices, it also gave rise to new ways to commit crimes,[23] and it was quickly adopted beyond business to the communication needs of everyday people. In the techie magazines of the times (such as *Electrical World*, the historical parallel to *PC Magazine*) many authors alluded to a possible loss of a world they idealized, a world threatened by new modes of electrical communication. As Carolyn Marvin writes, "electrical communication made family courtships, class identities and other arenas of society suddenly strange, with consequences that were entirely spun out in electrical literature."[24] The telegraph was felt to have limitless potential, for business and for men. Because the telegraph was supposed to radically improve business, the effort it took to send every letter of a message was deemed worthwhile to expend only when the message held military or commercial importance, realms that were at that time controlled and dominated by men. The telegraph used in other ways was a concern. "Frivolous" messages, messages that conveyed social gossip or home life, did not warrant the time and cost of instantaneous telegraphic communication. Thus, while the limitless access to communication possibilities was praised in the context of commerce, at the same time the limitless access to communication for women was condemned. Media critics of the times described the telegraph as used by "talkative women" who had "frivolous electrical conversations" about "inconsequential personal subjects."[25] Novels, like the 1879 *Wired Love,* and other popular culture texts expanded on this theme. The women portrayed in these narratives were naïve and incapable in the face of technical advances, and when they made forays into the world of the telegraph they ended up needing to be rescued, to be protected from technology, in sum. Nor were the women portrayed in these novels capable of learning about technology; they rarely learned from their mistakes or corrected their misconceptions. This technical ignorance was a virtue of "good" women. The moral was that women's use of men's technology would come to no good end.[26]

Paradoxically, in the early stages of mass communication, the only women who were able to use nondomestic technology were those employed as telegraphers. Most other women had very little exposure to machines outside of the domestic sphere. Women telegraphers had less technical ignorance than their peers who did not enter the work force, but they were nevertheless the object of discrimination and technical scrutiny. While at first, the telegrapher position was not gender-stereotyped, as men returned from the Civil War, women found themselves defending their presence in the industry. It was felt that men needed to protect their jobs, and that women should be kept out of the union and off the lines.[27] Published in *Electrical World* in 1905, the article "Women as Telegraphists" states: "Were it not for the docility of women there is no sufficient reason apparent to justify the favour with which they are viewed by administrative officers and others responsible for their employment." The author goes on to critique the role of women in managerial positions as he recounts his research in Italy's telegraph offices:

Despite the fairly broad academic education which they possess . . . this higher class of women is stated by the administration to not come up to expectations. They are found to be lacking in authority over their staff and unable to respond to heavy and sudden requirements of the service. From exhaustive inquires which I made on the spot in 1899, they would appear to be lacking in judgment and decision, and unable to apply effectively the technical knowledge they possess.[28]

Not only were they incapable of technical competence, young women, most vulnerable to losing their virtue, were also thought to be the most vulnerable to the vice of the telegraph. Interestingly, these very same young women were the most likely to be hired as telegraph operators, and the quickest to pick up the technical skills, despite the rhetoric about women's incompetence in the face of the technology. But, for the operators themselves, the job had double value—it was a job outside the home and it was an opportunity for romance.[29] Operators had relationships with each other, although most had never seen each other in the physical world. The same journals that published novellas about women's technical incompetence also published stories of mistaken identity, and clandestine affairs over the wire. In 1886, an article titled "The Dangers of Wired Love" recounted the real-life story of Maggie McCutcheon, who helped her father run a newspaper stand in Brooklyn, and operated the telegraph in her father's store due to his lack of technical skill. Soon Mr. McCutcheon found out that she was "keeping up a flirtation" with a number of men, and in particular one married man whom she had met online; she ultimately invited "Frank Frisbee" to visit her in the real world. Mr. McCutcheon found out and forbade his daughter to meet with the man, but Maggie nevertheless continued to meet him in secret. The father followed his daughter and threatened to blow her brains out for her bad behavior.[30]

These themes of parental technical deficiency and ensuing parental loss of control in the face of a daughter's appropriation of the technology for her own ends are common in the literature and publicity surrounding all the communications technologies. The telephone produced anxiety to an even greater extent than the telegraph.

In the early twentieth century, AT&T advertising campaigns associated the telephone with practical ends, like saving time. In the early years, the telephone promised ease for doing business, and later, when the telephone was marketed as a residential device, it was still for the household's efficient management.[31] Telephone companies knew about the telephone's potential to encourage sociability, but were tentative about promoting it as a tool for such conversations. Fischer explains that some industry men "worried that the telephone permitted inappropriate or dangerous discussions, such as illicit wooing."[32] Malcolm Willey and Stuart Rice in 1933 worried that the telephone had made social contacts brief and impersonal. Telephonic communication suggested a loss "of those values that inhere in a more intimate, leisurely, protracted personal discussion."[33] The telephone increased the pace of life and made privacy rare and difficult to achieve.[34] And, once again, the telephone threatened parental control over youth:

Again, while the result of modern communication may be to strengthen certain aspects of localism, it may simultaneously serve to break down the control hitherto exercised by relatively closely knit primary groups over individual conduct. For example, the telephone, utilized by the adolescent in "making a date," and the automobile, utilized in keeping it, may remove him from strict parental supervision to which he was formerly subject even within the same local community. Control may be further lessened through travel and increased mobility, as also through those agencies of mass impression which may easily lend themselves to the spread of patterns of delinquency no less than to the spread of more sociably desired patterns.[35]

As early as 1905, coextensive with the era when apologies were made for not owning a telephone, an issue of *Telephony* attacked women's telephonic relationships with male suitors.[36] "The invention of new machinery, devices and processes is continually bringing up new questions of law, puzzling judges, lawyers and laymen," the article stated. "The doors may be barred and a rejected suitor kept out, but how is the telephone to be guarded?" As Marvin describes it, the telephone not only created "unprecedented opportunities for courting and infidelity, but for romancing unacceptable persons outside one's own class and even one's own race in circumstances that went unobserved by the regular community."[37] "The potential for illicit sexual behavior had obvious and disquieting power to undermine . . . moral authority and social order." Once again, media pundits were uneasy and fascinated in equal measure with this new breed of women who were excited about the new contact between the sexes. It was commonly feared that these women might attract the wrong sorts of men, and that they were unaware of the powerful consequences of their appropriation of the technology.[38]

With the telephone, there was once again a contradiction between the push to employ women and girls as the operators of these new technologies, and a moral reaction of fear and condemnation of women using telephones and telegraphy. An Ontario newspaper, *The Watchman*, gave this account of female operators: "In the first place the clear feminine quality of their voice suits best the delicate instrument. Then girls are usually more alert than boys, and always more patient. Women are sensitive, more amenable to discipline, far gentler and more forbearing than men."[39] Boys, on the other hand, were dismissed for bad behavior or promoted to higher paying positions.[40] Companies insisted that women operators follow a course of "moral education" to make them pleasant "hello-girls" when interacting with subscribers. The purpose of such education and strict rules was primarily to increase call volume but also served another function: to keep employee attitudes consistent with the ideal values of society.[41]

As well as the societal regulation of female telephone operators, women subscribers were subjected to regulation by husbands and to societal scrutiny. For example, an etiquette column in 1930 warned "Patty" that to ensure that her boyfriend would "respect and admire her, she does not call him up during business or working hours . . . [and at home] she should not hold him up to the ridicule of his family by holding an absurdly long telephone conversation."[42] Frissen explains mildly:

> In spite of the crucial role the telephone seems to play in women's everyday life, the uses women make of the telephone are not taken very seriously. Even the industry had a blind spot for women's uses of the telephone. Domestic telephone use, particularly for sociable reasons, was not only weakly promoted, but even disapproved of. . . . Although many people, particularly women, used the telephone mainly for sociable reasons, it took the industry about twenty years to realize that sociability was a goal worthy of being advertised and marketed.[43]

Despite companies' efforts to direct how the telephone was used, women nevertheless cultivated their own purposes or "delinquent activities" as they were thought of—primarily social interaction.[44] It should be clear that women using technology for social purposes did not carry high social prestige.[45]

As we have seen, new communication technologies have always brought with them the hope for a society of open communication and unlimited access to knowledge, goods, and services. "All the inhabitants of the earth would be brought into one intellectual neighborhood" proclaimed Alonzo Jackman, advocating the Atlantic telegraph in 1848.[46] Much like automobiles and trains, when the telegraph and telephone were new, each increased the users' mobility. But access to others, access to information, access to opportunity—all these accesses, however partial (since it was only available to people of means who had access to the telegraph and telephone in the first place), also meant loss of social control.[47] Electronic media "led to a nearly total dissociation of physical place and social 'place.' When we communicate . . . where we are physically no longer determines where and who we are socially."[48] Uncontrolled movement in each case challenged the social order, particularly with respect to the role of young women.

Perhaps not surprisingly, it was the very same utopian characteristics of telegraphic and telephonic communication, where the symbols of status, gender, race, and ethnicity were putatively more difficult to discern, that fueled an increased panic over the loss of social control, and rather than making gender disappear, centered it in the public eye.[49] The promise of new communication technologies was supposed to be realized by men, but upheld—encouraged and supported, even rendered more gentle and less machine-like—by the female telegraph and telephone operators. But, when these same women appropriated the technologies to their own social and labor needs, the discourse soon turned to the misuse of technology, and the danger of the machine rather than its promise. Women's talk was negatively contrasted with the "efficient task-oriented, world talk of business and professional men."[50]

Historical evidence demonstrates that women and young people have long appropriated technology to their own ends in culturally important ways, but that very appropriation has proved a danger to the established social order, and by proxy has diminished in particular the female users in the eyes of those around them; has rendered them, in fact, "a threat to societal values and interests."[51] In the next section, before we turn to the modern "deviant activities" of female use of technology, we first take a more general look at the topic of delinquency among girls, and hence at the Victorian moral panic over the physical liberty of young teenage girls.

Victorian Predators and "Delinquent Daughters"

Victorian women were the subject of much scrutiny under the moral consciousness of social reform in the United States. Although a highly publicized "moral downfall" of women was at first thought by reformers to be the direct result of male vice and exploitation, women themselves soon came to be thought of as the deviant ones. The Purity Movement, which was launched by feminist women from various political and ideological backgrounds, and which worried about the effects of industrialization on the working-class girl, was soon replaced by a more conservative model of reform which held girls responsible for a perceived increase in sexually deviant behavior.[52]

This new model of social reform acknowledged the sexual agency of teenage girls, but emphasized the deviance of their behavior, and the need for social control. The awareness of female immorality and the perceived role of technology intensified during the first two decades of the twentieth century. Sexual promiscuity (often thought to lead to prostitution) among young working-class women in American cities was thought to pose serious moral, social, and health threats to the rest of society.[53] Alan Hunt argues in *Governing Morals* that "prostitution displaced poverty as the social evil which characterized, symbolized, and thematized Mid-Victorian society."[54]

New technologies of the time, such as the steam loom, meant that increasing numbers of women and girls worked outside of the home. In 1913, authors Woods and Kennedy wrote in their preface of *Young Working Girls* that "the problem of the adolescent girl of the tenement house family and the city factory or department store has come to be so keenly felt."[55] "Women have not only had to meet the general moral uncertainty of the age, but in addition have had to face the serious moral problems forced upon them by the reorganization of their sphere of life through its invasion by modern industry."[56]

In 1925, Winifred Richmond wrote in *The Adolescent Girl: A Book for Parents and Teachers* that "as would be expected, the most common form of delinquency in girls is antisocial sex behavior"; this was one of the only characteristics of delinquency that led to promiscuity, prostitution, and the lack of sexual hygiene.[57] In this new atmosphere where girls were felt to be at least partly responsible for general societal moral delinquency, it is perhaps not surprising that the conception of the sexual predator was also under debate. At about the same time, attention came to be focused on molestation by strangers, and away from incest and familial sexual abuse, and male sexual predators were considered as suffering from an illness that needed to be cured, rather than a moral evil that required punishment.[58]

In the classic American study, *Middletown*, the Lynds gave a then striking account of average adolescence:

... in such a grown up atmosphere it is hardly surprising that the approaches of the sexes seem to be becoming franker. 48 percent of junior and senior boys and 51 percent of 315 junior and senior girls marked true to the extreme statement, "nine out of every ten boys and girls of high school age have 'petting parties.'" 44 percent of boys and 34 percent of girls signified that they had taken part in a petting party.[59]

The Lynds attribute to the rise of the telephone an important role in the shift to a greater frankness between the sexes, especially among youth. The telephone affords a "semi-private, partly depersonalized means of approach."[60] The mothers of Middletown agreed: "Girls are far more aggressive these days. They call the boys up to try to make dates with them as they never would when I was a girl," and "Girls are much bolder than they used to be. It used to be that if a girl called up and asked a boy to take her somewhere she meant something bad by it, but now they all do it."[61] One parent wrote, in a 1905 issue of *Telephony*:

The doors may be barred and a rejected suitor kept out, but how is the telephone to be guarded. [It's providing] unprecedented opportunities for courting and infidelity.[62]

New technology, it was believed, removed girls from the safety of the home and invited sexual immorality. As Marvin documents, it was felt that allowing girls to be trained in the technology of the telephone was simply setting up opportunities for "seduction of the vulnerable by the cunning."[63] Consequently, its use needed to be controlled or restricted. What was largely ignored was the feminine use of the telephone for social networking, interpersonal relations, and extensions of identity beyond domestic life—the agency of the female telephone user.

As should be clear, the politics of both the Victorian era and early twentieth century— of rapid modernization and technological advancements—has many parallels with today's societal response to the advent of the internet. Control did not just exist within families or at the workplace. Women's new mobility and technical capability, even though it was not approved of, sparked a very broad-ranging societal response and was a large part of the Purity reform movement of the era. Several major elements of this movement, from blaming predators to blaming society, mirror current panic rhetoric about the internet.

Contemporary Moral Panic

Both boys and girls are subject to sexual exploitation, online and off. And sons, to a lesser extent than daughters, also worry parents when it comes to internet dangers. Thus, the fearful talk among adults can sound gender-inclusive on the surface. However, our argument is, on the one hand, that girls, significantly more than boys, bear the effects of being the target of the moral panic; and on the other hand, that the moral panic about girls' use of the internet is obscuring the positive benefits of girls using the internet. We do not mean that more girls than boys are sexually victimized (although that is the case), nor do we claim that we should somehow care more about girls than boys. Rather, in what follows, we intend to demonstrate the unique psychological and social effects of the moral panic on young women.

In July of 2006, the House of Representatives passed the Deleting Online Predators Act (DOPA) with a vote of 410–15. DOPA is based on three suppositions, of which the final is that:

... with the explosive growth of trendy chat rooms and social networking Web sites, it is becoming more and more difficult to monitor and protect minors from those with devious intentions, particularly when children are away from parental supervision.[64]

The bill's response is to require schools and libraries that receive federal aid to monitor a minor's use of the internet and to put in place filters that disallow any access to commercial social networking Web sites and chat rooms "unless used for an educational purpose with adult supervision." In addition, parents are to be informed of the dangers of sexual predators on the internet via a "consumer alert" and a Web site is to be created regarding the potential dangers posed by the use of the internet by children, including information about commercial social networking Web sites and chat rooms through which personal information about child users of such Web sites may be accessed by child predators.

DOPA is the official governmental response to widespread fear in the United States concerning the potential harm to young people of being online. The local and national news frequently quotes parents proclaiming the risk to the children of wayward, deviant men trolling the internet. But, reading the stories more closely, we find that the parents see their own children—primarily their daughters—as equally deviant, and that the attribution of blame is shared between the predators and the girls themselves, leading to a pattern of familial and societal reform similar to the Victorian era. For example, an article on MSNBC quoted a mother saying:

"And their pictures are very provocative," Marcy said. "There's shots with their butt in the air, with their thongs sticking out of it. They squeeze their elbows together to make their boobs look bigger."[65]

The local school technology coordinator added:

"The girls are all made up to look seductive . . . Parents have no clue this is going on," she said. "You think your kid is safe because they are in your house in their own bedroom. Who can hurt them when you are guarding the front door? But (the Internet) is a bigger opening than the front door."[66]

Note that these quotes highlight an image of girls that is explicitly eroticized. Adults describe the need to protect girls from their own sexual nature—to convince them to wait until they are older before they flaunt their bodies or describe their sexuality to their friends, for example. Little girls in the media, as Valerie Walkerdine has argued, embody this social conundrum of being objects both of desire and protection: "Are the little girls to be saved from this eroticization the very ones who are endlessly fetishized by adult desire when they are barely a few years older?" She claims that it is not over little girls and perverted pedophiles that there is a panic, but over adult suppressed and ever-present desires.[67] It is no surprise, then, that parents' panic over girls' growing connection to a network outside the family, and their own nascent sexuality, is bound to obscure those same parents' desire to encourage girls' confidence and interest in the computing technological fields. As one young woman said, in telling us about her relationship with a man she met online, and her parents' reaction, "Well, my parents like to blame him for everything bad that I have ever done, everything bad that has ever happened in my life ever since. If it's his fault, then it can't be my fault. And, if it's my fault then it would have to be either my genetics or my upbringing, which makes it their fault. . . . I think they've gone totally the wrong way with my sisters and not letting them chat. My sister, she actually chats online at her friend's place at the computer." This young woman is highlighting the ways in which parents may displace their fears about their daughter's growing sexuality onto the machine, and how the ultimate outcome may be not the diminished use of the computer, but lying about that use.

The term "moral panic" was first introduced by Stanley Cohen to refer to the perceived threat to societal values and interests posed by the 1960s Mods and Rockers. Intrinsic to his argument was the role of the media in producing a stylized and stereotypical representation of the deviants, and the role of the broad audience that consumed that representation.[68] In the case of the current internet moral panic, there is much to be said about the deviants, the online predators and child pornographers, and the audience, the parents, and otherwise normal public, who feast on the sensational elements of cybercrime. Adults who prey cause moral panic; adults who have children become fearful.[69]

But, what of the seduced and vulnerable youth? While every one of the sensational news stories on this topic is harrowing, it is the girls rather than the boys who come across as victims. For example, one of the more well-known online child pornography tales is that of Justin Berry, who operated a child pornography internet site featuring his own erotic performances, beginning at the age of thirteen. Justin is certainly a victim, but he is not portrayed in the media as helpless. He is described as an active producer of his own Web site, who helped other young people by turning himself in to authorities, so that he can now help catch other online child pornographers and solicitors.[70] The *New York Times* Web site devoted to his story is told primarily from Berry's perspective, and indeed videotapes of interviews are available on the site that show Berry telling his own story. Berry's story in this way stands in stark contrast to the majority of news items that deal primarily with the potential victimization of girls, and which rarely, if ever, quote the girls themselves. Instead, the majority of news articles about online predators rely on the police as key informants, not the victims, and these articles consequently highlight the magnitude of crime and play on parental anxieties.[71]

In Cohen's definition of a moral panic, the media relies on bias, exaggeration, and distortion to manufacture news.[72] In the contemporary case, the news has once again framed girls as victims in need of protection from cybercrimes and from technology itself.[73] In this way, they are "further marginalized by their absence as sources [in the articles] and by the police methods used to protect them." Edwards shows that "by appropriating girls' identities in cyberspace, and by extension, in the news, law enforcement officials substitute their voices and their experiences for those girls, effectively making these girls and the crimes committed against them, invisible to us."[74] It is time, therefore, to look to this often silenced group of players, beyond the parents, police and predators—young women online. For when girls are forbidden from posting profiles of themselves on blogs and social networking sites in order to prevent them from making contact with potential predators, they are also prevented from exercising some key skills in the online world.

In the next section, we will look at some of young women's online activities in terms of their role in adolescent development.

What Girls Do Online

Today's young people spend on average over six hours a day in front of some form of media, and of that time, at least one hour is spent in front of a computer.[75] Eighty-seven percent of U.S. adolescents aged 12–17 are online (compared to, for example, 75 percent of British teens), for a total of eleven million adolescent users.[76] This online activity takes place primarily in the home or at school. Fifty percent of U.S. families with online teens have broadband at home, while 100 percent of U.S. public elementary and secondary schools (and 93 percent of classrooms) have internet connectivity.[77] What are young people doing on the internet? In order of frequency, they send instant messages, get news about current events, look for information about politics, purchase things, seek spiritual information, or look for a job.

A 2000 study reported that girls between the ages of twelve and sixteen were the fastest-growing group of internet users.[78] Girls may use the internet differently than boys.[79] While boys are more likely than girls to play online games, girls are more likely than boys to send e-mail, use text messaging, read Web sites about movie stars, get information about school, and to look for health or dieting information. In fact,

Older teenage girls (aged 15–17) have driven the growth in many of the communication and information-seeking categories since our last survey. Older teenage girls have a much higher level of engagement with a wide array of these activities than do either boys of the same age or younger boys and girls (aged 12–14).[80]

In similar research, the Pew Internet and American Life Project found that girls also are most likely to be blogging. Twenty-five percent of online girls aged 15–17 write a blog, compared to 15 percent of online boys at the same age.[81] What are girls doing in these blogs? In a parallel to earlier, primarily female fan cultures surrounding television content,[82] today's girls often appropriate media conventions and media content in their blogs to create "riffs" on mainstream television, music, advertisements, and other kinds of mainstream media content.[83] Many of these girls choose to expose aspects of themselves that are often ridiculed, dismissed, and denigrated by mainstream society, to an online audience of potentially millions. In one example, in a study of message boards in an online, all-female forum, researchers found girls expressing sexuality in and through verbal expression. Posters shared feelings and stories "bringing sexual identities into being in the context of a community."[84] They found that the forum filled information gaps and encouraged exposure to diversity, not just of cultures, but also of ideologies. The research claimed that "in sharing a free affirming self-expression girls enact agency demonstrating and performing their ability and their right to make their own choices."[85] In another study, it was found that online magazines encouraged girls to become active seekers rather than passive recipients of information through the use of rhetorical spaces. Girls used the magazine to negotiate, resist, and reject dominant ideologies.[86] In a study of instant message conversations, likewise, girls were able to project themselves as

Girls vs. Boys		
The percentages of online teens who do the following activities, by gender:		
	Online Girls	Online Boys
	N=496	N=475
What online girls are more likely to do:		
Send or read email	93%	84%
Go to websites about movies, TV shows, music groups, or sports stars	88%	81%
Get info about a school you might attend	61%	53%
Send or receive text messages with a cell phone	45%	33%
Look for health, dieting or fitness info	37%	26%
Look for info on a health topic that's hard to talk about	27%	18%
What online boys are more likely to do:		
Play online games	76%	86%
What online girls and boys do at about the same level:		
Send or receive instant messages	77%	74%
Get news or info about current events	77%	75%
Look for news or info about politics and the presidential campaign	57%	53%
Buy things, such as books, clothing, or music	42%	45%
Look for religious or spiritual info	29%	24%
Look for info about a job	28%	32%

Source: Pew Internet & American Life Project Teens and Parents Survey. Oct.-Nov. 2004.
Margin of error is ±5% for online girls and ±5% for online boys.

Table 3
Girls and boys online

stronger and more forceful than how they presented themselves in person.[87] Looking at a teen chat room, Subrahmanyam et al. found that the teens focused primarily on the nexus of identity and sexuality in such a way as to allow them to engage in the all-important adolescent activity of "pairing off."[88] They argue that the virtual world of teen chat offers a safer environment for exploring emerging sexuality than the real world, in particular for adolescent girls, who may find it easier to inhabit an authoritative, agentive, and in-control persona online. Writing about social networking sites, danah boyd has described the ways in which teens use these online forums to reproduce, iterate, and refigure identity:

The dynamics of identity production play out visibly on MySpace. Profiles are digital bodies, public displays of identity where people can explore impression management. Because the digital world requires people to write themselves into being, profiles provide an opportunity to craft the intended expression through language, imagery and media. Explicit reactions to their online presence offers valuable feedback. The goal is to look cool and receive peer validation. Of course, because imagery can be staged, it is often difficult to tell if photos are a representation of behaviors or a re-presentation of them.[89]

It is not clear, however, whether the authors of these different genres of online content realize the extent to which their writings are public. Teenage blog and social networking site users describe their writings as read only by their peer network, express surprise that the writings are easily findable by others, and comment on the blogs that they feel comfortable exposing their innermost feelings in these contexts because of their anonymity (even though the same author may give identifying information in a neighboring post).[90] In another example of young women leading the charge with new communication technologies, in our own work on a closed (not visible to outsiders) teenage online community,[91] we discovered that the girls were more likely to be elected leaders of the forum, and more likely to set the tone of the discourse. That is, over the course of the forum, the girls' interaction style stayed constant, while boys adopted the language and interaction style of the girls, by using more emotion words, and also referring more to social process. However, our work has also shown the discomfort with which adults respond to children's sense of agency in these communities.[92]

It is clear that online participation is a key way of engaging in developmentally important activities for all young people, in the relative safety of the internet, where Web profiles can be erased and replaced with new and different representations of the self.[93] Teens' use of instant messaging, e-mailing, game playing, and Web site creation are key ways by which they grow into adults who manage, produce, and consume technology intelligently on an everyday basis. In particular, for young women, the internet appears to be a way to explore aspects of identity that may not be welcome in the real world, to project more forceful agentive personalities than they feel at liberty to do in the physical world, and to explore their technological prowess. With luck, there will be a single difference between the moral panic surrounding the telegraph and the telephone, and that surrounding the internet: that we will come to recognize young women as more likely to be empowered by technology than damaged by it. The internet allows for a tremendous potential of creative expression—expression that has not necessarily first been vetted by adults. Ultimately, it is when young women construct sexualized images of themselves, or contact strangers, that communication technologies are felt to become dangerous.

The Geography of Girls' Online Space

Learning and development do not just take place in schools, or under the tutelage of adults. Much of teen enculturation takes place in informal venues outside of school and outside of adult-constructed activities.[94] Young girls' behavior is often dependent on the space they exist in; and space, defined by social and cultural norms, is not stagnant. "Places are contested, fluid and uncertain" and both shape and are shaped by those who use them.[95] Adults, who tend to be afraid of digital media and how youth manipulate it, cannot ignore the important cultural function of the internet as a space for social and cognitive development. And yet, "identities are grounded in (if not tied to) the specificities of particular locations."[96] Local contexts and discursive practices influence how girls construct their identities. In many of the studies on teenage girls, the way they presented themselves shifted according to the kind of online venue in which they found themselves, and how they used that space as a stage.[97] As we have described above, young girls appropriate their space on the internet with fluidity. This "play" requires them to make a private space in a public sphere, and often uses much of the social constructions of womanhood, sexuality, and consumerism. Parental responses to girls identity play on the internet have primarily concentrated on the *product* of the play—text and photos that represent the girls in more or less transgressive poses. But the *process* of content production is rarely addressed. Navigating the complexity of modern life as a girl is a full-time job.[98] The work girls do online is legitimate work that should not be denied or ignored.

In fact, one useful way of thinking about girls' process-oriented work online is to construe it as a part of the developmental imperatives of adolescence.[99] In other words, there are a certain number of developmental milestones that young people must meet during their teenage years in order to pass into adulthood: they must come to rely less on the familial network and more on a peer network; they must explore alternative options for their future, and competing visions of their identity; and they must begin to engage in a sexual identity. These developmental imperatives will be met regardless of the technology that is to hand, or the era in which the young person is growing up. Girls will disobey their parents in order to be seen as cool by their peers, they will dress in a manner their parents deem too sexual, and so forth. And each of these activities serves an important role in the child's sociocognitive development. The internet happens to be an extremely effective way in which to pursue these imperatives—to construct networks of peers, to explore alternate versions of identity, to behave in sexual ways. At the same time, these girls are engaging with cutting-edge technology, and learning to be producers of media as well as consumers.

And yet, as we have seen in our examination of girls' uses of communication technologies throughout history, when girls move into spaces where they can—independently of adults—construct their identities, an alarm is sounded. Women have traditionally been limited by their movement, and while social, political, and economic activity is taking place in a distant public space, women are trapped in a shrinking private sphere.[100] In some cultural contexts, this limitation on mobility is a crucial means of subordination. "Moreover the two things—the limitation on mobility in space, the attempted consignment/confinement to particular places on the one hand and the limitation on identity on the other—have been crucially related."[101] Simply put, limitations on movement equate to limitations on identity.

Because the internet is a public resource that requires knowledge of technology, women are underrepresented in many areas of what would be considered legitimate online activity, and attempts to bring women into the field of technology can backfire. While the "girls' games movement" in the late 1990s was slated to get girls into Computer Science and other technology fields, the number of girls and women in Computer Science has gone *down* over the last ten years. Contrary to what we might have expected, the girls' games movement seems to have solidified a sense among both boys and girls that computers were "boys' toys" and that true girls didn't play with computers, while true computers were just for boys. As in so many domains, the marketplace has a hard time changing gender stereotypes on its own. Without a more general cultural sense of the diversity of gendered experience, girls games were just another tool with which to construct a gender divide.[102] The internet, on the other hand, has hardly suffered from a gender divide, and Web 2.0, where media creation trumps media consumption, seems to have brought the participation of women and girls to the fore.

Adolescent girls may alarm adults, in part, because as a group in transition, they frequently breach the confines of appropriate behavior.[103] Sibley argues that "moral panics articulate beliefs about belonging and not belonging, about the sanctity of territory and the fear of transgression." Danger, or at least uncertainty, lies in liminal zones where individuals and groups make their own spaces; where rather than viewing themselves as in transition, they stay a while.[104] The internet is a playground for this kind of activity because it is so easy to transgress spatial and social boundaries. When young girls go online to negotiate their identities, sexual and otherwise, they produce creative texts that are incompatible with the social space of either adulthood or childhood. Content is often private in nature, but public in exposure. Their bodies resemble those of children, but they are producing images of themselves as adult and fully mature. All the while they use traditionally male-dominated communications technology to perform this work. In a culture where the established rites of passage into adulthood are confusing or nonexistent, the activities of teenaged girls in transition threaten disorder. Whatever the threats that predators pose to young people online, it is the girls leaving their traditional domestic space and exploring the boundaries of their identities that may pose the greatest risk to the social order.

Conclusion

In this chapter, we hope to have demonstrated that the current panic over girls being online is not new. Vulnerable (usually young) women, unaware of the dangers of a new technology, fall victim to harassment and assault from sexual predators lurking on the wire. This same story was told about the telegraph and the telephone, and today it is being told about the internet and social networking sites like MySpace. In each case, unfortunately, the myth of girls' vulnerability online has unfortunate consequences, because it may result in positioning girls as disempowered with respect to technology. Our research shows that there has been a recurring moral panic throughout history about the putative danger of communication technologies to young women. However, when we investigate the kinds of statements made about the nature of the danger, in each instance it is less the technology per se that turns out to be the culprit (or even the kinds of relationships made possible by the technology), and more the potential sexual agency of young women, parental loss of control, and the specter of women who manifest technological prowess.

In each case that we have examined, when a new communication technology is introduced, upper middle-class Americans become afraid for their children—especially afraid about the noxious effects on girls. This is particularly the case when those technologies permit a kind of metaphoric mobility on the part of girls—movement outside the sphere of adult control. And in each case, whereas initially the anxiety is leveled at bad and transgressive predators, it quickly becomes displaced to the girls themselves who use technology. The girls' own behavior comes to appear counter to the image of a "good" girl: a nonsexual and nonerotic girl. As Marvin says:

In expert eyes, some of the most radical social transformations appeared to be brewing not around people at a distance, but around those close to home. Particular nervousness attached to protected areas of family life that might be exposed to public scrutiny by electrical communication. How would family members keep personal information to themselves? How could the family structure remain intact? . . . The escape from parental supervision made possible by the new communications technologies carried great risks.[105]

And in each case that we have examined, from the telegraph to today, the result of the moral panic has been a restriction on girls' use of technology. As we have described above, the telegraph, the telephone, and then the internet were all touted for how easy they were for young women to use, and how *appropriate* it was for young women to use them. Ineluctably, in each case, that ease of use and appropriateness became forgotten in a panic about how *inappropriate* the young women's use of these technologies was, and how dangerous the women's use was to the societal order as a whole.

In the current case, the panic over girls' use of technology has taken the form of believing in an increased presence of child predators online. But, as we have shown, there has been no such increase in predatory behavior; on the contrary, the number of young women who have been preyed on by strangers has *decreased*, both in the online and offline worlds.

Finally, as with uses of communication technologies by women in the past, it is clear that participation in social networking sites can fulfill some key developmental imperatives for young women, such as forming their own social networks outside of the family, and exploring alternate identities. Girls in particular may thrive online where they may be more likely to rise to positions of authority than in the physical world,[106] more likely to be able to explore alternate identities without the dangers associated with venturing outside of their homes alone, more likely to be able to safely explore their budding sexuality, and more likely to openly demonstrate technological prowess, without the social dangers associated with the term "geek." And yet, when moral panics about potential predators take up all the available airtime, the importance of the online world for girls is likely to be obscured, as are other inequalities equally important to contemplate.

Notes

1. Netsmartz Workshop, Parents Public Service Announcement: Family Concern, National Center for Missing and Exploited Children Boys and Girls Clubs of America (2006): 233. http://www.webcitation.org/5QYIxznkx (accessed October 18, 2006).

2. A Dangerous Net, *PC Magazine*, November 21, 2006, 23.

3. David Finkelhor, Kimberly J. Mitchell, and Janis Wolak, *Online Victimization: A Report on the Nation's Youth* (Alexandria, VA: National Center for Missing and Exploited Children, 2000), ix.

4. Chris Hansen, Catching Potential Internet Sex Predators, *MSNBC* (2005). http://www.webcitation.org/5JcD9Dul1 (accessed July 27, 2006).

5. One Hundred Ninth Congress of the United States of America, Adam Walsh Child Protection and Safety Act of 2006, Congress, 1st Sess. 2006.

6. Kurt Eichenwald, On the Web, Pedophiles Extend Their Reach, *New York Times*, 21 August 2006.

7. Julie Chen, Key To Protecting Kids Online? Talk! *CBS The Early Show* (2006). Retrieved April 5, 2006. http://www.webcitation.org/5JcC6BP8Z.

8. Bob Sullivan, Kids, Blogs and Too Much Information: Children Reveal More Online than Parents Know, *MSNBC* (April 29, 2005). Retrieved October 18, 2006. http://www.webcitation.org/5Jjav9Ch4.

9. Howard N. Snyder and Melissa Sickmund, *Juvenile Offenders and Victims: 2006 National Report* (Washington, DC: U.S. Department of Justice, Office of Justice Programs, Office of Juvenile Justice and Delinquency Prevention, 2006), 27. http://www.webcitation.org/5QYJ5Npyp (accessed October 18, 2006).

10. Ibid.

11. Ibid., 28.

12. David Finkelhor and Lisa M. Jones, *Explanations for the Decline in Child Sexual Abuse Cases* (Washington, DC: U.S. Department of Justice, Office of Juvenile Justice and Delinquency Prevention, 2004). http://www.webcitation.org/5JcCduEbH, 10 (accessed October 13, 2006).

13. Ibid., 2.

14. David Finkelhor, Kimberly Mitchell, and Janis Wolak, *Online Victimization: A Report on the Nation's Youth* (Alexandria, VA: National Center for Missing and Exploited Children, 2000). http://www.webcitation.org/5JcCpW6OR, xi (accessed October 18, 2006).

15. Janis Wolak, Kimberly Mitchell, and David Finkelhor, *Online Victimization of Youth: Five Years Later* (Durham, NC: National Center for Missing and Exploited Children, 2006). http://www.webcitation. org/5JjaqtjWF, 4 (accessed October 16, 2006).

16. Ibid., 17.

17. Snyder and Sickmund, *Juvenile Offenders and Victims*, 31.

18. Wolak et al., 13.

19. Ibid., 38.

20. Henry Jenkins and danah boyd, Discussion: MySpace and Deleting Online Predators Act, *Digital Divide Network* (2006). http://www.webcitation.org/5JcDJkn4u (accessed August 8, 2006).

21. Jeffery A. Dort, Internet Travelers, in *Medical, Legal, and Social Science Aspects of Child Sexual Exploitation: A Comprehensive Review of Pornography, Prostitution, and Internet Crimes*, ed. Sharon Cooper (St. Louis, MO: GW Medical Publishing, Inc., 2005), 2: 874.

22. Tom Standage, *The Victorian Internet: The Remarkable Story of the Telegraph and the Nineteenth Century's On-Line Pioneers* (New York: Walker and Co., 1998), viii.

23. Ibid.

24. Carolyn Marvin, *When Old Technologies Were New* (New York: Oxford University Press, 1988), 64.

25. Ibid., 22–24.

26. Ibid., 23.

27. Thomas C. Jepsen, Reclaiming History: Women in the Telegraph Industry, *IEEE Technology and Society Magazine* 19 (2000): 17.

28. Charles H. Garland, Women as Telegraphists, *The Economic Journal* 11, no. 42 (1901): 255.

29. Standage, *The Victorian Internet*.

30. Marvin, *When Old Technologies Were New*, 79.

31. Claude S. Fischer, *America Calling* (Berkeley: University of California Press, 1992), 62, 67.

32. Ibid., 78.

33. Malcolm M. Willey and Stuart A. Rice, *Communication Agencies and Social Life* (New York: McGraw-Hill Book Company, 1933), 240.

34. Ibid., 152.

35. Ibid., 154.

36. Quoted in Marvin, *When Old Technologies Were New*, 70.

37. Ibid., 70.

38. Ibid., 71–72.

39. Lana F. Rakow, *Gender on the Line* (Chicago: University of Illinois Press, 1992), 59.

40. Ibid., 59.

41. Ibid., 65.

42. Quoted in Valerie Frissen, Gender is Calling, in *The Gender-Technology Relation*, eds. Keith Grint and Rosalind Gill (London: Taylor and Francis, 1995), 234.

43. Frissen, Gender is Calling, 80.

44. Michele Martin, Rulers of the Wires? Women's Contribution to the Structure of Means of Communication, *Journal of Communication Inquiry* 12, no. 2 (1988): 95.

45. Frissen, Gender is Calling, 87.

46. Quoted in Standage, *The Victorian Internet,* 143.

47. Paul Starr, *The Creation of the Media: Political Origins of Modern Communications* (New York: Basic Books, 2004).

48. Quoted in Frissen, Gender is Calling, 11.

49. Rakow, *Gender on the Line,* 3.

50. Marvin, *When Old Technologies Were New,* 23.

51. Stanley Cohen, *Folk Devils and Moral Panics* (London: MacGibbon and Kee, 1972), 9.

52. Mary Odem, *Delinquent Daughters: Protecting and Policing Adolescent Female Sexuality in the United States, 1885–1920* (Chapel Hill: University of North Carolina Press, 1995); Anthony M. Platt, *The Child Savers: The Invention of Delinquency* (Chicago: University of Chicago, 1969).

53. Odem, *Delinquent Daughters,* 96.

54. Alan Hunt, *Governing Morals: A Social History of Moral Regulation* (Cambridge, UK: Cambridge University Press, 1999), 79.

55. Robert A. Woods and Albert J. Kennedy, *Young Working Girls* (Boston: Houghton Mifflin Company, 1913), v.

56. Ibid., 1.

57. Winifred Richmond, *The Adolescent Girl* (New York: Macmillan Company, 1925), 113.

58. Philip Jenkins, *Moral Panic: Changing Concepts of the Child Molester in Modern America* (New Haven, CT: Yale University Press, 1998).

59. Robert Lynd and Helen Merrel Lynd, *Middletown* (New York: Harcourt, Brace and Company, 1929), 138–139.

60. Ibid., 140.

61. Ibid., 140.

62. Quoted in Marvin, *When Old Technologies Were New,* 70.

63. Ibid., 72.

64. House of Representatives, *Deleting Online Predators Act*, 109th Congress, 2nd, HR 5319.

65. Sullivan, "Kids, Blogs and too much Information."

66. Ibid.

67. Valerie Walkerdine, *Daddy's Girl: Young Girls and Popular Culture* (Houndsmills, UK: MacMillan Press, 1997), 167.

68. Cohen, *Folk Devils and Moral Panics.*

69. Sharon R. Mazzarella, Claiming a Space, in *Girl Wide Web*, ed. Sharon R. Mazzarella (New York: Peter Lang Publishing, 2005), 141–160.

70. Kurt Eichenwald, Through His Webcam, a Boy Joins a Sordid Online World, *The New York Times,* 19 December 2005. http://www.nytimes.com/2005/12/19/national/19kids.ready.html?ex= 1292648400&en=aea51b3919b2361a&ei=5090.

71. Lynne Y. Edwards, Victims, Villians and Vixens, in *Girl Wide Web,* ed. Sharon R. Mazzarella (New York: Peter Lang Publishing, 2005), 13–30.

72. Cohen, *Folk Devils and Moral Panics,* 44.

73. Edwards, Victims, Villians and Vixens, 41.

74. Ibid., 41.

75. Victoria Rideout, Donald F. Roberts, and Ulla G. Foehr, *Generation M: Media in the Lives of 8–18 Year-Olds* (Washington, DC: Kaiser Family Foundation, 2005). http://www.webcitation.org/5JjbLsxVS (accessed October 18, 2006).

76. Amanda Lenhart, Mary Madden, and Paul Hitlin, *Teens and Technology* (Washington, DC: PEW Internet and American Life Project, 2005). http://www.pewinternet.org/report_display.asp?r=162; http://www.webcitation.org/5JjbvXdW4 (accessed October 18, 2006).

77. Basmat Parsad, Jennifer Jones, and National Center for Education Statistics, *Internet Access in U.S. Public Schools and Classrooms, 1994–2003* (Washington, DC: National Center for Education Statistics, 2005).

78. Anne Ricket and Anya Sacharaow, It's a Woman Wide Web, *Media Metrix and Jupiter Communications,* (2000): 19. http://www.webcitation.org/5JjbaIFSV (accessed October 18, 2006).

79. Mazzarella, Claiming a Space, 141.

80. Lenhart et al., *Teens and Technology,* v.

81. Amanda Lenhart and Mary Madden, *Teen Content Creators and Consumers* (Washington, DC: PEW Internet and American Life Project, 2005). http://www.webcitation.org/5JjbsYBAH, 4–5 (accessed October 18, 2006).

82. Henry Jenkins, *Textural Poachers: Television Fans and Participatory Culture* (New York: Routledge, Chapman and Hall, 1992).

83. Mazzarella, Claiming a Space, 156.

84. Ashley D. Grisso and David Weiss, What are gURLS Talking About? in *Girl Wide Web,* ed. Sharon R. Mazzarella (New York: Peter Lang Publishing, 2005), 45.

85. Ibid., 47.

86. Susan F. Walsh, Gender, Power, and Social Interaction, in *Girl Wide Web,* ed. Sharon R. Mazzarella (New York: Peter Lang Publishing, 2005), 80–81.

87. Mazzarella, Claiming a Space; Shayla Thiel, *I.M. Me: Adolescent Girls Negotiating Identity through Instant Messaging Communications* (Iowa City: University of Iowa, 2004), 136.

88. Kaveri Subrahmanyam, Patricia M. Greenfield, and Brendesha Tynes, Constructing Sexuality and Identity in an Online Teen Chat Room, *Applied Developmental Psychology* 25 (2004): 651–66.

89. danah boyd, Identity Production in a Networked Culture: Why Youth Heart MySpace, paper presented at the American Association for the Advancement of Science, St. Louis, MO (February 19, 2006).

90. David A. Huffaker and Sandra L. Calvert, Gender, Identity, and Language Use in Teenage Blogs, *Journal of Computer-Mediated Communication* 10, no. 2 (2005).

91. Justine Cassell, David Huffaker, Dona Tversky, and Kim Ferriman, The Language of Online Leadership: Gender and Youth Engagement on the Internet, *Developmental Psychology* 42, no. 3 (2006): 436–49.

92. Justine Cassell, We Have these Rules Inside: The Effects of Exercising Voice in a Children's Online Forum, in *Children in the Digital Age*, eds. Sandra Calvert, Rod Cocking, and Amy Jordan (New York: Praeger Press, 2002), 123–44.

93. Brendesha Tynes, *Internet Safety Gone Wild? Sacrificing the Educational and Psychosocial Benefits of Online Social Environments* (UIUC, 2006), 15.

94. Pamela Bettis and Natalie Adams, *Geographies of Girlhood: Identities In-between* (Mahwah, NJ: Lawrence Erlbaum Associates, 2005), 277.

95. Linda McDowell, *Gender, Identity and Place* (Minneapolis: University of Minnesota Press, 1999), 4.

96. Tom Hall, Self, Space and Place: Youth Identities and Citizenship, *British Journal of Sociology of Education* 20, no. 4 (1999): 501–13.

97. Bettis and Adams, *Geographies of Girlhood*, 4.

98. Ibid.

99. Penelope Eckert, Entering the Heterosexual Marketplace: Identities of Subordination as a Developmental Imperative, in *Working Papers on Learning and Identity* (Palo Alto, CA: Institute for Research on Learning, 1994).

100. Anne Scott, Lesley Semmens, and Lynette Willoughby, Women and the Internet, in *Virtual Gender: Technology, Consumption and Identity*, eds. Eileen Green and Alison Adam (London: Routledge, 2001), 3–27.

101. Doreen Massey, *Space, Place and Gender* (Cambridge, UK: Polity, 1994), 179.

102. Henry Jenkins and Cassell Justine, From Quake Grrls to Desperate Housewives: A Decade of Gender and Computer Games, in *Beyond Barbie to Mortal Kombat: New Perspectives on Gender and Computer Games,* eds. Yasmin Kafai, Carrie Heeter, Jill Denner, and Jennifer Sun (Cambridge, MA: MIT Press, in press).

103. David Sibley, *Geographies of Exclusion* (London: Routledge, 1995), 33–35.

104. Ibid., 33, 43.

105. Marvin, *When Old Technologies Were New*, 67–68.

106. Cassell et al., The Language of Online Leadership.

Wireless Play and Unexpected Innovation

Christian Sandvig

University of Illinois, Urbana-Champaign, Department of Speech Communication

At the age of nineteen, college student Shawn Fanning—nicknamed "Napster" for his messy hair—wrote the popular eponymous music-sharing software and demonstrated the viability of a "peer-to-peer" architecture for file sharing. "I was at Northeastern University playing with the idea and getting feedback from my roommates," he has said, "it was really my first Windows application." Two years later, Fanning was on the cover of *Time* Magazine, Napster had forty million users and Fanning eventually made an estimated $1 million.[1] For Fanning, the situation was unprecedented. He said, "If you're a musician or actor, you know that if you're successful, some level of fame goes along with that. You're prepared. But how often does that happen to a programmer?"

An answer to Shawn might be: "More often, these days." It is true that few programmers other than Fanning have been featured in *Rolling Stone* magazine, but stories like Fanning's are a staple of popular press coverage about new media technologies. Napster's story is captivating because it contains all of the elements of excellent drama: youth, humble beginnings, success, fame, hubris, failure, and a reversal of fortune (Napster went bankrupt in 2002 after legal challenges by recording artists). But it is also captivating because it seems to teach us about qualities of digital media. The large electronic communication systems that are familiar to everyday life are cable television networks, satellites, telephone systems, and the Internet. These systems and the popular cultural products that they carry (such as films and television shows) usually require millions of dollars in capital investment to produce. If teenagers can create their own infrastructure or popular content at home, out of software, this appears to be a dramatic shift in the ordinary state of things. It may be that digital media allow individual creators more power than ever before.

Napster is software infrastructure—it isn't music but it is a way to distribute music. Beyond Napster, this new power to create is celebrated even more regularly for content than for the infrastructure that carries it. For example, in 1997, Jyoti Mishra (a.k.a. "White Town") created the song "Your Woman" in his bedroom with free software and an Atari ST. Within four weeks it was #1 on the U.K. pop charts. *Wired* magazine, writing about the big business of music that year, wondered hyperbolically "how long they can hold out before cheap technology and the distributive power of the [internet] take over."[2]

The author would like to thank the authors and editor of this volume, participants in the 2006 Wharton Colloquium on Media and Communications Law, and Shane Greenstein for their helpful comments on an earlier version of this chapter. This material is based upon work supported by the National Science Foundation under Grant No. 0546409.

These are not singular examples. There are many exciting stories being told about digital media and innovation, and they posit this shift in power toward new forms of diverse or even distributed creativity. While the internet was generically reputed to increase anyone's ability to produce their own content, recent examples are more specific and well documented. To name just a few, blogs and MySpace allow fast and cheap online publishing for anyone. New video game "fan site kits," in-game scripting languages, and level editors allow the players to write portions of mainstream games. New audio software has greatly increased the ability to create digital music, and revitalized the genre of music that is composed entirely of other music, called a "mashup." To reiterate, this trend is not limited to the production of new content—it also includes some production of new communication systems themselves. For instance, new techniques to interconnect Web-based applications allow programmers to quickly create a "software mashup" by combining powerful existing Web applications without much new programming labor. Although the celebrated innovators can be any age, much popular attention has focused on the young. Lawrence Lessig, the most prominent advocate of loosening legal restrictions that encumber this sort of innovation, wrote recently about the application of copyright law to fan-produced Anime Music Videos. He observed "This will be the next big copyright war—whether this form of noncommercial creativity will be allowed." "When ordinary people hear both sides [of the argument], and more importantly, see the creativity their kids are capable of, 90 percent will be with us."[3]

The excitement is not limited to commentators and scholars: kids themselves relish the idea of more freedom and capability. Alister B. and Stuart C. Dunbar, finalists in the Global Kids Digital Media Essay Contest for teenagers, wrote about how the Linden Scripting Language (LSL) used in *Second Life* became an escape and a source of power for them. Alister was forced to home school after encounters with bullies, and turned to LSL development. ("Hey, I'm a nerd," he commented.) Stuart described LSL scripting as an escape he compared favorably to his earlier heavy use of marijuana. After turning to *Second Life*, Stuart wrote, "There's nothing I can't do."

This chapter will examine one example of new technology in some detail—wireless communication technologies—and attempt to determine what is really new about the present moment. Has digital media promoted creativity in some new configuration, and shifted power to individuals or the young? (In Fanning's metaphor, are young programmers the new rock stars?)

There Are Good Reasons to Expect Transformation

The writing about the power of the internet and of digital media in the 1990s has been charged and found guilty of hyperbole, utopianism, essentialism, determinism, ethnocentrism, and more. Most of the bombastic claims about the transformative power of new media may have been nothing more than the result of the affluence common in that decade, a millennial optimism that was filtered through the academy as scholarship.[4] Yet, there is good evidence that some things are indeed transformed as the result of digital media, and that there is some reason still to take notice of a transformation with respect to innovation.

The convergence of once-distinct media technologies is the reason that innovation on, in, and with communication systems has special characteristics.[5] Convergence literally means "coming together," but this distracts from the real significance of the phenomenon. The less exciting part of convergence is the idea that a common format or common ownership could allow a converged media system to reap substantial economies of scope and scale. Even though this is the less exciting form of the effects of convergence, it is worth reviewing here as it is a foundation for why one would expect a reorganization of media and communication at this historical moment.

Economists use the phrase "economies of scope" to refer to situations where producing more than one product can be more efficient than producing just one. For instance, if a cable company also offered telephone service (as many U.S. cable providers now do), the same marketing budget can be used to promote both products. Consumers could be offered one bundle including many media services, resulting in one price for a package including telephone calls, internet service, on-demand movies, television, and cable channels—all represented on one bill. This saves the company money when producing these products (i.e., it does not need a separate billing system for each), but it also can attract consumers who see media products as related and value the simplicity of making a single payment to one provider. In this sense, convergence refers to the coming together of media and telecommunications companies into merged enterprises that offer products across all media forms.

The conversion of media technologies into related digital formats also promises substantial economies of scale, a phrase that refers to situations where producing a larger number of units of the same product allows the cost of making each one to drop. This is familiar to most people as the rationale behind mass production. If convergence led to more sales, this could straightforwardly lower costs at a converged company, but in a slightly more subtle scenario, within a hypothetical converged company that provided content for film, television, and the internet, content developed for one media system could be slightly repackaged and transmitted over another, creating new efficiencies in production and duplication. In effect, what had been related but fundamentally different products (film, television) might become essentially the same product with economies of scale extending across all media forms.

It is worth pointing out that this situation in media is not new. The telegraph and related technologies sparked similar excitement about synergies with newspapers in the media convergence dreams of the nineteenth century (though this was not then known by the word "convergence").[6] New developments in telegraph technology such as the printing telegraph (invented in 1846) and then-new "online" media formats like the stock ticker or ticker tape machine (invented in 1857) convinced some newspaper companies that the future of media would see converged, integrated companies providing content simultaneously for multiple formats. This didn't come to pass for a number of reasons, but chief among them was that the new formats still required a large amount of effort to interconnect and demanded different sorts of expertise. This may be a cautionary note for the enthusiasms of today.

New Access to the Means of Production

While "convergence," meaning a coming together of producers for economies of scope or scale (or to produce the same content in related formats) is an old situation for communication technology, part of the recent excitement about convergence is different. The preceding section identified itself as presenting the less exciting dynamics of convergence for our purpose here. The more exciting portion relates to the properties of digital information. Once-distinct analog media like film, music, telephone calls, and television have been digitized and now share a common structure of binary code. Profoundly, this means that the means of reception in communications have also become the means of production and the means of distribution—all are now computers.

The simplest route to demonstrate this is by example. In 2007, if the owner of a relatively cheap personal computer installs the free software package *Asterisk*, the computer becomes a telephone exchange. If the user installs *Photoshop*, the computer becomes a photographic studio. *Audacity* or *Garage Band* produce an audio recording studio. *MythTV* or *Linux4.TV* produce a personal video recorder or a cable set-top box. That the means for media production and reproduction are so cheap and readily available is a new phenomenon, and it is remarkable that one common device may act as a receiver, editor, and transmitter for a variety of products. In addition, as the products are themselves digital data files, reproducing and manipulating them need not degrade their quality, require additional materials, or impose additional expense.

Most discussions of convergence until very recently treated these benefits as though they would only accrue to large corporations seeking efficiency gains in their operations. While it was clear to many scholars of digital media and telecommunications that a single platform—the computer—would change the production of cultural products, it was not clear until very recently that these benefits might extend to the general population of computer users.[7] Although commentators linked computers and the emancipation of information and production as early as the 1970s, this had been a minority view.[8]

In the previous examples of computer applications like *Garage Band* and *Asterisk*, note that the malleability of computing resources and its implication extends far beyond content to include the networks that distribute content. Before digital convergence, communication systems and their configuration consisted of relatively fixed arrangements of electro-mechanical components that were difficult to change. In fancier language, the logical architecture of the network and its physical architecture were the same.[9] Earlier, change involved building (or at least moving around) heavy and expensive wires and switches. With computerization, while manipulating these systems may not be trivial, at least it often involves the comparatively easier task of changing the digital instructions for how to do things. Significant changes in infrastructure may now be a *conceptual* rewiring like Shawn Fanning's peer-to-peer software. Napster only changes the instructions for how to transfer information, whereas with networks before convergence this sort of change could require an *actual* rewiring, with screwdrivers.

There is then some basis to believe that developments in digital media might actually prefigure new abilities to manipulate and reconfigure any of the systems of communication in society. The chance to reunite the traditional producers of communication in the oral tradition (the people) and the modern, technical means of production for communication is a heady possibility well worth investigating. Claims that digital media allow or cause new forms of creativity and production were part of the hyperbole surrounding the internet in the 1990s, it is true, but careful scholarship has found that tools like the internet have new potential to enable innovation and experimentation in ways that were formerly impossible (or at least very difficult).[10] After convergence, software and media can potentially be easily combined, reworked, and shared, and the results include important new artifacts and organizational forms such as open-source software.[11]

Despite this optimism, it is important to keep in mind that one major problem with earlier writing about digital media has been that technology was portrayed as an exogenous force outside history, politics, and culture. To demonstrate that anything is different or exciting about the present moment should require detailed and earnest consideration of the past as a point of comparison. At the same time, any investigation must remember that technology is built by people who spend money and time to shape its development to serve their own interest, not to simply facilitate the expression of a technology's innate potential. If digital media assists in a shift of any significance, there should also be signs of inertia and resistance. If a shift in power is underway, those who could be usurped should be expected to fight back.

Locating Production and Innovation in Digital Media

Garage, dorm, and bedroom producers of new digital media projects make for exciting headlines, but the excitement about those headlines begs the question: Where would one reasonably expect new innovation to come from? It may be that the garage, dorm, and bedroom are not such unusual places for technological production.

The claim that digital media allows new sorts of creativity and innovation from new or unusual sources tells as much about the preconceptions about how innovation ought to work as it does about the purportedly novel situation today. The story of garage innovation echoes many historical stories of invention that have been viewed skeptically by the scholarly literature on science and technology. While today's "inventor-heroes" usurp or bypass existing industries, older stories of invention also portray inventors who tinker in the garage and accidentally discover the foundation for a major industry. The birth of the personal computer, for example, is often told this way.[12] Whether David or Goliath comes first, both versions are very much in circulation. Noticing press accounts of younger people discovering things in garages does not yet demonstrate that innovation in digital media differs in a fundamental way from the innovation that came before.

Although professionalized research and development is an endeavor that has really flourished in the developed world only in the latter part of the twentieth century, it has a strong hold on consumer consciousness, and on the thinking in some branches of economics. Consumers might be likely to imagine that new media-related products originate at laboratories or product development facilities dedicated to that purpose by the same companies that normally supply them with these products. Indeed, "user" or "consumer" has been opposed to "producer" in most writing about media and computer technology.[13] However, a definitive work on this question, Eric Von Hippel's *Sources of Innovation,* convincingly demonstrates that in some fields, users develop most or even all of the innovations.[14] Consumers, after all, are the ones with the most intimate knowledge of the uses for a technology or product. They are the ones frustrated by missing features or services that could be commodified—omissions that to them are obvious.

In the area of cultural products, user-driven innovation seems almost obvious. This comes into focus by turning away from conduit for a moment and focusing on content. In the culture industries, it is readily accepted that stars were fans first; they were likely "users" of older instances of a media genre before contributing their own innovation. Rather than the "R&D" of the consumer products' world, media firms have evolved strategies like "A&R" (artist and repertoire departments) and independent film festivals to scout for new products rather than developing them in house. With cultural products, consumption can easily blur into production. One could argue that most truly committed music fans also play an instrument, and they might even learn to do so by playing their favorite song from the radio.

This may seem a far cry from infrastructure and technology innovation. After all, we are told that performers are artists and that they have something called "talent," while programming is a skill that can be taught. Yet since computing's early days, programmers have been "derided for their adherence to artisanal practices,"[15] and they have been compared to artists and surgeons as often as to coders.[16] The professionalization of programmers has been as incomplete as the professionalization of musicians and artists. (You can get a degree in computer science, in music, and in multimedia production, but the successful figures in every one of those fields agree that the superstars can be self-taught.) Detailed studies of programming labor have found that it is creative and performative, with some programming languages providing an infinite number of ways to resolve a single task of any complexity, just as there are an infinite number of ways to write a novel.[17]

Programmers are not being compared to artists here in order to congratulate them. By reminding ourselves that programming is an activity that may not require formal training and can be advanced by virtuosos, examples like Fanning seem less unusual. The advent of the internet has produced a pantheon of programming virtuosos (the rock stars of new media) from Tim Berners-Lee to Bram Cohen.[18] These innovators are often used to embody a "bottom up" or nontraditional path to innovation that lies outside the traditions of corporate R&D, but the situation is more complex than this.

It is true that while some of these "rock stars" had formal educations in computer science, they often pursued groundbreaking work well outside a traditional research and development context. While some held jobs in computing, these jobs were often not particularly related to the innovations they produced. Berners-Lee proposed the World Wide Web while working at a particle physics laboratory (Organisation Européen pour la Recherche Nucléaire), not while working in the R&D lab of an internet company. While Craig Newmark was trained in computer science, he developed the Web application *Craig's List* as a hobby and (like Berners-Lee) because he wanted to *use* something like *Craig's List*, not because he wanted to run it.

The distinction that is important here is not commercialization: Newmark would later commercialize *Craig's List* and incorporate as a for-profit company, but when he originally conceived of the project it was as a user of the internet, not as someone whose job was devoted to developing new applications. *Craig's List* started as a hobby. These user-driven innovations (to use Von Hippel's term) can be distinguished from the innovation path espoused during the dot-com boom of the late 1990s in trade press books about start-up companies.[19] That celebrated entrepreneurial path in digital media involves start-ups and venture capital funding and a desire to get rich, but this is quite different from hobbyists or college students who yearn to *use* the technology they are inventing.[20] Innovation in digital media is often portrayed as David versus Goliath, meaning "start-ups versus corporate R&D." But both the funded start-up company and the corporate R&D lab are Goliath if one is interested in the comparatively tiny user innovator. The young innovators like Fanning may represent the new promise of digital media.

The remainder of this chapter will seek innovation in digital media by turning to cases. Specifically, there should be case studies of technological development that help us to evaluate the present situation by putting in play all of the dynamics introduced so far. These include the young, convergence, production in a nontraditional context and dramatic shifts of function in the evolution of a technological system.

Geolocation, From Big Government to Small Subculture

In order to look more closely at this elusive notion of innovation in digital media, where innovation starts, and where innovation leads, it is essential to spend time with the gritty detail of examples of new media technologies and ideas about them. This section will do this via a discussion of some little-known developments from wireless communication technology, starting with geolocation. This particular example is useful because geolocation is a significant new technological ability, and the story of much of its development has not been written. (This relative obscurity will help avoid the distraction of hype and enthusiasm, as this technological area is obscure enough that it has little popular awareness and no popular inventor-heroes.) Today's wireless innovation makes an interesting case study because "new developments" in wireless is an old topic with a long history, studied extensively by generations of historians and media scholars, thus providing a useful point of comparison.[21]

For our purposes, this story begins in 1993, when the U.S. Air Force launched the last Navstar satellite required to complete the Global Positioning System (GPS).[22] GPS technology precisely locates moving people and objects on the Earth's surface, and in 1993 this was firmly a government effort. The same GPS devices that today produce driving directions for the affluent originally cost twelve billion tax dollars to build. GPS was developed by the U.S. Department of Defense and Raytheon, and they intended it as a means to guide intercontinental ballistic missiles to their target. GPS fits all of the criteria that have been proposed to define a "large technological project," a term of art defining that special sort of undertaking that includes "big science" and "big military" projects representing an expensive and complex societal effort.[23] These large projects (like Boston's "big dig" or the Apollo Program) address objectives that are thought to be impossible to achieve without a massive financial investment and a centrally managed sociotechnical system to control it. Large public projects like these are sometimes contrasted to networks and private systems that begin as small, isolated parts and then become large (like the railroads or telephone systems) through interconnection, consolidation, or some form of agglomeration. Unlike projects that can start small, by this logic, geolocation and landing on the moon both require a gigantic investment in infrastructure before the desired results can be achieved even once. While GPS has its stories of individual inventors and pioneers, the "S" for "system" in GPS required multiple satellites to be launched and millions of dollars to be spent before the first person could use them even once to locate anything.

GPS, in other words, is a system that was as far as possible from the decentralized, participatory ethos of digital media that now excites some commentators. But just a decade later in 2003, when the "next-generation" of geolocation technology was advanced by the Skyhook Wireless Corporation to improve upon performance of GPS, the new version was built on the backs of disaffected teenage digital media hackers. Without much fanfare, the innovative infrastructure for geopositioning had shifted from a network of military satellites to a network of emergent media practices—from big government to small subculture.

Generically called "software-only positioning," Skyhook's new replacement for (or supplement to) GPS takes advantage of the prevalence of wireless internet consumer products in cities. After 1999, short-ranged wireless internet access devices became a fantastically successful information technology product across the developed world, both in homes and in businesses of many types. The most popular type of wireless internet, called "Wi-Fi" (a term coined by a naming consultancy that does not stand for anything), allows high-speed communication without a cable between computers at a range of about 150 feet. These devices were often purchased by broadband subscribers who wanted to connect a cable modem or DSL line to their home office without the trouble of running new wiring.

Anyone who bought a $70 Wi-Fi access point for their house after 1999 has been steadily transmitting a unique number from it as long as it has been turned on. This number is part of the protocol that allows these devices to interconnect with your computer. In a massive survey, Skyhook inventoried these numbers across the twenty-five largest cities in the United

States, and compiled a database that identified exactly where in the United States each unique number had been found.

When a user of Skyhook's software-only positioning system opens their laptop in a moving car, the laptop's now-commonplace wireless internet chip listens for these numbers, and then Skyhook's database correlates them with locations from their earlier inventory. As long as most Wi-Fi users haven't turned off their access points (or moved, or bought new ones), Skyhook delivers an address more reliably than the Pentagon, and with more precision.[24]

This is a significant advance. In the urban canyons of cities, the line of sight from a GPS receiver to Navstar satellites is likely to be blocked or limited, causing the GPS system's notoriously poor performance in urban areas. But the denser the city, the more Wi-Fi signals there are, making the place where GPS is least accurate to be the most accurate for software-only positioning. GPS usually requires a specialized receiver (or at least a chip), and this provides a measurement of location that is accurate to within about 20 feet 95 percent of the time. In contrast, the promotional literature for software-only positioning claims accuracy rates within one foot.[25]

Wireless Play and Accidental Infrastructure

To say that all this came from disaffected teenagers isn't meant to imply inspiration or provenance, but to be taken literally. Skyhook's survey of Wi-Fi networks and its correlation of addresses originated in the folk practice of "wardriving," a quasi-legal hobby invented by computer enthusiasts.[26] As Drew explains in the underground instructional video "Responsible War Driving," wardrivers discover wireless signals by driving around the city with modified computers that "show us exactly where [people] are." All this is fun, Drew says, because of "the interesting maps you can create and explore."[27]

While driving around, a wardriver brings along a laptop or palmtop computer connected to a GPS receiver. Software like *Netstumbler* or *Kismet* logs the Wi-Fi networks that the computer has discovered along with the latitude and longitude where they were found. The results can be visualized using free mapping software like *GPSMap* or *JiGLE/DiGLE*.

Some of the pleasure in wardriving obviously comes from being privy to information that other people don't have, even if it is simply knowing where to find invisible signals. Typically, wardrivers don't use the Wi-Fi they find for any purpose other than to map it. Wardrivers like to trade stories about interesting Wi-Fi access point identifiers they have found ("im_watching_you" "garyisgay" "nojohnissupergay").[28] The fact that driving slowly and systematically down every street in a neighborhood is a suspicious activity adds excitement, and some wardriving sites refer to trips as "adventures." As one "tips and tricks" site advises: "Do not draw unwanted attention to yourself . . . do not be nervous of [sic] police officers."

It is difficult to get a clear picture of the average wardriver. Information on any small subculture is hard to come by (the most prominent Web service devoted to wardriving had 54,768 registered users in 2006), but wardrivers generally prefer anonymity or pseudonymity because of the uncertain legal status of their hobby.[29] They need to be old enough to have access to a car, but at least some are not much older than that. This younger group is joined by an older cohort that has previous experience in amateur radio. They appear to be predominantly male, and some of them are technically sophisticated when compared to the general population. Postings to Web forums that betray personal information say things like: "I have my rig running when I'm delivering pizza." "I wardrive between home and school."

"I need to do some college hw [homework]." "My gf [girlfriend] isn't into wardriving." "I've been a radio hobbyist all my life, a ham in the 80's."

Wardriving became more of a group activity, and more like a sport, with the introduction of opportunities for coordination, teamwork, and competition. Early efforts included "group" wardriving dates discussed on message boards in 2001–2002, attempts to wardrive at the same time in different places (and compare notes) like the "World Wide Wardrive" in 2002, and attempts to cultivate a Wardriving Meet-up at http://www.meetup.com.[30] Artists attempted to collaboratively produce Wi-Fi maps with volunteer wardrivers, while groups like NZ Wireless pioneered a way to organize treasure hunts using wardriving equipment (the treasure is a set of specific unique identifying numbers for Wi-Fi access points that have to be collected).[31] At this time, articles appeared in "serious" publications pointing out that wardriving might have useful applications.[32]

A major shift in the utility and character of wardriving as an activity arrived when Web services became popular that allowed pseudonymous hobbyists to pool their efforts into one shared dataset. That is, a shared dataset that allowed them to both cooperate and compete in a systematic way. Drew (introduced earlier) created the internet site http://www.wifimaps.com, while Arkasha, Bobzilla, and others (these are online pseudonyms) created "WiGLE"—the Wireless Geographic Logging Engine. These services allow wardrivers to submit their results over the internet and aggregate them. By 2005, thousands of young wardriving hobbyists using WiGLE had cooperatively mapped five million Wi-Fi networks.

Evoking open-source software production, these sites allowed individual hobbyists with no connection to each other to collaborate on producing a result that was much greater than each individual part: a global map of Wi-Fi.[33] But just as crucially, the sites defined a venue in which avid enthusiasts could compete against each other, creating a new incentive for the discovery of more networks. An example posting to the blog chroniclesofawardriver.org is illustrative. It reads: "Congratulations go out to mark571 for claiming 2nd rank earlier this morning.... Mark571 is currently 11,248 above my ranking and doesn't appear to be slowing down any—watch out 1st!"[34]

None of this was supposed to lead to geolocation. However, when entrepreneurs conceived of the possibility of software-only positioning and wanted to test its viability on a large scale, they found that wardriving enthusiasts were the ones in possession of the largest datasets locating Wi-Fi. Arkasha and Bobzilla of WiGLE allegedly sold their aggregated Wi-Fi database to Microsoft, creating a minor controversy among the wardriving community that was less about the hobby's commodification than it was about the sharing of the spoils. (One wardriver, mc_sikes, posted on the WiGLE forum asking "Now that wigle sold the data to Microsoft, are wardrivers going to get paid?") In this way, some of the same bits of data produced by the hobby have made their way into prototypes and even commercial software-only positioning products by Navizon, ekahau, Skyhook, and Microsoft.

General Prerequisites for Unexpected Innovation in Digital Media

From one perspective, the story of software-only positioning links terribly disparate actors, events, and technologies in a web of happenstance that is difficult to believe. To recap, a hypothetical middle-class urbanite in Pennsylvania buys a Wi-Fi access point to connect their cable modem in the living room to their computer in the upstairs den. Some time later, an anonymous hobbyist drives by (perhaps it was "SignalSeeker"), hoping to collect the device's ID number as part of a treasure hunt. In Chicago, Bobzilla and Arkasha like to play with maps and computers, and so in their spare time they build a system to share this hobbyist data online and rank "SignalSeeker" against "Psychic Amish Stumbler" and other players. Later, they sell SingalSeeker's early results to Microsoft Research. Back in Pennsylvania, this turns out to help a passing motorist in a rented SUV to find their hotel. The SUV's on-board navigation system uses software-only positioning, but this works especially well when it is combined with a guidance system for ICBMs (the GPS).

Is this an amazing sequence of events, or is it ordinary? While the details of this particular story are little known, it is only as strange as we need it to be. In fact, parts of the broad sketch might seem familiar. The internet, as its history is sometimes told, was invented as a Cold War communication system designed to survive nuclear attack. It was then transformed by computer geeks who wanted to summarize old Star Trek episodes and share pornography.[35] In another version, supercomputing exists because of the military need for complex simulations of nuclear weapons, but the National Center for Supercomputing Applications was the birthplace of the first graphical World Wide Web browser, written by a part-time college student and now used by everyone.[36] There are many other narratives like these. Wi-Fi and software-only positioning's juxtaposition of military technology, play, and production may seem particularly novel, but it is just this combination of purposes that Timothy Lenoir has highlighted with the brilliant phrase "the military-entertainment complex."[37]

The basic ingredients that unite geopositioning, the internet, and the graphical Web browser are a large-scale institutional or government investment refined or repurposed by upstart users. The pleasant surprise in these tales is the unexpected outcome: a technology has dramatically shifted function. These accounts of innovation invite the reader to celebrate the romantic notion of the individual, the "expressive, exploring, transfiguring idea of the individual" rather than the calculating utilitarian.[38] A handful of contrarian kids have created (or inspired) a new technology that has real economic value. Horkheimer and Adorno's classic rule that in the enlightenment "whatever does not conform to the rule of computation and utility is suspect," has been observed in part by finding new value and utility in media and software play and exploration. This play is linked with the young, as play is so often linked.[39]

Is this sort of innovation a new feature of digital media? Software-only positioning leveraged a number of other existing digital infrastructures to produce a new and unexpected resource. That is, the large technological project of the GPS first provided a centralized geolocation system that could be bootstrapped into a better decentralized one (software-only positioning requires GPS). The large technological project of the internet provided a converged digital communication infrastructure that could be employed to transmit and coordinate a variety of media, from e-mail to a wardriver's log files or mapserver. The large installed base of cheap consumer Wi-Fi access points accidentally provided the signaling mechanism that in the GPS would have required a satellite. The large installed base of Wi-Fi chips in laptop computers (and, more recently, some cell phones) provided the antenna that in the GPS would have required a specialized handheld receiver. "Playing with maps" and mapservers on the internet is an acceptable and encouraged pastime for programmers, thanks to the many popular examples of hobbyist programming provided by the open-source software movement. "Playing with Wi-Fi" and wardriving developed as a small but coherent subculture that provided its adherents an interesting pastime and an identity. Seen this way, the innovation of software-only positioning was a logical combination of these building blocks.

Speaking more abstractly, requirements for this innovation that could be applied to other examples could include that, (1) rich sets of information are freely available to be played with and repurposed, (2) information resides in a digital format that aids in its ready duplication, transfer, and manipulation, (3) cheap or free communication via the internet allows the coordination of disparate, distant actors, (4) important features of existing digital systems are documented and programmable so that they can be easily reconfigured by those who have the skill, and (5) a subculture exists or can be created that provides incentives to participate.

Stated in this more abstract manner, many of the new media technologies employed by youth subcultures also fit this general template, as do the interesting software recombination projects mentioned earlier called "software mashups." Social networking services like MySpace and Friendster have promoted themselves as a youth fad and induced individuals to produce a whole (e.g., a network) that is much more interesting than any single person's profile. The photo sharing service Flickr does much the same, relying on the extensive existing infrastructure of digital cameras. If the five-part template introduced above represents a real departure from previous innovation, 2008 could be the edge of a digital media renaissance, where form, tool, genre, and infrastructure are newly amenable to change and recombination. But this conclusion is premature because it asks us to assume that these features are new. Before generalizing about the "new" present, we should look for the Bobzillas and SignalSeekers of the past. Analog wireless play, after all, was pioneered by young boys and this led to what we now think of as radio.[40]

"New Wonders with 'Wireless'—And by a Boy!"

To those who have read the history of wireless innovation a hundred years ago, the parallels to the Wi-Fi experimenters of today are uncanny. The argument here is not that parallels can be found in history for the current situation—history is a large domain, and so it is almost always true that some sort of historical parallel can be found for any situation. The argument here is instead that wireless history offers exactly the same sorts of roles, behaviors, and activities: not a roughly comparable situation but an almost identical one. In the first days of Wi-Fi, much was made of the "Pringles Cantenna": a Wi-Fi antenna produced by enthusiasts who modified a potato chip can. A hundred years ago, the phenomenon was exactly the same, but the can used was Quaker Oats.

In the exemplary *Inventing American Broadcasting*, Susan Douglas coined the phrase "the cult of the boy operator" to describe the culture of radio amateurism and the press coverage that promoted it in the early years of the twentieth century.[41] As a point of departure, she refers to a 1907 article from the *New York Times Magazine* headlined "New Wonders with 'Wireless'—And by a Boy!" The star of this feature was twenty-six-year-old Walter J. Willenborg, an ordinary student with a facility for manipulating wireless equipment. A subsequent article in 1908 emphasized that "even today there are young folks who make [a] mistake in thinking that all great things that are worth doing have been done; all the great discoveries made; all the grand inventions finished."[42] Willenborg was an example of the white middle-class boys who were advancing the grand inventions of wireless. They did this by participating "in contests of strength, power, and territory,"[43] and by eavesdropping on otherwise inaccessible signals. Douglas asserts that for the amateur operators of 1908, technical prowess in wireless was an important new way to be a man. The middle-class masculinity of the day was dominated by physical and natural contest. As formal education increased in popularity and duration and everyday life became more urban for most people, there had to be some way to reclaim "a sense of mastery" using other means: technology.[44] Boy operators could still "triumph over nature if they controlled the right kind of machine."[45]

Scholars of media technology have given these boys enormous credit for shaping the development of radio as a system. The introduction of the inexpensive crystal set provided the means for amateurs to affordably experiment with radio, and the amateur audience that they developed foreshadowed the use of radio as a mass medium for entertainment. By many accounts, the most societally significant innovation in early radio was not a characteristic of the receiver or transmitter, but the idea of mass broadcasting itself. With radio, "it is not only that the supply of broadcasting facilities preceded the demand; it is that the means of communication preceded their content."[46] Radio companies of the time were focused on taking business away from cable and telegraph operators, and were reeling from the collapse of a speculation-related bubble in the stock market. After later developments in the regulation of radio, the significance of amateur operators would sharply decline, but in developing a very early audience of hundreds of thousands of users and uses for radio, amateurs demonstrated the viability of a system of mass broadcasting that would later be commercialized as "the media." What we know as radio was invented by young boys like Walter J. Willenborg. In their play, they invented the content and the audience.

A specific group of nonprofessionals in the past contributed valuable innovations to the social organization and the technological system of radio. They initially organized their activities as play and as "just fooling around," and they initially sought to serve only their own interests. While their greatest contribution was the idea of broadcasting (for instance, they were the first to transmit music over the radio), this was only one of many contributions. As they had limited resources, their contributions often emphasized overcoming these constraints. For instance, the American Radio Relay League managed the first transatlantic transmission by shortwave in 1921—a feat that without shortwaves required giant industrial machinery consuming large amounts of power.

Some of the rules and games of wireless play are identical, even after ninety years. NZ Wireless's Wi-Fi treasure hunts, mentioned earlier, are the same sort of organized seeking for particular signals that early radio amateurs pursued under a variety of names.[47] Much like the wardrivers of the twenty-first century, the early twentieth century pioneers often organized themselves while at play, and some activities took the form of a contest. Starting in 1916, the U.S. amateurs began to organize large-scale radio relays that would convey messages across the country (in 1916, a message from Iowa reached both coasts in about an hour).[48] These relays emphasized different characteristics of wireless technology at different times (e.g., some were speed contests, some experiments with reliability checks). The organizational vehicle for these relays, called the American Radio Relay League, became the dominant membership association for amateur radio.

Bobzilla and Arkasha's creation of WiGLE (the Wireless Geographic Logging Engine) on the internet to organize wardrivers was then a newer version of an old effort. Bobzilla and Arkasha used a dedicated Web server and computer programming expertise to harness the latest geographic information systems (GIS) and technologies. In 1916, W. H. Kirwan bought "a large map of the United States and a pair of compasses," and when he wanted to communicate with amateur stations, he produced mass mailings of 1,000 letters.[49]

So, the users of radio and software-only positioning both have some maverick teenagers to thank. With this in mind, the account of the wireless wardriver accidentally helping the driver of the rented SUV should start to seem less strange. The development of any technology involves a complicated tangle of associations that looks odd whenever anyone stops to look at it closely enough.[50] In these accounts, the involvement of youth, whimsy, and play often seems to be the most exciting and unexpected feature of invention. But this shouldn't seem strange either, as this combination is a leftover from the Enlightenment discovery of the imagination and its transformation through the eighteenth century into an attitude that glorifies creativity, "...freedom, originality, genius, the arts, and the innocent and uncorrupted character of childhood vision."[51] All of this is to say that linking teenagers playing around to new kinds of invention is in the longer view an awfully familiar "unfamiliar story."

The Prerequisites Revisited: What's Different Now?

Earlier, this chapter posited five general prerequisites for unexpected innovation in digital media. Summarized again concisely, they were as follows: (1) rich sets of data, (2) digital formats, (3) cheap communication, (4) open, documented interfaces, and (5) a subculture of innovators. After a short detour to the history of wireless play and radio amateurism ninety years ago, it should now be clearer that surprising things can also be accomplished with poor sets of data, expensive communication, and analog formats (the first three prerequisites).

If the new availability of data in a digital format combined with the cheap ability to communicate it is all that is truly new (our first three prerequisites), then there has been no revolutionary shift in innovation, but instead a simpler quickening. If the Shawn Fannings of the world are not a new phenomenon, it may still be that there are more chances to innovate in this manner now. Von Hippel depicts an acceleration of user-driven innovation across society in just this way: not as a wholesale transformation, but as a change in scale. "[R]apid technological advances in computer hardware and software and networking technologies have made it much easier to create and sustain a communal development style on ever-larger scales," he writes, due in part to "prepackaged infrastructural support" for subcultures of innovators.[52]

The fourth prerequisite—open, documented interfaces—simply isn't new. Open interfaces can be thought of both as a feature of a technology's development over time and as a decision made by the organizations involved in technology production. That is, radio was malleable by young boys in the 1920s in part because the knowledge of radio was so new (and so sparse) that it could be readily grasped and manipulated. The apparatus employed in early radio was much simpler than that used in later developments (such as satellite radio). While in the modern example of geolocation, GPS and Wi-Fi were open standards, freely available, there is no reason that they need be public, and in fact all of the operation of GPS used to be a government secret. Open interfaces can be found throughout the history of technology development in situations where firms found it more expedient to share information about technology and compete on some other field. (This is related to the business strategy of actively sharing technological innovations rather than keeping them secret, called "free revealing").[53]

While the fifth prerequisite (a subculture of innovators) has garnered a lot of attention recently, the young inventor-hero and the subculture of innovation is surely not a new phenomenon (as Walter J. Willenborg would agree, if he were still living).

This nuance separating a simple quickening of some features of innovation versus a wholesale transformation of innovation is of the utmost importance. This nuance has been lost in the public debate about the transformative power of digital media, and this has consequences for action. If fans of distributed creativity and decentralized innovation can locate some fundamental notion of positive empowerment inside the nature of digital media, they need to do nothing. As digital media marches across the landscape, power will shift, creativity will blossom, and we only have to pause and appreciate the results ("There's nothing I can't do," as Stuart wrote). Instead of this view, the preceding discussion suggests that there are historical precedents for the current excitement. "Programmers are the new rock stars" is nothing more than the latest installment of a recurring phenomenon, as amateurs were the new radio stars. In a longer historical perspective, doing nothing but waiting for the transformation won't work. The transformation won't arrive, and there is a need to figure out why not. Amateurs are not radio stars today—or to speak more generally, these positive phenomena seem associated with the birth of a communication technology, but then they disappear. It is also worth asking why these features of distributed innovation and creativity failed to transform society in the past—after all, here it is needing transformation again.

Innovation by Whom and for What?

A useful way to conceptualize the state of digital media and innovation today, then, isn't as a "transformation," but as something much more worrying: it is the predictable process of things staying the same while established centers of power and structure exert their influence. Arkasha, Bobzilla, Walter J. Willenborg, and Shawn Fanning have almost been collected from central casting to play the role of a young innovator. There is a reason that the role is typecast: the population of innovators in information technology is remarkably homogeneous. There is even a word to distinguish the class of people who can participate in configuring information technology, and that word is "nerd." (Remember Alister B. wrote, "Hey, I'm a nerd," to justify his own scripting habits.) Little systematic demographic data exist on the new or old waves of innovators, but a moment's examination reveals that information technology innovators inhabit an overwhelmingly privileged world. Recent reports of a new "participatory culture" arising from digital media beg the question: Who may participate, for what purpose?[54] The answers don't reveal a new world where anyone can be discovered to be a rock star or a rock star programmer. Instead, content and technology production seem to rest firmly with the same sorts of people we would expect after a review of radio amateurs: these are white, well-educated young men, typically from middle-class backgrounds.

Race and privilege are not raised here just to point out the ongoing inequality of society (although that would be reason enough). Instead, when considering the topic of innovation, the scholarship very clearly states that *who* innovates is absolutely critical to the kinds of innovations produced.[55] Creators of our new technologies overwhelmingly imagine themselves as the users (at least at first), whether they work in an R&D lab or not. Who they are, the kind of things they like, and the kind of things they want dictate the limits of their imagination for new inventions and features. As discussed earlier, many innovations come from users, and so it is uncontroversial to point out that the user and technology developer can be the same person, as in von Hippel's phrase "user-innovator." However, more fundamentally, scholarship in technology studies has found that any technological innovation is itself an act of projection where a designer actively constructs an idealized use and user for their product. This idealized or projected user—sometimes called "the reflexive user"—is intermingled with the developer's own identity, and this process is more prevalent during the earliest days of a technological system, as Bardini and Horvath have shown for the evolution of the personal computer.[56] While this concept has been used to describe technology production, there is no reason not to extend this idea to content. In the production of media content, it isn't a surprise that the directors, writers, and artists strive to produce film, text, and artwork that they would like, and to capture the attention of an audience like themselves and their friends.

This is a valuable shift in perspective because it invites us to stop searching for bottlenecks, or at least to reconceptualize them. In past fears about cultural domination, the concentration of cultural production, and technological disenfranchisement, the focus has always been on the few people that seem to get to decide "for the rest of us." The large technology producers, talent scouts, television executives, the Hollywood studio system are to blame, and have to be eliminated or bypassed. But today's excitement about digital media has bypassed the bottlenecks, and revealed a mass of creative people who often look just like, and aspire to be just like, large technology producers, talent scouts, television executives, and the Hollywood studio system.

Just a few examples will cement this point. In 2007, the potato chip brand Doritos followed a recent trend toward embracing consumer-produced marketing and partnered with Yahoo! Video to hold the "Crash the Super Bowl Contest." In brief, anyone could create and submit their own thirty-second commercial for Doritos, and Yahoo! Video users could vote for their favorite. Doritos would then pay to air the winning spot during the Super Bowl—long the most important and expensive (and therefore exclusive) venue for television advertising. The amateur users banded together and produced . . . a professional set of Doritos' commercials. One of the common remarks posted to the Yahoo! and YouTube sites of the contenders was that the videos were "so professional." Indeed, they were indistinguishable from the recent output of any professional ad agency, and the participants in the contest wrote about how they hoped for professional media jobs.

There is more to these Doritos than what has been made by recent cultural criticism. For instance, recent essays have pointed out that replacing mass media gatekeepers with distributed creativity hasn't unleashed a dynamo of creativity that was formerly repressed; it has only revealed the atrocious taste of the masses. (Jaron Lanier crystallized this critique with the phrase, "The hive mind is for the most part stupid and boring.")[57]

Most of the content and technology producers in the wireless case studies reviewed earlier do not aspire to a viable alternative infrastructure or new form of cultural organization, but this isn't because they have poor taste. They aspire to participate in the structures that exist already, or to build their own structures that are very similar, but have them in charge. This isn't their failing, it is their motivation—what makes their actions comprehensible. In the case of geolocation, Wi-Fi experimentation was a route for many technology amateurs to professionalize. Experiments with wireless systems, treasure hunts, and amateur collectives became items on the resumes of many who later went into some aspect of the information technology industry (if they didn't start there in the first place). Before Wi-Fi became widespread, wireless network engineering was not a common job classification and did not have a career path. When young wireless experimenters reminisce about their successes, they say things like, "it got us some consulting work," "I do consulting for [wireless] companies now," "it got him a job in Milwaukee in the end," "we split that off into a private company," "it attracted attention for my business," "it got you and me a skill set, which got us pretty nice jobs," and "now we have a business plan."[58] Studies of early technology experimenters across history have shown that technology tinkering can be an excellent route to becoming an insider.[59] But for this strategy to work, the tinkerer can't be that far from an insider in the first place.

Production Values: A Permanent Gulf

A meaningful confusion may still be lingering after the examples of wireless and Doritos. Above, Yahoo! Video and YouTube users were able to ape major advertising agencies using only desktop equipment, and wireless amateurs of the present were sometimes depicted conducting essentially the same activities as well-financed corporations (such as the assembly of national Wi-Fi databases). Is this, then, what is new about digital media—that producers with so few resources are able to perform the same way as well-funded institutions? Unfortunately not: recall that radio amateurs in the past also performed these feats, and better. They were able to provide both transcontinental and transatlantic message service. It is not new that poorly financed contributors can have a role in new technology or content development or that barriers to entry are low in some technological areas. The presence of user-driven innovation and peer production now does not particularly indicate that a transformation is underway. For the earlier writing about convergence, it was an error of reasoning to think that the benefits of digital convergence would accrue only to producers and corporations, and not to users. But it is another sort of error to think that this implies that the differential in resources between producers and corporations no longer matters. In media industries, production values have historically been the route to enforcing the boundary between professional and amateur content. In the United States, most people have been able to record their own music (or even their own television show) for some time and distribute it themselves, or air it on a local radio station or public access station. Still, there is an ever-evolving professional "sound" and a "look" that are difficult to emulate. Just as the style of one genre becomes widely imitable (as in the thirty-second Doritos television commercial), other forms slide farther out of reach as studios develop and invest in new technologies for lighting, editing, and computer-generated animation. Today, it may be easy to make your own Web page, but it is difficult to make a database-driven, Flash-enhanced, interactive site that looks the same as one produced by a large media corporation. The effects achieved by professional media industries are designed to look expensive and to be expensive in order to police this boundary. This may be one reason that the user interface has presented such an obstacle to open-source software development. By far the most successful open source products are server side and have little user interface and therefore little need for a look-and-feel that competes with Microsoft or Apple.

To scale the wall of production value and try to produce something that will be an entrée into professionalization, the amateur will face a number of daunting obstacles. Whether the vehicle is writing, photographs, film, or software, to even make an attempt requires literacy and entails a large investment in education. Worse, all of these objects contain cultural markers that do more than separate professional production values from amateur ones; they also reinforce the dominant conceptualization of the audience or the user. These range from male terminology in computing to the dominance of affluent perspectives in fiction writing.

Waiting for a Transformation, or Working for It

All this means that the people puzzling over interesting stories of peer production and unexpected innovation in digital media may not have discovered the route to any sort of revolution. Wanting a decentralized emancipatory technology badly enough may suffice for seeing one. This desire to build or find the "machine in the garden" (the American pastoral ideal resurgent, the preference for the diffuse over the centralized) is a powerful and alluring current in Western thought.[60] But taking von Hippel's earlier point seriously, *most* innovation may be user-driven. The innovator's garage, basement, and even youth may be completely normal. Peer production of content or infrastructure is then emphatically not a crack in the armor of an evil monolith, or a shift in power relations, but a more ordinary point of entry and commodification. A&R may be the new R&D, but the A&R department isn't run by artists, and any artist who has dealt with one will tell you that A&R's ascendancy doesn't mean that the talent will be getting a better deal anytime soon.

Reflect, for a moment, on the evolution of the newspaper as a capsule version of the other technological accounts developed in this chapter. While the newspaper has been written about as the epitome of the one-to-many, "mass" media form, the earliest newspapers in America were printed with blank pages at the end so that the readers could write in their own content. It is extravagant to think this affordance as "peer production" or as a way to redistribute the power of the press. Instead, it seems born of the material conditions of the newspapers of the day. They were infrequent, rare, expensive, and they tended to circulate through many hands and many sets of eyes. Indeed, before 1830, the American newspaper had no paid reporters (there was yet no profession of reporter), and instead relied upon the publisher's own writing and contributed letters. Again, it is too much to think that printing these letters was a democratic gesture (they usually came from the publisher's friends, and they were one more thing the publisher didn't have to write).[61] Today, nonprofessionals still have a means of entry into the pages of a newspaper: the "letters to the editor" section. Although they are often studied by journalism professors, letters to the editor have not been found to be a significant source of power to anyone. They may have the least power to influence the development of the communication technology that carries them (the newspaper). Indeed, professional journalists almost uniformly hold letter writers in contempt, and implement the letters' section in ways that are actively antidemocratic.[62] Even the accessibility of the technology of print itself is confusingly open to interpretation. While in democratic theory the press has been described as open to "anyone," it still requires literacy, technological expertise, cultural capital, and (for publishers, not letterwriters) it has been expensive. For much of its history, the American newspaper has been a discussion vehicle for affluent white men. The newspaper is surely not a perfect comparison to wireless, the internet, or digital media, but it does serve to highlight the longstanding history of user-contributed content and some of its complications. In secondary school civics classes, teenagers can start their own (small, badly financed) newspapers and contribute letters to existing newspapers, but this is stiflingly mainstream and not a transformative new practice with communication technology. It is no surprise that both scholars and teenagers themselves prefer to talk about the potential of *Second Life*.

This chapter has tried to portray the linkage of play, young people, and innovation in digital media as ordinary and not transformative. It has tried to replace the popular accounts of "young rebels" who seek to overturn the established order with a portrait of the usual suspects (i.e., well-educated, white, male innovators; nerds; literate and skilled content producers) who are looking for a warm place inside the establishment. In this effort, wireless has been a particularly useful case study, as the parallels across history are unusually apt. They demonstrate that subcultures of innovators and ease of entry into technological and content production are old features of media, not new ones. Today does feature the advantage of digital formats, widespread access to rich sets of digital data, and cheaper communication than ever before. Since great feats of amateur innovation were already possible without these advantages, it is not clear that these features are transformative. One might not even find them particularly encouraging when reminded that "amateur innovator" or "amateur content producer" is itself a privileged and difficult-to-obtain position depending upon literacy, other knowledge, social networks, class, race, and lifestyle. This is then the call for action for those who care about the democratic potential of decentralized production. Rather than wait for the technological changes to unfold, this analysis requires us to figure out why each instance of technological transformation from the 1920s to the 2000s never satisfies. "Participatory culture" will only move beyond the elite if the desire for decentralized control and widespread participation can animate changes in our society's fundamental structures of opportunity.

Notes

1. For a popular history of Napster, see Joseph Menn, *All the Rave: The Rise and Fall of Shawn Fanning's Napster* (New York: Crown Business, 2003).

2. Daniel Pemberton, Bedroom to Big Time, *Wired* 5, no. 6 (1997). http://www.wired.com/wired/archive/5.06/white_town.html.

3. lessig blog, The Read-Write Internet, 2006, http://www.lessig.org/blog/archives/003295.shtml.

4. James W. Carey, Historical Pragmatism and the Internet, *New Media & Society* 7 (2005): 443–455.

5. Milton L. Mueller, Digital Convergence and its Consequences, *Javnost/The Public* 6, no. 3 (1999): 11–27. http://dcc.syr.edu/rp1.pdf.

6. Dwayne Winseck, Back to the Future: Telecommunications, Online Information Services and Convergence from 1840–1910, *Media History* 5, no. 2 (1999): 137–157.

7. Yochai Benkler, *The Wealth of Networks: How Social Production Transforms Markets and Freedom* (New Haven, CT: Yale University Press, 2006).

8. For example, Ted Nelson's famous quote, "The purpose of computers is human freedom." See Theodore H. Nelson, *Computer Lib/Dream Machines* (Hugo's Book Service: Chicago, IL, 1974) and http://xanadu.com.au/ted/TN/WRITINGS/TCOMPARADIGM/tedCompOneLiners.html; For a review, see Fred Turner, *From Counterculture to Cyberculture* (Chicago: University of Chicago Press, 2006).

9. François Bar and Christian Sandvig, US Communication Policy after Convergence, Media, Culture & Society (in press).

10. Lawrence Lessig, *Free Culture* (New York: Penguin, 2004).

11. Steven Weber, *The Success of Open Source* (Cambridge, MA: Harvard University Press, 2004).

12. Martin Campbell-Kelly and William Aspray, *Computer: A History of the Information Machine* (New York: Basic Books, 1996).

13. Daniel Miller, Don Slater, and Lucy Suchman, Anthropology, in *The Academy and the Internet*, eds. Monroe E. Price and Helen F. Nissenbaum (New York: Peter Lang, 2004), 84–105.

14. Eric von Hippel, *The Sources of Innovation* (Oxford, UK: Oxford University Press, 1988). See also the literature on "Learning by Using," in *Inside the Black Box: Technology and Economics,* ed. Nathan Rosenberg (Cambridge, UK: Cambridge University Press, 1983).

15. Nathan Ensmenger, Letting the "Computer Boys" Take Over: Technology and the Politics of Organizational Transformation, *International Review of Social History* 48, no. 11 (2003): 154.

16. Frederick P. Brooks, *The Mythical Man-Month: Essays on Software Engineering*, 20th anniversary ed. (New York: Addison-Wesley Professional, 1995).

17. Sherry Turkle, *The Second Self: Computers and the Human Spirit*, reprint ed. (New York: Touchstone, 1985).

18. Tim Berners-Lee is credited with inventing the World Wide Web. Bram Cohen designed BitTorrent, the peer-to-peer file sharing system optimized to handle large files.

19. Examples of fiction in this genre include Po Bronson, *The First $20 Million is Always the Hardest. A Silicon Valley Novel* (New York: Random House, 1997), while trade press nonfiction summaries include Jerry Kaplan, *Startup: A Silicon Valley Adventure Story* (New York: Houghton Mifflin, 1995).

20. That is, programmers like Bram Cohen (designer of the peer-to-peer file sharing system *BitTorrent*) can be distinguished from Fanning and Newmark by their exact position of production—Cohen worked at a series of related start-up companies that were trying to commercialize peer-to-peer file sharing software before starting his own. Fanning and Newmark developed new applications as a creative experiment, and only later realized that their innovations had value.

21. For example, Erik Barnouw, *A Tower of Babel: A History of Broadcasting in the United States to 1933*, vol. 1 (New York: Oxford University Press, 1966); Clinton B. Desoto, *200 Meters & Down: The Story of Amateur Radio* (New York: American Radio Relay League, 1985); Susan J. Douglas, *Inventing American Broadcasting, 1899–1922* (Baltimore, MD: Johns Hopkins University Press, 1989); Susan J. Douglas, *Listening In: Radio and the American Imagination* (Minneapolis: University of Minnesota Press, 2004); Robert W. McChesney, *Telecommunications, Mass Media, and Democracy: The Battle for Control of U.S. Broadcasting, 1928–1935* (New York: Oxford University Press, 1995); Kristen Haring, The "Freer Men" of Ham Radio: How a Technical Hobby Provided Social and Spatial Distance. *Technology and Culture* 4 (2003): 734–761.

22. The National Academy of Sciences, The Global Positioning System: The Role of Atomic Clocks, *Beyond Discovery: The Path from Research to Human Benefit* (1997). http://www.beyonddiscovery.org/content/view.article.asp?a=458.

23. For a definition, see Bernward Joerges, Large Technical Systems: Concepts and Issues, in *The Development of Large Technical Systems*, eds. Thomas P. Hughes and Renate Mayntz (Boulder, CO: Westview Press, 1988), 9–36. For other examples, see Thomas P. Hughes, *Rescuing Prometheus: Four Monumental Projects That Changed the Modern World* (New York: Pantheon, 1998).

24. Several products combine GPS and software-only positioning. Ventures include Skyhook Wireless, ekahau, Navizon, and Microsoft Research's WiFi Positioning.

25. It is likely that this is not true. Still, software-only positioning offers more precision than GPS in urban areas.

26. Christian Sandvig, An Initial Assessment of Cooperative Action in Wi-Fi Networking, *Telecommunications Policy* 28, nos. 7, 8 (2004): 579–602.

27. See http://tv.seattlewireless.net/november/november2003.html.

28. See "best SSIDs you have seen" at http://www.broadbandreports.com/forum/remark,12349735~mode=flat.

29. See WiGLE at http://www.wigle.net/.

30. See http://www.worldwidewardrive.org/ and http://wardriving.meetup.com/about/.

31. See "Treasure Hunt Wi-Fi Style in Aukland" at http://nzwireless.org/content-3.html and "Use Wi-Fi to Play Access Point Games" at http://www.extremetech.com/article2/0,1697,1746269,00.asp.

32. Simon Byers and Dave Kormann, 802.11b access point mapping, *Communications of the ACM* 46, no. 5 (2003): 41–46.

33. Or perhaps a "global" map—these maps have holes where wardrivers do not go.

34. See http://www.chroniclesofawardriver.org/?p=285.

35. Janet Abbate, *Inventing the Internet* (Cambridge, MA: MIT Press, 1999); Hughes, *Rescuing Prometheus: Four Monumental Projects That Changed the Modern World*, 1998; Thomas P. Hughes, The Organization of Federal Support: A Historical Review, in *Funding a Revolution: Government Support for Computing Research*, ed. Thomas P. Hughes (Washington, DC: National Academy Press, 1999), Ch. 4.

36. Paul N. Edwards, *The Closed World: Computers and the Politics of Discourse in Cold War America* (Cambridge, MA: MIT Press, 1996).

37. Tim Lenoir, All But War is Simulation: The Military-Entertainment Complex, *Configurations* 8, no. 3 (2000): 289–335; Tim Lenoir, Programming Theaters of War: Gamemakers as Soldiers, in *Bombs and Bandwidth: The Emerging Relationship between IT and Security*, ed. Robert Latham (New York: New Press, 2003).

38. Thomas Streeter, "That Deep Romantic Chasm": Libertarianism, Neoliberalism, and the Computer Culture, in *Communication, Citizenship, and Social Policy: Re-Thinking the Limits of the Welfare State*, eds. Andrew Calabrese and Jean-Claude Burgelman (New York: Rowman and Littlefield, 1999). See also Thomas Streeter, The Romantic Self and the Politics of Internet Commercialization, *Cultural Studies* 17, no. 5 (2003).

39. Max Horkheimer and Theodor W. Adorno, *Dialectic of Enlightenment*, trans. J. Cumming (New York: Herder and Herder, 1944/1972).

40. Carolyn Marvin, *When Old Technologies Were New: Thinking about Electric Communication in the Late Nineteenth Century* (New York: Oxford University Press, 1988); Douglas, *Inventing American Broadcasting, 1899–1922*.

41. For other discussions of radio amateurism and alternative radio, see Desoto, *200 Meters & Down* and Jesse Walker, *Rebels on the Air: An Alternative History of Radio in America*, rev. ed. (New York: New York University Press, 2004).

42. Douglas, *Inventing American Broadcasting, 1899–1922*, 189.

43. Ibid., 191.

44. This only alludes to the large literature in feminist technology studies and anthropology linking the "technical" to the masculine.

45. Ibid., 191.

46. Raymond Williams, *Television* (London: Fontana, 1974), 18–19.

47. Radio amateurs, for instance, collect specific signals by gathering QSL cards (a paper version of the code QSL, meaning, "I confirm receipt of your transmission"). For more detail, see Danny Gregory and Paul Sahre, *Hello World: A Life in Ham Radio* (Princeton, NJ: Princeton Architectural Press, 2003).

48. William H. Kirwan, The Washington's Birthday Amateur Radio Relay, *The Electrical Experimenter* 64 (1916): 24–25.

49. Ibid., 24.

50. This sentiment has been made most clear by Actor-Network Theory in technology studies; see Bruno Latour, *Reassembling the Social: An Introduction to Actor-Network Theory* (New York: Oxford University Press, 2005).

51. Brian Sutton-Smith, *The Ambiguity of Play* (Cambridge, MA: Harvard University Press, 1997), 129.

52. Eric von Hippel, *Democratizing Innovation* (Cambridge, MA: MIT Press, 2005), 99.

53. See Eric von Hippel and Georg von Krogh, Free Revealing and the Private-Collective Model for Innovation Incentives, *R&D Management* 36, no. 3 (2006): 295–306. An earlier historical moment when "free revealing" became an important strategy is the emergence of open scientific research—this also coincided with major changes in communication technology, see Paul A. David, Common Agency Contracting and the Emergence of "Open Science" Institutions, *The American Economic Review* 88, no. 2 (1998): 15–21.

54. "[W]e need to confront the cultural factors that diminish the likelihood that different groups will participate. Race, class, [and] language differences amplify . . . inequalities in opportunities for participation." See Henry Jenkins, *Convergence Culture: Where Old and New Media Collide* (New York: New York University Press, 2006), 258.

55. This is a large literature, but for an introduction specifically focused on communication technologies, see François Bar and Annemarie Munk Riis, Tapping User-Driven Innovation: A New Rationale for Universal Service, *The Information Society* 16, no. 1 (2000): 1–10.

56. See Bardini and Bardini and Horvath (1998). Bardini and Horvath define the "reflexive user" as ". . . the conceptual user resulting from the thought process of the designer anticipating the potential use of his or her design. This anticipation is made possible by a set of representations understood both as cognitive practices creating an image of the user (a mental representation), and as political practices, a sketch of a strategic plan aimed at allowing the designer to speak and act in place of this user-to-be." (Thierry Bardini and August T. Horvath, The Social Construction of the Personal Computer User, *Journal of Communication* 45, no. 3 (1995): 41).

57. Jaron Lanier, Digital Maoism: The Hazards of the New Online Collectivism, *Edge 183* (2006), http://www.edge.org/3rd_culture/lanier06/lanier06_index.html.

58. These quotes are taken from interviews with wireless entrepreneurs and experimenters taken from 2003–2007 for a related research project.

59. For the most comprehensive discussion of this phenomenon in communication technology, see Marvin, 1988.

60. Leo Marx, *The Machine in the Garden: Technology and the Pastoral Ideal in America* (New York: Oxford University Press, 1964).

61. For a discussion of the evolution of reporting and newspapers, see Michael Schudson, *Discovering the News: A Social History of American Newspapers* (New York: Basic Books, 1980).

62. See Karin Wahl-Jorgensen, The Construction of the Public in Letters to the Editor: Deliberative Democracy and the Idiom of Insanity, *Journalism* 3, no. 2 (2002): 183–204. Although the inclusion of letters from the public might be seen to be a democratic impulse, letters sections are used within newspapers to actively deride the public and to portray them in sensational and unrealistic ways, "allowing them to be dismissed as crazy and irrational" (p. 200).

PART II: EXPLORING "NEW" MEDIA: CASE STUDIES OF DIGITAL YOUTH

Internet Literacy: Young People's Negotiation of New Online Opportunities

Sonia Livingstone

London School of Economics and Political Science, Department of Media and Communications

The "Internet Generation"?

It's just like life, you can do anything really.... My younger cousins, . . . they're now coming into an age where the Internet is all they've ever known. (Lorie, 17, from Essex)[1]

If the Internet is, as Lorie suggests, "just like life," for better and for worse, then the mother of ten-year-old Anna is surely observing a profound generational transformation when she says:

I'll have to come up to a level because otherwise I will, I'll be a dinosaur, and the children, when children laugh at you and sort of say "Blimey, mum, don't you even know that?" . . . Already now I might do something and I say "Anna, Anna, what is it I've got to do here?" and she'll go "Oh mum, you've just got to click the—" and she'll be whizzing, whizzing dreadfully.

For previously new media—books, comics, cinema, radio, and television—even if parents weren't familiar with the particular contents their children engaged with, at least they could access and understand the medium so that, if they wished to understand what their children were doing or share the activity with them, they could. With the advent of digital media, things have changed. The demands of the computer interface are significant, rendering many parents "dinosaurs" in the information age inhabited by their children. But, more importantly, attention to these demands blinds us to the real challenge of using digital media, namely the potential for engagement with information and education content, and for participation in online activities, networks, and communities. Indeed, the very difficulty of accessing and using the internet beguiles many adults into believing that if only they could master "clicking" on links with the mouse, then they—like their children—would be internet "experts." This is not a belief that we hold for the pen, else we'd stop teaching pupils English once they had learned to read and write, but the child who "whizzes" around the screen seems so skilled that, we conclude comfortably, they know all they need to know already.

Such a conclusion seems confirmed by the extraordinary news headlines of young hackers breaking national security codes or teenage entrepreneurs making a fortune on E-Bay, not to

This chapter draws on research funded by an Economic and Social Research Council grant (RES-335-25-0008) as part of the U.K.'s "e-Society" Programme, with co-funding from AOL-UK, BSC, Childnet-International, Citizens Online, ITC, and Ofcom. Thanks to Magdalena Bober, Ellen Helsper, Rodney Livingstone, Elizabeth van Couvering, and Nancy Thumim for their constructive contributions to the work presented here.

mention the youthful origins of such recent successes as Google and YouTube. Young people themselves, conscious of being the first generation to grow up with the internet, concur with the public celebration of their status as "digital natives."[2] Amir (15, from London) says confidently, "I don't find it hard to use a computer because I got into it quickly. You learn quick because it's a very fun thing to do." Nina (17, from Manchester) adds scathingly, "My Dad hasn't even got a clue. Can't even work the mouse. . . . So I have to go on the Internet for him." But while these claims contain a sizeable grain of truth, we must also recognize their rhetorical value for the speakers. Only in rare instances in history have children gained greater expertise than parents in skills highly valued by society (diasporic children's learning of the host language before their parents is a good example). More usually, youthful expertise—in music, games, or imaginative play—is accorded little, serious value by adults, even if envied nostalgically. Thus, although young people's newfound online skills are justifiably trumpeted by both generations, this does not put them beyond critical scrutiny, for the young entrepreneurs and hackers are the exceptions rather than the norm.

This chapter will engage with several claims illustrated by Anna's mother, above. First, I propose that the widespread struggle among educators, parents, researchers and policy makers to conceptualize what it is (young) people "know" or need to know when using the internet is usefully resolved by conceptualizing this knowledge in terms of literacy. This allows us to draw on, and learn from, a long intellectual history of debate over the nature of literacy (from print literacy to audiovisual and media literacies, information literacy, advertising literacy, cyberliteracy, games literacy, critical literacy, and many more), notwithstanding critical doubts over "literacy" as a normative or elitist project.[3] Through the concept of literacy, I suggest, we can weave together an account of basic and advanced skills, linking individual skills with social practices and crossing the boundary between formal and informal learning. Second, I show that the internet poses specific and new demands on the understanding of its users (and would-be users), which, as empirical work with children themselves reveals, not all manage. Third, and contrary to Anna's mother's assumption, I argue that mastering the technology means mastering not just the hardware, but all that the internet affords its users. Thus we should be satisfied with nothing less than an ambitious definition of literacy given the considerable social, economic, cultural, and political ambitions that society has for the information society and, especially, for the so-called "internet generation."

Introducing Three Children

To ground the present discussion, and without meaning either to celebrate or to criticize them, I will briefly introduce three children who participated in the UK Children Go Online project to convey the richness and subtlety of their knowledge of, and their continuing struggles with, the internet.[4] For behind the excited rhetoric of young online experts, the everyday reality is inevitably more complex, as ethnographic research on the domestication of new technologies readily shows.[5]

I first visited Megan when she was eight years old, in 1999. A bright girl from a working class family, Megan lived in a media-rich but small house with her rather "stay-at-home" parents and her older brother, a computer enthusiast. She loved writing stories and animals, especially her pet hamster. She also loved playing on the computer, and her parents proudly termed her "an information junkie," having high educational aspirations for her. At the same time, they kept an eye on her internet use from the living room, being cautious about her online activities and encouraging visiting trusted sites rather than bold exploration, gently restricting her to information rather than communication applications. When I sat with Megan while she showed me her online activities, my observations suggested that her skills were somewhat exaggerated by her parents, her internet use being narrowly concentrated on three sites—AskJeeves for searching, Nickelodeon for games (linked to her favorite children's television series Rugrats), and a few sites about pets (e.g., Petstore.com). Her use of these sites often proved frustrating and inefficient.

In 2003, I returned to the family, when Megan was 12. Though various aspects of family life had now changed—her father had a new job, her mother had returned to full-time work, her brother had taken over the father as the "computer buff," the computer had been upgraded, and Megan had begun secondary school—it is the constancies that were more striking in this close, quiet family. Lively and chatty as ever, grungy if not quite a teenager yet, Megan still reads and writes stories—now on the computer, using the AOL story-writing option on the kids' page. She still searches for homework or leisure-related interests, now using Google. As before, she follows her interest in animals onto the internet—for example, using Neopets to name and keep a pet.[6] She's become a fan of The Sims, visiting the Sims Web site and sites with game cheats and, having gained a taste for horror, she enjoys playing "against the grain" by murdering her Sims and writing gothic tales of murder and destruction.[7] Yet, as before, her online skills seem more limited than her confident talk suggests. She had lost the password for her "neopet," nor could she manage to get the Web master to e-mail it to her. She now has an e-mail and instant messenger account, but rarely uses it, and there is nothing in her inbox when she looks. She ignores invitations on sites to chat, vote, or e-mail. When I ask what is listed under "favorites," she says she does not know, having never looked, and when something goes wrong, she skims over the problem rather than stopping to figure out what happened. So though her online style is quick and competent, getting where she wants efficiently, her range is narrow, with little exploration. In addition, there seems little need to worry about online risks, for Megan has internalized the caution once explicitly impressed on her by her parents.

Megan's internet use illustrates several key features of the online experience—a continuity in interests offline and online (pets, stories), a continuity in individual learning style and family mediation over time (from child to teen), the gap between parental pride in a child's expertise and his or her ability to make the technology do what he or she wants it to, and parental ambivalence over the fact that encouraging confident exploration online also makes a child vulnerable to online risks. Although all of these features of internet use are supported by social science research,[8] research also shows that not all young people are as cautious as Megan in their online experience, as the next case study illustrates.

Fifteen-year-old Anisah is from a Ghanaian family and lives on a once-very troubled housing estate. We first visited Anisah, a middle child, lively and confident, when she was 12. The family lived in a small two-bedroom flat, the computer squeezed into the living room along with most other family activities. Her educated parents had not found work in the U.K. that matched their qualifications, leading them to place huge educational expectations on their three children—evident in their many encyclopedias and educational CD-ROMs, the emphasis placed on homework and computer access, and the parental support for children's offline and online learning. At 12, Anisah was active and outgoing—she danced, played netball, shopped, and socialized through the church—but as she lived far from her school friends and was often alone, she also used the internet on most days, enjoying making friends in chat rooms, liking to feel ahead of her classmates (most of her peers didn't have home access). Though she benefited from using the internet to research school projects (using Yahoo,

Excite, or BBC Online), her skills were imperfect: she told us about doing a project on China (the country) for which she needed an illustration; she searched, downloaded, and inserted into her work a picture of china (porcelain) from a Web site in Maine, United States, not realizing the problem.[9]

Anisah at 15 had become a charming, strong-minded, articulate teenager, doing well at school and hoping to become a designer. Having moved to a new house, she and her sister now have a bedroom to themselves and, to her delight, this also houses the computer. Interestingly, the family's serious, moral attitude has become even stronger in Anisah. Unusually for her age group, Anisah reads the news on the homepage of her ISP. She revises for exams online using the BBC's Bitesize. We discuss how—unlike her peers—she refuses to download music, it being both illegal and wrong. She claims to have seen no pornography, though her mother worries about this, checking up on Anisah and so invading her privacy, as Anisah sees it. The interview with her mother pinpoints an ambivalence between saying "children are children" who require guidance and seeing Anisah as part of the "guru generation" who know about the internet. Though she uses e-mail and instant messaging programs, often chatting to her friends late into the night (a practice of which her mother is unaware), Anisah is now scathing about chat rooms because of the risk from dangerous contacts and because chatting to strangers seems pointless (reflecting a widespread campaign in the U.K. about the risks of chatrooms).[10] Much of her internet use is purposeful—to research art work for a project, to follow her interest in design, to find a cheap flight, and so forth.

From Anisah's experience, we can add to the picture gleaned from observing Megan. Being both older and more experienced, Anisah has bypassed some of the struggles Megan has with accessing online content, but this means she faces the next level of challenge—what exactly did Anisah need to know about the porcelain pictures to avoid her mistake? And, did the mistake result from her poor searching skills (i.e., using an ambiguous search term, "china") or her assessment of the Web site's content and reliability (finding a commercial site on the wrong topic) or, even, a problem occasioned by poor Web site design or search engine algorithms? One also wonders what complementary knowledge would be required by the teacher, if he or she is to detect such a mistake and, in school, how the teacher could have better advised Anisah. Internet literacy surely is not simply a feature of the individual, but rather emerges (or fails to emerge) from the interrelation between individual skill, education, and interface design, a point I shall develop below. Anisah's case also shows the importance of family background in shaping internet use—her parents' cultural capital compensates for their lack of economic capital[11] in helping Anisah "get ahead," a motivation held, but not always achieved, by many parents for their children;[12] as Anna's mother said, "I think from the children's point of view they are so incredibly lucky to be able to have the information in their dining room . . . and I think they are at an incredible advantage to other children. Not every family has got a computer, and I think children are disadvantaged if they don't." Less typically, though characteristic of religious families, Anisah's parents' strong moral values guide and restrict the nature of her online activities in a manner that, for the most part, she accepts.[13] Where Anisah diverges from her parents—in seeking covert opportunities for peer-to-peer communication, she reminds us that literacy encompasses all skills—both those approved of by adults and those disapproved of.[14]

My third case adds further dimensions to our growing account of youthful internet use: Ted was 14 when we first visited. More affluent than either Megan or Anisah, Ted is privately educated and lives in a white, middle-class family. Perhaps because he is an only child and dyslexic, Ted is rather overprotected at home; he watches a lot of television, though he also spends time playing sports and out with friends. Education seems less emphasized in this household except as a means to gain a comfortable lifestyle. Like many children, Ted cannot remember a time before the family had a computer, though the internet is recent. Unlike many others, he does not profess much expertise about these technologies. "I haven't got a clue," he said, when things go wrong. Indeed, being a computer consultant, his mother is the expert at home, guiding Ted in his use of the internet. She bookmarked the BBC's Bitesize for him, though he does not use it, and also checks the history file to see what he does online. Indeed, internet use in this family is fairly social, with a parent often in the study while Ted researches his homework online or plays games, and he also goes online with his friend and internet "guru," Ted following Mark's lead.[15] They check on their favorite stars, television programs, sports stuff, send jokey e-mails to their mates, and they visit Yahoo Chat—pretending to be older, to be other people, to meet girls. For Ted, the internet is mainly "fun and funny, it's good, frustrating sometimes"—especially in relation to effective searching.

We revisited Ted when he was 18, about to go to university. Family life had changed, with fewer family activities and Ted spending a lot of time in his room. Yet Ted still says that his mother is better at using the internet than he is, particularly for searching (this seems likely, when we observe his rather poor searching skills). And when we ask, he has little idea why sites exist or what purposes they may serve. Like many teens, though unlike Anisah, who considers it wrong, Ted now spends a lot of time downloading music via the peer-to-peer file sharing system Kazaa while, multitasking, he conducts instant messaging with friends. Again unlike Anisah, Ted hardly searches the Web at all now—only checking out university sites for possible courses when he needs to; the internet has become for him a medium of communication and music, not of information or education.

Thus, Ted adds further features to our growing insight into youthful internet literacy. Regarding the discrepancy between economic and cultural capital, his is the contrary case to Anisah. Where Anisah illustrates the hopes of those who provide internet access for the otherwise disadvantaged,[16] Ted shows that simply having the resources (financial, educational, and parental) does not necessarily get you ahead if a genuine interest in learning and exploration is not cultivated early. Second, Ted's use of the internet is more social than either Megan or Anisah—where Megan takes turns with her brother on the internet, and Anisah uses it alone or to guide her little sister, Ted goes online with his friend or his mother and so gains from their greater expertise: literacy is, for Ted, part of a social practice, not just a cognitive skill.[17] Last, one should note that while Ted, like the other two, would appear to a superficial observer to multitask effectively, "whizzing around" in the manner that impressed Anna's mother, the benefits he gains from the internet are curtailed first by his lack of interest in information, education, or exploration and, second, by his poor skills in searching and evaluating Web sites, though one should not underestimate the importance of gaining communication-related literacy skills, especially for teenagers.

Indeed, we can compare their adoption of the interactive potential of the Internet[18] as follows: Megan mainly uses the internet to search Web sites and play games—what Sally McMillan (2006) terms user–document and user–system interactivity respectively.[19] For Ted, user–user interactivity (chat, e-mail) is more important. Anisah makes perhaps the broadest use of online options, treating the internet as a more flexible and diverse tool. These three rather different young people also share some common experiences: each, for reasons of gender, class, ethnicity, or special educational needs, is partly on the "wrong" side of the digital divide,[20] challenged to use their skills and resources to overcome this and get what they want from and through the internet. Each is treading a careful line between parent-approved and child-favored activities, raising issues of domestic regulation (and its dependence on national regulation), which balance freedom, safety, and privacy,[21] and each is developing valued expertise—"internet literacy," though they seem more focused on making the interface work rather than on developing the broader and more ambitious critical and creative literacies that internet use affords.

Why "Internet Literacy"? An Excursion into Theory

To those for whom "literacy" means "just" reading and writing, the notion of internet literacy (or computer literacy, cyber-literacy, etc.) will seem puzzling. To nonnative English speakers, the lack of a ready translation for "literacy" into some languages also poses a difficulty.[22] Raymond Williams (1983) traces the historical emergence of the English term "literacy" not from "ABC" or "pen and paper," but from "literature," a term that once combined the adjective meaning being discerning and knowledgeable according to "standards of polite learning" with the noun for a body of writing of nationally acknowledged esthetic merit.[23] Today, as he observes, "literature" has come to refer only to the noun, with its associated adjective, "literary," while by the end of the nineteenth century, "literacy" (and its adjective, "literate") "was a new word invented to express the achievement and possession of what were increasingly seen as general and necessary skills."[24] Significantly, this new word became necessary as the ability to read spread beyond the elite to the mass public, needed to characterize the growing body of people with the skills to read and write but who lacked familiarity with the literary canon. In other words, with the advent of mass education and the commensurate rise of mass literacy, many people became literate but not literary, and the "uses of literacy," as Richard Hoggart put it,[25] became increasingly subject to regulatory scrutiny and governance.[26] Indeed, the advent of a literate but supposedly uncritical public occasioned a series of "moral panics" accompanying each new mass medium (and, today, each new interactive medium) (Drotner 1992),[27] which focused precisely on the consequences of access without discernment.[28] Thus, the transition from print to audiovisual media has been accompanied by widespread cultural anxieties, particularly regarding youth that in turn position "media literacy" as a form of necessary critical defense against the standardized, commodified message of "the culture industries."[29]

In introducing these three children above, I have deliberately outlined an ambitious definition of young people's "internet literacy" that draws on the research literature so as to encompass three dimensions. First, literacy is a form of knowledge with clear continuities across communicative forms (print, audiovisual, interpersonal, digital). As regards the internet, this knowledge poses a phased series of challenges, from initial hardware difficulties of access through to more complex interpretative and evaluative competences regarding content and services that are distinctively afforded by (or socially inscribed into) the technology or text. Second, literacy is a situated form of knowing that bridges individual skill and social practices that is enabled (or impeded) by (unequally distributed) economic, cultural, and social resources (or capital). Crucially, this emerges from the interaction between individual activity, technology or interface design, and institutional shaping, and cannot be understood solely as "a neutral technical skill."[30] Thirdly, literacy comprises a set of culturally regulated competences encompassing both that which is normatively valued and that which is disapproved or transgressive. "Internet literacy" in particular may be distinguished from other forms of literacy to the extent that the specific skills, experiences, texts, institutions, and cultural values associated with the internet differ from those associated with print, audiovisual, or other forms of communication.[31]

Reviewing recent research on "media literacy," a field that concentrates primarily on broadcasting and audiovisual media forms, and that draws on both humanities and social science, James Potter (2004) cites over twenty definitions.[32] However, many of these broadly concur with the clear and concise definition proposed by the National Leadership Conference on Media Literacy held in the United States in 1992, namely "the ability to access, analyze, evaluate, and communicate messages in a variety of forms."[33] In the parallel realm of information science, the recent transition in the dissemination and management of information sources, from authoritative and controlled forms (encyclopedias, libraries, expert databases) to networked, diverse, flexibly specialized forms of representation of the information or knowledge society, has positioned "information literacy" as a vital skill in the competitive global marketplace. This field concentrates primarily on computing, telecommunications, and information technologies, and draws on the study of information processing, computer science, and library studies to theorize, especially, multiple levels of access competences, to identify a range of barriers and enablers to access, and establish initiatives for training or redistributing otherwise-unequal skills across the population. For, as Mark Warschauer puts it, "the ability to access, adapt, and create new knowledge using new information and communication technology is critical to social inclusion in today's era."[34]

Such an approach is, interestingly, strikingly parallel to that of media literacy.[35] The UNESCO-funded multinational gathering of experts organized by the U.S. National Commission on Library and Information Science and National Forum on Information Literacy stated that "information literacy encompasses knowledge of one's information concerns and needs, and the ability to identify, locate, evaluate, organize, and effectively create, use, and communicate information to address issues and problems at hand."[36] In this document, also known as The Prague Declaration, we see the same fourfold definition, now identified as "a prerequisite for participating effectively in the Information Society" and "part of the basic human right of life long learning."[37] So, with the widespread diffusion of information and communication technologies, the notion of information literacy has been developed to encompass the competences required to design and use complex digital systems for the representation and distribution of information. However, now that the internet converges multiple technologies, forms, and spaces of mediation and information—blurring hitherto distinctive social practices of information and entertainment, work and leisure, public and private, even childhood and adulthood, national and global—a convergence of media (or audiovisual) and information literacies is needed to map out a constructive route to understanding what (young) people know, and need to know, regarding that deceptively simple notion of "using the internet."

Charting the Limits of Young People's Internet Literacy

In thinking about young people's internet literacies, both the traditions of media literacy and information literacy are useful in recognizing the cognitive and social challenges posed by access (to hardware, software, content, and services) as well as the dimensions of literacy concerned with analyzing and critically evaluating content for its textual forms, genres, biases, and reliability. Undoubtedly, Megan, Anisah, and Ted's families are not alone in their struggles to appropriate this new technology—even to choose, locate, and operate the hardware, and deal with the constant and cascading demands to update and upgrade, let alone to access the content and services accessible online.[38] Megan's computer was inherited from her father's workplace and so came set up with many puzzling features that remained long after the computer had been brought home. Ted's inability to bookmark sites also limits his efficiency in accessing information, while Anisah's attempt to obtain illustrations of China shows the challenge of searching.

One observational session in thirteen-year-old Candy's middle-class household clearly illustrates the problems of access and its link to critical understanding and content creation. Candy was trying to find a German Web site on food and drink to help with her schoolwork. First she checked with her father that "du" is the German equivalent of U.K. He says yes, then thinks it might be dr. This doesn't work, so she tries www.esse.com.du. This doesn't work, so she tries .de, with no more success. The researcher suggests she tries www.esseundtrinke.com.de but this doesn't work either, because mistakenly she typed "trinke" without the "n." She notes that she couldn't access the site at school either. The observer suggests she puts an "n" in "essen" and she says that there should be one in "trinke" as well, but no luck (perhaps because the words are run together as one—searching for "essen und trinken" produces thousands of useful hits). Candy's father then suggests .dr for Deutsche Republik or "just to leave the last bit off and see if it finds it." Neither works. Her brother, Bob, comes across to try to help, but he can't remember any German sites. Now Candy is trying www.yahoo.co.du. Bob suggests Capital d, but still no luck. Her mother then comes into the room and tries to help. She suggests they try .uk to see if "the whole thing is working." Her mother goes to the refresh option on the ISP home page. Candy jokes "Don't do that! It goes on to a porn page!" Evidently, once she did this and this happened. She knows this must mean that someone in the house had accessed it earlier! The mother tries www.yahoo.co.uk and immediately the page comes up. So the family conclude that the problem lies with the name of the German site they are trying to access and is not a problem with their skills; so Candy gives up. This whole process took ten minutes, and the attention of the whole family.

Some of these difficulties have been effectively theorized within the information literacy tradition where, as noted above, "mere access" has long been recognized as posing significant barriers to many. In relation to media literacy, access has until recently been a minor issue; turning on the television or radio, picking up a newspaper, or going to the cinema are not challenging skills, oft-claimed to render these "democratic" media; although today, using the electronic program guide, installing multiple digital channels, or accessing interactive content raise questions familiar to those in the information/computer tradition. Where the media literacy tradition is arguably more advanced than that of information literacy is in relation to critical understanding. Mass media have been characterized by limited spectrum, expensive distribution channels, centralized organization, and strong state regulation, these combining to maintain a strong distinction between producers and consumers, with elite filters operating to select material to be distributed in accordance with criteria of cultural quality, editorial values, professional production conventions, and political or market pressures. Consequently, media literacy teaching especially has often centered on understanding and critiquing the operation and consequences of these elite public or private sector organizations.

But, to the extent that the internet enables cheap, accessible, diverse, and dispersed forms of knowledge distribution, the emphasis of critical literacy must be broadened to include information searching, navigation, sorting, assessing relevance, evaluating sources, judging reliability, and identifying bias. All these tasks increasingly fall to the ordinary user in a fast-changing environment in which familiar markers of authority, value, trust, and authenticity are lacking.[39] Nor are these tasks inconsequential, for they are applied in domains extending far beyond the entertainment or hobby activities associated with traditional media. Many young people find this exciting and empowering, affording diverse forms of expertise, expression, and exploration,[40] and the recent explosion of "user-generated content" certainly attests to the appeal of gaining expertise in this new online environment. Many, however, are less expert. In the "UK Children Go Online" survey, of those nine- to nineteen-year-olds who go online at least once a week, four in ten said they trust most or all online content—revealing, arguably, the scale of the challenge for media or internet literacy programs. For the majority who are more skeptical, one must ask how they decide what to trust: only one in three said they have been advised how to judge the reliability of online information.[41] As we saw with Ted, many have little idea of the motives that lead individuals or institutions to make information available online, and when asked to speculate, those interviewed in focus groups tended to assume benevolent and generous intentions to site authors. Steve (17, from Manchester) told me sites exist because "somebody's just thought this is my interest, and I'm going to share it with the world." So, critical literacy is a vital part of internet literacy, with trust a central issue in navigating the online environment. Yet most children and young people we interviewed in the focus groups appeared to be ignorant of the motives behind the Web sites they were using, and many, it was clear, had not thought about this question at all.

Moreover, the design of online resources often impedes the development of further skills or competences online. Even at 18 and at a private school with great IT facilities, Ted struggles to search effectively, typing in key words inappropriately, confused about bookmarking and so always retyping addresses, and not understanding why you can't always go "back" (itself a good question).[42] Similarly, why can't Megan work out how to get the Neopets site to remind her of her password? Since her teachers say she is an intelligent girl, perhaps the problem lies with the site design? Certainly, as I observe her attempts, the lack of any site feedback on her repeated mistakes seems a striking failure to encourage learning when needed.[43] In one visit, Megan (aged 12) shows me how the AOL kids home page offers a story-writing option. The site contains a standard story with gaps—you insert your own name, that of a friend, your favorite color, and so forth, and the result is a personalized story you can print out. The discussion then turns, and Megan switches to Microsoft Works to show me the story she is currently writing: this turns out to be a lengthy, closely written thriller, heavy on dialogue and drama, containing tragedy, murder, a mysterious beautiful foreign woman saying dramatic and intriguing things as she rushes about solving mysteries. The story uses elaborate forms of expression, a complex vocabulary, includes exciting and witty writing, if rather breathless and melodramatic. The same girl, two stories, one highly literate, yet enabled merely by the blank page, one minimally literate and positively impeded by some "creative" software.

Empirical observation of young people's internet use suggests that, conceptually, we must recognize that literacy emerges from the dynamic interaction between user and technology and that, consequently, politically, we must take care in criticizing individuals for limits of their online activities, for this is implicitly to assume that interfaces are well designed and that necessary resources are readily available. In practice, interfaces also obscure, impede, and undermine, especially in the new media and information environment where cultural conventions of representation are not yet familiar, cues to interpretation are inconsistent or confusing, and a critique of the new information environment is underdeveloped.

Furthermore, young people's internet literacy does not yet match the headline image of the intrepid pioneer, not because young people lack imagination or initiative, but because the institutions that manage their internet access and use are constraining or unsupportive—anxious parents, uncertain teachers, busy politicians, profit-oriented content providers. In recent years, popular online activities have one by one become fraught with difficulties for young people—chat rooms and social networking sites are closed down because of the risk of pedophiles, music downloading has resulted in legal actions for copyright infringement, educational institutions are increasingly instituting plagiarism procedures, and so forth. In practice, the Internet is not quite as welcoming a place for young people as popular rhetoric would have one believe, and in this, of course, it is not so different from offline social institutions concerned with young people.[44]

Convergent Literacies for Convergent Technologies

As audiovisual and information technologies converge, most notably but not only through the internet, people's skills and competences and, therefore, the research that seeks to understand them must also converge. The traditions of literacy scholarship discussed above each contribute to the analysis of internet literacy in complementary ways. Media literacy has developed a better account of the nature of the sensory, esthetic, and symbolic qualities of visuals, sound, and the moving image, and, therefore, of multimedia. However, it is heavily linear. Information literacy has a better account of the nonlinear, the database, the dispersed network. Since the internet combines these qualities, again we need to combine these traditions in theorizing internet literacy. This allows us to define internet literacy as the ability to access, understand, critique, and create information and communication content online.

To be sure, this is a definition tied to a technology (or domain, namely, online), and the technology is complex and changing, but this is not to fall into technological determinism, for precisely since technologies have been socially and institutionally shaped, they afford certain uses or embody certain preferences over others, and different forms of representation pose distinct interpretative demands.[45] Consequently, technologies invite or encourage the development of certain competences in preference to others, both in terms of basic skills (using a mouse, navigating hypertext, learning netiquette) and advanced skills (evaluating a Web site, contributing to a forum, inhabiting an online community). Thus, an interactive focus on user and text or technology is vital.[46]

The subfield of human-computer interaction, interestingly, treats computer or information literacy not simply as a skill, but rather as an interaction between skilled users and well-designed interfaces.[47] Similarly, the text reader model of interpretation (applied to both film and television, and itself derived from the domain of print literacy) stresses meaning as emergent from the activities of active subjects and polysemic texts.[48] Indeed, there is a thought-provoking parallel between the theorization of interactivity in the field of information literacy (through the contrast between the "inscribed user" and the actual users, plural, who interpret, normatively or otherwise, the meanings flexibly encoded into a technological system[49] and the theorization of the "inscribed subject" or "model reader" anticipated by the text and the empirical audiences, plural, who decode or read against the grain when faced with an audiovisual text in the field of media literacy.[50] We may add to this the growing literature on computer-mediated communication and its account of the specific communicative literacies associated with online peer-to-peer interactions but drawing, historically, on face-to-face interaction.[51]

Much in these converging traditions draws on a common origin in the analysis of print literacy, particularly in the stress on interpretation (or literacy not just as reading the printed word, but also as "reading the world"[52]). This legacy from print literacy remains crucial in relation to the internet, much of whose content is, after all, print—along with the associated reference frames of pages, reading and writing, sending, printing, looking up, filing, and so forth; the question of how representation is altered as we move from page to screen is a fascinating one.[53] Other dimensions of the print legacy are also important: Gunther Kress traces back to the dominance of print our cultural blindness to images compared with words; for though the power of images is widely recognized, our analytic and regulatory tools are more developed for words, hence the value of his development of an analytic toolkit to recognize the visual (hence, he proposes the concept of "visual literacy"), for "the exponential expansion of the potentials of electronic technologies will entrench visual modes of communication as a rival to language in many domains of public life."[54] He reminds us, further, of the important stress on writing in relation to print literacy when he observes that "writing has been the most valued means of communication over the last few centuries— the one that has regulated access to social power in Western societies."[55] It is especially the dual emphases on writing as well as reading—preserved in the fourth term of the definitions of both media and information literacy (as "communicate" or "create," respectively)—that has rendered literacy subject to close regulatory scrutiny. Not only does reading permit the dissemination of knowledge in a manner that may escape control, but especially, writing further democratizes knowledge in a move that challenges the authority of elites.[56]

Along with the emphasis on individual skills accompanying each new medium, historians identify an institutional (often, also a legal) history of regulatory interventions that manage the dissemination and use of these skills, resulting in critical scholarship on how the state intervenes—generally through educational institutions, though also the law and other agencies—in what might otherwise seem the private activities and pleasures of private individuals or private businesses (e.g., publishing, the press). Such normative concerns are now evident in the initiatives funded in relation to ICT literacy. As for print literacy, the purpose is often more to promote a skilled workforce, thereby advancing employment and economic competitiveness, than to support a critical, informed, and actively engaged citizenry. Hence, public policy resources are generally devoted more to enabling basic access and understanding than to critical evaluation or user-generated content creation. Critical scholarship must counter, therefore, by pointing out that the accepted definitions of media and information literacy are not satisfied with just knowing one's audiovisual "ABC"; one must also be able to communicate—to create content as well as to decode it; otherwise, one positions the public as mere recipients rather than also active producers and distributors of information and communication.[57] Yet the promise of literacy, surely, is that it can form part of a strategy to reposition the media user—from passive to active, from recipient to participant, from consumer to citizen.

Findings from the "UK Children Go Online" project suggest some positive prospects here, though again, some disappointing realities. They suggest that young people enthusiastically take the initial steps toward interactivity, communication, and participation, with some more active than others, but often, they do not sustain the activity or engage as thoroughly as those casually observing them might hope. For example, seven in ten nine- to nineteen-year-olds who use the internet weekly report at least one form of interactive engagement with a Web site (out of doing a quiz, sending an e-mail/SMS/picture/story to a site, voting for something online, contributing to a message board, offering advice to others, filling in a form or signing

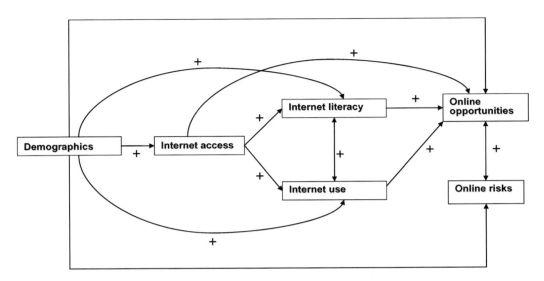

Figure 1
Explaining online opportunities and risks among teenagers.

a petition online), but on average, the total number of ways of interacting is 1.5 out of the eight asked about, suggesting that despite the many online invitations to interact, adoption remains low, especially among working-class teenagers. Similarly, the survey found that 34 percent of nine- to nineteen-year-olds who go online at least once a week have tried to set up their own Web page—more often boys than girls, and more often older than younger children (though younger children indicate that they would like to develop the skills to make a site). While over a third feel that making their own site is in some ways impressive, suggesting a considerable desire to be active and creative content producers as well as receivers, closer examination showed that of these, one in three never managed to get their Web page online, and a further one in three do not maintain their site—only one in nine, therefore, have created, uploaded, and maintained a site, and among these, doing so was often a requirement of their curriculum.

What might encourage a more ambitious use of the internet? The "UK Children Go Online" survey findings revealed that online expertise matters.[58] Measured in terms of the number of online skills that twelve- to seventeen-year-olds claim to be good at, as well as their reported self-efficacy, and assessed in terms of the range of online opportunities that the teenagers engage in, as well as the range of risks they have encountered online, the findings suggested that—as for learning to read or ride a bicycle—those with greater internet literacy take up greater online opportunities and, perhaps more surprisingly, encounter more risks also, as shown in figure 1. This diagram models the relations, direct and indirect, among demographic variables (age, gender, socioeconomic status), the quality (or variety) of the teens' internet access, the level of their online skills, and frequency/length of their use, together with the range of opportunities (e.g., education, civic participation, peer communication, information search, etc.) and risks (e.g., pornography, race hate, sexual harassment, stranger contact, or bullying) that they experience online.[59]

This empirical examination provides some encouragement for those who seek to overcome the digital divide by intervening in young people's internet literacy (whether via training, education, online provision, or better design); increased literacy results in increased opportunities over and above the positive effects of access and use. However, it points to a problem for policy makers and parents, for the positive correlation identified between the range of opportunities and risks that teenagers encounter online makes it apparent that initiatives designed to improve opportunities are also likely to increase risks, while those designed to minimize risks may also reduce opportunities. Indeed, as the absence of certain lines in the diagram conveys, access and use do not in and of themselves increase the likelihood of online risks, and nor does literacy reduce it; rather, the online risks are the outcome of online opportunities. The analysis also counters the technologically determinist view that merely providing access to the hardware could be enough; for, while better quality of access (e.g., more access locations, or having the internet for longer) was found to increase the range of online opportunities experienced by teenagers, the more literate among them gained an additional benefit over and above the less literate with equivalent access (or, indeed, equivalent amount of use).[60]

As soon as we inquire, however, into what these online opportunities might and should include, the normative character of internet literacy discussions becomes apparent. For society must ask what expectations it has for young people's internet use—what, in short, do we hope for young people and how much should their internet use be supported through institutional and other forms of support?

Internet Literacy as a Normative Project

Clarity over the purposes of literacy is often lacking, resulting in some crucially unresolved debates in both traditions discussed in this chapter, bringing, in turn, an unresolved and contested legacy to the analysis of internet literacies.[61] In the media literacy tradition, significant differences of opinion persist among theorists and media educators regarding their valuation of the media themselves: How much emphasis should be placed on critiquing or on appreciating media? One might here compare the notion of advertising literacy, seen as providing a cultural defense against the normative messages of media corporations, with that of film literacy, advocated for enabling a cultural appreciation of the esthetic, creative, and pleasurable potential of audiovisual expression.[62] This uncertainty in pedagogy influences, and undermines, the justification, implementation, and evaluation of media literacy programs, whether through either media education or citizenship initiatives, an uncertainty that now continues to shape contemporary discussions over the appropriate uses of internet literacy.[63] Similarly, information literacy advocates do not agree about the desired balance between technical skills and information skills, or the importance of motivational versus economic barriers to understanding, or the weight to be put on information literacy as a means of competing in an increasingly information-oriented labor market or as a means to participate fully as a citizen in the knowledge society. All these are debates, essentially, over the politics of literacy and literacy education. Concretely, one may ask not only whether Megan, Anisah, and Ted are "internet literate" but, also, what more should they know, and whose responsibility is this?

Being able to use the internet is of little value in and of itself. Rather, its value lies in the opportunities that it opens up, just as the history of debates over print literacy are, fundamentally, debates over the manner, inclusiveness, and purposes of public participation in society.[64] I have argued elsewhere that we can identify three broad purposes to which media and information literacies contribute.[65] First, democracy, participation and active citizenship: in a democratic society, a media and information-literate individual is more able to gain an informed opinion on matters of the day, and to be able to express their opinion individually and collectively in public, civic, and political domains, while a media and information-literate society supports a critical and inclusive public sphere. Second, knowledge economy, competitiveness, and choice: in a market economy increasingly based on information, often in a complex and mediated form, a media and information-literate individual is likely to have more to offer, and therefore achieve at a higher level in the workplace, and a media and information-literate society is innovative and competitive, sustaining a rich array of choices for the consumer. Third, lifelong learning, cultural expression, and personal fulfillment: since our highly reflexive, heavily mediated symbolic environment informs and frames the choices, values, and knowledge that give significance to everyday life, media and information literacy contribute to the critical and expressive skills that support a full and meaningful life, and to an informed, creative, and ethical society.

These purposes are deliberately framed to capture both the individual competences and institutional structures that, together, underpin literacy. For across diverse traditions, literacy research has often been strongly contested for its individualistic emphasis on skill. Literacy should, it is argued by these critics, be conceived as both an individual accomplishment or a social and cultural practice.[66] Just as competences can be conceptualized at several levels, from the basic (using the pen, the remote control, the mouse) through to intermediate skills (finding a book in the library, identifying a reliable Web page, contributing to a forum) and then advanced competences (creativity, specialized learning, participation, and critique), so too can the social structures that underpin these competences. At the basic level, then, internet literacy is enabled by and depends on the design of interfaces, software, and technical provision;[67] at the intermediate level, literacy requires institutional supports (education and other learning environments, accountable gate-keeping practices, well-resourced curricula, and information resources); at the most ambitious level, internet literacy requires societal encouragement both online and offline for democratic engagement, open and responsive civic organizations, an innovative and flexible economy, and a rich and diverse culture. In short, media and information literacies do not simply concern the ability to use the electronic program guide for digital television, or to complete one's income tax return online. Nor are the purposes restricted to becoming a more informed consumer or getting a better-paid job, though in methodological terms, these may be more readily evaluated against tangible outcomes.

However, research within media literacy and information literacy divides on the politics of literacy research. Some in the field of media literacy work within the administrative approach, in Paul Lazarsfeld's terms,[68] seeking directly to contribute to and influence policy on media literacy (for example, tracking ICT diffusion and access via government or commercial surveys). Other work takes a critical approach, exploring how people use media for their own sometimes non- or counternormative purposes, or critiquing the authorities that seek to "improve" literacy for administrative, economic, or commercial purposes. In the informational domain, similarly, research is bifurcated. For example, research on the search engine in the administrative tradition uses survey-based studies to examine access to and familiarity with search engines, the skills of different types of users, or the sophistication of users' search queries. In addition, studies using ratings and metrics examine the demographic trends in search engine choice and use, often to inform the advertising industry. Other research takes a critical viewpoint, integrating economic analysis, observation, and experiments, to question the adequacy of search engines for the public good, to critique the private structure of the industry and its lack of transparency in information provision, and so forth. Thus, the critical focus of the two traditions has been different. Media literacy—because of the focus on the dominant institutions of the mass media—has developed a critical focus on the value of media (appreciate or deplore, value culture or defend against harm), and an interest in the public's resistance to dominant meanings. Information literacy—because of its greater focus on the challenges of access, and their associated barriers and enablers—has developed its critical focus on in/equality, competition, and redistribution across the population. Both these foci are, clearly, critical points of intervention for the academy in responding to society wide initiatives to promote literacy of all kinds, including internet literacy for young people.

Conclusions

This chapter has stressed the historical continuities between internet literacy and print literacy, in order that the ambitious expectations society has for print literacy (notably, the importance of writing as well as reading, and the expectation of critical understanding at levels far beyond knowing one's ABC) can be extended to internet literacy in the information age; for these not only support a skilled labor force, but also ensure cultural expression, civic participation, and democratic deliberation. It has also noted the discontinuities, insofar as internet literacy poses some specific challenges, partly arising from the rapid pace of change and the consequent reverse generation gap regarding children's and adults' expertise, and partly arising from the unprecedented convergence of hitherto distinct spheres (public and private, work and leisure, education and home, information and entertainment, etc.) associated with the ubiquity of online technologies in developed countries; this, in turn, demanding a convergence of diverse forms of literacy.

Given such ambitious expectations regarding youthful internet literacy, this chapter has challenged popular claims regarding young people's online expertise, not in order to criticize young people themselves—who are undoubtedly enthusiastic, creative, and motivated in their exploration of online opportunities—but in order to make visible society's failure to sufficiently support their internet literacy through design, education, and regulation. The "myth of the cyberkid"[69] or "the digital generation"[70] (a rhetorical term whose technological determinism David Buckingham, 2006, critiques) may mitigate against increasing public policy resources to support young people's learning and participation. It also seems that asserting children to be in control of their online experiences legitimates a deregulatory regime that frees the market to the degree that it poses a risk to children's safety.[71] Undoubtedly, the prevailing tendency in communications' regulation across North America and Europe is toward "lighter touch" regulation or, preferably, self-regulation for an increasingly global industry. The consequent threat of harm to the public is countered by the claim that, conversely, such trends "empower" by providing more choice for an increasingly media-literate public.[72] To some degree, children are recognized as a special or "vulnerable" group in such policy debates, but the favored solutions are not to sustain industry regulation, but rather to increase educational initiatives to enhance media literacy.[73] While media literacy initiatives are much to be welcomed, a critical analysis requires that we recognize these as part of a broader shift from direct control by government to governance through "action at a distance" regulating parents, for example, through discursively established norms of "good parenting" and "appropriate children's conduct."[74] One consequence is that this creates a skills' burden that parents and children neither can nor should bear alone.

Today's connections between literacy, education, and individual responsibility are also foreshadowed in the history of print literacy. Carmen Luke (1989) links the historical emergence of discourses of literacy, child-rearing, and childhood to the confluence of the invention of the printing press in the late fifteenth century and to the "birth of the school" by the middle of the sixteenth century.[75] By the sixteenth century, she notes, "learning had been removed from the home, the streets, or the community and had been replaced by an organized and regimented institutional setting where rewards, punishments, and the ideas and skills to be learned were provided by an authority other than the more familiar and personal authority of family and community members."[76] Intriguingly, it seems that today this trend is reversed: public policy stresses putting learning back into the home and community, resulting in what Buckingham, Scanlon, and Sefton-Green have termed the "curricularization of leisure" and, partly in consequence, to the growing attention—public, policy, academic— to questions of literacy.[77] Both the removal from and then the reinsertion into the home of education, socialization, and learning form part of the same larger trend, namely the institutionalization of childhood, the incursion of the state into the realm of private life, including the repositioning of children from being the private property of families into a public, civil discourse.[78]

While the growth of state regulation over parents, children, and the home represents the downside of this trend, the concomitant rise of an international discourse of children's rights by the end of the twentieth century represents the positive side. Optimistically, then, literacy—including internet literacy—could represent a means of empowerment for young people in a mediated world.

Victor Quinn defines "empowerment" precisely not as the provision of adult or predigested information to children nor, simply, as free access to any information, but rather as enabling children to be able to do what they can do best.[79] In this view, it is not enough for adults to leave young people to get on with it, but rather it demands that they listen, respond carefully, providing feedback on creative or other forms of activity, encouraging critical reflection, taking their participation seriously. Yet the form of "empowerment" adult society provides through the internet is often a far cry from this: educational Web sites reinforce "right answer" learning as opposed to critical questioning, civic participation sites encourage youth to "have their say," but rarely listen to or act on what they say. Many information resources encode strategies of textual closure rather than openness—what Stuart Hall called the "preferred reading"[80] (frequently asked questions, recently asked questions, top ten lists, fact of the week, our favorites, etc.), and "sticky" commercial sites, acting in effect as walled gardens, tend to discourage the very exploration that a network structure could and should afford.[81]

No wonder that what excites young people about the internet is primarily the peer-to-peer opportunities it affords, in which they provide for each other the responsiveness, criticism, humor, feedback, openness, and networking that so often is absent from content designed for children by adults. Yet since information and communication technologies increasingly represent a key route to education, health, civic engagement, employment skills, participation in government, therapeutic advice, extended family relations, and so forth, it is here that we must ensure literacy is sufficient. Celebrating young people's enterprise and enthusiasm, while failing to support, respond, or engage with their online activities, risks failing to bring to fruition the ambitious hopes we hold not only for the internet but, more significantly, for young people. Overestimating their literacy is also hazardous, because anxieties about risk are, to some degree justifiably, enhanced in the risk society, and because support for the individual making these judgments (education, socialization, and institutional norms) is reduced as the burden of responsibility is shifted from provider to consumer, a process Ulrich Beck describes as "the individualization of risk."[82]

As more and more policy emphasis at national and international levels is placed on "media literacy" or "information literacy" or "internet literacy," critical scholars have all the more reason simultaneously to support internet literacy initiatives, to assert ambitious expectations in evaluating their effectiveness, to scrutinize the policy objectives that promote them and, last, to challenge the inflated public claims regarding the "internet-savvy" teenager that accompany them.

Notes

1. Quotations from children and parents are drawn from the "UK Children Go Online" project (see www.children-go-online.net).

2. Marc Prensky, Digital Natives, Digital Immigrants, *On the Horizon* 9, no. 5 (2001).

3. While some see literacy as democratizing and so as empowering of ordinary people, many others point to the uses of literacy as a source of inequality and so as elitist and divisive in its effects, including the stigma of "illiteracy."

4. Sonia Livingstone and Magdalena Bober, *UK Children Go Online: Final Report of Key Project Finding* (London: London School of Economics and Political Science, 2005).

5. Maria Bakardjieva, *Internet Society: The Internet in Everyday Life* (London: Sage, 2005); Thomas Berker, Maren Hartmann, Yves Punie, and Katie J. Ward, eds., *The Domestication of Media and Technology* (Maidenhead, UK: Open University Press, 2006); Ellen Seiter, *The Internet Playground: Children's Access, Entertainment, and Mis-education* (New York: Peter Lang, 2005).

6. Sara M. Grimes and Lesley Regan Shade, Neopian Economics of Play: Children's Cyberpets and Online Communities as Immersive Advertising in NeoPets.com, *International Journal of Media and Cultural Politics* 1, no. 2 (2005): 181–198.

7. James P. Gee, *What Video Games Have to Teach Us About Learning and Literacy* (New York: Palgrave Macmillan, 2003); Anne Jerslev, "Video Nights": Young People Watching Videos Together—A Youth Cultural Phenomenon, *Young* 9, no. 2 (2001): 2–18.

8. See Patricia Marks Greenfield, ed. Developing Children, Developing Media—Research from Television to the Internet from the Children's Digital Media Center, *Journal of Applied Developmental Psychology* 25, no. 6 (2004): 627–769; Karin Larsson, Children's On-line Life—and What Parents Believe: A Survey in Five Countries, in *Promote or Protect? Perspectives on Media Literacy and Media Regulations*, eds. Cecilia von Feilitzen and Ulla Carlsson (Goteborg, Sweden: Nordicom, 2003), 113–120; Amanda Lenhart, Mary Madden, and Paul Hitlin, *Teens and Technology* (Washington, DC: Pew Internet & American Life Project, 2005); Sonia Livingstone, Children's Use of the Internet: Reflections on the Emerging Research Agenda, *New Media & Society* 5, no. 2 (2003): 147–166; Ellen Seiter, *The Internet Playground*.

9. cf. Eszter Hargittai and Steven Shafer, Differences in Actual and Perceived Online Skills: The Role of Gender, *Social Science Quarterly* 87, no. 2 (2006): 432–448; Marcel Machill, Christoph Neuberger, and Friedemann Schindler, Transparency on the Net: Functions and Deficiencies of Internet Search Engines, *Info—The Journal of Policy, Regulation and Strategy for Telecommunications* 5, no. 1 (2003): 52–74.

10. Sonia Livingstone, *Online Freedom & Safety for Children* (London: IPPR / Citizens Online Research Publication, 2001).

11. Pierre Bourdieu, *Distinction: A Social Critique of the Judgement of Taste* (London: Routledge and Kegan Paul, 1984).

12. Keri Facer, Rosalind Sutherland, John Furlong, and Ruth Furlong, What's the Point of Using Computers? The Development of Young People's Computer Expertise in the Home, *New Media & Society* 3, no. 2 (2001): 199–219.

13. Stewart M. Hoover, Lynn Schofield Clark, and Diane F. Alters, *Media, Home, and Family* (New York: Routledge, 2004).

14. Sonia Livingstone and Magdalena Bober, Regulating the Internet at Home: Contrasting the Perspectives of Children and Parents, in *Digital Generations*, eds. D. Buckingham and R. Willett (Mahwah, NJ: Lawrence Erlbaum Associates, 2006), 93–113.

15. Maria Bakardjieva, *Internet Society*.

16. Lynn Clark, Challenges of Social Good in the World of "Grand Theft Auto" and "Barbie": A Case Study of a Community Computer Center for Youth, *New Media & Society* 5, no. 1 (2003): 95–116.

17. Brian Street, *Social Literacies: Critical Approaches to Literacy in Development, Ethnography and Education* (London: Longman, 1995).

18. Sonia Livingstone, Magdalena Bober, and Ellen Helsper, Active Participation or Just More Information? Young People's Take up of Opportunities to Act and Interact on the Internet, *Information, Communication and Society* 8, no. 3 (2005): 287–314.

19. Sally McMillan, Interactivity: Users, Documents, and Systems, in *The Handbook of New Media: Updated Student Edition*, eds. Leah Lievrouw and Sonia Livingstone (London: Sage Publications, 2006), 164–175.

20. Mark Warschauer, *Technology and Social Inclusion: Rethinking the Digital Divide* (Cambridge, MA: MIT, 2003).

21. Sonia Livingstone, Children's Privacy Online, in *Computers, Phones, and the Internet: Domesticating Information Technology*, eds. Robert Kraut, Malcom Brynin, and Sara Kiesler (Oxford, UK: Oxford University Press, 2006), 128–144.

22. In German, "Alphabetismus" means knowing one's basic ABCs while "Bildung" means culture/education, reflecting a common separation from basic literacy from being educated or cultured in many languages; more recently, the terms "Medienkompetenz" and "Internetkompetenz" are spreading. In French too, basic literacy ("savoir lire et écrire") is distinguished from advanced literacy ("très instruit et cultivé"). The lack of such a distinction in English gives rise to the problem that academics and educators may call for advanced (media/internet) literacy education, but policy makers may translate this into basic provision of skills training.

23. Raymond Williams, *Keywords: A Vocabulary of Culture and Society* (London: Fontana, 1983).

24. Ibid., 188.

25. Richard Hoggart, *The Uses of Literacy* (London: Chatto and Windus, 1957).

26. Carmen Luke, *Pedagogy, Printing and Protestantism: The Discourse of Childhood* (Albany, NY: State University of New York Press, 1989).

27. Kirsten Drotner, Modernity and Media Panics, in *Media Cultures: Reappraising Transnational Media*, eds. Michael Skovmand and Kim Schroeder (London: Routledge, 1992), 42–62.

28. As Richard Hoggart (*The Uses of Literacy*, 333) wrote in the early days of mass broadcasting, mediated communication seemed to permit "strengthening the hold of a few dominant popular publications on the great majority of people," driving out of business the quality papers and those catering to minority

interests, while generally reducing all content to that which appeals to the so-called lowest common denominator.

29. Theodore Adorno and Max Horkheimer, The Culture Industry: Enlightenment as Mass Deception, in *Mass Communication and Society,* eds. James Curran, Michael Gurevitch, and Janet Woollacott (London: Edward Arnold, 1977).

30. Ilana Snyder, Critical Literacy, Learning and Technology Studies: Challenges and Opportunites for Higher Education, in *The Handbook of e-Learning*, eds. Richard Andrews and Caroline Haythornthwaite (London: Sage, 2007), 395–415.

31. One could, further, break down the different literacies associated with the diverse activities—online games, communication, information, participation, and so on—afforded by the internet (as in games literacy, communication literacy, network literacy, etc.).

32. W. James Potter, *Theory of Media Literacy: A Cognitive Approach* (Thousand Oaks, CA: Sage, 2004).

33. Patricia Aufderheide, *Media Literacy: A Report of the National Leadership Conference on Media Literacy* (Aspen, CO: Aspen Institute, 1993); William G. Christ and W. J. Potter, Media Literacy: Symposium, *Journal of Communication* 48, no. 1 (1998).

34. Mark Warschauer, *Technology and Social Inclusion*, 9.

35. Sonia Livingstone, Elizabeth van Couvering, and Nancy Thumim, Converging Traditions of Research on Media and Information Literacies: Disciplinary and Methodological Issues, in *Handbook of Research on New Literacies*, eds. Donald Leu, Julie Coiro, Michele Knobel, and Colin Lankshear (Mahwah, NJ: Lawrence Erlbaum Associates, in press).

36. Information Literacy Meeting of Experts, "The Prague declaration: Towards an information literate society," 2003. http://www.nclis.gov/libinter/infolitconf&meet/post-infolitconf&meet/PragueDeclaration.pdf (accessed June 8, 2007).

37. Ibid.

38. André H. Caron, Luc Giroux, and Sylvie Douzou, Uses and Impacts of Home Computers in Canada: A Process of Reappropriation, in *Media Use in the Information Age: Emerging Patterns of Adoption and Consumer Use,* eds. Jerry L. Salvaggio and Jennings Bryant (Mahwah, NJ: Lawrence Erlbaum Associates, 1989), 147–162; Sonia Livingstone, *Young People and New Media: Childhood and the Changing Media Environment* (London: Sage, 2002).

39. Barbara Warnick, *Critical Literacy in a Digital Era: Technology, Rhetoric and the Public Interest* (Mahwah, NJ: Lawrence Erlbaum Associates, 2002).

40. Henry Jenkins, Quentin Tarantino's Star Wars? Digital Cinema, Media Convergence, and Participatory Culture, in *Rethinking Media Change: The Aesthetics of Transition,* eds. David Thorburn and H. Jenkins (Cambridge, MA: MIT Press, 2003), 281–312; Amanda Lenhart and Mary Madden, *Teen Content Creators and Consumers* (Washington, DC: Pew Internet & American Life Project, 2005); Sharon R. Mazzarella, ed., *Girl Wide Web: Girls, the Internet, and the Negotiation of Identity* (New York: Peter Lang, 2005).

41. Sonia Livingstone and Magdalena Bober, *UK Children Go Online.*

42. Ellen Isaacs and Alan Walendowski, *Designing From Both Sides of the Screen: How Designers and Engineers can Collaborate to build a Co-operative Technology* (Berkeley, CA: New Riders, 2002).

43. Richard Smith and Pamela Curtin, Children, Computers and Life Online: Education in a Cyberworld, in *Page to Screen: Taking Literacy into the Electronic Era*, ed. I. Snyder (London: Routledge, 1998), 211–233.

44. Jens Qvortrup, Childhood and Modern Society: A Paradoxical Relationship, in *Childhood and Parenthood*, eds. Julia Brannen and Margaret O'Brien (London: Institute of Education, University of London, 1995), 189–198.

45. Donald MacKenzie and Judy Wajcman, eds., *The Social Shaping of Technology*, 2nd ed. (Buckingham, UK: Open University Press, 1999); Barry Wellman, Anabel Quan-Haase, Jeffrey Boase, and Wenhong Chen, The Social Affordances of the Internet for Networked Individualism, *Journal of Computer-Mediated Communication* 8, no. 3 (2003).

46. Jonas Fornas, Kajsa Klein, Martina Landendorf, Jenny Sunden, and Malin Svenigsson, eds., *Digital Borderlands: Cultural Studies of Identity and Interactivity on the Internet* (New York: Peter Lang, 2002); McMillan, Interactivity: Users, documents, and systems.

47. Isaacs and Walendowski, *Designing From Both Sides*; Klaus Bruhn Jensen, ed., *Interface://Culture: The World Wide Web as Political Resources and Aesthetic Form* (Frederiksberg, Denmark: Samfundslitteratur Press/Nordicom, 2005).

48. Umbert Eco, Introduction: The Role of the Reader, in *The Role of the Reader: Explorations in the Semiotics of Texts* (Bloomington, IN: Indiana University Press), 1979; John Fiske, *Television Culture* (London: Methuen, 1987); Stuart Hall, Encoding/Decoding, in *Culture, Media, Language*, eds. S. Hall, Dorothy Hobson, Andrew Lowe, and Paul Willis (London: Hutchinson, 1980).

49. Wiebe E. Bijker, Thomas P. Hughes, and Trevor Pinch, eds., *The Social Construction of Technological Systems* (Cambridge, MA: MIT Press, 1987); Wanda Orlikowski, Learning from Notes: Organizational Issues in Groupware Implementation, *The Information Society* 9, (1993): 237–250; Steven Woolgar, Technologies as Cultural Artifacts, in *Information and Communication Technologies: Visions and Realities*, ed. Bill Dutton (Oxford, UK: Oxford University Press, 1996), 87–102.

50. Sonia Livingstone, The Challenge of Changing Audiences: Or, What is the Audience Researcher to do in the Internet Age? *European Journal of Communication*, 19, no. 1 (2004): 75–86; David Morley, *Television, Audiences and Cultural Studies* (London: Routledge, 1992).

51. Brian H. Spitzberg, Preliminary Development of a Model and Measure of Computer-Mediated Communication (CMC) Competence, *Journal of Computer-Mediated Communication* 11, no. 2 (2006): Article 12; John B. Thompson, *The Media and Modernity: A Social Theory of the Media* (Cambridge, UK: Polity, 1995).

52. Paolo Freire and Donaldo Macedo, *Literacy: Reading the Word and the World* (South Hadley, MA: Bergin and Garvey, 1987).

53. I. Snyder, ed., *Page to Screen: Taking Literacy into the Electronic Era* (London: Routledge, 1998).

54. Gunther Kress, Visual and Verbal Models of Representation on Electronically Mediated Communication: The Potentials of New Forms of Text, in *Page to Screen: Taking Literacy Into Electronic Era*, ed. I. Snyder (London: Routledge, 1998), 53–79.

55. Ibid., 55.

56. Luke, *Pedagogy, Printing and Protestantism*.

57. Content creation, is not just an optional extra: Article 13 of The UN Convention on the Rights of the Child states that "The child shall have the right to freedom of expression; this right shall include freedom to seek, receive and impart information and ideas of all kinds, regardless of frontiers, either orally, in writing or in print, in the form of art, or through any other media of the child's choice." See http://www.unhchr.ch/html/menu3/b/k2crc.htm (accessed January 12, 2007).

58. In the survey of 1511 nine to nineteen year olds and 906 parents, neither children nor parents claimed great expertise, though children claimed more than their parents: 28 percent of parents, and 7

percent of children, who use the internet described themselves as beginners; 12 percent of parents and 32 percent of children considered themselves advanced users (Livingstone and Bober, *UK Children Go Online*).

59. Sonia Livingstone and Ellen Helpser, *The Role of Internet Literacy in Mediating Online Opportunities and Risks Among Teenagers* (manuscript under review).

60. Access, predictably, is strongly influenced by demographic factors, with boys, and older or middle class teens having better quality access and so, as a result, using the internet more and gaining more skills and more opportunities online, see Livingstone and Bober, *UK Children Go Online*.

61. Douglas Kellner, New Media and New Literacies: Reconstructing Education for the New Millennium, in *The Handbook of New Media*, eds. L. Lievrouw and Livingstone (London: Sage, 2002), 90–104; Kathleen Tyner, *Literacy in a Digital World: Teaching and Learning in the Age of Information* (Mahwah, NJ: Lawrence Erlbaum Associates, 1998).

62. Cary Bazalgette, *Making Movies Matter* (London: British Film Institute, 1999), www.bfi.org.uk; Toby J. Hindin, Isobe R. Contento, and Joan D. Gussow, A Media Literacy Nutrition Education Curriculum for Head Start Parents About the Effects of Television Advertising on Their Children's Food Requests, *Journal of the American Dietetic Association* 104, no. 2 (2004): 192–198.

63. Rene Hobbs and Richard Frost, Measuring the Acquisition of Media-Literacy Skills, *Reading Research Quarterly* 38, no. 3 (2003): 330–355; Yves Laberge, Media Literacy and Public Citizens, *European Journal of Communication* 19, no. 2 (2004): 249–253.

64. Freire and Macedo, *Literacy: Reading the Word*; Luke, *Pedagogy, Printing and Protestantism*; Warnick, *Critical Literacy in a Digital Era*.

65. Livingstone et al., Converging Traditions of Research.

66. Street, *Social Literacies*; Snyder, Literacy, Learning and Technology Studies.

67. In Livingstone et al., (in press), we suggest the concept of content legibility to mirror that of user literacy, noting that if a book is badly written or typeset, we do not call the reader illiterate but we are critical of the book—its producers, its form or its address. Similarly, if the news provides no accessible information about its sources, fails in journalistic conventions of objectivity, or is inconsistent in its editorial policy, we do not say the viewer is at fault in struggling to evaluate the message, rather, we point the finger at the broadcaster, the newsroom, the text. If a search engine appears to offer unbiased access to information resources while operating with commercial priorities invisible to the user, again we do not ridicule users for failing to discern this and so misunderstanding the value of the information obtained.

68. Paul Lazarsfeld distinguished the approaches of positivist or liberal scholars from those in the Marxist tradition, defining administrative research as that which "is carried out in the service of some kind of administrative agency of public or private character" while critical research "is posed against the practice of administrative research, requiring that . . . the general role of our media of communication in the present social system should be studied." His purpose was to distinguish research that takes its agenda from, and produces recommendations useful for, public policy or commercial gain, from research that maintains a critical independence from established institutions. The former takes on the responsibility of actively shaping social and technological change; the latter seeks to produce independent knowledge that critiques the strategic activities of the establishment. See Paul F. Lazarsfeld, Remarks on Administrative and Critical Communications Research, *Studies in Philosophy and Science* 9 (1941): 3–16.

69. Keri Facer and Ruth Furlong, Beyond the Myth of the "Cyberkid": Young People at the Margins of the Information Revolution, *Journal of Youth Studies* 4, no. 4 (2001): 451–469.

70. David Buckingham, Is there a Digital Generation?, in *Digital Generations*, eds. David Buckingham and Rebekah Willett (Mahwah, NJ: Lawrence Erlbaum Associates, 2006), 1–13.

71. Livingstone and Bober, Regulating the Internet at Home; Janis Wolak, Kimberly J. Mitchell, and David Finkelhor, *Online Victimization of Youth: Five Years on* (University of New Hampshire: National Center for Missing & Exploited Children, 2006).

72. Andrea Millwood Hargrave and Sonia Livingstone, *Harm and Offence in Media Content: A Review of the Evidence* (Bristol, UK: Intellect, 2006).

73. For example, the UK Communications Regulator has a legal duty to promote media literacy. Yet it is set up primarily as an economic regulator, see Robert W. McChesney, The Internet and U.S. Communication Policy-making in Historical and Critical Perspective, *Journal of Communication* 46, no. 1 (1996): 100. Thus Robert McChesney worries that a focus on literacy distracts policy makers and cultural critics from questions of power; as he puts it, the question is less what people do with the technology than "who will control the technology and for what purpose?" Notwithstanding such justified skepticism, see The Council of Europe, Integration and diversity: The new frontiers of European media and communications policy, March 10–11, 2005, http://www.coe.int/T/E/Com/Files/Ministerial-Conferences/2005-kiev/texte_adopte.asp, with many good intentions, developing policy that will "give special encouragement to training for children in media literacy, enabling them to benefit from the positive aspects of the new communication services and avoid exposure to harmful content" and "support steps to promote, at all stages of education and as part of ongoing learning, media literacy which involves active and critical use of all the media, including electronic media." The European Commission's Audiovisual and Media Policy also supports a broad conception of media and information literacies; see http://www.ec.europa.eu/comm/avpolicy/media_literacy/index_en.htm (accessed January 12, 2007). http://www.ec.europa.eu/comm/avpolicy/media_literacy/expert_group/index_en.htm. In North America, the Center for Media Literacy (http://www.medialit.org/), the Media Literacy Clearinghouse (http://www.medialit.med.sc.edu/), Citizens for Media Literacy (http://www.main.nc.us/cml/), the Alliance for a Media Literate America (http://www.amlainfo.org/home/our-members/organizations/academic-institutions), and the Association for Media Literacy in Canada (http://www.aml.ca/home/) all seek to promote media literacy.

74. David Oswell, The Dark Side of Cyberspace: Internet Content Regulation and Child Protection. *Convergence: The Journal of Research into New Media Technologies* 5, no. 4 (1999): 42–62.

75. Carmen Luke, *Pedagogy, Printing and Protestantism.*

76. Ibid., 131.

77. David Buckingham, Marjorie Scanlon, and Julian Sefton-Green, Selling the Digital Dream: Marketing Educational Technology to Teachers and Parents, in *Subject to Change: Literacy and Digital Technology*, eds. Avril Loveless and V. Ellis (London: Routledge, 2001), 20–40.

78. Howard Gadlin, Child Discipline and the Pursuit of Self: An Historical Interpretation, in *Advances in Child Development and Behavior,* eds. Hayne W. Reese and Lewis P. Lipsitt (New York: Academic Press, 1978), 12: 231–261.

79. Victor Quinn, *Critical Thinking in Young Minds* (London: David Fulton Publishers, 1997).

80. Stuart Hall, Encoding/Decoding.

81. cf. Livingstone, 2002; Snyder, *Page to Screen.*

82. Ulrich Beck, *Risk Society: Towards a New Modernity* (London: Sage, 1992).

Looking BK and Moving FD: Toward a Sociocultural Lens on Learning with Programmable Media

Paula K. Hooper

Technical Education Research Centers (TERC)

When computers first entered schools in the early 1980s, programming was a major part of the taxonomies that were created to describe the types of applications and activities available for children's learning. For example, the book *Computers in School: Tutor, Tool, Tutee* categorized educational uses of computers according to the kinds of interactions students could have with them.[1] The *tutor* category referred to early forms of computer-assisted instruction. *Tools* at that time included microcomputer-based labs, word processors, or simulations. *Tutee* reflected students teaching the computer through programming language rather than being taught by the computer. Within that early landscape programming activities became widely used in schools, because in comparison to other uses, it was easy for educators to see how programming offered conceptually different ways of learning math and science.[2]

The growth of technology over the years has enabled a much wider variety of digital media for learning both in school and out than was encompassed by the original taxonomies. Although programming has not disappeared from the toolbox, it is no longer a mainstream tool, but is used within particular niches of children's experiences both in and out of school. In part the decline in use of programmable media is linked to the rise of other forms of digital media that are easier to use and more recognizable in their connection to subject-matter learning. But, the decline also arises from the paucity of research on why previous efforts have produced varying impacts on the mainstream of science, technology, engineering, and mathematics (STEM) learning.

Programmable media for learning is distinguished by its ability to encourage students to think differently about content than they would with other media. Andy diSessa described this ability as an expressiveness that programming environments offer by having representational forms that are uniquely suited to particular ideas.[3] He describes the power of learning to read and write with programming as a representational form of computational literacy.

In this chapter, I explore the work of children who came to be fluent programmers in the mid-1990s when some of the current capacities of digital media, such as easy manipulation of graphics, hypertext, and hypermedia, were just beginning to emerge. Looking back at their work provides lessons for the current development and analysis of programmable media and for expanding its use in current and future landscapes of digital media for learning.

I examine a vignette from a larger study of children in grades 2–6 who were learning through computer programming. The larger study investigated how children's computational ideas emerged through extended work with programmable media. The study spanned five years in an alternative African-centered school in an urban area. The vignette illustrates both how programming can be used as an effective learning tool and raises the issue of how cultural and social settings and personal experiences influence learning with programmable media.[4] The role of sociocultural context in this setting is unexpected from the standpoint of traditional constructionist orientations to learning and teaching with digital media, but elements of students' everyday cultural practices proved integral to their learning. I argue for a closer look at the cultural nature of learning as a way to better understand the benefits of learning with programmable media.

The chapter first identifies the relevant theories of learning as applied to programmable media and describes the kind of intellectual work that children do when programming. The second section features a case study of a media project created by African American girls in a school setting, where cultural connections and their relevance were made explicit. Analysis of the vignette reveals both the constructionist elements of learning and how the girls' participation in cultural and social contexts further buoyed their learning. The final section outlines implications for educators, policy makers, and researchers about programmable media and how incorporating a sociocultural lens can be used to extend the benefits of learning with programmable media to more children.

Constructivism, Constructionism, and Logo

The use of programmable media emerged as theories of learning evolved from transmission models to knowledge-construction models. This evolution has influenced the teaching of all subject matter, but particularly the role of tools and materials in math and science. Transmission models of learning claim that knowledge can be received by a novice from the mind of a more knowledgeable person, if the novice engages in traditional learning roles such as listening, following instructions, and practicing. *Constructivism,* the theory of cognitive development articulated by Jean Piaget, posits that people construct ideas from interacting with the world and interpreting their experiences from prior knowledge.

Seymour Papert, a student of Piaget's, viewed *constructionism* as an extension of constructivist theory. From his work with artificial intelligence at the MIT AI Lab in the 1960s and 1970s, Papert focused on the role that creating projects with accessible programmable materials can play in learning.[5] Both constructivism and constructionism draw on the idea of construction as both a metaphor and a model for learning. Individuals *construct* new ideas in the course of creating personally and socially meaningful artifacts.[6] From this standpoint, making things is a particularly good way for people to learn.

Programming as a Tool for Learning

In the 1970s, Papert and his colleagues at MIT, and Bolt, Beranek, and Newman created Logo as the first programming language designed with children's learning in mind. The development of Logo occurred well before Papert defined constructionism, and initially the theoretical foundation for its design was rooted in constructivism. Later, Logo was described as an instantiation of a constructionist learning environment.[7]

Many versions of Logo and a family of Logo-related environments have been developed over the years for learning a variety of content matter. Papert and others argue that the features of programming allow learners to form concrete ideas that are often too abstract for children or novices to grasp and use. A primary argument within research on children's learning with programming is that writing computer programs (also called procedures or methods) provides concrete representations of ideas and phenomena that are not possible with paper and pencil or other static models. Ideas, it is argued, become more concrete as learners connect to and use the computational tools and materials that they represent. The thinking that learners can do with computational objects that are integral to these environments led Papert to describe them as an "objects-to-think-with."[8] Andy diSessa further described the particular affordances of computational objects as representational forms, while others have noted the potential of programmable media to support collaboration, to reshape curriculum and teaching, and to enhance informal learning environments.[9]

Some brief examples of programmable media for learning include the following.

- *Boxer* is a programming environment that was developed to support children's learning of fundamental physics concepts as well as research on children's ideas about representation.[10] diSessa's research group at the University of California at Berkeley explored using Boxer with sixth graders to create interactive simulations of motion. In most standard curricula, students learn the representation systems of motion in high school algebra and calculus before they are asked to think about the physics of motion. diSessa shows that by playing with a simple set of programs to move an object forward at a uniform speed, students can begin to think earlier about the relationship between speed, distance, and time. In this environment, programs are written in boxes and the uniform speed program can be modified and coordinated with other simple programs to explore changes in speed. Creating programs to simulate a car stopping and starting, a spaceship landing, or a ball dropping helps students construct ideas about acceleration and other physics of motion without learning higher math first. These explorations illustrate how programming can become a representational form that is more expressive than standard mathematical forms.[11] As diSessa notes, "Programming turns analysis into experience and allows a connection between analytic forms and their experiential implications that even algebra and calculus can't touch."[12]

- Beginning with *LEGO/Logo robotics,* researchers have developed several environments that are hybrids of Lego building materials and Logo programming languages.[13] These tools allow children to explore engineering, design, and programming ideas. Examples of these environments include LEGO Mindstorms®, Crickets®,[14] PicoCrickets®, and the FIRST Lego League system of robotics competitions. These "microworlds" were designed such that math and science ideas are embedded in the building materials. Creating things in these programs allows children to playfully and personally discover interesting ways to think about science, technology, engineering, and math.[15] These programmable media for learning have been particularly popular in informal learning environments, such as museums, afterschool clubs, and out-of-school competitions.

- *Scratch* is a programming environment intended for teenagers in Computer Clubhouses and other afterschool environments to create their own forms of media expression, including games, cartoons, art, and interactive stories. It is based on the open source programming language *Squeak*, which is designed to make object-oriented programming paradigms accessible to novice users.[16]

- *Turtle graphics,* also referred to as *turtle geometry*, is a component of the Logo family of programming languages for teaching and learning geometry for young children.[17] Turtle geometry is the most well-known microworld (see below) among the Logo programming environments. The "turtle" is a graphical computational object that has several properties that make it a good tool for creating projects and thinking mathematically, including movement, heading, position, the ability to draw, and the ability to sense aspects of the environment. In early versions of Logo, children could easily begin interacting with a turtle by giving it commands such as PENUP (PU), FORWARD (FD) 50, LEFT (LT) 90, and PENDOWN (PD). As the turtle moves, it can draw a line that forms pictures, designs, or structures. Initially, learners figure out the path they want the turtle to "walk" to make the shape or design they desire. They can then create simple programs or procedures that contain the instructions for the pictures they create.

A classic example is directing the turtle to draw a square. A child can type the commands FD 100 RT 90 to direct the turtle from a starting position along a path that will create the first side of the square. Then, by repeating these commands a total of four times, the path of the square will be drawn. Another way to express the repetition of the commands for each side is REPEAT 4 [FD 100 RT 90].

In most mathematics curricula that are used in schools, children are taught to think of a square as a closed-shape with four straight lines for sides and four corners. This definition allows children to compare and identify properties of shapes; for example, triangles have three corners and circles have no corners. But ideas about the angles and relationships of sides that create the shapes are left for the study of geometry in later grades. Research on children's learning with turtle geometry has shown that this is a way of thinking about geometry that is epistemologically accessible to very young children.[18]

One of the most significant contributions of turtle geometry is illustrating that giving a computational object commands allows children to relate the movements of their body to the process of creating a shape. This thinking is an example of "object-to-think-with" as Papert described.[19] By drawing a square with the turtle, learners can think about and understand the square by imagining themselves as the turtle walking in the path of a square. They also think of giving the turtle commands as "talking to the turtle" in a way that is analogous to talking to a friend. The ideas of talking to the turtle and relating to its movements help make the turtle an object-to-think-with, where ideas that are abstract and inaccessible to their thinking can become concrete and expressive.

There are many examples of programming environments that provide excellent tools for learning. Yet, our understanding of how children learn with these tools has not yet adequately addressed the cultural nature of learning. Nasir et al. have made a strong call for the need to address the cultural nature of children's learning across the field of the learning sciences.[20] Recognition of sociocultural influences on children's learning with programmable media will allow us to see and include in our conceptions of their learning the resources that children bring from their experiences participating in multiple cultural groups. Youth culture, popular culture, family culture, school/classroom cultures, and cultures of racial experience create the overlapping sources of repertoires of practice that children bring with them to any learning experience.

Several questions are raised by opening up views of learning to include social and cultural perspectives on learning. Where do we see the influences of social and cultural experiences in children's learning with programmable media? What are the benefits of recognizing these influences? How can a sociocultural perspective influence the design of programmable media for learning? How can future research help to reveal more of the cultural nature of children's learning with programmable media? What will a sociocultural lens offer to teachers working with programmable media?

These were just some of the questions that arose in using MicroWorlds, a Logo-based programming environment, with a group of children in a culturally relevant school. Their work provides a window for us to see how a hybrid of constructionist and sociocultural approaches to learning, teaching, and designing with programmable media can advance the role of this media in the digital learning landscape.

Case Study: Making It Run Like a Movie

In this section I examine a vignette drawn from a longitudinal case study of children's learning with programmable media during the 1990s. Keanna and her third-grade classmates Shamia and Shanay are African American girls who were aged 8–10 at the time of this vignette. The discussion in this chapter is on how this group used programming to create an animation that they describe as a movie. This group did their work as a part of their computer class at Umoja Academy. Although the focus of this chapter is on the work and learning of this particular group, it exemplifies significant themes that emerged across observations of both this group over time and the work of several of the second- through sixth-grade students in the school.

The Sociocultural Context

Umoja Academy is an alternative African-centered school in an urban Massachusetts neighborhood that is slowly gentrifying. All three girls had attended the school since they were infants or toddlers and were in a mixed-age group of first to third graders. Observations revealed that the intertwined social, cultural, and instructional contexts of this school and its classes are different in some ways, and similar in others, from most public schools or other independent schools.

Several themes identified in the practices of students and teachers during both academic and informal parts of the day were very different from images often held about inner-city school settings. Some of these characteristics make the school day more like an informal learning environment or home school. Class sizes were very small (three to six children); students often worked on projects collaboratively by choice rather than by the teacher's design; students were often left alone without a teacher, with the expectation that they would work but with the acceptance that they might interact more socially than academically; and there was a schedule of classes, but it was often adjusted according to various needs and interests. Some practices helped to establish a home-like feel in the school environment. Students wore slippers inside the school buildings, which were converted houses. Meals were served in a family-style process. Field trips to local stores, museums, and parks often happened spontaneously. Frequent interactions across age groups before, during, and after school supported sibling-like relationships developing between students.

At other times, instruction was formed of more traditional teaching practices. Traditional practices included phonics workbooks, assignments given in traditional math textbooks, and some class sessions conducted in a "lecture style."

Symbols, beliefs, and practices within the school community reflected cultural orientation to African American identity as a source of self-esteem and academic striving.[21] One example of this cultural orientation is that the school community espoused the principles of Kwanzaa as a shared belief system.[22]

The goals of the computer class were to help children develop technological fluency, and over time become able to create their own programming projects. The classroom culture was designed to reflect the culturally relevant values and practices of the school. Computer class was held anywhere from once to three times per week over the duration of the study. Sessions ranged from forty-five minutes to three hours, depending on the assignment and students' other schedules. The focus was on using turtle graphics to help students become familiar with programming in Logo. Most of these projects involved using Logo for mathematics investigations. At the end of each exploration designed by the teacher, students were encouraged to make their own modifications. In this way, the practice of developing independent projects was scaffolded.

The L.S.O.H Project: Working Together to Create a Movie

Keanna, Shamia, and Shanay programmed an animated movie, based on the movie *Little Shop of Horrors* (*L.S.O.H.*), using the MicroWorlds version of Logo. They decided to work on this project after Shamia shared excitement about recently seeing the movie. They were also motivated by watching another student in their class, Andre, make a project he called *The Wiz3*, an animation of the characters from the movie *The Wiz* walking down the yellow brick road to the Emerald City.

The request of the girls to work together on a project was not unusual given the cultural practice of collaboration within the school. The girls organized themselves to work on different parts of the project by discussing the narrative and planning the scenes to create on each project page. Some, but not all, of the boys were working on video games for their project, and the themes they included were typical gender-related subjects, such as boxing, car racing, and action hero narratives. The girls' choice of creating a movie as distinguished from a video game, as well as the theme of the storyline, can be seen as a way to assert their gender identity in contrast to the prevalence of video games by boys.

The group worked on the L.S.O.H. project for six months beginning in March. Their original plan was that they would each design a set of three or four pages to depict a key scene from the original movie so that their movie would depict more closely the narrative of the original movie. One of the first changes they made was to make the major characters African American rather than white, reflecting their own racial-ethnic identity. It was easy to use the shape editor to create African American identities for the characters, and it was an incredibly important way for the girls to bring their own identities into the project. Once they had developed several pages in the project, they also decided to change the narrative to create their own ending. One motivation for the plot shift was practical: Shanay and Shamia were creating their pages more slowly than Keanna, and creating their own ending allowed

---

Figure 1
Screenshots of the final version of the *Little Shop of Horrors* project. Page 1 is an animation of the character they called "the Boy" walking across the screen, picking up the plant in the middle of the screen, and carrying it into his house. On page 2, the boy walks into his bedroom and the plant is sitting on his bed. Textboxes appear to show the characters' dialogue. The plant says, "Hey man, turn on the lights!" The TV and the lamp then turn on. Page 3 is a screen containing a textbox with narrative text that moves the story along, "Fifteen years later, when Little Shop of Horrors is a grown plant, we are going to see what he looks like." Page 4 depicts the boy yelling to the plant who has a man in his mouth, "Put down that man!" but the plant eats the man and says "Yummy! Yummy! Yummy!" Page 5 was made by Shanay. On this page, both the plant and the boy find female counterparts and fall in love. Shamia created page 6 where the plant and the boy both have large families. In the animation, each one of the characters disappears into a large house and the house bulges at its sides. The song "We are Family" is played on this page with a caption saying, "We need to move!" Page 7 is the credits' page with textboxes displaying credits the girls wanted to give to themselves and people who assisted them.

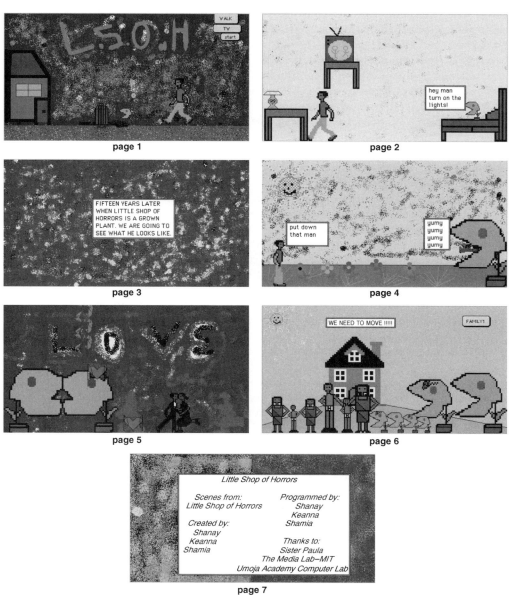

page 1

page 2

page 3

page 4

page 5

page 6

page 7

them to create a narrative that could be completed in two pages of animation. However, it also reflected several gender and culturally anchored ideas about story, as I will show below.

Style was also important to the girls. Once the shapes were on the turtles, the girls spent considerable time adjusting them in the shape editor to ensure that the character in the scene had clothes that reflected the style the girls wanted. For instance, it was very important to Shanay that the clothes worn by the boy and girl in the "love" scene were just right. She went back and forth choosing and coordinating the color of the clothes, length of the girl's dress, height of the girl's shoes, and so forth. She consulted with Shamia and Keanna several times to come to collective agreement about the style, almost as if they were designing outfits for a prom. This of course is an attractive task for girls of this age across many cultural groups. Other tasks in their project involved coordinating the motion of turtles to move simultaneously, recording the theme song and the closing song, the design, and setup of the credits' page. Finally, they wrote procedures to make the movements of the turtles, which formed the action of the scene.

The final version of the project was an animated "movie" that unfolded across seven pages (see figure 1). Keanna created pages 1–4 and her narrative follows the movie rather closely. Shamia worked closely with her on designing the first page. The plot twist starts on page 5. Shanay created this page after the group decided to shift the plot to focus on romance. Shamia created page 6, and they worked on the final credits' page together. As the storyboard reveals, reworking the narrative allowed them to create a powerful, imagined world of their own, extending beyond "remake" of commercial media to their own conceptual universe. Their story line reveals several factors of their cultural participation, including gender, race, age, and school, and community context.

"It Has to be a Movie not a Video Game": Emergence of Reasoning with Procedures

The major design goal that the girls were trying to accomplish was getting their project to be a movie, and not a video game. There were four major tasks involved in getting this result using the MicroWorlds programming environment: (1) merging the graphics pages, (2) copying and coordinating the shapes and turtles, (3) merging the procedures pages, and (4) editing the procedures so that the whole animation would run like a movie. Their decision to make it run "like a movie" is fascinating because they were drawing from popular culture while also remaking it. They were defining programming as a tool for movie making. The MicroWorlds environment essentially became their camera.

From a constructionist standpoint, making their project personally meaningful supported their learning of programming and the math ideas involved in their animation. Their main motive was to tell stories together that people could watch from beginning to end without having to interact a lot with the screen. This goal reflects their own cultural practices of storytelling and collaboration—movie making from experiences with media culture, youth culture, and African American culture, observations that I will return to below.

The fourth task framed a key moment in their thinking about procedures and the nature of their understanding structured programming as a way to tell stories, which is elaborated in the rest of this section. None of the girls had previous experience with merging projects from separate computers into one project. The teacher showed them how to do this in order to combine the separate parts of the story they initially created into one file. Once the projects were combined, the teacher took more of a facilitator role, allowing them to work

Figure 2
Shanay's page with buttons.

more independently on the problem of revising the procedures so that they would run the whole animation like a movie. The teacher listened to their work and offered comments and questions that seemed helpful to their thinking. This type of pedagogical move is resonant with constructionist approaches to helping children work with programmable media.[23]

The girls knew that figuring out how to edit the procedures was key to making the project run "like a movie." They defined "like a movie" as the whole project running by clicking buttons on the first page. Their plan was to put three buttons on the first page (one for setting up the pages, one for launching the animation, and one for the theme song). When each girl created her piece of the project on a separate computer, she wrote procedures for each of the animations in her scene and controlled each animation with buttons on her individual page (see figure 2). The goal of combining their parts of the project into one animation or "movie" set the stage for several conversations about how to write procedures that would combine the separate sets of procedures and allow them to control the project with just three buttons on the first page. When each page ran within the whole project, they did not want any buttons to be on the page. Their idea was that if the user had to press buttons to get things to move on each page it would make the project more like a video game than a movie.

In this way, their "movie-making" goal set up the programming task of coordinating procedural hierarchy. Each girl had enough experience with procedures to take on the intellectual work of structuring a program for the complete animation, although only Keanna had previous experience with writing a procedure that had subprocedures. Their conversations about combining procedures included elements of direct forms of discourse that are familiar in their cultural experience.

In the following dialogue, Keanna expresses her understanding of the idea of procedural hierarchy and how it will help them to accomplish their goal. She also takes on helping Shanay to make sense of this principle. The interaction in the transcript below occurred after the teacher told Keanna and Shanay that she didn't quite understand what they meant by getting their project to "work like a movie." The transcript excerpt begins with Keanna explaining to Shanay, M (another adult in the room), and the teacher how her WALK procedure needed to be changed by adding Shanay's procedures to it. As the interaction progresses, Shanay expresses her idea of how the procedures need to be written so that WALK will run everything.

Keanna: Now listen, Sis. P.

Teacher: OK, I'm listening.

Keanna: OK (pause) Go on the flipside, Shanay.

Shanay: Why?

Keanna: Just go on the flipside, Shanay. (pause) Thank you. OK. Do you see my WALK procedure? Wait. Wait, now you do that WALK procedure. This isn't my real WALK. But her WALK procedure, she would put her—What's your thing named?—Her BOY and GIRL procedure in my WALK procedure.

Teacher: You mean, her procedure called LOVE makes the boy and the girl move. Doesn't it?

Shanay: Yes.

Keanna: You put her LOVE, her G.WALK her B.WALK, her G.RUN and all her, both of her three procedures in **my** procedure.

M: I see, so LOVE, it launches GIRL.RUN and it launches BOY.RUN. So it makes them both do it at the same time.

Keanna: Yeah.

Shanay: And she wants to take—

Keanna: All.

Shanay: This procedure, the GIRL.RUN and the BOY.RUN and LOVE and put it in the WALK procedure.

Keanna: In one procedure.

Shanay: So that we only have three buttons on the screen instead of a whole bunch. We'll have WALK, START, and the music instead of a whole bunch of buttons over the whole screen.

Keanna: And so we put her PLACE and BEGIN procedure in my START procedure as one procedure.

Shanay: Yeah.

> (8/1/94 transcript excerpt)

Keanna was adamant about the strategy of adding Shanay's procedures into her WALK procedure as a way to accomplish their goal of making their project "like a movie." In the beginning of this interaction, Keanna used a direct form of talk to focus our attention on her explanation. Then, once she was sure we were "listening," she assertively explained her way of thinking about how, and why, the procedures needed to be combined. When she says, "You put her LOVE, her G.WALK, her B.WALK, her G.RUN and all her, both of her three procedures in **my** procedure," she is reasoning that putting the procedure called LOVE into her WALK procedure will also put G.RUN and B.RUN there.

Her description conveys the idea that G.RUN and B.RUN were subprocedures to LOVE. This idea is an indication that she understood that LOVE created the scene that needed to come next in their movie narrative. The task of putting all the procedures into one illustrates that she is reasoning with her own idea of the programming principle of procedural hierarchy or modularity/encapsulation. And in this case, putting procedures inside of other

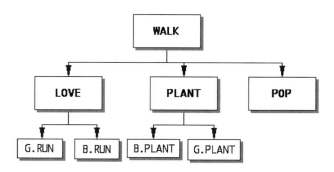

Figure 3
Tree structure representation of Keanna's idea.

procedures builds both their movie narrative and the movie form of interaction that was their goal.

Keanna was prepared to guide the coordination of the procedures because she had the prior knowledge about procedures from a project using turtle graphics to construct a picture of an apartment building. Keanna had been eager to stretch her abilities by creating the apartment building because she envisioned creating a street scene with cars and people passing. The apartment building was formed by a large rectangle for the outer frame, small squares for the windows, and a small rectangle for the door. She was guided by an activity book and wrote separate procedures for each piece and then a top-level procedure that created the whole thing. She had to put the pieces together into one picture, which introduced her to programming ideas of procedure hierarchy and local variable.

The use of these computational tools allowed her to make sense of both the programming idea of procedural hierarchy and to work with mathematical ideas such as perimeter, measurement, and symmetry. For instance, she quickly realized that "the window procedure can do it for you each time," meaning that the same set of commands could create all the windows rather than individually programming each separately. Later she generated her own idea about procedures—that "procedures make things happen automatically." Other key programming ideas that Keanna encountered included the idea that procedures can take inputs, in this case numbers, that influence how they work. This project was Keanna's first significant experience with the programming principle of procedural hierarchy or modularity. In this project, she began to think about the ideas that procedures can be parts of other procedures and procedures can be both part of a project and the whole project—a concept she would later successfully apply in the Little Shop of Horrors project.

Through their project construction, the girls are constructing a computational idea of procedural hierarchy or modularity (see figure 3). This idea is key to becoming expressive in this programming language. They are in the process of inventing the idea of procedural hierarchy for themselves for the purpose of collaborating to make their movie. With these goals in mind, the idea of program structure functions as a tool for them to collaborate and tell stories. The Logo environment provides the tools for them to create their project using programming, graphics, music, and interface design. The multiple forms of cultural participation that they bring to the work make collaboration, media remakes, storytelling, music, graphic style, and identity resources for their knowledge construction as well.

Discussion

I have argued that both constructionist and sociocultural analytic lenses will account for the nature of children's learning with programmable media by addressing the interplay between individual and collective activity that is present in their work. In the case of the L.S.O.H. project, the intertwined nature of elements of cultural participation and project construction is explicit and also unexpected from the standpoint of constructionist analysis alone.

The L.S.O.H. project is an exemplary constructionist project because the process of constructing this personally meaningful project facilitated the girls' ability to learn new ideas about programming, and the process of programming helped them to engage with other ideas, that is, narrative, interface design, and mathematics of scale. The thread of constructing the idea of procedural hierarchy began when Keanna drew on her prior experience thinking about procedural hierarchy in making her apartment project. Over the course of the movie-making project, Keanna and her friends clearly developed a greater fluency in programming. When they began the project in March, it was a big task for them to write procedures to simply animate the character they called "Boy" to move across the screen. When they finished the project in August, they had developed strategies for merging pages, coordinating shapes, consolidating several projects through merging and revising the procedures as well as for programming individual animations. Their familiarity with these tasks was evidence of their developing technological fluency.[24]

From a constructionist perspective, the pedagogical approach hinged on supporting the girls in making a complex construction with programming as a rich representational tool. MicroWorlds Logo functioned in this case as it was designed, as a construction kit that makes computational materials and ideas accessible to children. So constructionist views of learning, teaching, and design can explain some of how their project became more an expression of their ideas about narrative, identity, and interaction, and less a struggle with the intellectual overhead of learning how to program and use the technology. From a constructionist perspective, learning to use the technology for their construction enabled them to engage in these other forms of expression.

However, constructionism does not adequately address the evidence in their work that cultural context is doing more than just providing them an opportunity to make connections to new knowledge about programming and other ideas. Several elements of their work on this project reflect their participation in multiple communities of practice and the use of multiple cultural practices.

From the conception of their project as a movie, they created a purpose for programming as a way to create their own form of popular media. Working with Microworlds in a sense became their camera and editing tool. Their decision to make it run "like a movie" frames their work as an act of drawing from popular culture while also remaking it. This framing suggests that the kind of textual poaching that media scholars have written about is also at work here. The girls both scaffold their story on a popular media artifact and depart from the story to make it uniquely their own by rewriting the ending. They end up creating a space for themselves and their experiences in what began as a simpler remaking of a mass media culture product.

They continued to participate in using programming to express their ideas as participants in popular culture by reworking the narrative. The narrative they developed allowed them to create a powerful, imagined world of their own, extending beyond a literal "remake" of commercial media to their own conceptual universe. The content of their movie also reflects the girls' embeddedness, both in the African-centered context of the school and their community. For instance, the families that they construct mirror families in their own community and recreate images of family that are personally meaningful to them from their experiences.

Their use of "We are Family" as a kind of theme song at the end is an expression of African American identity from popular media. Elements of their experience of gender coupled with race are involved in decisions like their choice to make it a movie rather than a video game and in the focus on love, family, and domestic space. In their peer group, both boys and girls played video games, but only boys chose to make video games for their programming projects.

The point of programming for the girls was not to learn math or programming, but to tell stories together. This is an aspect of their constituting programming as a cultural practice. From a constructionist standpoint, the fact that their work is personally meaningful is viewed as a means to learning programming ideas and learning ideas in other subject matter through programming. From a sociocultural perspective, their work constitutes the activity of programming as a function of their own cultural practices of storytelling and collaboration—movie making from experiences with media culture, youth culture, and African American culture.

Collaboration is a cultural practice that comes from their experiences as members of multiple cultural groups and helps to form their goal of making a movie. Collaboration was a valued form of social interaction within the culture of the girls' school and classroom. Collaborative work functioned in this school community as a routine and enduring social practice inherited by membership in African American communities.[25] This function is marked by two of the Kwanzaa principles that the school adopted as an institutional belief system—Umoja, unity, and Ujmaa, collective work and responsibility.

While these are elements of the African American cultural experience, we should recognize that this experience is not the only influence, and it is not the sole reason why the girls chose to collaborate and work together as they did.[26] Their goal of working together was an expression of their membership in several cultural groups. Their goal to work together helped to structure the project and the programming ideas they used. For them, the structure of their programming is a way to tell their story together. Their cultural participation expands to their own family, to their neighborhood, to their city, and to their gender and position in the late twentieth century. It also expands to new forms of cultural participation, in this case, a new group cultural practice.

The girls continued to create narrative projects together for the next three years. The content and design of their projects carried on the tools that began with the making of this movie. They continued to tell collaborative stories, and they continued to use procedural hierarchy as a tool to tell their stories. The combination of storytelling and programming formed a cultural practice for this group. They used procedural hierarchy as a structure for the narratives they chose to appropriate or write together. In this series of projects, collaboration to tell stories in Logo involved both reappropriation of popular narratives and conceptualizing programming as a way to tell stories.

Implications for Learning, Teaching, Design, Policy

In this chapter, I have argued that adding a sociocultural lens will improve current constructionist views of learning. I have explored how the work of Keanna, Shamia, and Shanay on the L.S.O.H. project is instrumental in recognizing that sociocultural context plays an important role in learning that needs to be further explored in learning with programmable media. The girls brought elements of their experiences in youth culture, popular culture, family culture, school/classroom cultures, and cultures of racial experience to the content of their project and their process of making it. The activity of programming became a way to take ownership over a popular media artifact and make it their own. Their remake of this story inserts images that are personally meaningful from their experiences as African American preteenage girls, such as romance, family, and domestic space. The definition of their project as a movie, and not a video game, is an assertion of their gender identity because in their classroom culture, boys were more interested in video games than girls. They drew from their experiences as savvy movie watchers to construct their interface design so the user of their project would be watching, not playing, and, they drew on the cultural practice of collaboration that they experienced in both their school culture and as a practice with historical continuities within African American culture to both understand and use an important programming idea.

Focusing on the role that sociocultural context plays in learning with programmable media has important implications for the design of curriculum and programming environments, teaching practice, educational policy, and research on learning.

Design of Curriculum and Programming Environments   Recognizing the sociocultural nature of children's learning with programmable media can suggest directions in the design of programmable media and its use in both informal and formal settings. Programming environments need to do more than resonate well with content area knowledge. They need to be able to be used in ways that resonate with the sociocultural factors in students' learning. For example, from a sociocultural perspective, features of programming environments that allow children to represent their multiple identities are necessary to support their learning of computational knowledge. Programming environments can be designed with drawing and illustration tools that make it easier for students to create multiple iterations and fine adjustments to the ways that characters look and move. These tools might also provide easy options for the adjustment of skin color and clothing. These features already exist in environments like *Second Life*, where presenting your own identity is an important part of your experience in the world, but tools designed for educational use are not always as flexible.

Programming environments might also be designed to provide tools that support forms of social activity, such as collaboration, that are shared by groups of students and teachers. For instance, collaborative work was a cultural practice that was connected to African American historical themes in this school. In another setting, or in this setting for other purposes, competitive activity might be a cultural practice that it would be helpful for the designs to support.

Programming environments that contain features that students can use to express their cultural identities and enact cultural practices can be used to provide a curriculum that supports learning of a variety of subject matter. Ideas from mathematics learning and teaching suggest that framing problems with a narrative can support students engaging with a mathematical investigation. However, decisions need to be made about how to frame the problem so that living in the narrative is not more attractive than the math involved in solving the problem.[27] Curriculum design that uses programmable media has a similar problem that sociocultural perspectives can help to explore. For instance, Gee has argued that the literacy activities that students engage in for playing video games are at times much more complex than the literacy activities in school, but the problem then becomes how to understand these literacy activities so that they can inform the design of video games to be both engaging as games and as environments for literacy learning.[28]

Culturally relevant teaching offers the idea that in curriculum and teaching practice, we need to both support children in expressing their cultural identities and strive for academic challenge and success.[29] Thus, programming environments need to be designed to help children engage both their cultural resources from multiple experiences and their subject-matter ideas. For instance, a microworld that is designed for children to explore speed will allow children to draw on their cultural resources for learning by being able to use multiple objects for representing motion, not just cars. But the attention to the cultural nature of learning is more complex than just pictures and objects with which children can identify. Elements of discourse and organization of activity are also important. To some extent, programmable media can be designed to support this kind of curriculum, but it can't function well unless teachers and other adults who support children's learning are able to create learning environments that make use of these media in ways that attend to sociocultural factors.

Teaching Practice and Preparation   Extending constructionism with sociocultural perspectives also holds implications for rethinking pedagogical practice that is aligned with programmable media. Constructionist approaches to teaching emphasize a progressive pedagogy that involves having children make personally meaningful projects with programmable media and giving children models of projects to recreate and extend. Sociocultural perspectives on teaching emphasize that it is important for teachers to understand the relationship between language and social practices of students' daily lives and the practices of academic disciplines.[30] So, for example, teaching with programmable media in ways that acknowledge students' cultural lives could involve giving students example projects that are related to content that they care about. Another implication is using forms of talk that children bring with them to school from their various life experiences as resources for their subject-matter learning. For example, literacy scholars have argued from a sociocultural perspective that many African American and low-income students are more familiar with direct instruction modes of discourse from their experiences at home than indirect forms of talk that are often used in progressive pedagogy.[31] Teachers using programmable media need to recognize when children might respond more to direct forms of talk or more explicit guidance than is often involved in open-ended project development.

An implication for both curriculum design and teaching practice relates to encouraging children to create programming projects that are related to cultural contexts of their lives. Teachers need to be able to juggle the constraints of the projects that children define in relation to the constraints of classroom and school cultures. For instance, when students bring cultural practices such as storytelling to their programming, they define projects for themselves that are long and complicated. Teachers need to be able to respond to the investment that children want to make in creating their projects by providing the length of time that they need. They also need to be willing and able to help students break their projects into parts and help them learn the programming techniques and conceptual pieces they need for each part. Such approaches require flexibility in the classroom, an approach ill supported by rigid "teach-to-the-test" pedagogies.

Policies to Support Learning with Programmable Media   Incorporating a sociocultural perspective into constructionist views of learning, teaching, and design also has implications for how policy makers understand what programmable media can offer learning and teaching in schools and for what they can do to help realize the benefits of this form of digital media. We know from the lines of research that have been done on learning with programmable media that students can do some pretty amazing reasoning about STEM ideas when creating projects with this media. The case study presented in this chapter illustrates the sociocultural nature of students investing in complex learning of programming and various subject matter through programming. It suggests a potential for extending work with programmable media to support all children with using their cultural resources for the learning of STEM ideas and other subject matter. With an understanding of the potential benefits of this work, policy makers should enact polices that value the pursuit of this kind of innovation and flexibility by supporting teacher development and by developing appropriate assessment strategies and larger scale implementations of work with programmable media.

Research on Learning   Finally, the argument for a sociocultural perspective on construction-ism holds several implications for future research on learning. Here, I mention implications related to subject-matter learning, methods, and development of learning theory. We need to know more about the power that can emerge from interactions between what programming can do and what children can do with programming.

Constructionist research and practice has historically viewed programming as a represen-tational medium for mostly STEM ideas. Working on the L.S.O.H. project engaged Keanna and her friends in learning a range of ideas across disciplines. In fact, their work was largely driven by an interaction between programming ideas and narrative expression that is rarely addressed in research on learning with programmable media. Their work suggests the need to better understand how children construct ideas in multiple disciplines when they create programming projects that include their interests and identities. It also suggests the need to delve more deeply into their learning of ideas in particular content areas within the hybrid spaces that they create.

There are incredibly productive conceptions in the field about the resonance between subject-matter knowledge and the computational representations that programming can pro-vide. Andy diSessa calls this quality aptness or the expressiveness of particular representations for particular ideas, but his work addresses primarily the learning of physics and math ideas.[32] The case study described in this chapter calls us to ask what other ideas children bring to their learning of science ideas in the context of programming projects. It was unexpected from tra-ditional views of learning with programming that narrative would be such a strong part of the students' intellectual engagement. Sociocultural lenses help to recognize that their incorpo-ration of narrative was bringing their cultural resources to bear in the programming environ-ment. Future research on learning can benefit from broadening and deepening these lenses.

What methods are needed to further explore children's learning with programmable me-dia? More longitudinal studies of children's learning with programmable media that include attention to sociocultural context will help to answer this question. One aspect of methods that will come from further study is how different units of analysis will shape and elaborate our understandings. For instance, valuable insights can be gained from looking at classrooms over time, at out-of-school settings (i.e., Computer Clubhouses) over time, and at individual student projects over time.

It also will be helpful to conduct more fine-grained analysis of the work and interactions of different students on focused short-term projects. For instance, we might see more about the role of gender in constructionist projects by comparing the work of girls and boys on projects they choose to create.

Children in several different countries use programmable media, and there are possibilities of crosscultural analyses that can contribute to understanding the role of cultural practices in learning with programmable media.

Answering these research questions also involves further work in specifying theoretical frameworks that combine both constructionist and sociocultural perspectives. The vignette points to the importance of understanding the nature of learning with programmable media with additional analytical tools compared to the tools provided by constructionism. For instance, Carol Lee's conceptual framework of cultural modeling provides clear analytical tools for recognizing the cultural practices that students can bring from their experiences outside of school to forming literacy practices inside school.[33] How might this framework be used to support better understanding of children's learning with programmable media?

Over the past twenty years, the course of computer programming as a tool for learning for young children has gone from an area of great interest and fast growth down to very little use in schools (although there has been a recent and robust resurgence in particular niches both in and out of schools). Meanwhile, research on learning and teaching of various subject matter has continued to recognize the cultural nature of children's learning. In this chapter, I have presented a close examination of the children's learning with programmable media that revealed cultural practices having a strong influence on the course of their project development and learning. I have argued that designing programmable media and using it productively with all students must address multiple elements of learning. If learning environments that use programmable media only focus on the resonance between representational forms and disciplinary ideas, some elements of learning that are crucial to the learning of students who are underrepresented in academic achievement will be neglected (i.e., identity and cultural practices). My hope is that this chapter will contribute to new discussions of how an attention to sociocultural lenses will enable researchers, teachers, and designers to make better use of programmable media to improve the learning of all children, in a variety of settings and across racial and socioeconomic categories.

Appendix

Shanay's Procedure's 8/1/94

```
TO G.RUN
T5,
SETH 270
REPEAT 5 [SETSH 52 FD 6 WAIT 1
SETSH 53 FD 6 WAIT 1 SETSH 54 FD 6
WAIT 1]
END

TO B.RUN
T4,
SETH 90
REPEAT 5 [SETSH 37 FD 6 WAIT 1
SETSH 38 FD 6 WAIT 1 SETSH 39 FD 6
WAIT 1]
END
```

```
TO LOVE
LAUNCH [G.RUN]
LAUNCH [B.RUN]
END

TO PLACE
T4,
SETPOS [10 -95]
T5,
SETPOS [210 -95]
END

TO B.PLANT
T2,
SETH 0
REPEAT 5 [FD 6 WAIT 1]
```

```
RT 90 FD 13
SETH 180
REPEAT 5 [FD 6 WAIT 1]
END

TO G.PLANT
T1,
SETH 0
REPEAT 5 [FD 6 WAIT 1]
LT 90 FD 13
SETH 180
REPEAT 5 [FD 6 WAIT 1]
END

TO PLANT
LAUNCH [B.PLANT]
LAUNCH [G.PLANT]
END

TO BEGIN
T2,
SETPOS [-197 -71]
T1,
SETPOS [-70 -71]
END

TO POP
ASK [T10 T8 T7 T6 T3] [SETH 315
REPEAT 10 [FD 15 WAIT 2] SETSH 50]
END

TO POP1
ASK [T10 T8 T7 T6 T3] [SETSH 3]
T3, SETPOS [15 -117]
T6, SETPOS [15 -82]
T7, SETPOS [16 -48]
T8, SETPOS [17 -13]
T10, SETPOS [18 21]
END
```

Keanna's WALK Procedure 8/1/94

```
TO walk
t3,
seth 270
setsh "boy1 fd 85
setsh "boy2 fd 85 setsh "boy3 fd 70
setsh "boyb
setsh "boyp
t1,
seth 0
fd 55
launch [t1, seth 270
```

```
repeat 9 [fd 12 fd 12 fd 12]]
launch [t3, repeat 9 [fd 12 fd 12 fd 12]]
WAIT 10
page2
t1, setsh "boy1 seth 270
setpos [70 -83] repeat 10 [fd 20 wait 2]
t.lamp,
setsh "lamp setsh "lampb setc 44 fill
T6, SETSH "TD
WAIT 40
PAGE3 wait 40
page4
WAIT 10
T2,
SETSH "LITTLE
T1,
HT
wait 20
T2,
SETSH "G
end
```

Keanna's WALK Procedure 8/3/94

```
TO walk
t3,
seth 270
setsh "boy1 fd 85 setsh "boy2 fd 85 setsh
"boy3 fd 70
setsh "boyb
setsh "boyp
t1,
seth 0
fd 55
launch [t1, seth 270

repeat 9 [fd 12 fd 12 fd 12]]
launch [t3, repeat 9 [fd 12 fd 12 fd 12]]
WAIT 10
page2
t1, setsh "boy1 seth 270 setpos [70 -83]
repeat 10 [fd 20 wait 2]
t.lamp, setsh "lamp setsh "lampb setc 44
fill
T6, SETSH "TD
WAIT 40
PAGE3 wait 40
page4
WAIT 10
T2,
SETSH "LITTLE
```

T1,	LOVE
HT	PLANT
wait 20	POP
T2,	PAGE6
SETSH "G	IN
wait 10	wait 40
page5	PAGE8
	End

Notes

1. Robert P. Taylor, ed., *The Computer in School: Tutor, Tool, Tutee* (New York: Teachers College Press, 1980).

2. Yasmin Kafai, Constructionism, in *The Cambridge Handbook of the Learning Sciences*, ed. R. Keith Sawyer (New York: Cambridge University Press, 2006), 35–46; Douglas H. Clements, Longitudinal Study of the Effect of LOGO Programming on Cognitive Abilities and Achievement, *Journal of Educational Computing Research* 3, no. 1 (1987): 73–94; Seymour Papert, *Mindstorms: Children, Computers, and Powerful Ideas* (New York: Basic Books, 1980).

3. Andrea diSessa, Can Students Re-Invent Fundamental Scientific Principles?: Evaluating the Promise of New-Media Literacies, In T. Willoughby and E. Wood (eds.), Children's Learning in a Digital World (Oxford, UK: Blackwell Publishing, 2008).

4. Na'ilah Suad Nasir, Ann S. Rosebery, Beth Warren, and Carol D. Lee, Learning as a Cultural Process: Achieving Equity Through Diversity, in *The Cambridge Handbook of the Learning Sciences*, ed. R. K. Sawyer (New York: Cambridge University Press, 2006), 489–504.

5. Seymour Papert, Situating Constructionism, in *Constructionism*, eds. Idit Harel and Seymour Papert (Norwood, NJ: Ablex, 1991), 1–11; Seymour Papert, *New Images of Programming: In Search of An Educationally Powerful Concept of Technological Fluency*, proposal to the National Science Foundation (Cambridge, MA: Massachusetts Institute of Technology—The Media Laboratory: Epistemology and Learning Group, 1991); Seymour Papert, *The Children's Machine: Rethinking School in the Age of the Computer* (New York: Basic Books, 1993).

6. Ibid.

7. Papert, *The Children's Machine*; Mitchel Resnick, *Turtles, Termites, and Traffic Jams: Explorations in Massively Parallel Microworlds* (Cambridge, MA: MIT Press, 1994).

8. Papert, *Mindstorms*.

9. Andrea diSessa, *Changing Minds: Computers, Learning, and Literacy* (Cambridge, MA: MIT Press, 2000); Kafai, Constructionism.

10. diSessa, *Changing Minds;* Andrea diSessa, Meta-representation: Native competence and targets for instruction, *Cognition and Instruction* 22, no. 3 (2004): 293–331; diSessa, *Can Students Re-Invent*.

11. James Paul Gee, *Game-Like Learning: An Example Of Situated Learning And Implications For Opportunity To Learn* (Madison, WI: Academic Advanced Distributed Learning (ADL) Co-Laboratory, 2006).

12. diSessa, *Changing Minds,* 34.

13. Mitchel Resnick, Steve Ocko, and Seymour Papert, LEGO, Logo, and Design, *Children's Environments Quarterly* 5, no. 4 (1988): 14–18.

14. Mitchel Resnick et al., *The PIE Network: Promoting Science Inquiry and Engineering through Playful Invention and Exploration with New Digital Technologies,* proposal to the National Science Foundation (The Media Lab at MIT, 2000).

15. Mitchel Resnick, Robbie Berg and Michael Eisenberg, Beyond Black Boxes: Bringing Transparency and Aesthetics Back to Scientific Investigation, *Journal of the Learning Sciences* 9, no. 1 (2000): 7–30.

16. Mitchel Resnick et al., *A Networked Media-Rich Programming Environment to Enhance Technological Fluency at Afterschool Centers in Economically-Disadvantaged Communities,* Proposal to the National Science Foundation (The Media Lab at MIT, 2003); John Maloney, et al., Scratch: A Sneak Preview. Second International Conference on Creating, Connecting, and Collaborating through Computing, Kyoto, Japan (2004): 104–109.

17. Papert, *Mindstorms*; Douglas H. Clements and Michael Battista, Geometry and Spatial Reasoning, in *Handbook of Research on Mathematics Teaching and Learning,* ed. Douglas Grouws (New York: Macmillan Publishing Company, 1992).

18. Douglas H. Clements and Michael Battista, The Effects of Logo on Children's Conceptualizations of Angle and Polygons, *Journal for Research in Mathematics Education* 21, no. 5 (1990): 356–371.

19. Papert, *Mindstorms*.

20. Nasir et al., "Learning as a Cultural Process."

21. Na'ilah Suad Nasir, Milbrey McLaughlin and Amina Jones, What does it mean to be African-American? Constructions of Race and Academic Identity in an Urban Public High School, presented at the American Educational Research Association Annual Meeting, Chicago, IL, 2007.

22. Maulana Karenga, *Kwanzaa: A Celebration of Family, Community and Culture* (Los Angeles: University of Sankore Press, 1998).

23. Kafai, Constructionism; Molly Watt and Daniel Watt, *Teaching With Logo: Building Blocks for Learning* (Menlo Park, CA: Addison Wesley, 1986).

24. Papert and Resnick 1997.

25. Nasir et al., "Learning as a Cultural Process"; Lee 2002.

26. Lee 2002.

27. Deborah Ball, Hyman Bass, and Geoff Saxe et al., *The Laboratory Class: A Multidisciplinary Approach to Studying the Teaching and Learning of Mathematics* (Chicago: American Educational Research Association, 2007).

28. James Paul Gee, *What Video Games Have to Teach Us About Learning and Literacy* (New York: Palgrave Macmillan, 2004).

29. Gloria Ladson-Billings, But That's Just Good Teaching! The Case for Culturally Relevant Pedagogy. *Theory into Practice* 34, no. 3 (1995): 159–165.

30. Nasir et al., "Learning as a Cultural Process."

31. Lisa Delpit, Skills and Other Dilemmas of a Progressive Black Educator, *Harvard Educational Review* 56, no. 4 (1987): 379–385.

32. Andrea diSessa, *Changing Minds*.

33. Carol D. Lee, Is October Brown Chinese? A Cultural Modeling Activity System for Underachieving Students, *American Educational Research Journal* 38, no. 1 (2001): 97–141.

Whispers in the Classroom

Sarita Yardi

Georgia Institute of Technology, Department of Human-Centered Computing

Introduction

"Let's face it — our school doesn't have a book for everything." —Autumn[1]

Online chat rooms are a novel communication medium that provide an opportunity to transform classroom learning in unexpected and powerful ways. Youth are a demographic of highly engaged, core members of the "always on" crowd—active users of the internet, instant messaging, video games, and social networking sites. Numerous studies have documented how young people use instant messaging and online chat rooms in their personal lives. Some youth today perceive technologies to be entirely new and in the position of setting unprecedented opportunities for interactions online. One high school student stated that, "I can't see how people in the past survived without digital media." Similarly, another asserts that, "My generation, those born in the early 90's, are the first humans to be so profoundly impacted by today's new technology."[2] Their familiarity with and enthusiasm for these tools suggests a valuable opportunity to examine how such communication media can be transferred into more formal educational settings to enable both formal and informal learning through student discussions and interactions online. Students can learn from one another through collaborative knowledge sharing, while educators can use the tool to gain more insight into what and how their students are learning. Kyle, a high school teenager from Wyoming, captures many of the most important factors in chat room use when he says:

Chat rooms can be a way to experience intelligent conversation and try out new ways of saying things, often without having to deal with the fear of being wrong or being laughed at. Kids are using this great tool to enhance personal relationships based on simple dialogue. I'm not going to encourage such behavior, but it is better than what could be going on. Chat rooms and other forms of online communication provide a launching pad for the great thinking minds of America's youth, with little or no consequence for failure.[3]

As wireless networks have been introduced in conference halls, hotels, university auditoriums, and in particular, the classroom, laptop users have realized that they do not have to sit idly during a lecture or presentation. Behavior can range from surfing the Web and checking e-mail while blatantly disregarding the frontchannel speaker to actively engaging in the frontchannel discussion through concurrent related discussions, debates, fact checking, resource sharing, and collaboration. The recent surge in interest has generated a number of conference-based case studies that look to describe the implications of backchannel chats.

Participants in these conferences have expressed a wide range of opinions about the useful-ness of the backchannel in context of the frontchannel discussion. Similarly, a number of educators have considered the effects of unrestricted wireless access in the classroom, and some have attempted to incorporate these technologies into their lectures and lesson plans.[4] However, little research has been conducted on how chat rooms affect learning experiences and environments. Chat rooms could transform how course material, learning behaviors and practices, and interactions between students and teachers, fundamentally change the ways in which teachers and students create and disseminate ideas, knowledge, and understand-ing. This chapter first describes a backchannel chat room that has taken place over multiple years in a large university student community and then explores some unforeseen and ex-citing opportunities—as well as possible limitations—for redesigning teaching and learning practices in educational environments.

Background: What is a Backchannel?

Chat rooms can be accessed through any Web-based chat sites or by downloading a chat client to one's computer and then connecting to an online server through this local client. Internet Relay Chat is a client-based chat environment that enables groups of people to collaborate and chat from any physical location. It was first used in the 1980s and has since grown into one of the most popular real-time chat systems around the world. It is a multiuser system where people meet on channels to talk in groups or privately. There are no restrictions on the number of people who can participate in a given discussion or the number of channels that can be formed. Chat room conversations tend to be thought of as ephemeral and impermanent due to their synchronous nature. The interaction is rarely thought out in advance, and conversations occur spontaneously. Similar to face-to-face conversation, there is little archiving of chat conversations. Although chat logs may be maintained, they are rarely referred to after the chat has occurred.

The central function of the backchannel chat room is its use as a secondary or back-ground complement to an existing frontchannel. The frontchannel may consist of a profes-sor, teacher, speaker, lecturer, conference panel, or other similar environment containing a centralized discussion leader who is usually colocated in the same physical space as the participants. The frontchannel usually implies a single focus of attention. The backchan-nel can function to enhance the frontchannel discussion by encouraging user participation and interaction, changing the dynamics of the room from a strictly one-to-many interac-tion to a many-to-many interaction. Activities in the backchannel may include establishing guidelines, inviting participants, excluding outsiders, posing questions, providing answers, critiquing what is being said in physical or digital communication channels, or sharing information and resources.[5]

With a thorough understanding of the opportunities and limitations of the backchan-nel, educators and instructional designers could transform the classroom experience from a passive lecture model to one of active, collaborative, and engaged knowledge production. Students can learn through a different communication medium, while educators can use the tool to gain more insight into what and how their students are learning. Some questions addressed in this chapter include:

- In what ways does chat augment class discussion and how can this information be used by educators?

- What can chat data say about classroom interactions?

- What types of interactions occur in this backchannel and how do they contribute to the academic learning space?

- How does this communication medium change techniques for information and knowledge sharing?

- Is there a compelling story to be told or is it simply noise-wasted bandwidth that distracts participants from their face-to-face environment?

A Case Study in a University Backchannel

The notion of "the academy" as an institution of modern higher education has been transformed from a tradition of an intellectual quest for truth, philosophy, and the arts, with an often stark and disciplined rigor into a socially-oriented, student-empowered learning space. The sense of entitlement in the modern undergraduate student is significant. They want to be able to select which courses they are taking, participate in fully-funded sports teams, have access to clean and often luxurious living standards, and complain if an academic setting has a dearth of social options, food selection, or entertainment opportunities. Such is the environment at the university described in this case study. It is an internationally renowned academic institution, highly sought after by undergraduate, graduate, and faculty scholars.

A student set up a designated Internet Relay Chat channel at this university in which fellow students could easily chat together in an online social environment. No specific purpose or use was attached to the chat room, and an automated login welcome message simply declared that it was to be used by university community members and guests. The chat room experienced an enormous surge in traffic within a matter of weeks. Activity then maintained an overall steady state, amassing a few hundred postings on any given day, and generating a total log of over 300,000 user entries within the first year. In the following year, the new incoming class quickly assimilated into the existing virtual community, integrating into and redefining its culture and social dynamics.

Students login throughout the day, during class, outside of class, and in the evening. With the goal of better understanding patterns of behavior, chat log users and time stamps were plotted in information visualization software to highlight trends in adoption and usage within the classroom. In figure 1, user count is plotted versus the first six weeks of the spring academic semester, showing a general increase in user participation. This suggests that students become more engaged in the chat room community over time. Figure 2 shows total entries by user. The curve shows a power log trend in behavior, indicating that a few users participate most often.

While these tools help to measure quantitative trends over time, they do not help to shed light into the constantly evolving, organic, and unstructured social dynamics of the chat room. In this environment, there is no sense of ownership, nor is there a moderator or leader within the virtual community. It is a self-generated, self-sustained, and thriving online community. Nobody anticipated that from this community would emerge a powerful new genre of computer-mediated learning. As students became comfortable with the affordances offered by the chat room, while simultaneously developing a growing sense of community through their physical social interactions, the channel was unintentionally appropriated into a space for self-directed learning. It provided an open and unrestricted bandwidth through which to engage in a professor's lecture. They had created an environment that was rich

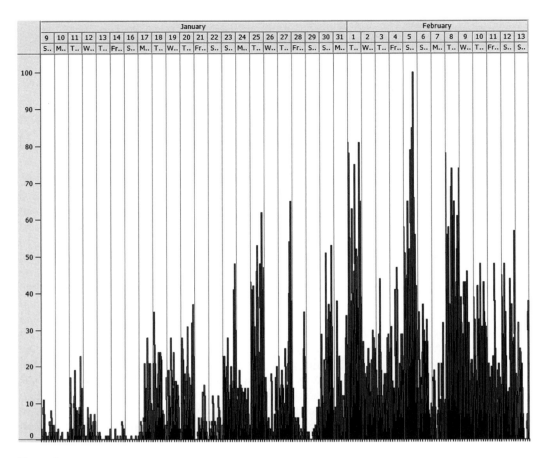

Figure 1
Number of chat entries over first six weeks of spring academic semester.

for collaborative learning and knowledge production, a communication medium through which to engage in active, creative, discovery-based learning. Students who may have been too shy and inhibited in the physical classroom had an opportunity to express themselves in the backchannel. The chat room transitioned from a simple tool for social communication to a tightly knit community. This conversion was both unanticipated and unexpected and elicited a wide variety of reactions from students and teachers. They were surprised, confused, curious, excited, eager, and intrigued. Regardless of their perceptions, there was a clear lack of understanding about the future of the backchannel in classrooms, but nonetheless, a sense of enthusiasm about its potential for change.

The backchannel presents a unique toolkit through which people can create, identify, and filter new modes of interaction. Young people adopt and appropriate new forms of communication technologies and digital media in order to experiment with their self-identity, develop their social networks, and nurture their personal friendship and relationships. This suggests a powerful opportunity for engaging them by incorporating these practices into new classroom teaching and learning paradigms. The emerging experiences offered by this

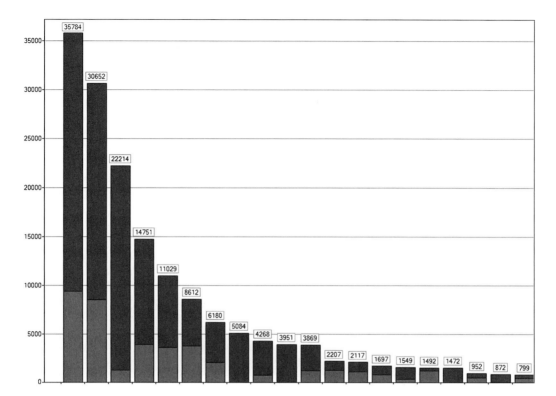

Figure 2
Total chat entries by user over one year.

digital backchannel offer an exciting space in which to explore new directions in collaborative learning. In light of the increasing role of new media technologies and computer-mediated communication as ubiquitous tools in our everyday lives, researchers need to address the need for a better understanding of how these tools can be incorporated into the classroom environment to facilitate enhanced teaching and learning.

Historical Background: Conflicts and Context

Conflicts in backchannel use have their theoretical underpinnings in historical and ongoing power struggles over who maintains ownership and control within the classroom. Should teachers run the classroom or should students direct their own learning environment? Can the two pedagogical models coexist? Educational pedagogy has evolved over time in parallel with the cultural, societal, and governmental influences in which it is embedded. For example, Pink Floyd's famous and controversial song, "Another Brick In the Wall" reflects the counterculture sentiment of its time with a chorus line: "We don't need no education. We don't need no thought control. . . . Teacher! Leave the kids alone. Hey! Teacher! Leave the kids alone!" As the lyrics suggest, the traditional educational classroom setting has historically been perceived by some as an environment of oppression. Friere describes such oppression as banking, in which students are the depositories and the teacher is the depositor.[6] In this model, students are given agency only so far as to receive, file, and store the deposits, rather than to engage in creative, transformative, and knowledge construction processes. Students are force-fed facts and information, required to regurgitate the teacher's personal mantra. Unmotivated students fail the system and uninspired students may despise the system. Students who learn to work within the system align themselves on the fast track to success.

More recently, teachers, educators, parents, and policy makers are paying increasing attention to the implications of enabling online access in classrooms. In the wake of recent legislative acts, such as the No Child Left Behind Act[7] and the Deleting Online Predators Act,[8] the question of ownership and regulation in schools is revisited in this context of internet use. These acts seek to protect youth in their online environments and to enable more equal access of these environments to all students. Yet, by demonizing the negative effects of youths' online activities, these laws may have inadvertently caused a culture of fear and moral panic surrounding online environments that limit the potential for designing powerful and novel learning opportunities that take advantage of Web-based opportunities, such as chat rooms and backchannels. Despite the negative perceptions that are frequently perpetuated by mainstream media, the large majority of youth are not looking to engage in unsafe behaviors online, but instead want ownership over their online activities. In particular, recent studies show that teenagers are often more aware of the implications of their online activities in terms of safety, learning, and privacy than they may be given credit for.[9] Amber, a teenager from Wyoming, suggests that "technology is changing things so rapidly that the control procedures need to change with it.... The only real answers would be the ones worked out by students and adults alike."[10] Dahye, a teenager from Brooklyn, asserts that "we own these new digital medias, we shouldn't be slaves to them."[11] Teens are looking to use the internet to socialize with their peers, for entertainment, and to search for information.

The students who use the backchannel may simply be looking to engage in an environment in the classroom that is not forced, regardless of the actual interactions that play out within this space. Ironically, because regulation in schools prevents free access to the Web, those youth who may be the most in need of free access to information are cut off from the ability to utilize these resources. Furthermore, schools are well equipped to serve students at the most crucial points in their stages of technology adoption, during introductory and educational phases of adoption and when a high quality, reliable connection is otherwise unavailable. Educators are in, perhaps, the best position to be a watchdog for youth's online activities. Educators can teach youth about empowerment and professionalism and the necessary means for articulating and understanding credibility and assessment in their online worlds. A good educational environment requires teachers who motivate their students, facilitate knowledge building, engage participation, and foster a passion for lifelong learning. To deny students this right is to deny them their fundamental right to learn. Such deprivation would be to deconstruct the very premise upon which our economic and cultural existence rests. Thus, the role of chat rooms in the classroom and the contradictory notions of ownership that are suggested uproot the very premise upon which traditional classroom learning has been constructed. The polarization of opinion in who *should* have control in this learning environment can lead to embittered debates that may be motivated by personal agendas and politically and historically rooted beliefs. This chapter, therefore, discusses the role of a backchannel chat room in context of such political divisions, seeking to overcome these challenges to harness the potential of the backchannel as a communication medium for enabling new forms of learning.

The following sections examine some of the potential affordances and struggles surrounding the use of a backchannel in a school setting. These include its role in establishing social trust and individual identity, its ability to create a sustained sense of space, its function as a site of power negotiations, and its capacity to improve learning using strategies for situated pedagogy and knowledge creation. The section below highlights some of the potential benefits of the backchannel, and is followed by a description of its primary disadvantages that are drawn from the case study environment. These dynamics are then used to explore ways in which the backchannel could be used in the classroom and to dissect the conflicts and challenges in doing so. The final section suggests rules and methods for designing a productive backchannel environment with recommendations for changes in educational pedagogy and teaching and learning styles.

Benefits: Innovations in Learning

As the emerging participatory culture on the internet has clearly demonstrated, new technologies can help to enable equal participation across domains that have previously been restricted to authorities within a particular field. How might this change the classroom learning environment? "People with expertise contributed answers, tidbits, essays, pages of software code, lore of astonishing variety," Howard Rheingold writes in Smart Mobs.[12] People want to establish themselves as an authority on a subject by becoming both producers and authors in digital media. If students can participate in a lecture, how they make sense of the transmitted information will not be the same as if they were simply listening. On one hand, their shared social construction may create a homogenizing of opinions as they share their perspectives with one another. On the other hand, students are empowered to argue, debate, and discuss with one another, creating an environment in which they can take on as much power as they want.[13] Johnson states that "To understand how these new media experiences work, you have to analyze the message, the medium and the rules. What's interesting here is not just the medium, but rather the rules that govern what gets selected and what doesn't."[14] However, without a common ground upon which to understand its power to engage students, enable new modes of learning, and facilitate teaching, the power of the backchannel may be lost as yet another poorly understood medium that is unsuccessful in school environments.

The potential success of peer-to-peer learning in a chat room is rooted in the theory of constructivist learning. According to this theory, learning is an active process in which learners construct new ideas or concepts based upon their current and past knowledge. The learner selects and transforms information, constructs hypotheses, and makes decisions, relying on a cognitive structure to do so.[15] Classes in which students participate in discussions encourage them to go beyond merely plugging numbers into formulas or memorizing terms.[16] Similarly, Brown, Collins and Duguid argue that students learn best when given the opportunity to learn skills and theories in the context in which they are used, then construct their interpretations of a subject, and communicate those understandings to others.[17] In the backchannel, students can create their own knowledge by having the freedom to direct the discussion in ways that are relevant, contextual, and instructional for their own learning purposes. The ways in which students use chat rooms emulate their culture of learning, communicating, and interacting. Peer-to-peer interactions support flexible, learner-centered designs in which learning is active and organic rather than static.

The backchannel offers students the opportunity to interact with the teacher, the presentation, and one another in a relatively unrestricted, open environment. Far from the traditional presentation environment where they are at the mercy of whoever is standing in front of the classroom, chat offers the possibility for engagement through multiple modes of transmission. Students can experience a positive engagement with the backchannel, suggesting that they can conduct backchannel discussions that are on-topic, and can even lead to a more involved audience and better interaction with the presenter.[18] Giving students access to a public ubiquitous backchannel also broadens the scope of discourse within the shared physical space. Students are able to ask questions, receive answers, and solicit information without having to interrupt the frontchannel presentation. The signal-to-noise ratio in the frontchannel classroom discussion is improved because only the most important and salient questions are posted verbally, while more peripheral or irrelevant questions can be filtered through the backchannel discussion. Students can ask their peers questions, such as:[19]

10:48:10   Student1: so whats constructionism?

10:48:21   Student1: same as constructivism?

10:48:39   Student2: no, it is more about making things in learning, like learning by building artifacts

Similarly, they can help explain or link relevant material to the discussion topic.

10:51:08   Student1: Did [lecturer] show us where he got his dataset?

10:51:30   Student2: I don't think he did

10:52:17   Student3: but you can find it in [source]

10:52:47   Student2: Actually, I think this is the link

10:52:48   Student2: [URL]

The backchannel provides a means through which to challenge and verify the authority of the teacher without actually challenging him or her explicitly. Students may be more willing to brainstorm over chat when it is considered a backchannel and the social cost of failure or being wrong is low, or at least, is perceived to be low. They also ask questions about material the teacher already covered in class that they may not feel comfortable asking about again.

14:25:10   Student13: what is microformats again? sorry

14:25:59   Student66: http://microformats.org/about/

11:25:29   Student44: what does participatory design mean? I know he explained it but I forgot.

11:25:33   Teaching Assistant: it's a type of design that brings the users into the process

Students frequently shared resources based on their own expertise. In this way, the backchannel can enhance the professor's lecture, without interrupting the flow of the in-class discussion. The backchannel also enables people who have not had a voice, whether because of educational, economic, social, or cultural barriers, to build an equitable reputation in the classroom by participating in the dialogue.

Disadvantages: Distracted Youth or Engaged Students?

Many opponents to using backchannels in the classroom highlight its potential for distraction. Although students have always been subject to distractions during class, in a modern wireless-enabled physical space, the possibilities for distractions increase exponentially. Some participants have suggested the term "continuous partial attention" to describe an audience member's cognitive ability to pay attention to the speaker's presentation when simultaneously engaged in the backchannel. Others, somewhat cynically, suggest that "continuous partial inattention" is a more appropriate description.[20] Regardless of how well intentioned a student may be, a backchannel is going to elicit reactions and engagement from the group that will be asynchronous and off-topic to the frontchannel presentation. This can cause confusion and disruption for the students as well as the teacher. For example, in the two admissions below, the students acknowledge that they missed part of the lecture because they were not paying attention.

10:51:22   *Student4:* Yeah, I missed that, was reading the news headlines

10:51:28   *Student4:* what's that about usability?

18:42:31   *Student6:* Wait, what did she say? I wasn't paying attention. Oooh, a birdy . . .

Similarly, the discussion below took place in class but was unrelated to the professor's lecture:

17:31:28   *Student12:* yeah. I had a roommate who went running with friends and ran like 14 miles.

He came home and was eating honey directly out of the jar. It was funny.

17:32:01   *Student12:* I never saw an adult eat honey directly out of the jar before.

17:32:1   *Student31:* i eat jelly straight from the jar sometimes

Furthermore, discussions can become improper and disrespectful. For example:

13:27:32   *Student4:* i think we should have a goal this semester

13:27:53   *Student18:* to get [Student3] a girlfriend?

It could be argued that these students would be distracted even if they were not in the chat room. Weighing the costs and benefits of the backchannel in this case may reveal that the chat room is beneficial for the student because he or she is able to ask a classmate about what was missed, rather than simply conceding it as a lost opportunity. At the same time, students recognize that the backchannel does offer an opportunity for distraction that is more exciting and stimulating than traditional forms of distraction, such as staring out the window or doodling on paper. In an unmoderated classroom environment, multitasking online may easily deteriorate into a range of activities that are unrelated to the professor's lecture. One student revealed this perspective:

I do occasionally feel kind of guilty about it, I should be paying attention to the class. Especially when things "get out of hand" people start laughing, I think, "we shouldn't be doing this. . . . " I try not to let it overtake my attention. I don't feel like it's a problem. If I can concentrate, it's helpful. If not, I probably wouldn't be paying attention anyway.

In their study of undergraduate students, Kinzie et al. found that students in the open laptop condition suffered decrements on traditional measures of memory for lecture content even though the students felt they were capable of engaging in on-task discussions and of expressing opinions and exploring instructionally relevant topics.[21] Although students routinely multitasked in classrooms as they attended to lectures, processed the material, and took notes, both students and the instructors expressed some discomfort with discussion occurring synchronously with classroom lectures. Furthermore, students' experience with and ability to use forms of technology will affect their levels of distraction while using it.

For those youth who are advanced chat room users, the backchannel may enable them to intuitively appropriate the technology to maximize their learning experience. Others who have not interacted in chat rooms may expend significant energy trying to overcome the learning curve of the technology before being able to actually engage in the actual classroom discussion. What may be an innovation in technology and practice to one student is familiar, and perhaps even antiquated, to another. Therefore, the use of backchannels may be helpful for some students while others are better off not using it, depending on the personal experiences of each individual student.

Power Plays: Who Rules the Classroom?

In the midst of the pervasive culture of fear that surrounds many forms of popular new media, the backchannel may be perceived to be a medium that encourages transgression. Those who oppose it may argue that to participate in the backchannel is to purposefully upstage the teacher's role in the classroom. Their claims highlight the politically charged pedagogical implications associated with the backchannel. Cohen states that "passing notes in the classroom is probably as old as formal education itself, but the advent of cell phones and other sophisticated handheld devices has elevated this communication to a digital art form."[22] McCarthy et al. similarly suggest that "the term 'backchannel' is a political term, implying not only the existence of a primary 'frontchannel,' but also carrying implications of an unofficial, unwanted, illicit quality. In the lecture-oriented classroom, backchannels have always had a rich life, enabled by the technology of the day—from whispering, hand signals, and note passing, to today's e-mail, instant messaging, and mobile phone-based SMS."[23] The meaning of the term backchannel thus varies with context and usage. To some it suggests an intangible, clandestine community. To others it suggests an empowering toolkit for participation, collaboration, and informal interactions.

There are a number of ways in which the backchannel could be rude or disrespectful to the teacher. First, if the teacher is not aware of the existence of the backchannel, he is placed in a compromisingly uninformed position about the dynamics of the classroom environment. Second, the context of the backchannel discussion could very likely contain negative or disrespectful comments about either the lecture content or personal characteristics of the teacher. Third, as has been described already, students' presence in the backchannel suggests a partial or complete lack of attention to the teacher.

Interviews with professors, teachers, and students revealed a challenging disconnect in perceptions of ownership within the backchannel. There is an ongoing power struggle between teachers and students, both explicit and implicit, which creates a division in approaches to adapting the backchannel in the classroom. This struggle is not new, as educators have always been challenged to maintain a balance of control and power in the classroom. David Labaree, a Professor at Stanford's School of Education, declares that "one reason that teaching is such a difficult profession is that its aim is to change the behavior of the client, and . . . its success depends on the willingness of the client to cooperate. . . . "[24] Teachers can succeed only if they can convince or motivate students to cooperate with them. Given that student attendance is mandatory, many develop an inherent resistance to following classroom instruction. However, existing norms do not necessarily apply to new technologies, and must be reconsidered in context of the affordances of the new technology. Is there a possibility for rethinking and reconstructing teaching paradigms using the backchannel that is satisfactory, even embraced, by educators and students alike?

For example, the introduction of computers in the classroom creates a shift in dynamics from one-to-many to many-to-many between the teacher and the students. In a many-to-many interaction, such as that enabled by a backchannel, student culture dominates over the traditional teacher-generated ecology. Therefore, a self-policing model may be needed to facilitate a productive learning culture. Whether in a lecture or a seminar, students have acknowledged the instructor as the moderator of the discussion and rely on the instructor to provide structure and to manage the discussion.[25] Nonetheless, professors have lamented the use of wireless technologies in the classroom, resorting to banning classroom usage or attempting to turn off access. "Some have banned the technology from classes, some turn off the Internet during instruction, while others struggle through lectures knowing that students are instant messaging, looking at photos, writing papers, and playing games instead of focusing on teacher-relayed information."[26] At the University of Virginia, a law professor decided to turn off wireless access during class times. At the University of Texas, a law professor climbed a ladder and disconnected the wireless transmitter due to his frustration with students' inattention. "Laptops are a real problem," says Charles M. Grisham, a professor at the University of Virginia. "You can stand at the door and see students surfing the web, e-mailing to each other.... We wanted to bring this knowledge [technology] into the classroom, but it may be crippling in other ways."[27]

Professors at the university in this study expressed varied opinions about the university backchannel and its use during their lectures. One professor felt that he now had to teach in shorter bursts in the hopes of holding students' attention better. He was not happy about this, since he felt that his subject material required a lot of concentration on complex topics. Another professor, who had not been previously aware of the chat room, expressed discontent at having no awareness of it. This professor asked, somewhat cynically, if she could also be given access to this chat room. She did not appreciate that students might be talking about her without her knowledge. This latter reaction was expressed by a number of professors, lecturers, and teachers. In Golub's study, the lecturer's initial reaction was one of anger and apprehension that students were talking about her behind her back.[28] However, when she realized that the participants in the chat room had been talking about topics related to her presentation, she became more enthusiastic about the idea.

Another university professor confided that the university backchannel was disconcerting for him because he did not know what was being said. "When a whole bunch of people start smiling broadly or snickering, you sometimes go, wait, did I say something weird or what?" He emphasized that he experienced a feeling of disconnection when he did not know what was going on and what people were doing on it. He felt that it could play an interesting role if it were incorporated into the classroom through professor endorsement or a frontchannel display. It would provide an interesting dynamic for teachers and students to combine lecture and debate at the same time. If it were incorporated into the classroom, this professor asked, would it change the entire content of the discussion? "Would it poison the well?" Another professor in the university program expressed a contrasting perspective on the backchannel. He knew that students were chatting online during class because he could easily perceive their engagement with the computers as such. However, he stated that it did not bother him as it did many of the other professors. Although this particular professor did not feel that the possibility that students were chatting about him was a challenge to his authority or self-esteem, many university students we interviewed felt that insecurity could explain a professor's opposition to the backchannel:

Some professors think, "if you don't have anything else to do, then you'll pay attention." I feel like it's almost insecurity, that professors are worried that people aren't paying attention, they get a little pissy about it.

Although it may be partially attributed to their unfamiliarity with technologies, there is also a greater sense of loss of power that could occur. If students are able to direct their own learning styles and materials, the power structure in the classroom could easily transfer from the teacher to the student. While the transition away from a teacher-centric classroom may simply take time to evolve, it could also be argued that it may be time to reinvent teaching. "Faculty may argue that computers are distracting and so should be eliminated from or controlled in the classroom," says John G. Bryan at the University of Cincinnati. "The problem isn't that computers are distracting. The problem is that many faculty work against the computers or in spite of the computers instead of really using the computers to accomplish their instructional goals."[29]

A better understanding of the social dynamics around the technology is essential to improving its use in the classroom. "We must learn from social trends, capture the power of student–technology interactions, and consider how such relationships engender students' motivation for learning. The stipulation is that we as educators must be willing to reshape our traditional norms of communication, as well as be open to drawing upon skills students bring to the classroom."[30] The backchannel offers a relatively moderated environment in which students can assert some ownership and control over their own learning environment. Given the flux in educational goals and teaching theories, teachers are often uncertain about what skills they are ultimately seeking to enable in students. Is the goal of the backchannel to enable students to be more engaged? To seek out their own fields of expertise? To teach the new forms of media literacy? To take advantage of the opportunity to learn from their peers? The use of the backchannel in the classroom could foreshadow a revolution in the classroom in ways that are as yet undetermined but that harbor real potential.

Building Community Identity

Establishing identity and reputation in a virtual community has long been understood to be one of the most important characteristics to increasing participation and engagement within that community.[31] Social recognition was one of the biggest motivators for participants in the university chat room. The most common form of identity recognition is a participant's username. Core community members rarely change usernames, and when they do it is usually because of server or connection problems with their preferred nickname, and they will choose a similar alternative name. Because of the synchronous nature of the university channel and its very strong sense of community, trust is a crucial dynamic of the backchannel environment. Chat's real-time synchronous affordances make it difficult for people to mask their identity within the community. "Rapid responsiveness in communication begets trust. [Chat] forces rapid response, a basis for trust, which if backed up by short message quality provides deeper context for an initial relationship."[32] For both regular community members and new participants, a sense of trust within the channel is mandated at all times. The auto-message upon login explains the chat room community: "[Chat room name] is the [university name]. If you are looking for discussion of [similar sounding name], you are in the wrong place. Unidentified lurkers will be kicked." This is primarily maintained by requesting all users to reveal their true identity. In fact, all regular users on the backchannel know the real identity of any other user at any given time. If a username is present that is not recognized by the backchannel core community, users will immediately query the unidentified user to reveal his or her true identity.

17:54:30   Student23: hello Student4

17:54:33   Student12: whois Student4?

17:54:35   Student4: hi

17:54:42   Student4: [Student4 name]

17:54:55   Student7: Hey!

17:55:02   Student9: hi Student7

17:55:10   Student2: welcome to [chat room name]s

17:55:10   Student4: hello everybody

In a separate episode, two recent alumni of the university who had graduated the previous year entered the chat room to check it out. The current class members knew the identity of the alumni, but the incoming class did not. They immediately questioned the identity of the new participants, but were ultimately willing to trust that they were welcome members of the channel as long as the current members could vouch for their identity.

21:37:58   –> Student17 has joined

21:38:06   Student54: [student17 name]?

21:39:11   Student17: yes, [student name]

21:40:22   Student54: how's it going [student name]?

21:40:44   Student17: good, just checking out the [class] topic of the day

21:41:37   Student14: who is [Student17]?

21:41:47   Student17: [Student17 full name]

21:42:01   Student24: incomings meet the alumni

21:42:09   Student14: . . . heh. i don't know who that is, but okay - so long as someone does :P

Other key contributors to increasing trust include rules, personal disposition, history, shared category membership, and roles.[33] In particular, establishing a shared context between users is essential to maintaining trust online. For the university community, the sense of a shared context is easily increased through the daily personal interactions that users experience in their face-to-face environment. By chatting informally in the classroom hallways, during lunch, or in outside social settings, users establish a sense of trust that is quickly transferred to their interactions in the online environment. The sense of shared context facilitates discussions and conversations online. The more shared context participants have, the easier it is for them to negotiate their sense of interpersonal trust and reputation.

You hear an idea, make a joke of it, you've just used something you've just got. Some professors might not like something going on outside of their ideas. Being able to form a joke means you've got it. Some people think it's funny, some don't, it fuels the social network.

There should be a reciprocal relationship between group members and the environment that the chat room provides that will fulfill the social desires of its members for sustained participation. Social presence is high in the university backchannel. Participants acquire instant gratification, approval, and acceptance upon entering the chat room. For example, a student entered the chat room for the first time over a year after matriculating in the program:

11:09:04   ->Student18 has joined

11:09:34   Student12: wow, guest appearance by Student18!

11:09:40   Student18: ;D

A chat room that is devoid of social affordances will likely lose participants and isolate the remaining members from one another. Regardless of whether this motivation is selfish or altruistic, participants often go to extreme lengths to enhance their social capital with the community, which serves to then build their reputation in the community, inserting them into a cycle of increased participation and acceptance. People tend to categorize themselves as part of the group if the salience of perceived differences among these individuals is minor, relative to the perceived differences to other individuals. Thus, perceived similarities between different university community members concerning attitudes, beliefs, norms, and values, a common task, or a shared history are significant contributors to social identification and group cohesion. Because participants share a physical space on a regular basis, their ability to build a community and recognize other people with whom they are conversing virtually is significant.

Community as a Third Place

Participants in the university chat room were driven by a desire for a sense of community. They may be "searching for a feeling of community that's been lost as many 'third places' which are neither work nor home, but a third place where people congregate and interact, have closed down."[34] Oldenburg describes how many parents and community members have lamented youth's declining participation in community activities, such as Boy Scouts, local Park and Recreation teams, and hobby-inspired clubs, which have instead been replaced with participation in online communities, such as MySpace, Friendster, Doom, Neopets, and countless others. Similarly, adults are participating in online card games, chat rooms, and other virtual communities in place of knitting clubs, poker gatherings, or Tupperware parties, as may have been the norm thirty years ago. For this reason, many chat room participants are using their virtual community as a replacement for the camaraderie and support system previously offered by membership in community organizations. The virtual community offers a home away from home.

In the same way, the university backchannel provided a place for students to develop their third place. Participant usage increased during class time, but also in the evenings. For example, participants often reveal their physical location with other participants, creating a sense of shared physical space, even when participants are not actually colocated. Research suggests that digital technology can improve communication in many ways, such as by providing the "virtual hallways" for students and instructors to meet."[35] Subjects who participate in the backchannel stated that they first heard about the channel directly through a social contact. In these cases, they were approached and specifically told about the channel's existence and how to access it. One participant stated that he originally viewed the channel as a way to meet people when he first started school and did not know anyone in the area. In this case, he used the channel as a way to actively seek out friends. He perceived the channel as open to any university community member:

I don't think there's anyone that's unaware that it exists. Some people think they'd have trouble con-centrating or whatever. I feel like not that it's excluding people, but *including* people. I don't know if that makes sense. People who are on [chat] are more of a group. It's building group cohesion where there wouldn't be one otherwise, but I don't think it's an exclusion.

In contrast, those who do not participate said that they had heard about the channel in public spaces, but did not know much about it. Nonparticipants also stated that their social circle did not use the channel or did not use laptops in class at all. This suggests the possibility of a relationship between *existing* social networks and chat participation. It is not necessarily the case that chat participation mirrors social networks within the school, but they may generate strong ties that reinforce existing dynamics. The sense of community also exists outside of the classroom environment. Participants like to share their evening activities, especially regular daily events like cooking, visits to local eateries, and sleeping. In particular, university students who were single would choose to share their common daily activities:

22:21:18   Student9: I think I might sleep soon

22:21:22   Student9: I know it sounds lame

. . .

22:29:11   Student9: I think I am going to crash

22:29:14   Student23: nite Student9

22:29:14   Student9: see you all tomorrow

This behavior is usually seen in the evenings and outside of class settings when there is a smaller group of core users logged into the chat room. Because the core users are often the same participants every evening, there is a distinct subculture within the university chat room that encourages this sharing of personal lifestyle activities. The offline interactions thus reinforce online interactions as a third place.

Pedagogy of Hope: Designing the Backchannel

How might a backchannel be designed to maximize its potential as a learning environment and tool for both students and teachers? The complex interplay between teacher and stu-dent, teaching and learning, and pedagogy and practice creates a challenging but potentially rich learning ecology. Is it possible to design a sustainable backchannel? Can productive backchannel discourse be fostered without being forced? What are the ideal conditions under which a backchannel will thrive given varied classroom sizes, student ages, subject material, and teaching styles? Abrahamson suggests that designing for emergent situativity can help to merge learning pedagogy and scientific inquiry, creating a potential for an en-gaging, personally meaningful, and authentic exploration into content.[36] Rick and Guzdial similarly highlight the importance of situating a new medium within its sociocultural con-text, grounding it in the culture of its users and their practices.[37]

However, the inherently clandestine nature of the backchannel is problematic, implying that there is the possibility that it simply cannot be designed for. One might argue that, by definition, a backchannel is only a backchannel if it has evolved organically through its user community and contextual behaviors. Therefore, in one sense, designing a backchannel is not possible—it is a contradiction in terms. Can a chat room framework be documented or does it have to be learned through experience? Is its emergence and evolution so ingrained in each instance that the only possible form of documentation is through indoctrination? Returning to Friere's antibanking theory of education, it may be that "The important thing . . . is for men *[students]* to come to feel like masters of their thinking by discussing the thinking and views of the world explicitly or implicitly manifest in their own suggestions and those of their comrades *[classmates]*."[38] The backchannel characteristics could be designed by suggesting certain norms, roles, signals, and behaviors, with the intention of encouraging the backchannel community to adopt such practices. The sections below highlight how such characteristics might be designed and implemented.

Rules of Participation

Craig Smith suggests the development of a protocol for virtual classroom etiquette, "chatiquette," which he bases it on research on classroom discourse and conversational turn-taking.[39] While this protocol does reduce the free-flowing interaction characteristic of most chat sessions, it does not constrain the interaction to the extent that often occurs with a designated moderator controlling the chat session.[40] Instead, it allows all participants to monitor themselves and others in contributing to the discussion. The socialized conventions that structure and organize face-to-face conversation are lacking in the online environment of synchronous communication. Without the nonverbal and verbal cues that indicate a request to speak, such as a raised hand, synchronous discussions can become disjointed. In a learning context in which the exchange of complicated or sophisticated concepts and principles is being attempted, a lack of coherence and flow can quickly degrade into worthless chatter or confusion.[41] The university chat room differs from many other chat rooms in that it is highly unmoderated. The original channel creator purposely set it up with few rules or regulations, empowering the chat room participants to develop their own ecological community. The underlying purpose of rules is often about establishing control. Who governs the roles that participants play, how they interact with others, and any sense of ownership within the community?

The rules of participation are defined by a number of characteristics, ranging from the technology itself, such as rules that are built into the software, to rules defined by the host. Although the university community has no established moderators or community members who are appointed to moderate the discussion flow, a set of rules has evolved, of which participants maintain a general knowledge and awareness. For example, some of the rules were more explicit, such as the automatic message that is sent each time a user joins the chat room. On the other hand, other rules are learned over time, such as identifying oneself if the username does not clearly indicate real life identity, or not repeating certain discussions outside of the users who were present in the chat room during the specific conversation. Over time, the community can rely on the protocol that has evolved through the sense of flow in the chat room environment. Nonverbal cues are constructed online when participants know one another and learn one another's styles of interactions such that the same type of cue becomes equally transparent. An explicit set of rules and protocol can help to build these intuitive practices. This protocol provides a way to make apparent to all participants the usual nonverbal cues used in turn-taking, and in giving and relinquishing the discussion floor. Once the students become familiar with the protocol, they become self-monitoring and self-regulating. Their ability to facilitate this structure and sustain it emphasizes the importance of building community to create a constructive learning environment.

Guiding the Discussion

Failed exploratory peer-to-peer discussions may occur when ideas are accepted unchallenged or because continuous disputation leads to a breakdown of communication within the group. Exploratory peer discussions rarely broke down in this manner in the university community. As a graduate student community, the learning dynamics are more advanced than those in elementary, high school, or undergraduate classrooms. Failed peer discussions might occur far more frequently in younger learning environments where students are more susceptible to competition or immature group behaviors. In these environments, it would be important to have rules to minimize breakdowns during group communication. These might include guidelines that describe the information, assumptions, tasks, and evaluative criteria for constructive collaborative group work. This could be implemented through the presence of a teacher or teaching assistant within the chat room or a postmortem review of the chat logs on a regular basis in which the dynamics of the group could be studied and improved for future classes. Similarly, the ways in which the backchannel is used in the classroom would influence the types of discussions that took place. One option is to publicly project the chat rooms using one or more screens, where they are separated by comments and questions. In the latter chat room, students could post questions for the teacher. A second option is to use a chat room robot to monitor a channel and provide basic information as well as perform a heuristic analysis of events for postanalysis. For example, entering the command "Define: copernicus" would automatically return a definition from a dictionary lookup robot. A third option is to display the backchannel discussion on the screen in front of the classroom so that students would be less inclined to contribute off-topic postings and would instead focus on the academic discussion. Similarly, a teaching assistant could participate in the backchannel and help facilitate interactions by guiding the discussion and providing scaffolding for the learners.

Assigning Roles

One type of protocol to encourage the development of such rules might be the assigning of roles within the backchannel. Howard Rheingold is designing an innovative new participatory media syllabus (described elsewhere in this series) in which he suggests that assigning roles in a chat room backchannel may help to facilitate order and constructive interactions among students. In an unmoderated chat, students must decide to prioritize a single voice and follow it; in an ideal learning environment, however, all voices would be heard, and none would be disposable, spoken over. Rheingold suggests that students have assigned roles, on a rotated basis, such as "google jockey," "wikipedian," "expert," and "cybrarian." In addition to role assignment, structure in the backchannel may be increased through an informed design of curriculum and uses based on its affordances to minimize disruption and unproductive behavior.

Constructing Culture

A successful learning backchannel must be designed based on the classroom culture in which it is being used. For example, the ways in which a backchannel could be used in a fifth grade classroom will differ significantly from its use in a third-year law class. Teachers may need to implement a more controlled and disciplined environment in younger grades, whereas, law professors could assume that a Socratic teaching method will effectively command their students' full attention and that the backchannel will therefore be used strictly as a knowledge resource, not as a source of distraction. In smaller groups and seminars, the instructor may choose to explicitly relinquish some of his or her control in order to facilitate a more open discussion, although in these cases students must accept the burden of making sure that the discussions are meaningful and productive. In a small seminar, the backchannel will generally be unnecessary because students are supposed to interact in the physical classroom environment. In a large lecture hall, with hundreds of students, a backchannel could become swamped with too many simultaneous users and conversation threads to be of any use. An ideal class size might be between twenty and forty students, where most know each other and are able to develop a community and sense of trust in their channel, but where there are not so many participants as to weigh it down beyond any academic value.

Teaching Teachers

Education researchers have long emphasized the fact that technology in itself cannot improve instruction.[42] However, technology can enhance the effectiveness of a good instructional design.[43] Many teachers will be more likely to adopt chat room technology in their classrooms if they are first provided support and instruction on how to use the technology.[44] Teachers may need to teach in shorter cycles to hold students' attention. They should adjust their curriculum and teaching styles to provide different and improved environments for scaffolding than the standard lecture format. As students become more accustomed to multitasking in their everyday activities, teachers may find that they need to redesign their teaching styles in order to keep their students engaged. For example, they could intersperse lectures with group activities and individual activities, allotting shorter time spans to each section. A tighter integration of the backchannel may require their lectures to be more permeable, and the right level of focus and formality will need to be determined. As student's learning styles evolve over time and with changes in technology, teachers can adjust their skill sets in order to facilitate ongoing engagement.

Conclusion: The Backchannel, Up Front

The backchannel in the classroom offers an exciting innovative space for a new learning paradigm. There are a number of salient factors that can be taken advantage of to construct a positive learning environment in the classroom. However, as has been shown, it is not a panacea in itself, but must instead be understood within the greater context of its use for it to offer an improved learning experience for youth. This includes the cultural influences within this technology-mediated learning environment, such as ethnicity, gender, access, experience using technology, and individual student personalities and learning styles. Lessons learned through repeated histories of technological determinism remind us that technology does not have inherent preexisting manifestations, but that meaning and implications emerge as computers and social actors come together in different communities. Innovations in its use are only enabled through a complex interplay of multiple requisite behaviors, practices, and external factors. If we can tease out the variable uses of the medium and understand how they influence its construction as an artifact, then can we encourage innovative and unexpected uses? And for that matter, do we want to? Are youths' innovations with digital media a naturally evolving learning opportunity with an embedded unpredictable and exploratory nature that we should encourage? The institutional contexts of the backchannel are multilayered and complex—from teacher to student to school to parent to district to national standards.

Will Richardson, a teacher, author, and educational researcher, suggests that "shouldn't we hear what [students] are saying, that in a world where the answers to the test are easily accessible that *the test becomes irrelevant*?"[45] Students need to learn how to share ideas and knowledge ethically and appropriately. They need to take ideas that they are taught and make them their own, by exploring and massaging them into their own experiences, as the university students often did on the university backchannel. Richardson continues that, "we need to say to kids 'here is what is important to know, but to learn from it, you need to take it and make it your own, *not just tell it back to me*. Find your own meaning, your own relevance. Make connections outside of these four walls, *because you can and you should and you will*.'"[46] The balance of power in the classroom can be mutually constructed by the student and teacher if both parties are able to facilitate constructive discourse about rules and roles of the backchannel in the classroom. Younger students may not have the experience online through which to develop their own learning environment, although their varied levels of engagement and learning within these environments can be used as a metric for designing the most productive educational experience. As students develop the ability for metacognitive self-reflection on their own experiences, they are better equipped to design and coconstruct their ideal personal learning activities by taking advantage of the varied opportunities that the backchannel can facilitate.

The backchannel may therefore enable a type of education that is progressive but meaningful and has long been needed in the American school system. "It means basing instruction on the needs, interests and developmental stage of the child; it means teaching students the skills they need in order to learn any subject, instead of focusing on transmitting a particular subject; it means promoting discovery and self-directed learning by the student through active engagement; it means having students work on projects that express student purposes."[47] This notion of constructivism may be the ticket to avoiding the learning paradox that plagues much of student motivation in the classroom. Once a student knows how to complete a task, he or she is no longer motivated to learn or participate in that task, and performance in that task will not improve. However, the organic, evolving, and ever-changing dynamics in the backchannel prevent students from succumbing to this sense of stagnancy in learning. Students may be encouraged to learn through a self-motivated eagerness to explore the opportunities and novelties offered by the backchannel on an ongoing basis. Furthermore, as an online, Web-based medium, it allows youth to continuously refine their existing media practices in parallel to their backchannel use. As digital natives, they can produce, consume, remix, and generate their own learning opportunities. They may truly be creating their own classroom of the future.

Notes

1. Digital Media Essay Contest (DMEC), Global Kids' Digital Media Initiative 2006, supported by the John D. and Catherine T. MacArthur Foundation, http://globalkids.org/olp/dmec/.

2. Ibid.

3. Ibid.

4. Campbell and Pargas 2003; D. Franklin and K. Hammond, The Intelligent Classroom: Providing Competent Assistance, in *Proceedings of Autonomous Agents* (Montreal, Canada, May, 2001),

(ACM Press, 2001), 161–168; M. Ratto, R. B. Shapiro, T. M. Truong, and W. G. Griswold, The Activeclass Project: Experiments in Encouraging Classroom Participation, in *Computer Support for Collaborative Learning* 2003; H. Hembrooke and G. Gay, The Laptop and the Lecture: The Effects of Multitasking in Learning Environments, *Journal of Computing in Higher Education* 15, no. 1 (2003).

5. J. F. McCarthy and d. m. boyd, Digital Backchannels in Shared Physical Spaces: Experiences at an Academic Conference, in *CHI '05 Extended Abstracts on Human Factors in Computing Systems (Portland, OR, April 2–7, 2005),* 1641–1644 (New York: ACM Press, 2005).

6. P. Freire, *Pedagogy of the Oppressed* (Harmondsworth, UK: Penguin, 1992).

7. http://www.ed.gov/nclb/landing.jhtml.

8. http://thomas.loc.gov/cgi-bin/query/z?c109:H.R.5319.

9. A. Lenhart and M. Madden, *Social Networking Websites and Teens: An Overview* (Washington, DC: Pew Internet & American Life Project, 2007), http://www.pewinternet.org/PPF/r/198/report_display.asp.

10. Digital Media Essay Contest, 2006.

11. Ibid.

12. H. Rheingold, *Smart Mobs: The Next Social Revolution* (Cambridge, MA: Perseus Books, 2002).

13. Jack Vinson, More Backchannel Via CSCW, *Knowledge Jolt with Jack* 2004, http://blog.jackvinson.com/archives/2004/12/02/more_backchannel_via_cscw.html.

14. Steven Johnson, *Emergence: The Connected Lives of Ants, Brains, Cities, and Software* (New York: Scribner, 2001).

15. J. Bruner, *Toward a Theory of Instruction* (Cambridge, MA: Harvard University Press, 1966).

16. National Research Council, *Science Teaching Reconsidered: A Handbook* (Washington, DC: National Academy Press, 1997).

17. J. Brown, A. Collins, and P. Duguid, Situated Cognition and the Culture of Learning, *Educational Researcher* 18, no. 1 (1989): 18–42.

18. T. Kennedy, E. Golub, B. Stroope, K. Kee, A. Powell, and S. Zehnder, Wireless Communication in the Classroom: A "Back Channel" to the Learning Process? paper presented at Internet Research 6.0: Internet Generations (Chicago: 2005).

19. All names and direction quotations are changed to maintain anonymity

20. McCarthy and boyd, "Digital backchannels in shared physical spaces."

21. M. B. Kinzie, S. D. Whitaker, and M. J. Hofer, Instructional Uses of Instant Messaging (IM) During Classroom Lectures, *Educational Technology & Society* 8, no. 2 (2005): 150–160.

22. D. Cohen, Digital Note-Passing Gains Respect Among Adults, *USA Today*, 2005, http://www.usatoday.com/tech/products/services/2004-11-26-im-gains-cred_x.htm.

23. J. F. McCarthy, d. boyd, E. F. Churchill, W. G. Griswold, E. Lawley, and M. Zaner. Digital backchannels in Shared Physical Spaces: Attention, Intention and Contention, in *Proceedings of the 2004 ACM Conference on Computer Supported Cooperative Work (Chicago, November 6–10, 2004),* 550–553 (New York: ACM Press, 2004).

24. David Labaree, Progressivism, Schools and Schools of Education: An American Romance, *Paedagogica Historica* 41, nos. 1,2 (2005): 275–288.

25. R. West and J. C. Pearson, Antecedent and Consequent Conditions of Student Questioning: An Analysis of Classroom Discourse Across the University, *Communication Education* 43 (1994): 299–311.

26. K. Phalen, Taking a Minus and Making it a Plus, *Information Technology & Communication* 7, no. 1 (2003).

27. Ibid.

28. Kennedy et al., "Wireless Communication in the Classroom."

29. Phalen, "Taking a Minus."

30. D. DeGennaro, Should We Ban Instant Messaging in School? *Learning and Leading with Technology* 32, no. 7 (2005).

31. S. Turkle, *Life on the Screen: Identity in the Age of the Internet* (New York: Simon & Schuster, 1995); B. Wellman and M. Gulia, Virtual Communities as Communities: Net Surfers Don't Ride Alone, in *Communities in Cyberspace*, eds. M. Smith and P. Kollock (New York: Routledge, 1999), 167–189; Etienne Wenger, *Communities of Practice: Learning, Meaning, and Identity* (Cambridge, UK: Cambridge University Press, 1998).

32. Ross Mayfield, Social Networks, Jobs & the Third Place, *Ross Mayfield's Weblog*, 2003, http://ross.typepad.com/blog/2003/08/social_networks.html.

33. J. Pyysiainen, Building Trust in Global Inter-organizational Software Development Projects: Problems and Practices, in *Proceedings of the International Workshop on Global Software Development* (ICSE, 2003).

34. R. Oldenburg, *The Great Good Place: Cafés, Coffee Shops, Community Centers, Beauty Parlors, General Stores, Bars, Hangouts and how They get you Through the Day* (New York: Marlowe & Company, 1989).

35. D. Abrahamson, What's a Situation in Situated Cognition? A Constructionist Critique of Authentic Inquiry, in *Proceedings of the Seventh International Conference of the Learning Sciences* (ICLS), eds. S. Barab, K. Hay, and D. Hickey (Bloomington, IN: ICLS, 2006).

36. Ibid.

37. Jochen Rick and Mark Guzdial, Situating CoWeb: A Scholarship of Application, *International Journal of Computer-Supported Collaborative Learning* 1, no. 1 (2006): 89.

38. Freire, *Pedagogy of the Oppressed*.

39. Craig Smith, Synchronous Discussion in Online Courses: A Pedagogical Strategy for Taming the Chat Beast. http://www.innovateonline.info/index.php?view=article&id=246&action=article.

40. G. Motteram, The Role of Synchronous Communication in Fully Distance Education, *Australian Journal of Educational Technology* 17, no. 2 (2001): 131–149.

41. M. Pimentel, H. Fuks, and C. J. P. Lucena, Mediated Chat Development Process: Avoiding Chat Confusion on Educational Debates, in *Proceedings of Computer Supported Collaborative Learning (CSCL) 2005*, eds. G. Stahl and D. Suthers (Mahwah, NJ: Lawrence Erlbaum Associates, 2005), 499–503.

42. D. Hestenes, M. Wells, and G. Swackhamer, Force Concept Inventory, *The Physics Teacher* 30 (1992): 141–158.

43. C. Hoadley and N. Enyedy, Between Information and Communication: Middle Spaces in Computer Media for Learning, in *Proceedings of the Third International Conference on Computer Support for Collaborative Learning*, eds. C. Hoadley and J. Roschelle (1999), 242–251.

44. L. Cuban, *Teachers & Machines: The Classroom Use of Technology Since 1920* (New York: Teachers College Press, 1988).

45. Will Richardson, Weblogg-ed. What Do We Do About That? 2005, http://www.weblogg-ed.com/2005/10/25#a4126.

46. Ibid.

47. Labaree, "Progressivism, Schools and Schools of Education," 275.

Found Technology: Players as Innovators in the Making of Machinima

Henry Lowood

Stanford University, University Libraries

. . . while to adults the Internet primarily means the world wide web, for children it means email, chat, games—and here they are already content producers. Too often neglected, except as a source of risk, these communication and entertainment-focused activities, by contrast with the information-focused uses at the centre of public and policy agendas, are driving emerging media literacy. . . . Bearing in mind that the elite realm of high culture has already been breached, who is to say that this form of content creation counts for little?—Sonia Livingstone[1]

The focus of this essay is a new narrative medium, called machinima, which has sprung out of computer game technology and play since the mid-1990s. Machinima is "filmmaking within a real time, 3D virtual environment."[2] This means producing animated movies with the software that is used to develop and play computer games. The growth of machinima as a creative medium within digital game culture certainly reveals much about the creativity of players. Homing in on machinima as a form of player-driven innovation also teaches us lessons about how and what players learn from game technology and gameplay, how they share knowledge about what they learn, and how these engagements lead them to come to grips with issues that threaten to limit the potential of machinima as an expressive medium. Player creativity and innovation then is the focus of this investigation of machinima as an outgrowth of computer game culture. Computer games are providing new opportunities for performance and expression mediated by computers and networks; players enjoy game-based replay movies and machinima videos, and they are equally fascinated by the activities of the player behind them as they try to understand the mix of skills and tricks that go into making them. Put another way, the development of machinima over roughly a decade is about how players have learned to master computer technology, gameplay, and performance practices. How players have learned to be creative may well be the most significant story in game culture today.

Introduction: Koulamata's "The French Democracy"

For many observers outside game culture, perhaps the first visible example of the expressive power unlocked by machinima was provided by a game-based movie created in November of 2005, Koulamata's "The French Democracy."[3] The story behind its creation shows us that community players—players who create and circulate game-based performances within communities of game players—can contribute to public discourse about current events. This is an important enough claim, but just as significantly, "The French Democracy" provides a convincing example for another assertion: machinima has become accessible, putting a

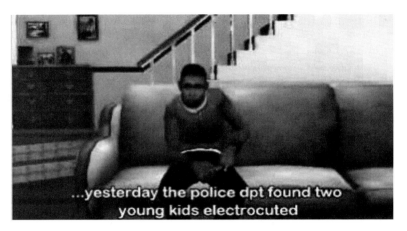

Figure 1
Koulamata (Alex Chan), "The French Democracy" (2005).

powerful technology for real-time animation production in the hands of a widening circle of players. In other words, digital games and game technology have a place among new media forms that have translated entertainment technologies into engines for the creation of content. Sonia Livingstone has described the impact of networked media in empowering children and young adults as "content producers." The example of Koulamata's "The French Democracy" suggests that game-based moviemaking is capable of empowering a variety of age groups as moviemakers.

Let us begin by taking a closer look at Koulamata's project. In late October 2005, riots broke out in the largely African and Arab Parisian suburb of Clichy-sous-Bois and other parts of France after incendiary remarks by Interior Minister Nicolas Sarkozy and the electrocution of two teenagers fleeing from police in an electrical substation. These riots spread and smoldered for about two weeks, reaching a peak between November 6 and 8, followed by the declaration of emergency powers on November 9 to quell the violence. Concurrently, on November 8, Peter Molyneux's Lionhead Studios in England released a game called *The Movies,* part Hollywood studio simulation, part toolkit for making animated movies by setting up simple scenes and manipulating actor avatars. The obvious reason for players to make these movies is that as virtual studio heads, that became their job within the simulation space. However, many players found a different reason to play the game: they figured out how to move straight to the movie studio and the production of movies. This was no surprise to Molyneux, who revealed that "one of the dreams for the game was that as you play, you realize you could direct a movie of your own."[4] His vision of the player as creator was confirmed within days of the game's release, as dozens and then hundreds of movies were posted to Lionhead's community Web site. About two months after the game's release, more than 3,000 movies were already available for viewing on this site[5] alone. Over a year later, in November 2006, movies were still being uploaded to this Web site at a rate of nearly seventy per day, not to mention those posted to viral media and other distribution points on the World Wide Web.[6]

Back in the Parisian suburb of Seine-Saint-Denis, twenty-seven–year-old Alex Chan, a freelance industrial designer with absolutely no experience making movies, decided to buy *The Movies* and make his own filmic statement about the French riots. It was still mid-November 2005; the turmoil was just subsiding around Paris and the game was brand new. These two unrelated facts were connected by Chan's drive to craft an immediate response to the events around him. As Chan put it himself, "through these tools you can get some more spontaneous reaction or reflection, not from mass media, but from a simple citizen like me."[7] Remarkably, under the name Koulamata, he was able to post his thirteen-minute movie to the Lionhead site on November 22, hardly two weeks after both the end of the riots and the release of the game. His movie told several stories about the victimization of French minority groups through harassment, job discrimination, and daily events in an attempt to explain the tensions and emotions that fueled the riots. Despite awkward English-language subtitles and cinematography—or perhaps because of these qualities—the movie comes across as immediate and authentic, directly striking a heartfelt note of sorrow for the loss of French historical ideals such as liberty and fraternity. MTV News admitted that the first film about these events came "courtesy of a video game."

"The French Democracy" was rapidly distributed through numerous game Web sites, blogs, and movie download sites on the Web and ignited a passionate discussion on "The Movies" Web site and elsewhere. On the Lionhead site, for example, more than 400 viewers rated the movie within the first six weeks of its release; a year later, in November 2006, viewers were still posting comments. The main thread for discussion of the movie offers a similar number of comments, both in French and English, from the very first posting on November 22 ("Magnifique, tout simplement! Very great job!") to reflections that document the continuing resonance of this project around the world nearly two months later ("I think those events can be linked to our own here in Quebec in 1970 when our own country called the army on us.") These examples document the roles that gameplay and the online forums in which communities of game players gather can powerfully extend participation in public discourse about current events in "real life," not just game culture. They also suggest the new modes of informal learning that were taking place in these forums, as participants traded ideas about the events and the project in ways set up by engagement with the game. News of Koulamata's project also flowed into mainstream media channels. It was covered by a range of outlets from *The Washington Post, USA Today,* MTV.com, and *Business Week* to the important Socialist daily, *Libération*.[8] It was shown widely via viral media and machinima sites on the Web and continued to be shown during 2006 at venues such as the Centre Pompidou's Flash Festival in May and the World Wide Short Film Festival the following June in Toronto.[9] By then, Chan's movie had become something more than a commentary on recent events in his own country. It had become a poster for the potential of machinima as a medium. Paul Marino, a veteran machinima artist and executive director of the Academy of Machinima Arts & Sciences, concluded that Chan's movie had proven "that Machinima can be a powerful medium—showing that it can extend the thoughts of individuals into areas the game developers might not be so quick to embrace."[10] Xavier Lardy, founder of the leading French Web site devoted to machinima, told *USA Today* that "there has never been a machinima with such a clear and prominent political message."[11]

During the unrest and in its aftermath, Jacques Chirac publicly bemoaned a lack of diversity and minority representation in French media. He insisted that mainstream media must "better reflect the reality of France today" precisely as Koulamata was learning to use *The Movies* in order to answer this challenge in his own way.[12] Subsequent discussion in France during December 2005 focused on the specific solution of the hiring of more minority television reporters and newscasters. This proposal was important, but it bypassed equally critical issues surrounding point of view and the power to create new narratives. In this sense, the public discussion missed the contribution of "The French Democracy." Indeed, Chan told reporters that he made a game-based movie in order to bypass mainstream media as well as to correct the errors carried by them. So, the story with regard to Chan's project is that it filled a gap not only in minority representation, but also by utilizing a new format that while under the mainstream media radar, nevertheless responded immediately, was widely viewed, and offered a point of view that was different from what could be seen on established news outlets. The Web-magazine *Alterités* of the Cité nationale de l'histoire de l'immigration, which has highlighted media-related issues of concern to French immigrant groups, pointed out in December that from "blogs to videogames," new media were dedicating themselves to "all the youth of color in the world." Mogniss H. Abdallah cited "The French Democracy" in an article for *Alterités* specifically as evidence that "technological innovations are being used to satisfy the thirst for public expression (expression ambiante)."[13]

It is of course important to acknowledge that the production and circulation of game-based content might open up new means of public and creative expression, and not just for gamers. And yet, reducing a positive assessment of gameplay to its potential for leading to "more serious" forms of activity is neither the only nor the most compelling rationale for turning our attention to machinima. From a strictly historical perspective, this move wrenches the motives of game players out of the original context of their innovative uses of game technology. Overvaluing "serious" goals as an end point of the creative use of entertainment technologies leads to an anachronistic, even Whiggish justification for these uses of technology: the value of those activities *then* is seen through a lens that only shows us their recontextualized value *now*. If that were the only problem, however, perhaps only historians would have reason to be upset. If the payoff of projects like "The French Democracy" adds value to public discourse or creates new outlets for artistic expression, so what if we misread the interests and motivations of the players who created the techniques that can be exploited in this fashion? In fact, there really are important reasons to pay attention to the lessons we might learn from machinima. The first is that it illustrates the full reach of the do-it-yourself culture that has emerged so powerfully from game culture, not just for modifying game technology and content, but also as a move across media technologies from interactive digital games to animated filmmaking. Second, if we fail to contextualize the emergence of the practices associated with machinima production inside player communities, we lose the essential association of these practices to a mix of technology, gameplay, and public performance inside game culture. Perhaps most importantly, the history of machinima provokes discussion of frequently debated points in the valuation of new media associated with "fans, bloggers, and gamers,"[14] as well as others of their ilk: in unlocking game-based moviemaking, what have players learned about connecting innovative uses of technology to the emergence of new cultural modalities made available to them?

This essay addresses these questions by presenting three takes on the development of machinima. *Take One*: What do the origins of game-based moviemaking tell us about the relationship among learning, demonstration, and performance in the uses of technology associated with computer games? The story about how game players learned to make machinima becomes easier to understand when it becomes more than an answer to the question, "who invented machinima?" It also must show how some players learned to use this technology and develop practices of extroverted performance and production around it, as well as how others acquired skills as spectators and began to watch these movies. *Take Two*: How has the status of machinima creators as players and users of game technology redefined them as players—or as "moviemakers"? How has the dependence of machinima on game engines, that is, on a particular technology, interacted with the context of machinima as emerging from game culture and player communities? Following the lead taken by recent technology studies, this take explores not only whether players as consumers matter, but also how *use* matters.[15] I will explore the notion of the "game engine," stabilized in games like *DOOM* and *Quake* that also propelled the creation of replays and machinima, as a "found technology," ready-made for appropriation by players. *Take Three*: As machinima emerges from the geeky edge of game culture, does the context of its creation offer special advantages, or alternatively, noteworthy constraints for convergence with other forms of cultural expression? We know that today a young Frenchman can acquire an animation studio in the form of a commercial game costing about $50. Might "The French Democracy" be a signal that game technology and culture has established new means for cultural and political expression? Or will limitations embedded in this culture ranging from steadfast self-referentiality to scant regard for intellectual property throttle the expansion of machinima spectatorship to a wider audience?

Public Demo: Origins of Game-Based Moviemaking

In December 1993, id Software released the first-person action game *DOOM*. The authors were a group of programmers led by John Romero and John Carmack, who had founded id in February 1991 to develop shareware games for personal computers. From the beginning, Carmack in particular focused on the development of cutting-edge game technology as a platform for frantically paced, competitive action games. *DOOM*'s gameplay, for example, consisted largely of slaughtering (shooting) demons or opponents in the game world. What was innovative about id's games was that they depicted this world as the player's character would see it, from a 3D first-person perspective that was rapidly redrawn as that character moved through the environment. This innovation established a game genre that would dominate the development of game technology during the 1990s: the "first-person shooter" (FPS).

DOOM immediately left its imprint on almost every aspect of computer gaming, from graphics and networking technology to styles of play, notions of authorship, and public scrutiny of content. Id followed up, in June 1996, with the release of *Quake*, built on the modes of competitive play introduced with *DOOM*. *Quake* was a technological tour de force. Its built-in client/server networking was an improvement over the peer-to-peer networking in *DOOM*, greatly stimulating the popularity of internet-based multiplayer games. *Quake* also offered what is generally acknowledged as the first graphics engine capable of providing true 3D graphics.[16] The reception of *DOOM* and *Quake* offers an object lesson in the importance of distinguishing public reactions to game content from practices associated with the use of technology provided by the same games. The subject matter of *DOOM* (bloody, rapid-fire killing of demons in outer space), its moody graphics and audio, and the vocabulary associated with its gameplay ("shooters," "death match") increased public attention to the levels of violence depicted in computer games. Coincidentally, the game was released just as congressional hearings convened by senators Herb Kohl and Joseph Lieberman were getting underway to examine media violence and its influence on children, and of course a few years later *DOOM* came under particularly close scrutiny in connection with the tragic shootings at Columbine High School. The portrayal of computer games such as *DOOM* or *Quake* as "murder simulators"[17] and "bloodlust" games obviously reflected on players, who were often portrayed as disconnected and desensitized, or as engaged in mindless, repetitive, or addictive play.

I do not mean here to enter debates about the presentation of violent content in computer games or its effects on players. I am looking instead at how *DOOM* and especially *Quake* opened up the medium of the computer game to unexpected kinds of player creativity. Practices associated with FPS play and the technical configuration of these games together made new modes of creative play possible, among which were making animated movies using id's real-time graphics engines. What was it about these games' technology that inspired player creativity? In order to answer this question, we have to begin with the idea of the "game engine" as worked out by Carmack. Inspired by programming hacks that altered games, such as the "Barney patch" for Silas Warner's original *Castle Wolfenstein* (Muse Software, 1981), he had often altered computer games as a teenager. He built modifiability into *DOOM,* but in a manner that simplified the process and didn't require such hacks. He did this by separating the core "game engine" from the code for specific "levels" of the game defined by maps, objects, monsters, graphics, sound, and so on, which came to be called the "game assets." The explicit intention of this separation was to make it possible for players to create their own content by designing their own maps or "levels." Level-specific information was captured in so-called "wad" files, which were loaded separately into the game to play these levels; editing or creating wad files changed a game's content without hacking at the game engine. It thus protected critical software code that produced fundamental functionalities of the game, such as graphics or physics. Carmack's design decision to separate game engine from assets spawned independent and third-party level design, as id expected, and encouraged the development of software tools to make new content, whether by id, other companies, or players.[18] The game engine also represented a new business model for id, now positioned as a game technology company as well as a game developer. Standardizing game production also opened up the gates for a flood of player-created content, which in turn would extend the commercial life of the game. According to id's own corporate history:

The team of innovators also made *DOOM*'s source code available to their fan base, encouraging would-be game designers to modify the game and create their own levels, or 'mods.' Fans were free to distribute their mods of the game, as long as the updates were offered free of charge to other enthusiasts. The mod community took off, giving the game seemingly eternal life on the Internet.[19]

Beginning with *DOOM,* much of the fun began after an FPS game was published, as players (and other independent designers) would create their own levels and maps, or modify other game assets. Computer games such as *Quake* essentially could function as design tools, and learning how to use id's software to make mods, even the smallest personalization of the game, became part of the player's engagement. This also meant a "letting go of authorial control" by game developers that media curator Randall Packer has called a distinguishing characteristic of computer games, in contrast to other artistic or entertainment media.[20] And why not give up some of this control? Carmack was particularly skeptical about the game designer as auteur, arguing in one widely circulated statement that "there is not a hell of a lot of difference between what the best designer in the world produces, and what quite a few reasonably clued in players would produce at this point."[21] Indeed, players came to see customization of *Quake* as another way to show other players the superiority of their skills.

Carmack's configuration of the game engine and assets was not the only aspect of his games that unexpectedly led to game-based moviemaking. The other was more closely tied to gameplay than game development. *DOOM* could be played as a single player or even as a cooperative game, but it also introduced a new mode of competitive play devised by id cofounder John Romero called "deathmatch." Players connected via Local Area Networks to

Figure 2
The Rangers, "Diary of a Camper" (1996).

compete by recording kills (or "frags") against opponents. *Quake* was fundamentally a multi-player and competitive game, and was playable over the Internet. Immediately after *Quake*'s release, players formed groups held together by its improved multiplayer connectivity and chat options. Like hacker gangs dissecting the intricacies of computer networks, these *Quake* Clans shared techniques of high-performance gaming, both play *and* programming. Multi-player was not just linking up to frag opponents online; it also described chat, discussion, and sharing of exploits *among* players. Competition led to community; networked death match led to networks of players. The Ranger Clan provides a telling example. Arguably the most famous clan of all, its top-notch players also helped shape the *Quake*'s technically inclined community. They had participated in the first prerelease test of the *Quake* engine. One member designed the original Capture the Flag mod; another founded one of the major sources of information about *Quake* development, Blue's News; in all, about half the twenty-five or so members remained active in game development or went on to work in the game industry.[22] Being in such a clan meant being a community player; it meant visibly performing skills and demonstrating abilities, showing how to do things, spreading information, and building software tools and content to share with other players. With their reputation for stellar performances as players and programmers firmly established, the Rangers surprised the *Quake* community in October 1996 with a new kind of exploit. Barely a month after its commercial release, they circulated a movie made inside *Quake*, "Diary of a Camper." It established id's first-person shooter as the first platform for game-based movies, known for several years simply as *Quake* movies.

These *Quake* movies were closely related to a form of in-game performance known as the demonstration or "demo" movie. The demo as a means of performance, skills certification, and training runs through the history of computer game culture. It goes back to *Spacewar!*, arguably the first modern computer game. Developed at M.I.T. in 1962 by a group led by

Figure 3
NoSkill, *DOOM2* demo, 1995.

Steve Russell, *Spacewar!* established the computer game as a method for demonstrating the capabilities of computers. Russell's group disdained previous methods for showing off what a computer could do and believed that a good demonstration "should involve the onlooker in a pleasurable and active way—in short, it should be a game."[23] *Spacewar!* did just that, showcasing the new PDP-1 computer, its graphics, I/O, and display technology; the M.I.T. group confidently told the new PDP users' community that *Spacewar!* "amply demonstrates the real-time capabilities of the PDP-1" and verified its "excellent performance."[24] But at the same time as it showed what computers could do, this game demonstrated the technical mastery of programmers and hardware hackers. An immensely popular competitive game available in any U.S. computer science laboratory of the 1960s and 1970s, *Spacewar!*'s community of programmers and players grew rapidly. Stewart Brand, writing in the early 1970s, considered this game to be a "flawless crystal ball of things to come in computer science and computer use." He cited it as evidence of a new culture, part coproduction, part player performance. In "days of batch processing and consumerism," it was a "heresy, uninvited and unwelcome. The hackers made *Spacewar!*, not the planners."[25]

So public demonstration as a mode of computer-based performance was associated with computer games right from their origins in academic computer science laboratories. *Spacewar!* players demonstrated computer-mediated performance through play. Recasting the player as a performer settled into not one, but two predominant modes: the superior player, the God of the joystick and mouse, and the player-programmer able to hack into game code and show off mastery of the technology. Both sorts of performance occurred as public demonstrations in ways that would later influence the use of games to make movies, while also illustrating the degree to which important kinds of experimentation and informal learning have long accompanied computer gaming.

Technically, *DOOM* demos were essentially replay files, saved sequences of instructions from a previously played game that, when executed by the game software, would show the same game from the same (first-person) perspective of the original player. As one guide put it, "in the *DOOM/DOOM II* universe, the term "demo" refers to a file that contains a recorded session of gameplay."[26] *DOOM* demos demonstrated player skills. The rapid action of *DOOM* as a multiplayer, competitive game; the growth of a networked player community, and the technology of the replay facility all came together in the demo to establish a performer–spectator relationship. A critical aspect of this relationship was a learning experience. *DOOM* required skills. Some players excelled in marksmanship, others in movement tricks, others in stealth and the psychology of stalking their opponents. Star players emerged, and mere mortals wanted to see these "*DOOM* Gods" play, to gather insights into their play tactics and learn how to improve the quality of their own play. As BahdKo, a veteran of the *DOOM* demo scene points out, "Use of demos for their educational value has been going on since almost the beginning." Demonstrations of skill by admired players such as NoSkill, XoLeRaS, and Smight circulated widely. In a typical use of these movies, "a new player who wants to get better requests that a game with a higher-skilled player be recorded, and then the new player watches the demo (where presumably he lost) from the higher-skilled player's point of view, hoping to learn ways to improve his own skill. Such a player is then able to plainly compare his own movement, aim, and possibly strategic ideas with those of the higher-skilled player, enabling him to practice on his own in order to improve or otherwise attempt to adjust his own performance."[27] Single-player, death match, and clan demo movies certified the status of star players while helping everyday players compare and improve their abilities. Beginning in 1994, the Doom Honorific Title (DHT) Program, a game rating system, became "the means by which good players can objectively prove to the world that they are as good as they claim."[28] The certification process explicitly promoted the performance of gameplay through demo movies. Another project, COMPET-N, started in 1994 to collect demos and a variation of them known as speedruns (completing a game or game level as quickly as possible), joined before long by the Public Demo Archive of the Non Gods, DOOMed Speed Demos Archive, and other collections of demo movies established so that players could find demonstrations of any skill or game level. Establishing a basis for spectatorship through recorded gameplay fed back on the growth of the player community as well. *DOOM* clans sought to establish reputations through demos just as individual players did. These various practices of showing, viewing, and learning via *DOOM* replays showed that multiplayer collaboration could be derived from competition.[29]

Evidently, the notion of the demonstration is fraught with implications for the computer game as a site for skill performance, certification, and acquisition. This was again the case in the distinctive scene associated with a particular kind of demonstration program known simply as the "demo." These demos were noninteractive animated movies, in the sense that they combined sights and sounds, and like *DOOM* and *Quake* demos, they were typically generated in real time. The main difference between demo movies and demos is that the so-called demoscene emerged from practices of game piracy and hacking of the 1980s, particularly on home computers such as the Apple II and Commodore 64. By then, the open, cooperative culture of game design associated with computer science laboratories, games such as *Spacewar!* and *Adventure* or the people's computing movement of the 1970s, had collided with a business culture founded on proprietary development and the closed technology of the game cartridge. The failure of the Atari generation of console manufacturers coincided with the success of games such as *Pac-Man*, intellectual properties controlled by closed industrial studios that produced games to be played not toyed with. The next generation of companies, led by Nintendo, carefully guarded their console technology and intellectual property. Games published for home computers followed this business model for the most

Figure 4
A crack screen.

part, but with the important difference that it was possible, and often acceptable (at least among players) to copy software acquired on formats such as audio cassettes and floppy disks. This provided an opening for players to create an ironically clandestine sort of open culture around computer and video games. The availability of BASIC interpreters built into most of these machines provided the often irresistible temptation, particularly among younger users of home computers, of not just copying, but often altering software as a form of resistance, the 1980s version of taking computer power to the people.

As players acquired the chops for disassembling and rebuilding programs, defeating copy protection schemes or cracking code became means for modifying games or simply for un-licensed, free distribution. Some crackers, as they came to be called, with names like the German Cracking Service, AEK Crackware Essen 2099, 1103, or JEDI, acquired reputations as masters of code that circulated with the copied games; we have already seen that repu-tations are important in the social networks of players. Crackers documented their prowess when they added credits or load screens to the beginning of games they marked as having been opened up by them. Like tattoos on the body or sprayed tags on a city wall, these introductions became personal (or group) signatures. They also became a basis for compe-tition among crackers. They played a new game with the goal of being the first to post a newly cracked version publicly. This competition intensified during the late 1980s as copy protection systems began to provide more intelligent opponents on this playing field. After cracking a new game, groups celebrated each exploit with ever more elaborate and visually impressive title or load screens, including graphics, sounds, and even animations. These cracktros (cracker intros) became a self-standing form of hacker performance, the cinematic "demo," on emerging multimedia platforms such as the Commodore 64 and Amiga, the Atari ST and the PC.

Demoscene groups began to compete publicly, especially in Europe and California. Their programs were turned into real-time multimedia shows of coding prowess, not just intros

Figure 5
Axios Copy Party Announcement, 1988.

but standalone graphics-and-sound productions lasting roughly as long as a music video or even longer. At a live demoparty (originally known as a copyparty), greatness was no longer demonstrated simply by being the fastest to crack software, it also meant putting on a good party, sharing and socializing; being the best was not just about cracking the most games, it also meant providing an exquisite, yet tightly coded presentation, doing it within prescribed constraints such as available memory or a particular console or home computer platform, and sharing it.[30] The founder of the cracker group Sledgehammer (SLH, interviewed by JS) described its social network:

JS: How old are you?

SLH: I am 22 years old (22-10-65)

JS: When did you found Hotline?

SLH: I founded HOTLINE in beginning of August 1986.

JS: How many members does HTL have at the moment?

SLH: HOTLINE has now 15 members!

JS: What was your first crack?

SLH: It was DONKEY KONG from OCEAN!

JS: How many swappartners do you have?

SLH: 10 real ones! 4 in Holland 3 out of them are Hotline members, 1 of the SRG, POPEYE in Denmark and 5 guys in England. I swap by express with them!

JS: How many packages do you send per week?

SLH: 4 express ones and 26 or 27 to the rest![31]

The demoscene fed off the same impulses as other forms of game-based skill demonstration, while showing another move from playful competition to exhibition, and from mastery of computing technology to creation of new social and performative spaces defined by computer games and their players. As a few years later with game-modding or machinima, players learned about demos from demos, and they kept right on learning when they gathered together (whether in parties or online). Curiously, this very public demo culture within various player communities remained one of its best-kept secrets, because the cost of entry was exactly the high level of involvement, motivation, and time commitment that nurtured the demo as the center of an informal learning network. It was probably not until the mid-1990s perhaps that modding connected demo culture both to mainstream game technology (via the standardized game engine) and to the game industry (via targeted recruiting). But demo coders nevertheless learned skills of direct relevance to eventual careers in the game industry, and many of them moved in that direction. As one coder put it, "at the time I did it for 'the love of the code,' not because I planned to get into the games industry. Being part of the scene you also get to discuss your ideas with other people, and show off, which all helps improve your skills. Also, you get some experience with building something through working with a few other people, both other coders and 'arty types,' which is just like the real world."[32] At the same time, these same practices set the stage for *Quake* movies and machinima by completing the idea of the demonstration program in an important way. In the demoscene, the hacker was no longer demonstrating technology; he was demonstrating the hacker, and it was his performance that mattered. The public demo as skills demonstration set the stage for game-based moviemaking.

From *Quake* Movies to Machinima: Players as Moviemakers

So, was machinima invented by game developers or players? Did the player clans who made the first *Quake* movies simply connect the dots from real-time play to real-time moviemaking, or did they only see this possibility through immersion in the practices and community of multiplayer gaming? Was machinima an invention or an innovative use of existing technology? We have seen so far that game-based moviemaking emerged from an existing culture of performance that included showing, sharing, and competing in forms enabled by real-time competition, replays, and skill demonstration. But is it necessary to separate practices emerging from what we typically call the "culture" of computer games from those directly enabled—or constrained—by innovation in computer game technology? Not at all. Game-based performance and spectatorship associated with machinima depended on specific design decisions (e.g., Carmack's architecture of the game engine), but at the same time they were unlocked by players. These players were users of game technology who discovered rather than invented new uses for it.[33] Their excitement about exploiting, hacking, and demonstrating uses of game technology emerged out of engagement with computers—a form of engagement that can only be described as playful, but can also be recognized as a powerful mode of informal learning.

Following the model introduced by id Software, game developers produce or utilize software called "game engines" to manage sophisticated real-time graphics, physics, lighting, camera views and other facets of their games. Games are interactive; prerendered animation has limited applicability in software that must immediately respond and redraw the screen in response to player actions.[34] Fast-paced action games drawn from the dynamic perspective of the player/avatar—first-person shooters being the exemplar—significantly increased the technical challenge for game developers. In order to immerse the player in the rapid action of the game, FPS developers had to render a compelling 3D space from the player's point of view. Software (later, with the assistance of specialized graphics boards) constantly recalculates and rerenders at high frame rates as the player's character moves through that space. The insight that led to Quake movies and machinima was to see this technology as providing a robust system for real-time animation production, as opposed to the painstakingly drawn (whether by hand or server farm) animation delivered, say, by artists at Pixar or Disney studios.

This is not to say that game developers and programmers missed or ignored the potential of their games for making animated movies. They were busy enough making computer games, to be sure, but more fundamentally, moviemaking with games was a user-driven innovation. It was another form of play that evolved out of the particular context of multiplayer, competitive games and the forms of demonstration, learning, and performance that grew out of technologies and communities associated with those games. We can see the impact of competitive play more clearly in an idea that predated Quake movies, that of the "game film." This notion opens game-based moviemaking up to replay, and from there to other forms of mediated or archival performance, such as televised sports spectatorship (introduced as Ampex's "instant replay," first utilized by CBS in a football game telecast in 1965). It is also connected to practices of "proto-performance,"[35] such as rehearsal and training, both in dramatic performance and, especially, in sports (such as the football team that spends endless hours "studying game film"). Dani Bunten Berry, the designer of the head-to-head multiplayer strategy games *Modem Wars* (1988), *Command HQ* (1990), and *Global Conquest* (1992), brought this idea to game development. Berry designed these games to reward hand eye coordination and interface mastery as well as strategic thinking, so that "each person had their own specialized style of play." The technical design made it possible to store data from which replays, or "game film" as Berry called it, could be created. Players could watch these movies to rerun and study their performance. Supporting this kind of informal learning was precisely the role that replays played later in the *DOOM* community. Berry also noticed the ease with which players slipped back and forth between the replay as learning material and as a story about games remembered. She was amazed at "how people used this opportunity the game films offered to rationalize their loss and to create stories out of the intense and ephemeral experience of the battle." Berry believed that player communities would thrive on replay's capacity to make "legends out of their best performances."[36] Game film was included in both *Command HQ* and *Global Conquest*, but the vision would not be realized until multiplayer social and computer networks required for making the reputations of community players were more closely synchronized with replay technology, that is, until *DOOM* and *Quake*.

Over and over, already, we have seen that demonstrating skills through competitive player performance was behind the replay captured as a demo movie; learning about gameplay through replay implied practices of spectatorship, witnessing, and certification. They both provided means and motives for community players—again, players who put on their own display for other players—to learn more about how to record their gameplay. Not only were replays usually circulated as skill demonstrations, but the very code that made *Quake* movies possible was embedded in something called a "demo" format and saved in a DEM file (with a filename ending .dem). This convention was carried forward from *DOOM* to many other games: *Quake/Hexen, Half-Life, Unreal Tournament,* and so on. The Rangers' "Diary of a Camper" resembled the demo movies of *DOOM* gameplay, with short bursts of frantic action punctuated by flying blood and bits of body parts. Yet, "Diary of a Camper" broke with the *DOOM* demo movie in one essential respect: the independence of the spectator's view from that of any player/actor. Their movie was not "shot" from the first-person perspective of the shooter. An independent camera view framed the action. This innovation illustrates *Quake*'s significance as a platform for high-performance play. Strictly speaking, *DOOM* demos were not really movies. Rather, they were sequences of commands or scripts that told the game engine what to do essentially by repeating the effects of keyboard and mouse input in the same sequence as the player had. One consequence of the separation of game engine from asset files in Carmack's architecture was that the demo or "intro" movie was stored in a discreet file with its own format, the LMP ("lump") file. This was a game asset in the form of the gameplay movie shown when a player started up the game. Players could also record their own game sessions as demos and play them back inside the game by loading and running these LMP files. Due to the design architecture, making these movies required no hacking of the game engine, in effect creating a new performance space. This technical change differentiated the makers of *DOOM* and *Quake* demo movies from previous modes of game-based performance.

The real-time animation engine inside the computer game was discovered by players, who found the technology and learned to use it to produce animated movies in a new way. Certainly, it was the game developers who built this technology, but they did not foresee this application of it, which was instead discovered, tested, and improved by those players. Uwe Girlich became the leading technical authority on *Quake* moviemaking; he found in his analysis of its new demo format that "player coordinates and the camera positions may be different," in other words, that different camera views could be presented in replay demos. This discovery led him to observe that, "for people with too much spare-time *Quake* can replace a full 3D modelling system for cartoons or the like."[37] When the Rangers figured out how to move cameras in *Quake,* they programmed their own tools to do this, thus demonstrating coding skills alongside gameplay. Girlich showed how this approach could be taken a step further, focusing on careful analysis of *Quake*'s architecture and operation, especially the demo format and network protocol; he revealed what he discovered to the player community and provided tools such as the "Little Movie Processing Center" for replay recording in *DOOM* and other games. Others followed his lead, notably David "CRT" Wright, who wrote the Keygrip and Keygrip2 utilities for "no compromise demo editing," that is, postproduction work on *Quake* movies.[38] Clearly, these contributions to *Quake* moviemaking were another mode of game-based performance, as these code mechanics opened up the hood of the game engine and revealed their talents by unlocking capabilities hidden inside the *Quake* programming code. *Diary of a Camper* used the Rangers' homebrew tools, but later projects drew increasingly on a reservoir of knowledge and skills shared with a growing community of players and moviemakers. Players were once again demonstrating multiplayer learning derived from demonstration, competition, and collaboration.

During the first year after *Quake*'s release, projects such as the "Quake done Quick" team's filmed "speedruns" and Clan Undead's "Operation Bayshield" showed how playing with the camera in computer games could be enhanced by techniques such as "recamming" (editing demo movies to alter the camera view) and postproduction editing with player-created software tools.[39] Every new project seemed to introduce a technique or push game-based moviemaking forward in some unanticipated way. Once players learned how to redeploy sophisticated game engines to make movies, they began to see themselves as moviemakers. They discovered that their knowledge of play *and* technology translated into acting and directing, literally turning players into "cameras" to make these animated movies inexpensively on the same personal computers with which they fragged monsters and friends in *DOOM* or *Quake*. Id continued to open up access to *Quake* in order to make it easier for players to customize or modify the game. Carmack supported open discussion of id's technology as beneficial, because "programming is not a zero-sum game. Teaching something to a fellow programmer doesn't take it away from you." Abrash, the 3D programming expert who helped Carmack with *Quake,* followed this "enlightened attitude." He published articles about their programming tricks "even before *Quake* has shipped" and noted "when it's legally possible, sharing information benefits us all in the long run." He called this philosophy, "learn now, pay forward."[40] These values trickled down to *Quake*'s player community, including those who made *Quake* movies. Just as FPS players shared knowledge about how to modify games, progressing together from map and level design to add-ons and eventually to full-scale total conversion mods, machinima makers likewise helped each other. The Rangers learned how to change the camera view, "Operation Bayshield" was the first *Quake* movie to utilize custom artistic assets, and so on. At each step, the Rangers, Clan Undead, and other players shared their techniques as they learned them. As other players did for game mods, they created skins for avatars, designed visual effects, added sounds, and produced game graphics (for sets, characters, etc.) in order to make more ambitious movies. Projects following on their work through the late 1990s taught methods for revising game assets as surely as they demonstrated gameplay and provided entertainment.

The impact of the modification of game software and assets on the cultural economy of game design is well documented, particularly with respect to modding. Id's "enlightened" attitude about discussion of its innovative programming techniques encouraged the player community to dive into investigation of the game software and eventually to produce tools and assets, especially with each eagerly anticipated (and sometimes unanticipated) release of source code. But even if sharing is caring, are these practices sufficient to take players into a sphere of activity we might call codesign or cocreation of the technology itself (as opposed to the media content produced by that technology)? Put another way, when players use game technology to make mods and movies, in what sense are they innovators? Perhaps these activities are better depicted as an extension of their use of technology rather than part of the process that invents it? As players figured out how to use computer games to make animated movies, were they inventing a new technology for real-time animation production or coming up with a new way to play these games? And, if they were not coinventors, does that mean that they were just playing around?

Historians of technology for a long time focused on the process of invention in a way that paid far more attention to invention, design, and even production than to how technologies are continuously redefined, stabilized, and redefined again through use. In a variety of disciplines encompassing the history of technology, business, innovation, and media, more critical attention has been paid in recent years to consumers and users, especially in terms that emphasize how they take part in shaping, modifying, and repurposing the technologies that they use. Studies of technological innovation are paying attention not just to *users* as consumers, but also to *use* and the practices associated with it as part of the process of innovation.[41] This perspective emerged during the late 1980s in technology studies under the rubric of "social construction of technology" (SCOT). The SCOT manifesto was a group of essays published as *The Social Construction of Technological Systems* in 1987.[42] As an approach to innovation, SCOT initially focused on interactions among producers (including inventors, designers, etc.) and users as a process of negotiation leading to "stabilization" of a technological artifact. Space here does not permit a detailed history of demand-side innovation studies. However, it is important to note that during the 1990s, criticism of SCOT's focus on the stabilization of design through interactions between suppliers and the demand side (consumers and users, treated interchangeably) shifted to an approach that encompassed users of mature technologies and producers. In brief, SCOT began to address "how technologies are actually used in practice."[43]

This "turn to the users"[44] is allied with similar impulses from other disciplines. Cultural studies, fan studies, innovation studies, business history, and a broad range of writings on contemporary media have shifted the focus of creativity and innovation to the user or consumer of technology.[45] This diverse set of approaches includes a variety of models to describe users as active and creative, rather than just passive consumers, ranging from resistance to distributed innovation. An important common characteristic of these approaches has been the idea of *negotiation* as part of an overarching process that shapes technologies as well as their users from innovation and design through consumption. In studying this process, researchers have worked out a claim made by Kline and Pinch in their study of early rural use of the automobile in the United States, "that the use of an artifact or system has not only resulted in unforeseen consequences, but that users have helped to shape the artifact or system itself."[46] In working out the dynamics of this process, it is crucial to identify different participants in such a process of negotiation and the meanings they attach to a particular technology under discussion. SCOT proposed the "interpretive flexibility" of an artifact as a way of articulating that it can have different meanings for various interested social groups. This notion was coined for a model that showed how this flexibility eventually led to "closure" as technologies stabilized and disparate notions faded away. Later studies explored "how interpretive flexibility can reappear at the use stage of technology."[47]

Of course, as business historian JoAnne Yates has pointed out, the "very notion of closure in interpretive flexibility is problematic" in the realm of software.[48] Machinima provides a good example. Certainly, Carmack achieved a dominant design for game engines, but players opened up this design by using it as a real-time animation engine for making movies; they reshaped the technology by establishing needs and desires for a new group of users (moviemakers, let's call them) with a different set of expectations for how the technology would be used. This may be conceived as users pushing back on the configuration of a technology established by designers, but this tells us little about how the technology likewise configured the users, that is in the case of machinima, how the use of game engines for making movies created a certain kind of player and moviemaker.[49] As we have seen, at least through 1998, there was no machinima community, only a *Quake*[50] movie community. This is important to acknowledge, because even though the movies produced were growing in scope and ambition, the community that produced and consumed them was limited to players of a particular, albeit very popular, computer game. Whether creator or spectator, if you knew about *Quake* movies, you were a *Quake* player; indeed, the demo format required access to the game even to play the movies.

The popularity of the game was drawing in new players, however, and some of these players imagined that game-based moviemaking could lead to a meaningful convergence of interactive gameplay and linear, story-driven entertainment forms. They began to think of themselves not so much (or not always) as players, but as moviemakers. Players with training or professional experience in video, improvisational comedy, film or television production began to explore the possibilities of moving "beyond the world of *Quake*,"[51] notably the Ill Clan in the United States and Strange Company in Great Britain. For example, the Ill Clan's

Figure 6
The Ill Clan, "Hardly Workin'" (2001).

"Apartment Huntin'" (1998) and "Hardly Workin'" (2000) added voice talents, improvisational comedy, and custom artwork to skills derived from *Quake* gameplay, resulting in a comedic short good enough to win the Best of SHO and Best Experimental Short awards at the Showtime Network's Alternative Media Festival. Paul Marino, the director of "Hardly Workin'," cited these awards as an indicator of "the recognition of Machinima by a mainstream media venue."[52] Only viewers familiar with *Quake* (or *Quake II* in the case of the second movie) would have recognized that the Ill Clan's movies had anything to do with a computer game. But that realization pointed perhaps to a problem in terms of increasing the visibility of these movies; if only *Quake* players could see them, what difference did it make if nonplayers would find them entertaining to watch?

By the late 1990s, players had learned that they could make animated movies from computer games. While on the one hand, it could be said that game engines were ready-made for making movies, on the other hand, finding that the technology could be used in this way did not feed back significantly on the subsequent development of the game engine as a technology. This is an important issue for a better understanding of how users of game technology (players) interact with roles traditionally understood as inventors and producers (programmers, developers), whether by changing game content or reshaping game technology. One might think that if making movies with game engines is such a compelling idea, producers such as game developers, makers of 3D modeling and rendering software or even graphics processor manufacturers would have responded with a dedicated technology, a flexible real-time animation studio perhaps. There was in fact little incentive for game developers, or anyone else for that matter, to spin off such animation engines as a new technology just for players who chose to make movies using *Quake*.[53] The question of why game-based moviemaking technology has not emancipated itself from game technology compels a closer look at how platform-independent machinima "broke out" from the relatively closed world of *Quake* movies. Furthermore, these matters focus attention on whether players making movies aspired to break out from the culture of computer games to a broader media audience, that is, to cross over into other media and engage with an increasingly diverse set of issues and genres in their movies. In fact, the dependence of *Quake*-based moviemaking on id's game engine development played an important and unexpected role in stimulating the development of machinima beyond *Quake* movies.[54]

Quake II, the successor to *Quake,* was released in 1997 and continued as the dominant platform for making demo-based movies. Productive groups, such as Ill Clan, Zarathustra Studios, and Strange Company used the game for influential projects, some of which (such as Strange Company's multipart *Eschaton,* which took place in the fantasy world of H. P. Lovecraft's "Chtulhu mythos") spanned development in *Quake* and *Quake II.* At the end of 1999, id released *Quake III Arena* (henceforth, *Quake III*), published by Activision. With an updated and improved version of the *Quake* engine, such that *PC Magazine* called it "the current state of the art in gaming graphics,"[55] and id's apparent encouragement of player-created content, the new game seemed to offer nothing but benefits for game-based moviemaking. The initial enthusiasm among demo moviemakers soon dissipated, however. *Quake*'s developers had become concerned about cheating in competitive versions of the game. The potential effect on the success of the game was obvious; as one player of FPS games put it, the knowledge that other players were cheating online made him "ready to walk away from the game in disgust and tell every one else to do the same."[56] It turned out that as players gained more knowledge about the network code underlying multiplayer games, they learned not only how to make mods and movies, but also to cheat more effectively. Girlich had done more than anyone to reveal and disseminate the intricacies of the demo format, but even he had to admit that "existing demo formats are only variants of the network data flowing between the server and the clients. So any existing demo format description leads directly to the network protocol. Many cheaters misuse this information to write proxy-bots." Indeed, the network messages sent back-and-forth by the Quake server and clients were identical to those used in demo files. Girlich concluded that he could no longer provide information about the *Quake III* demo format to the moviemaking community, noting that there were also "legal reasons" for this decision.[57] Wright, the creator of Keygrip and Keygrip 2, likewise announced that there would be no new version for *Quake III*.[58] An expert on *Quake* movies concluded that "it looks highly unlikely that any tool will ever be released with the capacity to edit Quake III demos."[59] Suddenly, it looked like the neat linkage of peer-to-peer learning and multiplayer innovation accidentally nourished cheating technology. The social organization of players into competitive clans and communication patterns that promoted the sharing of these techniques for high-performance play also abetted those who would propagate cheats drawing upon this knowledge. Clan members shared these hacks as they would other programming exploits that publicized the superior skills of their clan. Lone players were more likely to keep such tricks to themselves.[60] The *Quake* movie scene threatened to grind to a halt.

From id's perspective, what was a game developer to do? The company decided to throttle access to *Quake III*'s network code to protect the game. Demo-editing tools such as Wright's Keygrip and Girlich's LMPC that made use of this information were out of luck. Now that circulating detailed information about this aspect of the game was forbidden, to the extent that id threatened legal action against anyone who revealed the code or how it worked, these tools would not be available for making movies with *Quake III*. The crisis initiated by id's decisions with regard to *Quake III* technology forced a response from those moviemakers who until then had found the game engine so hospitable. Now they began to see the gift of a found technology as a limitation on their creativity. As Paul Marino, a member of the Ill Clan put it, "This started a turning-point for the movie community. The newness of imbuing fantastical environments with mundane situations and commentary seemed to wear off. Simply said, the joke was getting old. This coincided with id's decision to protect *Quake III Arena*'s network code, and hence the amount of productions slowed to a crawl. The community was forced into survival mode—either reinvent itself or succumb to the harsh realities that the allure of *Quake* movie production would slowly fade away."[61]

The *Quake* movie community reinvented itself around a more general conception of game-based moviemaking as a new media form. Hugh Hancock, founder of Strange Company, and Anthony Bailey, renowned as a founding member of the *Quake done Quick* team that had popularized the class of *Quake* movies known as speedruns, coined a term that would redefine the community's work: machinima. Bailey, in a private e-mail to Hancock during May 1998, had devised the term as a portmanteau of machine and cinema, so he originally spelled it "machinema." In the original e-mail he noted that "it's a bit of a contrived term . . . but what in general *are* we going to call these pieces of cinema that are made using 3D engines?" He also predicted accurately that, "Not only is 'Quake movie' an ugly and confusing term, it's also fast going to become outdated as other technologies become relevant."[62] For a while, the term was rarely used in public forums.[63] At the end of 1999, about when *Quake III* would be published, Hancock, while working on the Web site for Strange Company, proposed "machinima" as an improvement. It suggested animation generated by machine (game engine). He registered the domain name and shortly afterwards launched the machinima.com Web site at the beginning of 2000; almost immediately, it became the de facto community site and resource for machinima makers.

Bailey and Hancock's conscious use of "machinima" to describe an expanded scope of game-based moviemaking not limited to the *Quake* engine coincided roughly with id's decision to restrict access to the demo format in order to protect its network code. Players and developers pulled their oars in synch with each other, but without a common notion of their destination. However, machinima continued to include projects created with the various versions of *Quake* technology, and id supported such player-created content in principle, even if its design decision had the effect of driving projects away from the game. The first movie to be made with *Quake III* was Triton Films' "Quad God," and the effects of these crosscurrents are illustrated by the circumstances of its creation and release. Work on the project began in June 1999, long before the game's release, and the movie was released in early January 2000. The Triton team had responded to a contest set up by Katherine Anna Kang of id Software to create the most original work of art making use of the *Quake III* logo. They made more than fifteen custom maps and thirty character skins on the way to releasing a thirty-three-minute movie made with the test engine for the game (as it had not yet been released). Even though "Quad God" was clearly a *Quake III* movie, the circumstances of its release previewed characteristics of a more widely accessible medium. It was one of the first movies to be released via Hancock's then brand-new machinima.com site; just as important, it was released not as a demo movie that required viewers to own and execute the game, but encoded in a conventional video format that could be played using easily available media players. One could now with a bit more sleep deprivation encode game movies as video files that could be viewed almost by anyone.

Figure 7
"Tritin Films Movie Set for QUAD GOD 1999." Source: Tritin Films.[64]

The shift away from *Quake* movies and the gradual demise of the demo format accelerated during 2000. The crisis gave way to the emergence of machinima. More movies appeared that were based on other engines, such as *Unreal* and *Half-Life*.[65] Ill Clan's "Apartment Huntin" at the end of 1998 was the first machinima piece encoded in the RealMedia format, but two years later video files could be distributed over the internet (at almost no cost) either as the original game replay file or in an encoded movie format. A few years later, nearly all machinima movies were released in one of the common video formats, and today nearly every one of the major viral media sites includes a channel devoted to game movies. The decline of the *Quake* movie can be seen as a consequence of the tight connection between game-based moviemaking and a particular technical configuration of the game engine and demo format. The unexpected impulse id's decision gave to *Quake* moviemakers was that it pushed them harder to think of their work as defining a new and more generally accessible cinematic medium with the potential to be viewed as meaningful by a wider audience than *Quake* players. Therefore, what we have here is an example of how the stabilization of use by players does not necessarily follow from what technology studies might describe as closure of design. Machinima resulted from the breaking of the connection between the game engine designed by id and the practices of moviemaking created by players. The innovation of game-based moviemaking was not achieved through the stabilization of design and use to create a new artifact (technology). Instead, players found that they could extend the practices and culture learned from these movies—in fact, the essence of what they had created—by other means.

Screen Capture: The Politics of Found Technology

Players have learned through making machinima that the dissemination of accessible tools—even if they are not necessarily easy-to-use—creates opportunities for the emergence of unexpected content. Player culture values playful experiments and throwaway pieces alongside startling and original instances of creative expression, much as other forms of viral media today.[66] In this sense, we can think of machinima as exploiting a found technology. I borrow this idea of a found technology from that of the found object (*object trouvé*) of the art world, the readymade, everyday, recycled object that is appropriated or reinterpreted as a form of artistic expression, ready to use, but also readily discarded for something else. Marcel Duchamp coined the term "readymade" for the found objects he used for works such as "Bicycle Wheel" (1913)[67] and "Fountain" (1917). Whether or not they remained in their original form, however, the essential point was that the artifact has not been created for or by the artist, nor generally for the purpose of display or artistic statement. The artist selects unexceptional objects and gives them a new context or purpose. The bicycle wheel chosen by Duchamp is like any other. Even if the artist lays no claim to having created the artifact itself, he creates something new with the visual or conceptual statement that emerges from its recontextualization.

Depicting machinima as a found technology emphasizes certain of its characteristics as a player-created use of computer games, such as the availability of game technology as "ready-made" for a purpose other than making movies, or the ease with which machinima creators move to new game engines or from demo to screen capture techniques. Hugh Hancock of Strange Company has been fond of citing William Gibson in this regard, that "the street finds its own uses for things."[68] At the same time, there is an important difference. In the artistic notion of the found object, the process of reworking elevates the object as artwork and infuses it with new meaning. The artist offers a reenvisioning of the artifact. In machinima, the transformation stimulated by the artistic process revises the technology that produces the artifact. Not by altering the game engine, but by turning the found technology of the game engine into an animation engine, that is, by finding a new purpose and context for it. When technologies are revised in this unanticipated way, the user operates in a hybrid space, mixing practices learned from the familiar, found technology and reworking them as an application of these skills to new purposes. Paul Marino, looking back at his experience making Quake movies as part of the Ill Clan, observed that the work on these projects was "a combination of playing multiplayer *Quake* and shooting a live film." The language used to describe machinima techniques became a pastiche of gaming and performance terminology, such as making sure that "key configs were set and that we knew our marks in the game maps."[69] The recontextualization of the computer game led to a related layering of practices. Early machinima "definitely took some modding skills"[70] as well as the use of tools to capture, edit, and reassemble files that could be viewed with game software; later work in games such as *World of Warcraft* typically called upon facility with model viewers, compositing techniques, and postproduction video editing to radically reassemble game assets. As Hancock put it, machinima makers do not create proprietary technology, but rather they "take a bunch of disparate and varied technologies—mostly things that have come of the Digital Video or gaming world—and weld them together, using their various capabilities to make films."[71] Casting machinima as found technology helps us to move away from an idea of user creativity focused on invention of new artifacts to one that traces new player commitments and uses, often by learning how to mash up practices imported from other activities and contexts.

The hybrid nature of machinima as a found or readymade technology carried important implications as the new medium broke out into a variety of media spaces less closely tied to the hard-core computer game culture of FPS games. As we have seen, video files are easily distributed over the internet at virtually no cost. Significantly, the machinima movies that became most popular with the largest audience relied on a mode of production quite different from *Quake*'s demo movies. Instead of capture in the game, editing with special tools, recompilation into the demo format, and playback inside the game, these movies followed the path pioneered by Tritin's "Quad God," capturing the screen display to video, editing

Hitchcock.

Spielberg.

Tarantino.

Guy with an Xbox.

Explore the evolution of animation and filmmaking.

Animated filmmaking, videogame style.

The 2006 Machinima Festival
Saturday, November 4th and Sunday, November 5th, 2006
Museum of the Moving Image

Figure 8
2006 Machinima Festival announcement, *Computer Gaming World* no. 268 (November, 2006): 73.

the video (with nonlinear video editors such as Adobe Premiere), and then distributing and viewing the movies in common video formats. Instead of FPS games, console games and massively multiplayer online games became the dominant modes of machinima production based on screen capture. The breakout title was Rooster Teeth's "Red vs. Blue," a comedy series now in its fifth year based on the Xbox games *Halo* and *Halo 2*. In 2006, huge numbers of machinima titles are produced in massively multiplayer games (*World of Warcraft*), virtual worlds (*Second Life*) or games that export directly to video (*The Movies*); in each case, the predominant mode of production is direct capture to a video format. The issues raised by screen capture as the dominant method of machinima technology are manifold. How should the screen content, which clearly includes content and intellectual property owned by developers, be licensed and marketed? Who owns an artistic product based on contributions from a mix of sources and creators? What constraints will a potentially contested ownership of the assets (not just the technology) used to create these movies place on freedom of expression?

Players have made changes and improvements to game software and assets since *Spacewar!* and *Adventure*. Such modifications have been a permanent part of the business culture of game design since the release of *DOOM*. This is undeniably a quality of game culture that has inspired some observers to value its creativity as a kind of resistance to passive consumption, or as a participation in content creation. In fact, I have been less concerned with an aesthetic evaluation of machinima than with the ways in which this new medium reveals modes of creativity and innovation associated with playing computer games, learning how to play them better, and figuring out what the technology that produces them can do. It is important to see the ready availability of game-based moviemaking evident in the making of "The French Democracy" not only as a validation of computer games as being culturally expressive. Rather, we should dig deeper and discover why playing these games leads some players to want to make movies for other players and to explore found technologies independent of gameplay. While the creativity expressed through authorship, invention, or intellectual property is important, other aspects of computer games as technology, as the basis for player communities, and as a site for performance techniques and practices have given game movies their particular significance. Those players whom I call "community players" are not only creative and theatrical, but they also take care to exhibit mastery of technology and cyberathletic skill. It is important to recognize the extroverted and expressive play performance of the community player for what it is. Part stage actor, part activist, the community player plays for other players. The complex cocreation of machinima and other game-based movies benefits from consideration of the player not only as a "consumer who also produces," but also as a "user who also innovates" and the computer game itself as a found technology capable of being appropriated for the new application of real-time moviemaking. An important issue illuminated by the development of machinima is the capacity for users of a technology not only to shape its development, but also to transform its purpose and, in effect, to create a new technology out of an existing one through redeployment for a new purpose. The payoff was more than the delivery of entertaining video clips, even more than creating a new moviemaking technology; it included showing how to *do* it. In this sense, the core innovation was the *demonstration* itself as a paradigm for multiplayer learning fueled by engagement with digital play.

We have seen that the replay culture of game film and screen capture supplemented the demo format as the basis for game-based moviemaking. This has made possible a broadening of appeal, primarily through the replacement of game files by downloadable or streamed movie formats that anyone can view. Of course, conflicts can arise when the free donation of time, effort, and invention is entangled with, indeed dependent upon, technology and content developed by commercial enterprises and professional artists. In machinima, this occurs when a game provides virtual locations, studios, and cameras, or a pop song serves as the soundtrack for a dance video. To get at these conflicts, I will revisit a machinima project that I have covered elsewhere, Tristan Pope's "Not Just Another Love Story," made with (and in) the *World of Warcraft (WoW)*.[72]

Until moviemakers learned to extract models and maps with new tools such as *WoW* Model Viewer, server-based games such as *WoW* denied direct access to code and even to game assets outside their use in-game; moviemaking was limited to edited screen captures. This means that early *WoW* movies were essentially replays grabbed via screen capture, then cleverly edited, perhaps with voice-overs or painstakingly lip-synced dialogue. A player dubbed JuniorX made the first *WoW* movies to be widely distributed.[73] His movies were essentially training films, introducing potential players to the game, giving an indication of its pace, challenges, and tactics through lengthy recordings of adventures encountered in the game, little more than unadorned gameplay. His movie on the hunter class, for example, showed every moment in the career of a dwarf character up to level ten in the game; more than an hour long and claiming nearly 400 MB of storage space, it was nonetheless downloaded more than 11,000 times from warcraftmovies.com, a new Web site devoted entirely to *WoW* machinima and replays. These movies get us back to the skill training that motivated DOOM demo movies or the replay sharing among players of other Blizzard games, *Starcraft* and *Warcraft III*. JuniorX recast the training replay as entertainment when he made "Dancemovie" and "Dancemovie 2." He combined the discovery of dance movements built into the game, the presence of other players as coperformers or spectators, and the showcasing of neat tricks and exploits (such as being able to activate dance movements during combat, a fleeting "feature" quickly eliminated during the beta test) to put together his recorded performances. Dance videos became a staple of the *WoW* movie scene, remediating MTV music videos through gameplay set to music, with particular attention to matching lyrics and images, synchronization of character movements to soundtracks, and elaborate choreography of players. For the new *WoW* player community, the novelty of these videos dovetailed with replay culture to show *WoW* players how to perform for other players in a virtual world.

WoW movies, from game film and dance videos to memes of viral culture, such as Pals for Life's "Leeroy Jenkins," became an integral part of the *WoW* player culture. Moviemakers in *WoW* have discovered, however, that increasing popularity magnifies the creative constraints on their work due to issues of intellectual property, social dynamics, and politics. The production and reception of Pope's "Not Just Another Love Story" illustrates the new performance politics of the community player, suggesting both the payoffs and problems he or she faces. Its reception pointed to the potential for creative conflict beneath the surface of the relationship between machinima and game developers. Pope, like JuniorX, was an early *WoW* player. He released his first *WoW* movie, "I Surrender," near the end of the beta period. Completed after playing *WoW* for only three days, he was inspired by other beta period dance and party movies available around that time and soon created the Crafting Worlds Web site to facilitate the distribution of his projects to the *WoW* community. With each of his movies from "I Surrender," released in November 2004, through "Onyxia Eliminated," completed in April 2005, he worked through remediations of various movie and even game replay formats, such as the music video, sketch comedy, and guild demo. In April, he coyly introduced a more ambitious project, "Not Just Another Love Story":

I want to give you a full description of this movie, but that would ruin the surprise.
I'll give you a hint: I only executed what the pixels in WoW suggest...
And it has something to do with something that was removed in patch 1.3.
Ok, that's all you get![74]

Beginning with the disclaimer that "this movie contains material that may not be suitable for all ages," Pope's movie tells a Romeo-and-Juliet story, but with a game-specific twist. It sets up the story by showing his Troll Rogue character, Tristanmon, heading off to work in the desert for another day of monotonous creature kills. In the middle of combat, he notices and falls head over heals in love with a human female who can match him kill for kill. Alliance and Horde characters do not mix in this world, but despite such taboos, they become engaged and marry. Pope uses editing, character positioning, and carefully chosen camera angles to depict the pair consummating their love in various ways. The highlight of Pope's movie is a spectacular rave during which the Troll emerges from his shell and is fully transformed by love into a wildly dancing party animal. The masterfully choreographed series of scenes would not have been possible without dozens of player-actors, choreographed actions and spell effects, cleverly chosen locations, and immense preproduction planning. In a stunning reversal, the troll's new life is later shattered by the death of his spouse in combat. His luck holds, however. She is resurrected by an equally attractive human female, and the threesome live happily ever after.

But there was more to this love story. Pope had purposefully sharpened the narrative edge to give voice to the player community. The story specifically drew attention to issues of creative ownership of the story world. Since the first *Warcraft* game, subtitled "Orcs vs. Humans," the narrative momentum pushing forward the single-player campaign was

Figure 9
Tristan Pope, "Not Just Another Love Story" (2005).

faction and racial hatred. While the opposed races and their relative moral elevation could be remixed from version to version of the game (such as the focus on the reawakened nobility in the Orcs of *Warcraft III*), the role of relentless and unremitting conflict in shaping the history of the fictive world remained constant and fundamental. As players descended from the strategic perspective of the RTS games to play on the ground in *World of Warcraft,* they discovered that these conflicts had been built into their characters. This fundamental fact of *Warcraft* life translated into the inability of Horde and Alliance characters to communicate directly in-game through language. Chat was impossible, and shouted speech was rendered as unintelligible gibberish; the game software even recognized and filtered out subversive attempts to communicate by embedding text in descriptive gestures, known as "emotes." Beginning in the beta version of the game, players discovered that the language of game culture provided the key for unlocking a system of universal speech. They found that it was possible to embed the number- and special character-based misspellings of "1337 speak" ("leetspeak," or elite speak) in emotes, thus bypassing Blizzard's text filters and making it possible for, say, trolls to speak with their human enemies. Just as an earlier generation of hackers and gamers had used it to circumvent mail and bulletin board language controls, they used it to speak across an in-game cultural divide and they shared the workaround. This was a clear transgression of Blizzard's control of the relationship between gameplay and story world, so in the aforementioned 1.3 patch of the game the development team announced that henceforth "numbers and punctuation will not be passed through chat communication to members of the opposing faction."[75]

In the context of this assertion of Blizzard's control, Pope's depiction of the marriage of Troll and Human characters, as well as the massive collaboration of Horde and Alliance players evident in the movie itself, put an alternative vision of the game world into play. In the movie, Pope directed a final comment to Blizzard after the credits had wound down and the waning notes of The Darkness' "I Believe in a Thing Called Love" had faded away:

Figure 10
Tristan Pope, "Not Just Another Love Story" (2005).

"Even without leet speak you cannot take away our love!" The mature content creatively constructed through character positions and camera angles in the video intensified this point, but it also sharpened the ensuing controversy. An often-overlooked implication of the *WoW* moviemaker's inability to modify the server-based MMO was, as Pope argued with a wink, that he had merely showed "what *WoW*'s pixels imply ☺." Even sexual imagery, therefore, was nothing more than a rearrangement of what Blizzard's artists had drawn, or more accurately, what its game engine generated during gameplay. Rather than asserting his right to subvert the game's content, Pope reasoned that he had in fact not created anything on the screen, merely captured it.

Since the release of this phenomenally successful game, Blizzard had eagerly sponsored *WoW* events such as screenshot and stunt competitions, encouraging players to use the game's visual assets as Pope had as a means of generating new content as part of the shared culture of its millions of players. (Indeed, Pope went on to become a Blizzard employee and played a key role in the machinima portions of South Park's notorious "Make Love, Not Warcraft" episode.) Community managers encouraged announcements about game movies in official *WoW* forums, allowing creators to provide links to facilitate downloading of video files. Pope was allowed to post such a link, but within two days the volume of complaints, flames, and counterflames about "adult" scenes in "Not Just Another Love Story" caused Blizzard to cite the user agreement concerning language or images that are "pornographic in nature" and lock the discussion thread about his project. It barred links to any of the movie's download sites in subsequent discussion threads.[76] The marketing of in-game creativity collided head-on with the game's demographics and success, which by then had brought many young players to the *WoW* player community. Players argued over the implications; some supported Pope, others supported Blizzard: "How can making an IN GAME movie with only IN GAME animations, on a forum about THAT GAME be inappropriate?" or "Let me go take Ken and Barbie at Toys R Us and pose them in sexual ways, and say 'But whoamygod~ their joints BEND that way so its not sexually suggestive or inappropriate for us to advertise that way!!!' Plus you're overlooking the simple fact that there ARE forum rules prohibiting these things."[77] Pope conceded Blizzard's right to some measure of control and understood that

Figure 11
Ruby (Tilda Swinton) in Second Life (April 2006).

rights to freedom of expression on the forums were not governed "by the Constitution," but at the same time he argued that "I also don't want censorship over something that took what is already in game and just made it more provocative."[78] By acting as the lightning rod for commentary on the contested boundary between developer and player control of a complex, multiplayer game world, Pope's "Not Just Another Love Story" showed that game movies could function as a medium for negotiation of issues important to the player community.

Pope's movie brings us back to an optimistic view of the potential for game-based moviemaking implicit in "The French Democracy." It suggests that players are learning to use digital media that matter to them in order to express ideas and opinions that are equally important in their lives. Note well that we have seen that these issues of importance extend from the politics and conflicts of real life to those of virtual worlds and game communities. We have also seen that the expressive potential of machinima brings into focus the ways in which player-generated practices and uses of digital technology may be limited by the use of digital games as a found technology for moviemaking. Whatever the accuracy of the substantial claims I have made on behalf of player-driven, innovative use of game technology, the fact remains that most of the technology and many of the images, music, and, in some cases, even texts remain contested intellectual property, thanks to a wild mix of benign neglect by game developers, player-created content, and other sources of content, such as commercially published music. At this early stage in the historical development of real-time animation and game-based moviemaking, the bottom line is that players are learning how to deploy technologies from computer games to develop new practices for expressing themselves through game-based performance. The capacity of a medium based on computer games to venture forth beyond the self-referential is at the heart of player practices that, as we have seen, encourage a sense of co-ownership (however misled it may be in legal terms), and the freedom to replay, reinvent, and redeploy. These practices include performing for other players, skills certification, showing by doing, and multiplayer learning across networks of players. In particular, performance practices around the demonstration as a key moment show us that "high performance play"[79] is capable of taking players from their deep engagement with games and game technology to the discovery of new uses of digital technology for learning, as well as cultural production.

Notes

1. Sonia Livingstone, The Changing Nature and Uses of Media Literacy, *Media@LSE Electronic Working Papers* 4 (2003): 13–14. Retrieved September 2006. http://www.lse.ac.uk/collections/media@lse/pdf/Media@lseEWP4_july03.pdf.

2. Paul Marino, The Machinima Faq, (updated 8.03.2005), Academy of Machinima Arts and Sciences. Web site. http://machinima.org/machinima-faq.html; for the history of machinima, see Henry Lowood, High-Performance Play: The Making of Machinima, *Journal of Media Practice* 7, no. 1 (2006): 25–42. Also to appear in: Andy Clarke and Grethe Mitchell, eds., *Videogames and Art: Intersections and Interactions* (Bristol, UK: Intellect Books, 2006).

3. The French Democracy. A film by Koulamata. *The Movies*. http://movies.lionhead.com/movie/11520.

4. Mike Musgrove. Game Turns Players into Indie Moviemakers. http://washingtonpost.com (1 Dec. 2005): D1.

5. http://www.lionhead.com/themovies/, with the movie database at http://movies.lionhead.com/movies.html.

6. 460 movies uploaded in the last 7 days. http://movies.lionhead.com/recent.html.

7. Stephen Totilo, First Film about French Riots Comes Courtesy of a Video Game. *MTV News* (5 Dec. 2005).

8. For example, Musgrove, Game Turns Players...; Totilo, First Film...; Joelle Diderich, French Film about Riots Draws Applause, *USA Today*, December 15, 2005; Carol Matlack, Video Games Go to the Movies, *BusinessWeek online* December 9, 2005. Retrieved January 2007. http://www.businessweek.com/technology/content/dec2005/tc20051208_639203.htm; Marie Lechner, La cité animée d'Alex Chan, *Libération*, December 12, 2005.

9. http://www.worldwideshortfilmfest.com/schedule/programme_details.php?program=Machinima; http://iarvers.free.fr/pages/evenement.html.

10. Paul Marino, The French Democratizer. Post to Thinking Machinima blog (16 Dec. 2005). Retrieved January 2007. http://www.machinima.org/paul_blog/2005/12/french-democratizer.html.

11. Quoted in Diderich, French Film....

12. "Je rencontrerai également l'ensemble des responsables de l'audiovisuel. Les médias doivent mieux refléter la réalité française d'aujourd'hui." Déclaration aux Français de Monsieur Jacques Chirac, Président de la République, November 14, 2005, Présidence de la République Web site, http://www.elysee.fr/elysee/francais/interventions/interviews_articles_de_presse_et_interventions_televisees./2005/novembre/declaration_aux_francais.32000.html.

13. Mogniss H. Abdallah, Quand les banlieues s'embrasent. Entre révolte "ethno-religieuse" ou colère sociale, une opinion publique divisée, Alterités (Médias) Web site, December 22, 2005, http://www.alterites.com/cache/center_media/index.php.

14. Henry Jenkins, *Fans Bloggers and Gamers: Media Consumers in a Digital Age* (New York: New York University Press, 2006).

15. Nelly Oudshoorn and Trevor Pinch, *How Users Matter: The Co-Construction of Users and Technology* (Cambridge, MA: MIT Press, 2003).

16. Designed by John Carmack and optimized by Michael Abrash. A good summary of the technical innovations in *Quake* is provided by Abrash, Ramblings in Realtime, esp. chap. 6: Quake's 3-D Engine: The Big Picture (2000), gamedev.net Web site, http://www.gamedev.net/reference/articles/abrash/abrash.pdf. These essays were revisions of chapters in Michael Abrash's *Graphics Programming Black Book: Special Edition* (Scottsdale, AZ: Coriolis, 1997).

17. Jack Thompson, Bloodlust Video Games Put Kids in the Crosshairs, *Denver Post*, May 30, 1999, G1.

18. However, the original version of *DOOM* was not released as open-source software; rather, id issued a "Data Utility License" that allowed modification of the game software under strictly defined conditions. With the release of *DOOM II* in 1994, Romero released more information about the game program. Carmack released the *DOOM* source code as a Christmas present to the player community in December 1997.

19. Id Software, n.d. id Software Backgrounder, n.d. From: id Software Web site, at: http://www.idsoftware.com/business/home/history/.

20. Randall Packer, Net Art as Theater of the Senses: A HyperTour of Jodi and Grammatron, *Beyond Interface* (2004). http://www.archimuse.com/mw98/beyond_interface/bi_fr.html (accessed June 2007).

21. John Carmack, Re: Definitions of Terms. Discussion post to Slashdot. 2002. http://slashdot.org/comments.pl?sid=25551&cid=2775698 (accessed January 2007).

22. Hugh Hancock, Ranger Gone AWOL. *machinima.com*. http://www.machinima.com/articles/Ranger_Gone_AWOL/index.shtml.

23. Stewart Brand, SPACEWAR: Fanatic Life and Symbolic Death Among the Computer Bums, *Rolling Stone*, December 7, 1972. Also available from http://www.wheels.org/spacewar/stone/rolling_stone.html.

24. D. J. Edwards and J. M. Graetz, PDP-1 Plays at Spacewar, *Decuscope* 1, no. 1 (1962): 2–4. See also J.M. Graetz, The Origin of Spacewar!, *Creative Computing*, 1, no. 1 (1983): 78–85.

25. Brand, SPACEWAR.

26. Ledmeister, What is a DOOM/DOOM II Demo (or LMP File)? *Classic Doom.* http://www.classicdoom.com/.

27. E-mail from Laura "BahdKo" Herrmann to Henry Lowood (28 Jan. 2004). Interestingly, it has long been suspected that some star players abstained from the practice of delivering demo movies of their gameplay in order to maintain their competitive edge. However, such reluctance seems to have been unusual and the absence of demo movies from players such as Thresh (whose fame is based on his dominance in *Quake* death match) is now seen as evidence that they were not as active in the *DOOM* scene as word-of-mouth would have it. This shows the necessity of spectatorship and community, as well as skill, in achieving the status of a "God-like" player.

28. Welcome to the *DOOM* Honorific Titles! *DOOM Honorofic Titles.* http://www-lce.eng.cam.ac.uk/~fms27/dht/dht5/#dht5. An excellent compilation of demo movies of all sorts can be found at the *Doom2.net* Web site, http://www.doom2.net/, along with recording and training tools.

29. Within limits, of course. Some players were known not to reveal all their best tricks.

30. Extensive documentation on the history of copyparties and demoparties has been lovingly preserved by the demoscene itself. For one example, see "CSDb: The C-64 Scene Database," http://noname.c64.org/csdb/.

31. Interview of the Month! This time: SLH/Hotline. *Illegal: The Cracker Magazine 2* (1987). This, appropriately, is from an unauthorized excerpt of the English-language sections that apparently circulated as a text file, though the original was printed in Germany. CSDb, entry for Illegal #22, http://www.df.lth.se/~triad/triad/ftp/Illegal/illeg22.txt

32. Saxon Druce, quoted in Vincent Scheib, Introduction to Demos & the Demo Scene: How They Relate to Games, and Their Appearance at SIGGRAPH, *Gamasutra* (2001). http://www.gamasutra.com/features/20010216/scheib_01.htm#a1.

33. E.g., Uwe Girlich's unlocking of the *DOOM* and *Quake* demo formats.

34. Examples of pre-rendered games would be Don Bluth's *Dragon's Lair* or the enormously successful *Myst*. But these are exceptions that prove the rule with regard to games based on 3-D engines.

35. Richard Schechner, *Performance Studies: An Introduction* (London: Routledge, 2002), 191.

36. Berry, n.d.

37. Uwe Girlich, The Unofficial DEM Format Description Version 1.02, July 30, 1996: 3.2 and 3.4. http://www.gamers.org/dEngine/*Quake*/Qdem/dem-1.0.2-3.html#ss3.2.a.

38. Cf. the Keygrip 2 Web site, http://keygrip.planetquake.gamespy.com/.

39. For more detail on this phase in the early history of machinima, see Henry Lowood, 2006; Andy Clarke and Grethe Mitchell, 2006.

40. Michael Abrash, *Michael Abrash's Graphics Programming Black Book. Special Edition* (Albany, NY: Coriolis, 1997), xxxii, xxxiii, 1190.

41. JoAnne Yates, How Business Enterprises Use Technology: Extending the Demand-Side Turn. *Enterprise and Society* 7 (2006): 423

42. Wiebe E. Bijker, Thomas P. Hughes, and Trevor Pinch, eds. *The Social Construction of Technological Systems: New Directions in the Sociology and History of Technology* (Cambridge, MA: MIT Press, 1987).

43. Nelly Oudshoorn and Trevor Pinch, *How Users and Non-Users Matter* (2003). See Ronald Kline and Trevor Pinch, Users as Agents of Technological Change: The Social Construction of the Automobile in the Rural United States, *Technology and Culture* 37 (1996): 763–95 for a pioneering study.

44. Oudshoorn and Pinch, 4.

45. A small sample of important texts, in addition to those already cited: Stuart Hall, Encoding/Decoding, in *Culture, Media and Language,* ed. Stuart Hall (London: Hutchinson, 1980), 128–38; Henry Jenkins, *Textual Poachers: Television Fans and Participatory Culture* (New York: Routledge, 1992); John Fiske, The Cultural Economy of Fandom, in *The Adoring Audience: Fan Culture and Popular Media,* ed. Lisa Lewis (London: Routledge, 1992), 30–49; Susan Strasser, Consumption Conspicuousness: Transgressive Topics go Mainstream, *Technology and Culture* 43 (2002): 755–570; Cornel Sandvoss, *Fans: The Mirror of Consumption* (Cambridge, England: Polity, 2005); Eric von Hippel, *Democratizing Innovation* (Cambridge, MA: MIT Press, 2005); Jenkins, *Convergence Culture: Where Old and New Media Collide* (New York: New York University Press, 2006).

46. Kline and Pinch, *Users as Agents*, 765.

47. Kline and Pinch, *Users as Agents*, 767.

48. Yates, *How Business Entreprises Use Technology*, 442.

49. Cf. Keith Grint and Steve Woolgar, eds. Configuring the User: Inventing New Technologies, in *The Machine at Work: Technology, Work and the Organization* (Cambridge, UK: Polity, 1997), 65–94; Hugh

Mackey, Chris Crane, Paul Beynon-Davies, and Doug Tudhope, Reconfigure the User: Using Rapid Application Development, *Social Studies of Science* 30 (2000): 737–757.

50. Including *Quake II,* released in 1997.

51. Strange Company, Company History (2005), http://www.strangecompany.org/page.php?id=19.

52. Ill Clan press release, February 12, 2001, http://www.illclan.com/ILL%20Clan-Showtime-PR.htm.

53. Exceptions include the Lithtech Film Producer/Player, co-developed with the machinima group Strange Company, and Epic's sponsorship with NVidia of the "Make Something Unreal" machinima contest.

54. Other reasons for the demise of the *Quake* movie included aspirations among machinima makers to produce for Web video or other media and improvements in game technology introduced by other game systems.

55. Michael E. Ryan, Quake III Arena, *PC Magazine*, June 26, 2001: 176.

56. Matt Pritchard, How to Hurt the Hackers: The Scoop on Internet Cheating and How You Can Combat It, *Game Developer*, July 24, 2000. http://www.gamasutra.com/features/20000724/pritchard_01.htm.

57. Uwe Girlich, The OpenDemo Project: Mission Statement. http://www.machinima.com/opendemo/od-about.html. His only recourse was to invent his own protocols through this OpenDemo project.

58. Hugh Hancock, Upcoming Technology: 2/00, *machinima.com*, http://www.machinima.com/article.php?article=403.

59. Hancock, *Upcoming Technology*.

60. Pritchard, *How to Hurt the Hackers*.

61. Paul Marino, *3-D Game-Based Filmmaking: The Art of Machinima* (Scottsdale, AZ: Paraglyph, 2004), 11.

62. Machinima, *The Word Spy*, Posted August 9, 2002. http://www.wordspy.com/words/machinima.asp.

63. The only exception I have found is Bailey's use of "machinema" in "Suggested Quake1 toolkit," (28 Jan 1999), ReMaic Web site, http://www.machinima.com/remaic/index.shtml.

64. http://www.machinima.com/tritin-films/.

65. Though *Half-Life* was based on *Quake* technology.

66. I am indebted for this line of thinking to Galen Davis of the Stanford How They Got Game Project. He is preparing an article on machinima and performance theory for publication. On camera phones and the emergence of new content, see: Daisuke Okabe and Mizuko Ito, Camera Phones Changing the Definition of Picture-Worthy, *Japan Media Review*, August 29, 2003. http://www.ojr.org/japan/wireless/1062208524.php, also Justin Hall's reports on weblogging and camera phones in *The Feature*, such as Rehearsing the Future: First International Moblogging Conference Report, *The Feature*, July 8, 2003. http://www.thefeature.com/article?articleid=24815&ref=30721.

67. From The Sidney and Harriet Janis Collection on view at Museum of Modern Art, New York, http://www.moma.org/collection/browse_secondary_images.php?criteria=O%3AOD%3AE%3A81631&page_number=1&template_id=1&sort_order=1&sec_img=1.

68. Strange Company, *Company History*.

69. Xavier Lardy, An Interview with Paul Marino, www.Machinima.fr, February 11, 2006. http://www.machinima.fr//index2.php?option=com_content&task=view&id=16&pop=1&page=0&Itemid=41.

70. Xavier Lardy, An Interview with Paul Marino.

71. Hugh Hancock, Making Machinima: Part 1, *machinima.com*, July 31, 2002. http://www.machinima.com/article.php?article=302.

72. Much of what follows on *WoW* movies is taken from my Storyline, Dance/Music, or PvP? Game Movies and Community Players in *World of Warcraft*, *Games & Culture* 1 (Oct. 2006): 362–382.

73. United Canadian Alliance Web site. http://clanuca.ca/index.php?content=about&PHPSESSID=2383368b5ff886e3c04ba1f0f1baab7c.

74. Tristan Pope, Crafting Worlds Web site (2005). http://www.craftingworlds.com/. Movies available at http://www.craftingworlds.com/videos.html.

75. *World of Warcraft* 1.3 patch notes (2005). http://www.worldofwarcraft.com/patchnotes/patch-05-07-04.html.

76. Caydiem, *Subject: Re: Rated M for Mature: LOCKED Was a good run!* Posted April 22, 2005 to General Discussion Forum. 2005. http://forums.worldofwarcraft.com/ (accessed May 2005).

77. Necrotus, *Subject: Re: Rated M for Mature . . .* Three posts dated April 22, 2005, and response by Fairon dated April 23, 2005. General Discussion Forum. 2005. http://forums.worldofwarcraft.com/.

78. Before the controversy ran out, two discussion threads devoted to it would gather nearly 800 replies with more than 200,000 views. Pope. 2005. *Subject: Rated M for Mature . . .* Posted April 22, 2005 as "Tristanmon," in General Discussion Forum. http://forums.worldofwarcraft.com.

79. Henry Lowood, 2006; Andy Clarke and Grethe Mitchell, eds., *Videogames and Art: Intersections and Interactions* (London: Intellect, 2007), 59–79.

PART III: DELIMITING SOME FUTURES: ISSUES AND CONCERNS

Growing Up Digital: Control and the Pieces of a Digital Life

Robert A. Heverly

University of East Anglia, Norwich Law School

Entanglement, Persistence, and Growing Up Digital

When young people speak about digital media, they generally speak about it as something they use, a tool called upon to do a general or specific task or tasks. They show an awareness of digital media's promise, its pervasiveness, even its potential misuse by themselves and others. They use the medium. It may not be perfect, but almost without fail they externalize it—it is apart from them, different, exogenous. It may change what they can do, how they can do it, even how they live, but it does not change them as such (though it may help them to change themselves).

There is little, if any, explicit recognition among young people that digital media may not only be used by them, but in fact, may use them. That is, when young people become the subject (or object, if you will) of digital media, they are used by it; when a digital media artifact—a digital media file of any type, for example video, audio, still image, text—that features them is created, part of them becomes entangled with the digital media and forms the substance of it. Yet, children (and many adults) tend not to recognize this, preferring to retain the familiar conception of using a tool to achieve an end and then casting that tool aside without further thought. Even where it is considered in greater detail by scholars, where changes in the person who uses (or views, in some cases) digital media are expertly analyzed, almost no attention is paid to how being enmeshed in digital media actually affects people.[1] That being "in" the media can change people has always been true of media and those featured in media artifacts, but changes in how we create media and what we can then do with those media are changing the importance of these observations for our youth (and adults).

For example, now forty years old, I have relatively few pictures of myself from when I was very young, and those that I do have are either at my father's house or in boxes in my garage where they are difficult to find. There are a few videos of me here and there, made by parents first using an eight millimeter film camera and then later using a VHS video recorder. If anyone wanted to find a photograph of me, either online or off, the ones they would find would most likely be modern ones, after I turned thirty, when the internet, and especially the World Wide Web, began growing and flourishing. Older pictures or videos, especially those that might have the capacity to today embarrass me in some way, are probably outside the ability of anyone other than the most dedicated detectives to procure. This is true of many people who grew up in the "analog world" where photographs were things you held in your hand after getting them back from the photo lab, and for whom home videos were made up of the complete video footage shot by a person with a bulky video camera.

In contrast to this story of the "ancient art of analog media," I have a young daughter who, as of this writing, is nineteen months old. My wife and I have taken more than 1,500 digital pictures of her in the year and a half since she was born, and over ten hours of "raw" digital video. She will be able to look back at her life over time, from moments after her birth until she has her own children, and find media files made by us, by her, and by others. These media files will be the pieces of her digital life, created as she lives as a digital person. Her friends will take and share photographs and video of her, and she will do the same with them. Early performances in school, athletic events, dressing up for Carnival or Halloween, sleigh riding in the snow, all will be part of various digital media files. In the end analysis, the digital record of her life may not be complete, but it will be extensive. She will be able to search this digital record, find specific digital media files, and share them with others.

Here, in this latter story, the story of children growing up today, my daughter will still grow up in a variety of ways, as has always been the case. But a new way of growing up has been added in recent years, due primarily to the technological and cultural changes that have brought us into the information age. As have others in the past, she will grow up female, white, and probably tall (though the jury will be out some number of years before this latter element is decided for certain). But, importantly, she will also grow up digital. Parts of herself, and her life, will be embedded into the digital media artifacts that are created using digital media devices throughout her life, used by herself and by others. This growing up digital is distinct in crucial ways from growing up analog, as those of us now grown experienced growing up. Some of these differences are teased out above in the nature of a world where people's memories are extensive and accessible to them. The differences, however, between the analog and the digital go further, and the panacea of life's memories easily and quickly available is juxtaposed against the negative potential of digital media persisting over longer time frames than was generally true for analog media. Where this persistence allows digital media artifacts to reappear at inopportune or unwanted moments, they are pernicious in nature, being negative and unwanted. Identifying that negative potential and the effects that the persistence of digital media artifacts may have on the lives and futures of our children are the critical issues addressed in this chapter.

The negative possibilities, as is usually the case when technology meets society, are legion; we will, however, attempt to avoid the rhetoric and the hyperbole of doom, the urge to yell "Danger, Will Robinson!" when confronted with the new potential for persistence of digital media. We will instead focus on cognizable harms that are already beginning to be seen, both as to boys and as to girls,[2] and on the reasonably logical extensions of these developing situations. It is especially the persistence of the media—defined as its longevity of existence and the ease with which it can be located—that will form the basis of our discussion, and likewise that forms the basis for the claims here of potential negative consequences.

This persistence raises the question of control, for control could potentially obviate the negative consequences of that persistence. This places the question of control of digital artifacts after they are created and distributed within the core of our inquiry, and the perceptions and realities of control of and over digital artifacts will point our predictions in various directions. We will look at the question of control primarily through the lens of the law, a discipline that is often seen as playing an important—at times critical—role in control over the creation and distribution of the kinds of creative works with which we are concerned here.

While control as seen through the law's lens will be the continuing theme we will address, we will also use it to consider why children are different from adults when it comes to evaluating the potential for future and long-term harm from present actions. Law is likely to follow its established practices in this area, and we will touch upon areas such as juvenile offender law, contract law, and even the law relating to drinking alcohol and smoking cigarettes, while considering this question. In the end, we will recognize the challenge the persistence of digital media creates for our future, and we will think about the role that law might play in relation to minimizing the long-term effects of childhood decision making on young people's choices when it comes to creating and embedding themselves in digital media artifacts.

It thus seems we have two stories to tell, one of long-term access to life's memories and events, and one of the danger that flows from being embedded in digital media artifacts that persist across time that are identifiable and can be found across time. We are not describing here alternate futures of pure technological bliss opposed to "a sick future society glued together around communication technologies" (Angell, discussing William Gibson's "Neuromancer").[3] This is a false dichotomy (as dichotomies often are). Our two stories are actually one and the same—they run together, not separately. But even this is not a story of inevitability, either of positive outcomes or negative ones, nor is it a tale of the ability of technology to determine outcomes to the exclusion of other realms of influence. Rather, it is a story told based on our evolving understanding of and experience with these new technologies, with an admonition that the negative is perhaps just as likely as the positive, and that the positive and negative will coexist, playing off of and into each other. We must consider the negative effects along with the positive when we think about technology and our youth. We must not forget the negative potential of digital media technologies while pursuing the positive benefits of their use. We must also consider what these technologies do to and with our children as well as what our children do to and with these technologies. In other words, where children are entangled in and become a part of digital media artifacts, we must consider the nature, importance, and future potential of that entanglement when thinking about the creation of and control over those artifacts. These contentions give us a great deal to think about as we walk the crossroads from the analog to the digital world, and the stories we will consider here will help us to see how and where we might end up based on choices we are making—or in some cases remaking—today and in the near future.

To help us to think more deeply about the interactions and interconnections of the negative and positive aspects of the lifelong creation of digital media artifacts—of growing up and living digital—this chapter will first lay out some scenarios that show the potential negative effects of the distribution of digital media featuring young people, stories that temper the story outlined above of memories preserved over a lifetime. We then turn to a consideration of why control matters, with a specific inquiry into why it matters for our children and how digital media have increased the importance of these questions, followed by looking at responsibility and autonomy through the eyes of the law, seeking to understand how the law views children in relation to these two areas. We then revisit control, this time specifically of digital media artifacts, and provide some modest suggestions for how we might actively engage with the questions at hand and provide some relief from the negative potential we identified earlier. We close with thoughts on digital media artifacts, growing up digital, and our children, with cautious optimism for the lives that will be lived digitally.

Some comments before we proceed further. The story told in this chapter is one of unintended and unexpected outcomes of technological progression and adoption throughout society. They are unintended because digital media were not developed so that digital media artifacts could become perniciously persistent. In this vein, to the extent they have already begun to appear, these effects were largely unexpected. We can change at least that; that is, in a semantic sense if not more, no outcome that we are discussing can be entirely unexpected. Once we discuss it, it is at least theoretically possible. Changing these outcomes from unexpected to being within the realm of our predictive understanding is one small hope of this chapter.

Finally, the lessons learned here are not unique to the age group that features as the primary focus of its analysis—young people under the age of eighteen. Indeed, many of the lessons here are very relevant in today's world to adults, and especially to college-age young adults who are over eighteen but under twenty-two. Many adults formerly in married or committed relationships who created digital media of personal moments can also attest to the deviousness of their distribution after the relationship broke down; yet, the importance of these effects, and the nature of them, is qualitatively different when we consider children as opposed to adults, even young adults. In this chapter the choice is made to play up these differences and focus on the perniciousness of digital media as they relate to children or young people who are not yet adults (under the law). This choice, however, does not alter the fact that similar issues are raised for adults in confronting their digital selves. Whether the law should step in for adults, however, in the way it is argued that law might step in for our youth, is a question left for future consideration.

Control: Why We Care

It might seem easy to work from a position that assumes that digital media artifacts, as the expressions of their creators, are mere speech with limited ability to harm those who are their subjects. The following scenarios are designed to show that, in these circumstances, the creation of digital media artifacts has the potential to have significant and potentially severe negative effects on those whose digital selves are captured within the boundaries of those artifacts. The following scenarios are based in reality, many times backed by actual facts lived out by real people, people who were growing up digitally as well as physically.

We start here with four examples that show digital media's pernicious nature through its apparently spontaneous appearance, its potential for viral distribution, and its expectation of permanence. These examples are a mix of truth and fiction, but each is rooted not in hysteria, but in some reality of digital media. None is intended to be hyperbolic; they are all offered as examples of the reality that this chapter later takes up.

Everyone Does It: Why Not Me?
After an evening out with her boyfriend, Katie, then seventeen, goes back to his house with him, where he encourages her to take some sexy pictures. She says, "Why not; lots of couples do it, why not me?" Her boyfriend takes the pictures with her camera, but she leaves the camera with him. The relationship later ends, and after it does, the digital photographs are distributed: some are distributed electronically by her boyfriend, others are distributed by his friends both in physical form and electronically. The photographs are eventually sent to her parents, with her relationship with them being damaged, possibly beyond repair. Criminal charges are eventually filed against the ex-boyfriend and his friend, and convictions on charges of distributing child pornography are obtained against them. Yet, the photographs persist on the internet, and each time they are seen she is again subjected to feelings of disgrace and shame.

Just For You

The year is 2001, the internet bubble is bursting, but the internet itself is growing by leaps and bounds. In Madison, Wisconsin, a college boy—we'll call him Mark—makes and sends to his girlfriend a number of videos of him engaging in rather personal behavior. These often end with a kiss blown at the Web camera on which they were recorded. This couple's relationship subsequently ends, and the videos are distributed on the World Wide Web (how they come to be distributed is a question for which there is no certain answer, and which is not entirely required for our purposes). Internet rumors say the girlfriend was charged and convicted of distributing child pornography, but as Mark was over eighteen when the videos were made, this is likely to be myth. Other rumors have Mark changing his name, his university, and his life to avoid further detection. Again, this is unconfirmed, and there are no major media stories describing this scenario. It was lived out wholly on the Web. Yet, by running a correctly phrased search in a modern search engine today, you will still find these videos being distributed by numerous Web sites, not to speak of peer-to-peer users, and private or registration-only bulletin boards. Mark created these videos; he sent them to someone he loved, and now, they may "follow" him for the rest of his life. Each time one is viewed, a stranger is allowed to see his deepest secrets and watch him in private acts meant for only one other person; each time one is redistributed, he is injured once again. He wonders whether one day his children will find these digital media artifacts and ask him why he behaved this way at this time in his life.

Persistent Embarrassment

Jack is a respected teacher in a poor area of an urban city. He struggles to keep control over his class, which is made up of some of the most difficult learners in the school. They are constantly questioning him and spreading stories about him to the other kids at the school. One day, one of the students finds a picture of Jack from when he was younger, and brings it to class. It is a straightforward picture of Jack on a bicycle winning a race. Because he now knows what Jack looked like when he was younger, another student finds a video of him and also brings it to school. In this video, Jack is being picked on by some larger students at his middle school: they approach him, pull off his pants and underpants, spray his body with paint, and run away, leaving him there, degraded and partially naked. Jack is clearly aware of the existence of the camera, but can do nothing to stop what is happening. Students' laughter from off-camera echoes in the closing moments of the video and the word "punct" appears at the end of it. Jack's students spread the video throughout the school, sharing it with friends and acquaintances alike via their portable media devices. The last of Jack's control over his classroom, and of his self-respect as an adult, fades into the background after being forced to repeatedly relive this experience from his childhood, an experience he had tried hard to leave behind.

The Hidden Camera

Susan had been the victim of bullying for much of her life. Since entering high school, she had been taunted and teased at every turn. Some of this teasing happened in the locker room after physical education classes, when Susan had to be naked along with her tormentors. Susan dreaded these encounters, and did her best to protect her dignity and pride. One day one of the other girls snuck a camera phone into the shower, and recorded a video of Susan trying to keep herself covered while she showered. The video was shown around school, and led to Susan's parents removing her from that school and moving to avoid the continued teasing. Susan graduated from college with a political science degree and got a job in the legislature, eventually running for and attaining elected office herself. During one campaign, the video of her from so long ago is "found" and redistributed, bringing Susan back into the emotion and heartache of her youth and bullying her again.

These scenarios show us a number of things. Initially, they also help us to see the potential for both immediate and long-term harm from the creation and distribution of digital media artifacts. But, from law's perspective, they help us start to see who might have legal rights over the distribution of particular media artifacts we are concerned with, a question we will return to later. There is a continuum of digital media artifact creative activity and involvement that moves from active creation to a passive object. "Active creation" involves young people who embed themselves in digital media artifacts not only by choice, but both by directing the creation of the media files and by embedding themselves within them. The "passive object" is the pure subject of digital media's creation; the object neither participates in the decision to create the artifact nor directs any part of its coming into being; in fact, the pure object may not even know that the digital media is being created (though he or she may later learn of its creation). Between these polar extremes exist situations where the object may have knowledge, or may acquiesce to the artifact's creation, but does not exercise control over its creation. These matter to who has control, often technological, often legal, and the effects of these elements of control on the actual practice of control in the real world is the next step in our journey.

Digital Media: Why Control Matters Even More Today

Types of Media: Differential Similarities

Not all media are created equal. As McLuhan taught us, the medium is the message, a lesson that at times has been a bit overstated. Yet, we recognize that human beings perceive media in different ways. A written text is different from a photograph, a photograph is different from a recorded moving image, a recorded moving image is different from a live moving image, and a live moving image is different from live action viewed directly. Add in audio and the differences are multiplied further.

The point here is thus a fairly straightforward one: all digital media are not equal. If we consider a young boy who writes a "racy" e-mail to a girl for whom he has strong affections, should that e-mail appear later in his life, his first line of defense would be to simply deny his affiliation with it. It is incredibly easy not only to create text and pretend that it was created by another, but even to create false e-mails that appear to be from one person when they are in fact from another (thus the wide distribution of spam and viruses via e-mail). It is similarly easy to fictionalize an account of a particular event, including who participated and what occurred. If we read a text account, especially from an untrustworthy source such as a personal Web page, we are likely to be quite doubtful of its authenticity, both as to origin and as to claims of truthfulness. This will be exacerbated where the subject of the textual account denies their participation, that the events took place as told, or both, especially where we are personally familiar with the person making that denial.

Visual media has a significant effect on our perceptions, our beliefs, and our understanding of the world around us. But even following the advent of visual-based media, such as photography and television, because of the significant cost of both creating the relevant media artifacts and the difficulties of distributing them, our perceptions could be rationally based on generally accepting visual depictions at face value. Our neighbor could not broadcast a video into our homes; in fact, until quite recently, any video camera owned by our neigh-bor was likely to produce video media artifacts of a quality that they were easily seen as "nonprofessional," and the neighbor's attempt to alter the video, or to undertake such post-production as to alter the reality captured within it, was unlikely. It was simply too expensive to capture and alter visual depictions.

This state of affairs is rapidly changing. The price of digital still and video cameras has fallen such that they are now within the financial grasp of a large number of people, and the integration of capturing video with computer generated postproduction, and your neighbor now can make "professional" visual images. He can clone out red eye in photographs, or even convincingly remove an entire house; he can add graphics, additional images, and undertake animation with video cameras. The analog methods of creation and production, once in the hands of the "trusted" few, are now increasingly in the hands of the many. We are now all potential creators, leaving only our senses and our critical thinking skills to keep us from being convinced that Martians have landed in Washington and are taking over the world.

As we move on in our inquiry here, the thing to remember is that the shift to easy and inexpensive creation of digital media files means that these differences are critical to the problem we are predicting here. Without this ease, children themselves would not likely have the ability to embed themselves or to be embedded in digital media artifacts to the extent that currently appears likely. Add to this—as we shall see—the potential for persistence of these digital media files, and it appears likely that young people who create digital artifacts as the offshoot of growing up digital—with their likeness and actions embedded in digital media files—will suffer from unexpected outcomes in relation to these digital artifacts due at least partially to a lack of control—legal, cultural, normative, technological—over them after they are created. How distribution has changed, and especially why it plays this critical role, is the point we take up next.

Strangers, Networks and Storage, and Persistence

We reach now an integral part of our story. Digital media creation is potentially in the hands of everyone. We all may be the objects of those digital media, with various pieces of our digital lives or of our growing up digital embedded within them. We may have actively participated in the creation of those artifacts of digital life, or we may be only their objects. So what?

The answer is that the transition to digital media, accompanied by the increased availability of the tools for digital media creation, also alters another fundamental element of media creation: distribution. We have already seen that the creation of digital media artifacts is now easier than ever, and it is likely to become even easier and less costly over time, becoming a pervasive part of everyday life as media creation devices are embedded in other technologies, such as mobile phones. But, how has distribution, another essential piece of the puzzle, changed?

In the past, duplication and distribution of media files was more expensive, both in cost and in quality, when those files were in analog formats. Recording a vinyl record onto a cassette tape took as long as it would take to play the album through, including flipping the album over halfway through. Making further copies of the tape required another connected cassette deck, and each copy—even the first cassette—was of a lower quality than the original. This is described in media terms by saying that such copies were "lossy"—each subsequent generation of copies was a bit worse than the original. Finally, to share the media created, some physical connection was required. That is, they had to be sent through the post or handed over in person. So, creation, duplication, and distribution were all quite difficult. You could, generally, only share with people you knew (unless you were willing to risk being caught selling such goods in a flea market).

If an analog videotape had been made by a young woman for a young man, she would have had to deliver it to him personally or by mail, and if their relationship had later ended, he would have been hard pressed to show it to more than his direct circle of friends. Preventing further distribution would have been the difficulties of distribution, such as his likely inability to get a video production company to be willing to release it without his ex-girlfriend's consent, and the loss in quality if he wanted to make duplicate copies himself. In addition, if he had offered to show the video to strangers, perhaps those passing by in the local shopping mall, he would likely have been ignored, and probably asked to leave that public space. If, ten years later, someone wondered whether this young woman had ever made such a video, he would have had to hire a private investigator to inquire of her past friends and boyfriends, something most people would not be willing to do. Discovering the existence of such a video, let alone finding a copy, would have been a practically impossible—or at least highly improbable—task.

These examples show us that a number of obstacles to the creation and distribution of the artifacts of growing up analog would have limited the effect that these artifacts could have later in life: readily available technologies only allowed relatively poor copies to be made, with each copy generally taking the same time to make as the media artifact being copied; distribution was limited to physical means, and was generally limited to personal acquaintances (perhaps even as limited as "good friends"); and trying to determine the existence and location of such files in later years was so difficult that most people would not have attempted it.

Digital technology has "solved" these problems, or at least allowed most people to overcome them. Our first objection disappears as the computer and digital media devices allow us to make perfect copies of all of our digital media. If we change the format—say from CD audio to MP3—the quality may be somewhat degraded, but copies of the MP3 file will duplicate the original MP3 file exactly. In addition, digital copying can take place in mere fractions of the time of making an analog copy, as it is the speed of the computer processor and related technology that matters, not the time length of the original file.

Our next obstacle—that of distribution—falls as digital devices such as computers are interconnected and networked or as digital media technology is introduced into mobile phones. We can now widely distribute files of any type, without knowledge of who the receivers or potential receivers are. This can happen through Web pages, peer-to-peer technologies, file transfer protocol (FTP) servers, or other networked technologies (widely grouped around use of the internet). But, as we shall see, not only can we easily distribute, we can just as easily lose control of the file. Once it's been released "into the wild," it may be impossible to ever get it fully back under control. As media companies have learned, finding and deleting or even inhibiting access to digital files once they are released is difficult, if not impossible. Restrictions on access need to be included at the file's creation; if they are not, or if they are overcome, they most likely cannot be restored later. We will explore some of the implications of setting digital artifacts free in the digital wilderness as we move further through this discussion.

Our last analog obstacle—that of discovering and locating media artifacts—is again solved in the digital age. This time, our saviors appear in the form of search engines, archive sites, and online communities that share digital media files, often by niche or type. Thus, amateur sex videos are distributed on many internet sites, while others specialize in distributing strange, odd, embarrassing, or even disturbing videos, photographs, and stories. Some of these sites even maintain tutorials describing how to capture and prepare digital media artifacts for distribution to others. Still, other sites, rather than collecting, simply locate existing videos or photographs and make them available—from the original Web site—in a gallery format for viewing or downloading. In addition, the major search engines together have indexed file data on a large number of pages available on the Web, and often on the files that those Web pages include. Archive sites allow material that used to be available on the Web, but no longer is, to be found. This form of data indexing is now pervasive and user friendly. If you want to find it, and it's out there, there is a technology available to help you do so.

All of this together makes discovering the existence of and identifying particular copies of media files now easier (though not necessarily "easy") to do. Even media content that was originally in an analog format may have been converted to digital and can now be shared. Today's technology allows us to communicate personal digital media content to strangers, and it allows the personal digital media content to remain available and findable over long periods of time.

This point deserves further elaboration. Even with the ability to create and distribute, there is little to support the claims here if the digital media artifacts do not persist across time. Persistence, and especially the kind of pernicious persistence described here, is not simple existence. It is the ability to learn not only the existence of the artifact, but to be able to locate and obtain a copy of it. The case is being made that digital media artifacts are yet again qualitatively different in this respect when compared with analog media files. Something has changed in the way that media artifacts exist in the shift from analog to digital creation and distribution, and that something makes the files not just easier to create and easier to distribute, but also easier to find, both in terms of finding out about them (i.e., of their existence) and in terms of finding where they are (i.e., their actual location).

Think back to a time when music lovers had collections of record albums, pressed on vinyl, on shelves in their living rooms. They may have recorded cassettes from these albums, either full copies of the albums or "mixed tapes" (given names appropriate to their use, such as "driving tape" or "music for the beach"). Now recall how hard it may have been to find a particular song on a particular album, or worse yet, on a mixed tape made by someone else. If they had not written the order of the songs down, finding a particular song on a particular tape involved first locating the cassette tape and then fast forwarding and rewinding through it.

This continued with the advent of videotapes, whether recorded for private use and time shifting, or recorded on an analog video camera. If a person failed to label the tape and name it something useful, finding video content later was something of a nightmare. Even if the date of creation was known, finding specific content on an unlabeled tape, especially where large numbers were unlabeled, was a difficult task.

Add the element of time to the mix. Consider the example of a videotape recorded ten years ago, showing the camera operator's young friend falling off of his bicycle because he wasn't paying attention to what he was doing. That tape sits in a pile of unlabeled tapes in a box in a dusty corner of the camera operator's garage, forgotten and unknown. The video's subject—the bicycle rider—is now a bicycle safety instructor, and he claims as he badgers his students about paying attention to their riding that he has never in his life let his attention wander when he rides. He is particularly hard on one young man who doesn't seem to be getting the message. This young man broods over the instructor's directions, sure that at some point the instructor, too, was not focused on his task. Yet he has no way to know of the videotape's existence, let alone its location. Even if the person who knew of its existence remembered that it existed, it would be difficult to find. The original tape exists, but it is not persistent as that term is used here, because it is largely forgotten. Even if it had not been forgotten, it would not easily be found.

Digital media in the networked environment changes this. Alter our scenario to make the video recording a digital one, showing the same events. Perhaps the boy—now our instructor—who fell thinks the video is quite funny, and asks his friend to post it to an "embarrassing moments" Web site. It is uploaded, and at the time of upload is categorized, named, and its content described. The friends then tell all their friends about it, and everyone watches it. Google, Yahoo, MSN and other search engines index the site, so that anyone searching for this boy's name will find the video. Eventually, archive sites, dedicated to making sure materials that are available online remain so over time, archive the video and its attendant metadata—that information about the artifact, information that relates to it and describes it—where it remains available over time.

We return to the present, except now the young man who has been the focus of the instructor's attention simply goes home and searches the Web for the instructor's name. If the original site is still operating, the video is easily found using whatever is the main search engine of the day. If the original site is no longer available, then archive sites may provide a means to both identify and locate the video. The digital age has again altered how things were in comparison to the analog age, that is, digital media artifacts now exist more persistently across time, and have an increased potential for long-term effects when compared with analog media artifacts.

It is persistence across time that is the point here. Digital media artifacts, whether made by young people or made by adults, persist across time. They are created, categorized, and stored in a way that makes them easier to find across both time and geographic distance. We will make more of them (quantitatively), and they will be distributed more widely. They will persist, and the implications of their existence will be extended across time and space in a way that is qualitatively different from similarly produced analog media artifacts.

There is an argument that incompatible file formats could prevent later viewing or reading of data originally saved in a file format that is no longer used. The brief history of the Web shows us, however, that where there is a need for a conversion technology to make "old data" or "old files" that have become obsolete through technological change usable today, a conversion utility will be created and made available, often for free. This has occurred in relation to games originally played on the first gaming consoles, which cannot be played in their native format on either current computers or current gaming consoles. A number of Web sites and Web communities exist to make such games available again, including creating and maintaining the application software required to make them function on today's powerful PCs.[4] So far, our experience has been that if a file is digital to begin with, someone, somewhere, can design a way to make that file readable again today. Because digital files are flexible, or "plastic"—they are, after all, in a binary form, made up of zeros and ones—it seems that this is likely to continue.[5] Thus, it seems that digital media artifacts are likely to be persistent, that is, their existence and location will likely be known or knowable, and they will likely exist in a usable form.

An Aside and a Retreat

Some of the assertions above may be made too strongly, especially given continued changes in technology. Remember, this chapter does not flow from the perspective of technological determinism. We will make it such that in the future, with our technology, our futures will not be determined for us by that technology. A critical element of this current issue is that the costs of creation and distribution of digital media have declined, leading to the widespread use of digital technologies to create digital media artifacts. Is it not that other technological costs are likely to decrease, as well, that might mitigate the impact of the "If I can see it, it must be real" perceptive phenomenon? There is no strong reason to argue that they will not. In fact, it is possible that soon anyone working with digital media will be able to alter video and photographic images so easily and so effectively that we will, within society, simply learn to distrust those images as much as we may distrust bare text. Remember, there was a time when the written word, signed under wax seal, was truth. That day is long gone, but the potential for "seeing is believing" to follow in its wake given current changes in technology does not seem impossible or even improbable.

Persistence and Pernicious Effects: Maturity, Responsibility, Autonomy

There is potential harm, and potential long-term unanticipated harm, to children from the creation of and their entanglement with digital media artifacts. Spouses, partners, lovers, and friends are already learning about the pernicious effects of digital media today. We are concerned here with these harms as well, but injuries such as these cannot be viewed or reviewed outside of the society's structures for addressing such harms. Protections against harm cannot do more damage to society than they prevent in terms of individual harm. We thus must balance any response to the largely unforeseen pernicious persistence of digital media artifacts against the problems that may arise in crafting a solution to the persistence problem.

We are concerned with adults whose lives are disrupted by the appearance or reappearance of digital media artifacts made by them as adults and that they reasonably thought were private, or about which they had no knowledge, but we are also constrained in our responses by the institutional and regulatory structures that we perceive as holding society together. Individual autonomy and individual responsibility are two important parts of the theoretical groundwork that justifies both criminal and civil law. The pernicious persistence of digital media artifacts created by or featuring adults may thus place us squarely in the middle of rather intractable debates regarding freedom of expression and individual responsibility. This is not the place, however, to dive into this debate, though diving in will likely be necessary at some point in the future. Law treats adults as individuals and holds them responsible for their actions.

A different case arises, however, when it comes to our children. The law treats children differently from adults across a range of enterprises and experiences. It often does so based on the arbitrary establishment of an age, only upon the attainment of which can the relevant person undertake the relevant action. There is no set age used by law to determine when the shift to a future-oriented perspective occurs for our young people. In the United States, the law uses the ages of eighteen to signify sufficient maturity for purposes of voting and twenty-one for drinking alcohol, while in the U.K. those ages are eighteen for both voting and drinking alcohol. In Germany, young people must be eighteen before they can independently bind themselves contractually without the consent of their guardians. These ages are based as much on perception and ad hoc (adult) experience than on hard scientific fact, but we are generally in agreement that young people need to be mature before they will understand the effects of certain of their actions. The law sometimes seems to go to extremes to prevent young people from suffering long-term harms from their "youthful indiscretions."[6]

Yet, we do not shield our children in every way and from everything they do that might follow them throughout their lives. The marks a child receives in school may be important to entering college, which may then affect their path in life, and though the "permanent record" may not exist, the effects of early decisions on children's later choices in life are noticeable. This is especially true with regard to having choices as to which University to attend, a choice that can often be highly determinative of later opportunities in life. Law does not shield children from the long-term effects of these decisions. In fact, in many countries the performance of children in primary school determines their choices of secondary school.[7]

Our focus on the global nature of the distribution network for digital media artifacts has taught us that it is difficult, indeed perhaps impossible, to strictly control the distribution of such artifacts once they are "in the wild" given the current state of the law. We return to this international focus now, seeking a useful description of when the law acts, and does not act, to protect children and young people from the potentially harmful effects of their actions. Our purpose remains to consider whether the law should act specifically in the interests of children to strengthen their control over digital media artifacts in which they are embedded.

At times, minors are prohibited ex ante from engaging in certain acts—smoking cigarettes, drinking alcohol, driving automobiles—because minors are viewed by the law as being insufficiently mature to deal with the implications and potential negative effects of their actions in these situations. In some cases, such as smoking cigarettes, it is both the current decision that young people are seen as being insufficiently mature to understand, and the long-term implications of that current decision. At other times, minors are released after the fact from the long-term implications that would be suffered by an adult who has taken the same actions. Thus, minors who sign contracts might be released from their terms, depending on the law of the contracting jurisdiction.[8] Minors who commit crimes might have their records cleared or expunged ex post upon reaching the age of twenty-one.[9]

In both the ex ante and ex post scenarios, action is taken by the state—through law—to address questions of the perceived inability of minors to make certain decisions. Whether this is actually effective or not is often open to debate,[10] and it should be noted that the law acts in this paternalistic fashion not only in regard to minors, but also in many cases—such as prohibiting suicide or requiring helmets for motorcyclists, for example—to adults as well.[11] In addition, the question of maturity and capacity for decision making is often politicized, such as in the area of requirements for parental approval for abortions sought by their children.[12]

The reality is, however, that the law—at least in common law jurisdictions such as the United States and the U.K.—does not have a clear track record of addressing these questions. It is yet another murky patchwork of provisions arising from separate legal doctrines, and lacks a common juridical thread that might be seen as holding it together, though attempts to bring order to the chaos have been made.[13] Reactionary movements to lower the threshold under which minors are charged as adults help little to settle the law.[14] This might perhaps best be identified as law's schizophrenic side, an element that makes it difficult to predict how law would intervene in affairs such as these. There is a desire to recognize children as autonomous actors, while at the same time insulating them from the repercussions of some of their actions. This conflict seems to underlie the current movements to remove minor protection where the action taken is perceived as adult, even if the minor could not—from a developmental standpoint—fully understand the implications of their actions.

With all of this, the only generalized conclusion we can reach here is that there are circumstances under which the law will intervene on behalf of young people to prevent them from doing harm to themselves, to prevent others doing harm to them, or to prevent them from suffering the long-term effects of certain decisions that they might make. In all cases, it is a community choice based on the cultural norms of a particular society.

This is a story of how the law sometimes shields and protects children, and sometimes does not. Here, the kinds of effects that may ultimately result, and the way in which they have come into being, are a fairly straightforward result of the immaturity of the young people involved in making or being featured in the artifacts we are discussing. In addition, the injury is to that young person, not to another person, such as in the case of a murder committed by a fifteen-year-old. Intervention on the part of the law—protection for children—thus seems warranted.

Here, law might take up young people's cause because the pervasiveness and persistence of digital media have the potential to increase the long-term effects of what is an otherwise healthy and necessary part of development. Where a youngster shares his or her experimentation with others, especially using visual media, there is the potential for this digital media artifact to reappear at a later time in life. Because society is not particularly good at accepting embarrassing moments as simply a natural part of life, these videos have the potential to cause significant embarrassment later in life, especially if they appear at inopportune moments or are found by people who would use them against their subjects.

This need to experiment, to try and determine for themselves what is good, right, interesting, and fun, is natural—it is a part of life. Some experimentation is expected, and recording some of this experimentation, this growth, would not likely have any negative effect on the future. In fact, a mother being able to show her daughter that she too once learned to ride a bicycle would likely be positive. It could create shared memories and help solidify the bond between parent and child. But, where there is a potential for negative effects, especially long-term negative effects, the solution most societies have chosen is to insulate children from them in whatever ways are possible.

The question thus remains whether special intervention on the part of children is required here. To answer this question we must investigate whether the law already provides young people with the control they need, control over the digital media artifacts in which they are entangled while living their digital lives. We must therefore ask to whom the law currently gives control of these artifacts, and if we are dissatisfied with the answer, we must consider what the law might do beyond what those provisions it already has in place to address the issues raised by those who become entangled in digital media artifacts.

The Law and Control of Digital Media Content

The initial question for investigation at this point is the law's application and its relevance in determining who has legal control over the digital media artifacts created while growing up—or living—digital. As we shall see, for a variety of reasons, it is initially unlikely that a subject that appears in a digital media artifact will be given control over that artifact by the law. There are circumstances where this does happen, but they are limited and do little to allow us to address the problems that might result where control is not awarded to the individual in question.

Legal control over digital media artifacts flows from a variety of doctrines in a variety of areas. In the United States and the United Kingdom, intellectual property law—specifically, copyright law—is relevant. Privacy would also seem to have some pertinence to our question, though as we shall see, privacy law often has little substance that is related to what we perceive as private outside of the law. Other law is relevant, as well, such as laws against creating and distributing child pornography. Our task here is not to provide an in-depth, comprehensive review of every legal nuance across a host of national legal structures. Instead, we will endeavor to touch only the surface with an eye toward gaining an understanding of the structure of control. Much of what appears here will of necessity oversimplify what are at times complex issues, but not so much that they will be inaccurate, and hopefully the balance struck will be between complexity and comprehensiveness on one hand, and not losing focus on our ultimate goal of dissecting potential futures in a world in which our existence is entangled within persistently pernicious digital media artifacts on the other.

Copyright law provides "ownership" over creative works that meet its rather low creativity or originality requirement (essentially that the creative works not be directly copied from existing works, and that the required level of effort was put into their creation). Copyright protects expressions of ideas, but not the ideas themselves.[15] When a digital media artifact is created, unless it is a copy of an existing work, it is likely to qualify for protection under copyright law, even if it uses existing works as part of its content (though doing so may itself be a violation of the copyright in those existing works). The important element to note here is that copyright law generally protects the authors of works, giving ownership of the created work to that author[16] (the author being a legal term of art that essentially equates with the legally prescribed "creator" of a work). In some cases, authorship is quite straightforward—a poet who writes a poem has created it, and is therefore its author (and first owner), for example—though there are of course exceptions (such as "works for hire" or works created within the course of employment). Where copyright attaches, the copyright owner has the authority to stop unauthorized distribution, copying, and public display of the work. Copyright law would thus seem to be a strong potential ally in our search for control over digital media files with young people as their objects.

The difficulty in utilizing copyright law for this purpose, however, is that the author of a digital media work is unlikely to also be its subject. For example, under U.S. law, motion picture ownership is most often subsumed under the "work for hire" doctrine (wherein the studio employer becomes the owner of the copyright).[17] In our scenarios above, there was no employer, no work for hire, and so we need to understand copyright's perception of a film's author outside of the traditional commercial film studio. In that capacity, the author of a film is uncertain; it may be the camera person, or the producer, or both of them and others jointly (where both exist). It may be the actors, but this appears unlikely, as they may undertake the acting, but play little part in the creation of what is considered the motion picture. In the U.K., the authors of a "film" are the principal director and the producer,[18] the "producer" being defined as the person who made the arrangements necessary for the film to come into being.[19] There is little question that in the U.K., actors are not "authors" of films in which they appear. Similar results are obtained in relation to photographs, where it is the photographer, not the subject photographed, who "earns" the right under intellectual property law to "own" the rights to that photograph under copyright law.

In the scenarios presented near the start of this chapter, only one person—Mark, who made and sent videos of himself to his girlfriend—was both the maker (and thus author) of the digital media artifacts as well as their object. He entangled himself in these digital media artifacts, and as such was likely their legal owner. In all three of the other scenarios, the person with whom we are concerned, the one the digital media's pernicious persistence may later affect—was object only (willing participant, knowing participant, or unknowing object aside), and therefore likely has few if any rights under copyright law in the artifact with which their digital selves has become entangled.

We are forced then to turn to other areas of law that may provide help in the kinds of situations we are discussing here. Privacy law is one, but to even begin to delve into the legal conception of privacy is to open a can or worms that could not be returned to their can by the end of this entire series of volumes, let alone the end of this chapter. In the United States, privacy law is seen as ill prepared to deal with the demands of technology and digital media distribution.[20] In addition, privacy law is not cohesive; it is an amalgam of different legal doctrines that are oftentimes lashed together, but that lack unifying themes or structures. One of these disparate areas is particularly pertinent here, however, the right of publicity or personality.

Using the United States as our first example, the right of publicity is a right based primarily in state law. That is, each of the fifty states has its own law governing the matter. They generally prohibit commercial use of an image.[21] New York's law (contained in the N.Y. Civil Rights Law) is illustrative:

§50. Right of privacy. A person, firm or corporation that uses for advertising purposes, or for the purposes of trade, the name, portrait or picture of any living person without having first obtained the written consent of such person, or if a minor of his or her parent or guardian, is guilty of a misdemeanor.

Much of the distribution we have discussed is not commercial in this respect. It is public, but not for "trade." The laws of many U.S. states would not apply to prohibit the kind of digital distribution at the heart of the matter here, taking place through peer-to-peer file-sharing networks and online forums.

In the U.K., there is no specific "right of publicity," but rather a patchwork quilt of other laws that are used to obtain something that looks like a publicity right. In many European countries, however, the right of personality is stronger. In Germany, for example, the right is notably stronger, with each person having the right to determine when and which photographs of them are published. This is a legally enforceable right in Germany, and similar rights exist in France. In Canada, the right to anonymity—ostensibly part of the right to privacy—may also be implicated here, but the application of this right to files that you personally created and initially distributed is far from certain.

Other methods of control not directly focused on digital media artifacts may also be used. Child pornography laws may be brought to bear should the digital media artifact consist of illegal content (even where that content was created by the child involved acting alone). A school may suspend children who inappropriately use digital media to disrupt the learning environment, for example. There is some control provided by law that may be used to obviate some of the harm that might come from the pernicious persistence of digital media artifacts.

Note here that this does not assume that simply through the enactment or potential application of law the results will be guaranteed. The underground culture that the internet has helped facilitate has many technological ways to make "end runs" around the law, and so law should not be seen as having a claim to perfect enforcement or efficiency. National boundaries, the places at which the edge of a country's authority extends, present additional obstacles to the law's assistance here. But this does not mean that we should not at least attempt to have laws in place that are addressed to preventing harm, especially where that harm may be to children. To accept such an argument would be to give up on law altogether, something not many of us would likely be willing to do.

Moving Forward or Forced to Stand Still?

For the problem we have set out here, law is not determinative (in fact, law is not determinative of the outcome of any problem, but that is a discussion for another chapter in another book). Does that mean we are without any means of moving forward, of trying to take some steps that might at a minimum mitigate the potential for negative consequences to flow from our youthful entanglements in digital media artifacts? Of course it does not; just as this chapter is not bound by notions of technological determinism, it is also not determined by a defeatism in the face of technological change and legal challenges. There are a number of things that can be done, and though not likely to be a silver bullet solution on its own, law does play a role. In addition to law, we might make moves in education, technology and cultural and societal awareness. In this, the penultimate section of the chapter, we consider these areas together, thinking again of the law, but looking forward, and considering—briefly and for the first time—steps we might take in these other areas. Alone, none of the potential options is notable; together, they may make some difference to whether and to what degree digital media artifacts created by our children today are perniciously persistent tomorrow.

Starting with law, we have made the case that our children differ in maturity in important ways from adults, and these differences are sufficient to justify differential treatment when it comes to the effects that being embedded in digital media files will have on their lives. To that extent, while national governments often cannot take dispositive steps to enforce their laws outside their borders, and so to the extent media files are distributed globally, children cannot be protected alone by the law itself, adopting laws that give greater control to children over the digital media artifacts in which they are embedded would still be a useful step. Adopting either a German style "control over image publication" right for minors (or in relation to digital media artifacts that contain minors), or even a copyright-style distribution right in favor of children who are the subjects of digital media artifacts, is one possible step. Applying such a step to digital media artifacts featuring adults could run headlong into freedom of expression on the part of those wishing to distribute such artifacts, and would require a greater balancing of interests. For children, the result is possibly easier to achieve.

Add to the mix the potential for education to bring at least a minimal level of understanding of the issues of becoming embedded in digital media artifacts to children, and things look brighter still. Currently, digital media education is focused on a number of tracks, from how to use digital media in all its many forms to media literacy or understanding of how media work and how to understand the different messages media bring to us. There has been little, if any, work done on how to educate children regarding the long-term effects of either creating digital media files that include themselves within them, or allowing themselves to be included in such files created by others. It is important that new works addressing digital media, whether from a literacy standpoint[22] or a skills' standpoint,[23] include discussions of the persistence of digital media across time and the importance of considering this point when creating digital media artifacts.

Education in this sense will do little to overcome situations such as Jack's and Susan's, where they were included in digital media artifacts without their explicit consent. Where knowledge or consent is not a part of the digital media artifact's creation, educating children as to these effects has little chance of contributing significantly to overcoming the long-term perniciousness of these files. That does not mean that education should not take place; it should, while acknowledging that it is likely to attack only half of the potential for the pernicious persistence of digital media artifacts.

Other opportunities are presented by technology. Major media producers have long used content encryption to protect DVD content for many years. Currently, Apple and other online MP3 distributors use similar but more advanced technologies to protect MP3 files. Developing and placing in the hands of young digital media creators affordable, useful technologies of this sort may help to keep files under control that—if released now—would be gone with the cyberwind. As with education, however, this part of the solution helps only so far as the media artifact in question was at one time under the control of the young person embedded within it. To the extent that its creation was practically outside the control of the person featured in it, this solution may actually counter the subjects' attempts to control the file, as they themselves may not be able to see it without the permission of the person who added the technological protection to it. In addition, all such systems are subject to being broken, as has happened with traditional DVD protection, Apple's MP3 protection, and now the protection newly put in place to protect high definition DVDs, even before such DVDs have even been firmly established in the marketplace.

As our last potential piece of the puzzle here, we consider how society itself might adapt to a future that includes perniciously persistent digital media artifacts. What will these artifacts show? They will reveal society's child or adult members in a light that many of us share, doing things not unlike things that many of us have done or had done to us, and as such, could become viewed as vestiges of a normal youth. That they are recorded in digital media files could be viewed not as a perversion or an oddity, but just as something that happens and is likely to continue to happen. Some have argued that this is likely to be true with respect to people, technology, and sex, where society is predicted to adapt to changes in this area.[24] Why not to this as well? In addition, and to the extent that such artifacts are created without the consent of their subjects, entangling youngsters against their will or without their consent, they could come to be viewed as evidence of injustice, regardless of the actions shown within them. That is, their viewing and distribution could be viewed by society on the whole not as embarrassing to their subjects, but as embarrassing to those who created them and to those who now continue to distribute them.

This does have the potential to address the "noncontrol" issue that arises in situations like Mark's and Susan's, and could be a possible safety net discouraging even the creation of such artifacts. But this solution, such as it is, is extremely simplistic in its worldview. We know that societal views on issues such as sex and other embarrassing situations change slowly, if at all. If victims of rape are still often considered to "have asked for it," and campaigners have limited success in overcoming the stigma attached to cases of domestic and sexual abuse, there is little realistic cause for optimism regarding society's ability to adapt to and overcome attaching stigma to the types of personal situations likely to be preserved in digital media artifacts. Add to this the tendency of some to do and act exactly opposite to the norms of the society in which they live, undertaking such activities "underground" if necessary, and the problem remains quite deep.

Considering these together, there is reason for hope, but it must be tempered by the reality of digital media as we understand it. We must encourage our children to think about how what they do today with digital media will affect them tomorrow. We would do well to do the same ourselves.

Special Futures, Future Shock or Both?

We have woven here a story of a technological nature that has the very real potential to have unexpected outcomes in relation to the entanglement of young people into the substance of digital media artifacts. These artifacts result from children who grow up digital, similar to how they grow up a particular race, or to a particular height. In fact, children who are featured in digital media artifacts will leave digital pieces of themselves within those files. Digital media permeates our existence, and as the current trends toward more powerful and more affordable digital media creation and distribution technology continue (as they are likely to do), it is likely to further advance our digital lives and our digital selves.

These are not the digital selves we manufacture while online, the embodiments of our efforts to portray ourselves a certain way, though these may be part of our growing up and living digital. They are instead the digital pieces of digital lives that are created with more and more frequency in current times, and which may spin out of our control, leading to unexpected, unintended, and even surprising outcomes in the long term. These digital pieces are the digital media artifacts that have been the focus of this chapter, whether visual, audio, or even text based. They break off from us—and from our children—as we live our lives, as we live and grow as digital beings as well as analog ones.

Growing up digital will change our children from children who grew up before them. It has the potential to give them a solid grounding in their childhood throughout their adult lives, allowing them to relive memories, and to keep loved ones close in memory after they are gone through digital media files made, stored, and accessible due to digital media technology. They will have aids to memory when it comes to friends, trips, aunts, uncles, fathers, mothers, and life beyond those even imagined by our own parents. In this way the potential persistence of digital media files is a potential boon, bringing about progress for the good for our children. But this is balanced by the potential for perniciousness in these same kinds of digital artifacts.

Within this context, our children are "better" at technology than we are, and will expect things we never expected, accept things we would never have accepted.[25] They will have access to and will learn to use digital media technology. They, their friends, and even their enemies will create digital media artifacts, and these will follow them over their lifetimes. The effects they feel from them may be negative, or they may be positive, but most likely they will be a complicated mix of the two. Where popular or mainstream culture learns to accept that kids do stupid things, and to look past the content of these artifacts to the mature adult, the impact may be mitigated somewhat. Where law is adjusted to give rights to the objects of digital media artifacts to control their legal distribution, the impact may again be mitigated. Where technology can be made to effectively and efficiently control access to and distribution of digital media artifacts, at reasonable cost, again, these effects may be mitigated.

But none of these options separately can do the whole job, and this leaves us in largely uncharted territory. We have identified a potential problem in the way our youth interact with digital media, creating artifacts with potentially pernicious permanence, yet we have identified no clear way to prevent it. As Youniss and Ruth have phrased it:

The question we have is, how to begin this process of choosing among the alternatives that will determine the future of youth and the long-term well-being of our society.[26]

Without some movement on—or at least consideration of—the issues of control addressed in this chapter, some societal recognition of their importance, and changes in law to protect children, we risk a future where the bullied remain bullied throughout their whole lives, where the space that children need to grow is wiped out by the permanence of the digital artifacts that are created when they err, where sharing the intimate steps of life with strangers—strangers who laugh, or point, or make fun—is an everyday fear. We have a choice to move toward a more tolerant, understanding, compassionate future, or a harder, more strident, darker one.

The time to make this choice is now.

Notes

1. Don Tapscott, *Growing Up Digital: The Rise of the Net Generation* (New York: McGraw Hill, 1998); Donald F. Roberts, *Kids & Media @ the New Millennium: A Comprehensive National Analysis of Children's Media Use* (Kaiser Family Foundation, 1999); Dorothy Singer and Jerome Singer, eds. *Handbook of Children and the Media* (London: Sage Publications); Patricia Valkenburg, *Children's Responses to the Screen: A Media Psychological Approach* (London: Lawrence Erlbaum Associates, 2004).

2. This is not a chapter outlining dangers of pernicious persistence only to women or girls, and as such, the claims and analyses that follow here are consistent with the claims of Cassell and Cramer in this volume. That is, these potential futures will have an effect on boys as well as girls, women as well as men. While the effects themselves are viewed through culture and society, and so the stigmatization that follows them will inevitably differ based on the sex of the digital media object, there is at least a colorable argument that technology equalizes some gender differences, if not putting women in a position better than that that exists in the "real world," see Donna Harraway, A Cyborg Manifesto: Science, Technology, and Socialist-Feminism in the Late Twentieth Century, in *Simians, Cyborgs and Women: The Reinvention of Nature* (New York: Routledge, 1991), 149–181.

3. Ian Angell, *The New Barbarian Manifesto: How to Survive in the information Age* (London: Kogan Page Ltd., 2000).

4. See, for example, Abandia: http://www.abandonia.com/index2.php; see also, The Abandonware Ring: http://www.abandonwarering.com/ (accessed June 12, 2007).

5. Yochai Benkler, *The Wealth of Networks: How Social Production Transforms Markets and Freedom* (New Haven, CT: Yale University Press, 2006).

6. This is the terminology that President George W. Bush often employed when asked about his alleged drug and alcohol abuse during his first campaign for election as President of the United States. See, for example, Blue-blooded rivals: Men In The News Al Gore and George W. Bush: Mark Suzman assesses two US presidential hopefuls who are more alike than they would care to admit, *Financial Times*, London (UK), November 7, 1998, p. 9.

7. The Bavarian state in Germany has such a system, with distinctions being made among the "Gymnasium" "Realschule" and "Hauptschule," with the school level providing an indication of the level of instruction and expectations of the students, placement being based explicitly on performance in the lower grades, see Thorsten Schneider, Hauptschule, Realschule oder Gymnasium? Soziale Herkunft als Determinante der Schulwahl, in *Generation und Ungleichheit*, hrsg. Mark Szydlik (Opladen, Germany: Leske und Budrich, 2004), 77–103; Mark Ashwill, ed., *The Educational System in Germany: Case Study Findings* (Washington, DC: US Department of Education, 1999.

8. Martijn Hesselink, Capacity and Capability in European Contract Law, *European Review of Private Law* 4 (2005): 491–507; Anna-Karin Larrson, Robert Perrson, and Sara Cronlund, National Report: Swedish Contract Law, Intensive Programme on Commercial Contracts, Rome (2001).

9. See David Brink, Immaturity, Normative Competence, and Juvenile Transfer: How (Not) to Punish Minors for Major Crime, *82 Tex. L. Rev.* 1555 (2004).

10. Irving Kaufman, Protecting the Rights of Minors: On Juvenile Autonomy and the Limits of Law, *52 N.Y.U. L. Rev.* 1015 (1977).

11. Anthony Kronman, Paternalism and the Law of Contracts, *92 Yale Law Journal* 763 (1983).

12. Stephanie Zavala, Note: Defending Parental Involvement and the Presumption of Immaturity in Minors' Decisions to Abort. *72 Southern California Law Reviews* 1725 (1999).

13. Ngaire Naffine, Who Are Law's Persons? From Cheshire Cats to Responsible Subjects, *Modern Law Review* 66 (2003): 3.

14. Jeremy Shook, Contesting Childhood in the US Justice System, *Childhood* 12, no. 4 (2005): 461–478.

15. Trade Related Aspects of Intellectual Property Law (TRIPS), Annex 1C to the Final Act and Agreement Establishing the World Trade Organization (1994), Article 9, no. 2.

16. (Berne, Article I).

17. 17 U.S.C. §201(b).

18. CDPA 1988 s 9(2)(b)

19. CDPA 1988 s 178.

20. David Holtzman, *Privacy Lost: How Technology Is Endangering Your Privacy* (New York: Jossey-Bass, 2006); Keyon and Richardson, eds., *New Dimensions in Privacy Law: International and Comparative Perspectives* (Cambridge, UK: Cambridge University Press, 2006).

21. Tara B. Mulrooney, Note: A Critical Examination of New York's Right of Publicity Claim, *74 St. John's Law Review* 1139 (2000).

22. Len Unsworth, *E-Literature for Children: Enhancing Digital Literacy Learning* (London: Routledge, 2006); Jackie Marsh, *Popular Culture, New Media and Digital Literacy in Early Childhood* (London: Routledge, 2005).

23. Gigi Carlson, *Digital Media in the Classroom: Increase the Learning Potential of Today's Digital Generation* (San Francisco: CMP Books, 2004).

24. Kate Hellenga, Social Space, the Final Frontier: Adolescents on the internet, in *The Changing Adolescent Experience: Societal Trends and the Transition to Adulthood*, eds. Mortimer and Larson (Cambridge, UK: Cambridge University Press), 208–249.

25. Ronald Anderson, Youth and Information Technology, in *The Changing Adolescent Experience: Societal Trends and the Transition to Adulthood*, eds. Mortimer and Larson (Cambridge, UK: Cambridge University Press, 2002), 175–207.

26. James Youniss and Allison Ruth, Approaching Policy for Adolescent Development in the 21st Century, in *The Changing Adolescent Experience: Societal Trends and the Transition to Adulthood*, eds. Mortimer and Larson (Cambridge, UK: Cambridge University Press, 2002), 250–271.

Auto-Modernity after Postmodernism: Autonomy and Automation in Culture, Technology, and Education

Robert Samuels

University of California, Los Angeles, Writing Programs

This chapter argues that in order to understand the implications of how digital youth are now using new media and technologies in unexpected and innovative ways, we have to rethink many of the cultural oppositions that have shaped the Western tradition since the start of the modern era. To be precise, we can no longer base our analysis of culture, identity, and technology on the traditional conflicts between the public and the private, the subject and the object, and the human and the machine. Moreover, the modern divide pitting the isolated individual against the impersonal realm of technological mechanization no longer seems to apply to the multiple ways young people are using new media and technologies. In fact, I will argue here that we have moved into a new cultural period of automodernity, and a key to this cultural epoch is the combination of technological automation and human autonomy. Thus, instead of seeing individual freedom and mechanical predetermination as opposing social forces, digital youth turn to automation in order to express their autonomy, and this bringing together of former opposites results in a radical restructuring of traditional and modern intellectual paradigms. Furthermore, the combining of human and machine into a single circuit of interactivity often functions to exclude the traditional roles of social mediation and the public realm. For educators and public policy makers, this unexpected collusion of opposites represents one of the defining challenges for the twenty-first century, and it will be my argument here that some innovative uses of new technologies threaten to undermine educational and social structures that are still grounded on the modern divide between the self and the other, the objective and the subjective, and the original and the copy. To help clarify what challenges automodernity brings, I will detail ways that new media technologies are shaping how digital youth learn and play, then I will discuss how these automodern technologies challenge contemporary theories concerning education and self-hood, and I will conclude by suggesting different techniques for the integration of old and new media in education and political culture.

A New-Media-Writing Scene

I am sitting with my fifteen-year-old nephew Benjamin as he works on a paper for his ninth-grade English class. Benjamin has Microsoft Word open, and he is also in a chat room with some classmates who are exchanging parts of their own first drafts. Their assignment is to write individually a five-paragraph essay on the novel they have just read in class. To complete this traditional assignment, Benjamin has his book open on his desk, but he also has on his computer screen a list of Web sites that discuss the novel, and his Instant Messaging program keeps on dinging him to warn of another incoming message. Meanwhile, he is downloading a new movie, and he is also playing a multiuser game that includes live chat with people from all over the world. He is thus multitasking at the same time as he is using multiple media to write his paper and entertain himself. If this scene is typical for many digital youth in the developed West, then these students may come to school with a radically different conception of writing and technology than their teachers have;[1] furthermore, this high level of multitasking points to the virtually seamless interplay of work and leisure activities that can be operated on a single personal computer.

This new-media-writing scene not only shows a breakdown of the old cultural opposition between work and play, but it also challenges the structural conflict between self and other. For instance, when I ask Benjamin if he is supposed to work with his friends on this paper, he responds with a quizzical look. From his perspective, like the movies and songs he is file sharing, information and media are always supposed to be shared and distributed in open networks.[2] Moreover, he reminds me that he still has to hand in his own paper, and thus he is only collaborating on the research part of his paper, and he will "write the real paper on his own." After I ask him if he is afraid that all of his multitasking will get in the way of him writing a clear and coherent paper, he informs me that he will use his spell and grammar checkers to make sure, "everything looks professional." Benjamin therefore retains a high level of personal autonomy at the same time that he is sharing information and employing automated programs and templates. In other words, instead of technological automation creating a sense of mechanical alienation and impersonal predetermination, digital youth turn to new media technologies to increase their sense of freedom and individual control.

Moreover, Benjamin and students like him are now quite used to seeing knowledge and research as collaborative processes, while they retain more traditional notions of reading and writing. In fact, the ways Benjamin and his friends copy and paste texts from the Web and then distribute them in chat rooms and e-mails depicts an important transformation in the "modern" conception of property and individual work: these young adults have become habituated to sharing all different types of media and information with little concern for property rights or plagiarism.[3] It is also important to point out that the way Benjamin jumps from writing agrammatical instant messages to typing extended essayistic prose displays the ability of young writers to transform the style and voice of their composing according to the context and the audience.

One can argue that Benjamin and his friends are using new technologies and media in innovative and unexpected ways, which in turn challenges the traditional educational structure centered on judging the work of the individual student. While many educators would simply castigate these students for cheating, I want to argue that these digital youths are leading the way for a new type of education that might be more effective and productive. For it may be that the types of collaborative activities in which students are engaging outside of school are very much like the types of activities they will be required to perform in the workplace and in their everyday lives when they finish their education. However, schools have for the most part resisted incorporating these digital innovations because the new media stress on collaboration, multitasking, automation, and copying does not fit into the older model of book-centered learning.

Since so many educators, parents, and administrators are locked into the rigid definition of education defined by the testing of memorized knowledge retained by the isolated learner, our educational systems have helped to create a strong digital divide between students' home and school uses of technology. One of the results of this divide is that students who are now used to employing new media in innovative and unexpected ways when they are at home are often alienated from school because these institutions still concentrate on outdated modes of communication and information exchange. Therefore, on a fundamental level, our schools are still structured by the modern celebration of the isolated individual who is rewarded for individual acts of creativity and/or conformity, while our students have embraced a more collaborative and distributive mode of learning and working.

Some educators who have acknowledged this growing divide between students and educational institutions have developed "postmodern" theories to account for the current undermining of traditional and modern beliefs and practices. However, I will argue below that most of these postmodern theorists have failed to account for the ways digital youth are combining automation with autonomy. In fact, I will posit that we have moved into a new period beyond postmodernity, and it is important for educators to understand how automodernity undermines postmodern theories and educational efforts. Therefore, just as the development of postmodernism was based on a critique of modernism, I will begin my analysis of automodernity by critically examining postmodernity. This analysis of postmodernity is especially important, because in many ways automodernity represents a popular reaction to the postmodern emphasis on social determinism.

Four Versions of Postmodernity

Before the reader stops reading because of the use of this word, "postmodern," I would like to posit that this cultural category has many different possible uses: some of them helpful and some of them not. In fact, I turn to this term because it helps us to enter into discussions occurring in many different disciplines about our current cultural order and how new technologies and social movements are changing the ways we think about education and learning. While some people have sought to dismiss the whole idea of postmodernity by labeling it an intellectual fad or a nihilistic radical movement, my intention is to show that postmodernism describes a series of contemporary social transformations.[4] To be more precise, I want to rescue this term from its misuse by arguing that there are in fact four separate forms of postmodernity that have often been confused.

Perhaps the most important postmodern idea is the notion that our world is made of multiple cultures and that we should respect the knowledge and cultures of diverse communities. In fact, multiculturalism is a reflection of the important social movements of the twentieth century, which fought for civil rights, minority rights, women's rights, workers' rights, and political self-determination. Thus, in recognizing the vital values and historical contributions of diverse social groups, multiculturalists have posited that there is no single, universal source for knowledge or truth.[5] Unfortunately, this multicultural idea has often been confused with the extreme postmodernist notion that there are no truths or moral values since everything is relative to one's own culture.[6] This mode of cultural relativism is often a caricature of the more subtle idea that all truths and values are socially constructed. Therefore, a more accurate statement of multicultural relativism and social constructivism is that while there are truths and values in our world, we can no longer assume that they are universal and eternal, particularly when "universal and eternal" often function as code words for "white and male."[7]

Besides multiculturalism and social constructivism, a third mode of postmodernity concerns the cultural model of combining diverse cultures in entertainment and art through the processes of collage, remixing, and sampling. On one level, we can say that all cultures feed off of other cultures; however, some people have rightly claimed that our incessant recombining of diverse cultural representations does not necessarily help us to understand or encounter other cultural worlds.[8] I would add that while this esthetic version of post-modernity is probably the most prevalent, it is also the easiest to dismiss for its tendency to be superficial and short-lived.

Finally, I would like to define a fourth form of postmodernity, which concerns the academic critique of modern culture and philosophy. This mode of academic discourse often comes under the title of deconstruction or poststructuralism and has been attacked for offering the extreme idea that our world is determined by language. But, language can never escape its own domain, and thus ultimately all knowledge and meaning is suspect.[9] While this overly generalized representation of postmodern philosophy can be questioned, what is often missed is the way that this theory of rhetoric has worked to hide the important connection between postmodernity and social movements. After all, what has fueled multiculturalism and the critique of modernity is the rise of collective action around minority rights, civil rights, and women's rights. These social movements of the twentieth century have challenged many of the presuppositions of modern culture, and it is important to not confuse these vital cultural changes with their reflection in various academic fashions. Indeed, many of those most involved with these social movements as activists or theorists have challenged the extreme focus on difference within postmodernism, positing instead a kind of navigation between "sameness" and "difference."

It is also essential to emphasize that if we want digital youth to use new media to engage in the social and public realms, then we must be able to point to the social movements of postmodernity without being caught up in the more extreme forms of academic discourse. In short, while we desire our students to see how culture, knowledge, and subjectivity are influenced by important social forces, we need to avoid the pitfalls of promoting theories that destroy the foundations for any type of stable meaning, argument, or social action. Moreover, as I will stress below, since one of the determining aspects of automodern youth is that their seemingly seamless combination of autonomy and automation often excludes the social realm of cultural differences and collective action, we need to show the importance of the social realm in contemporary, postmodern culture.

Postmodern Theories of Education and Society

In surveying several texts defining postmodernity from the perspective of multiple disciplines, I have found that the one consistent factor in the circumscribing of this historical period is a stress on the transition from the modern notion of Enlightenment reason to an emphasis on the social nature of all human endeavors. Thus, whether one is speaking about the contemporary loss of master narratives, the critique of universal science, the rise of multiculturalism, the downgrading of the nation state, the emergence of the global information economy, the mixing of high and low cultures, the blending of entertainment and economics, or the development of new communication technologies, one is dealing with an essentially social and antimodern discourse. According to this logic, modernity represents the rise of capitalism, science, and democracy through the rhetoric of universal reason and equality. Moreover, the modern period is seen as a reaction to the premodern stress on feudal hierarchy, religious fate, cosmic belief, and political monarchy.[10] This coherent narrative moving from premodern to modern to postmodern modes of social order and collective knowledge can be challenged and debated, but what is certain is that this schema plays a dominant mode in contemporary intellectual history. However, what I would now like to show through an analysis of the representation of modernity and postmodernity in various fields of study is that this prominent intellectual narrative does not help us to account for the major modes of subjectivity and culture employed by digital youth today, which I have labeled automodernity.

In the field of education, the movement from modernity to postmodernity has often been tied to a belated acknowledgment of the multiple cultures that make up our world in general and our educational populations in particular. For example, Marilyn Cooper has argued that the central guiding force behind the development of postmodernism in education is the acknowledgment of cultural diversity:

Postmodernism is, above all, a response to our increased awareness of the great diversity in human cultures, a diversity that calls into question the possibility of any "universal" or "privileged" perspective and that thus values the juxtaposition of different perspectives and different voices and the contemplation of connections rather than a subordinated structure of ideas that achieves a unified voice and a conclusive perspective.[11]

By stressing cultural diversity and "the contemplation of connections," Cooper points to a social and cultural mode of postmodern education challenging the modern stress on universality and unified subjectivity. Therefore, in this context, postmodern theory can be read as a response to multicultural diversity and the juxtaposition of different voices and disciplines in an environment where social mediation trumps universal reason and individual autonomy.[12]

Like so many other theorists of postmodernity, Cooper's understanding of this epoch is based on the idea that our conceptions of what knowledge is have shifted away from the previous modern stress on universal truth and unified individualism:

The transition involves a shift from the notion of knowledge as an apprehension of universal truth and its transparent representation in language by rational and unified individuals to the notion of knowledge as the construction in language of partial and temporary truth by multiple and internally contradictory individuals.[13]

According to this common academic argument, the movement away from the "modern" conception of knowledge as universal truth pushes people in postmodern culture and education to sift through competing forces of temporary truths, and this destabilized conception of knowledge and truth leads to the undermining of the modern individual of unified consciousness. In turn, under the influences of postmodernism, education and culture become social and nonuniversal.

This social definition of postmodernism is linked by Cooper to the role played by new computer-mediated modes of communication in culture and education: "in electronic conversations, the individual thinker moves . . . into the multiplicity and diversity of the social world, and in social interaction tries out many roles and positions."[14] According to this description of electronic discussions, new technologies help to create a situation where individuals enter into a multicultural environment that stresses the social, dialogical, and interactive foundations of knowledge, communication, and education. However, I will later argue that this emphasis on the social nature of new communication technologies does not take into account the contemporary dominance of automation and individual autonomy in the production of automodernity. Moreover, due to their desire to promote a more socially responsible and multicultural society, many educators have made the questionable assumption that networked collaboration equals an acceptance of cultural diversity and so-cial responsibility. Not only do I think that this easy equivalency between new technologies and multicultural awareness is too simple, but I will argue that many new technologies can foster a highly antimulticultural mode of communication and actually inhibit an under-standing of or experience of difference.

Another serious problem with the theories stressing a radical shift from modern universal reason to postmodern social mediation is that they are predicated on a strict linear conception of historical development, and this progressive model tends to ignore the continuation of modern and premodern influences in postmodern culture. An example of this common mode of argumentation can be found in the "new science" idea that we are now witnessing a radical shift in the transition from modern universal knowledge to the postmodern stress on the social construction of truth. Thus, in George Howard's understanding of the conflict between objectivism and constructivism in the natural sciences, we find the postmodern critique of modern universality:

All across the intellectual landscape, the forces of objectivism are yielding to the entreaties of con-structivist thought. But it is rather surprising that even our notion of science has been radically altered by recent constructivist thought. Briefly objectivism believes in a freestanding reality, the truth about which can eventually be discovered. The constructivist assumes that all mental images are creations of people, and thus speak of an invented reality. Objectivists focus on the accuracy of their theories, whereas constructivists think of the utility of their models. Watzlawick (1984) claimed that the shift from objectivism to constructivism involves a growing awareness that any so-called reality is—in the most immediate and concrete sense—the construction of those who believe they have discovered and investigated it.[15]

According to this social constructivist interpretation of the sciences, the modern conception of knowledge as being universal and objective has been challenged by the postmodern notion that knowledge is always an act of interpretation and invention.[16] Furthermore, by seeing science as the formation of shared constructed versions of reality, postmodern scientists often take on a social and anti-individualistic conception of reality.

This contemporary movement in the sciences from the modern individual as a neutral observer to the postmodern social construction of accepted theories is linked to the rhetorical turn in all aspects of current academic culture. In fact, Alan Ryan has made the following argument about how postmodern rhetoric changes our definitions of the self and the very process of recording our perceptions:

Postmodernism is a label that embraces multitudes, but two ideas especially relevant here are its skepti-cism about the amount of control that a writer exercises over his or her work, and a sharp sense of the fragility of personal identity. These interact, of course. The idea that each of us is a single Self consorts naturally with the idea that we tell stories, advance theories, and interact with others from one particular viewpoint. Skepticism about such a picture of our identities consorts naturally with the thought that we are at the mercy of the stories we tell, as much as they are at our mercy. It also consorts naturally with an inclination to emphasize just how accidental it is that we hold the views we do, live where we do, and have the loyalties we do.[17]

Here, individual autonomy is seen as something that has to be constantly negotiated and revised, and is thus not a finished product, and this conception of subjectivity feeds into the social definition of postmodernity. However, as my students often posit in reaction to these postmodern notions of social construction, they do not feel that their autonomy and self-hood are being challenged and rendered transitory; in fact, students most often report a high level of perceived individual control and freedom.[18] Furthermore, the conflict between how students experience their own lives and how postmodern theorists describe contemporary subjectivity often works to make students simply reject these academic theories, and this student resistance to theory is one reason why we may want to rethink postmodernism through the development of automodernism.

Thus, as academics are concentrating on critiquing modern notions of universal reason and unified subjectivity, students are turning to modern science and technology to locate a strong sense of individual unity and control. However, I am not arguing here that we should simply reject all postmodern academic theories because they do not match our students' experiences and perceptions; rather, my point is that we should use these students' resistances to better understand how people today are influenced by the technological access to a heightened sense to individual control that can downplay social subjectivity and multicultural differences. Therefore, by seeing what postmodern theories have gotten wrong in the underestimating of virtual subjectivity, we can gain a better idea of what new educational theories need to get right. For instance, in fully articulating both a social and a psychological theory of student subjectivity, we can show why it is important to defend the social realm at the same time that we expose the reasons why new media caters to a psychological downplaying of social mediation.

In fact, what the social or postmodern theory of self-hood tends to neglect is the psychological and virtual foundation of autonomy and subjective unity. It is important to stress that if we examine how the sense of self is developed psychologically, we learn that one first gains a sense of individual identity by looking into a mirror or external representation and seeing an ideal representation of one's body as complete, whole, and bounded. This mirror theory of self-hood (Lacan) teaches us that since we never really see our whole body at a single glance—at least not without several mirrors or cameras—our internal body map is actually an internalized virtual image and not a concrete material fact. In other words, our sense of self is psychological and virtual and not primarily social and material. Moreover, our subjective feelings of autonomy are built upon this imaginary level of self-hood: To have a sense of self-direction, one must first have a sense of self, and to have a self, one needs to first internalize an ideal body map.

Social theories of subjectivity are thus misleading when they claim to depict a generalized undermining of unified subjectivity; yet, these same theories are vital when we want to discuss the possibility of social and cultural change. In the case of automodernity, I will be arguing that the power of new automated technologies to give us a heightened *sense* of individual control often functions to undermine the awareness of social and cultural mediation, and this lack of awareness can place the isolating individual against the public realm. Therefore, when my students reject postmodern theories because these self-denying concepts do not jive with their own self-understandings, we can posit that students and postmodern theories are both failing to distinguish between psychological and social models of subjectivity. In other terms, many of the postmodern theories discussed here stress the social determination of subjectivity, while many contemporary students focus on their sense of psychological determinism, and we need to offer models of education that integrate both perspectives.

However, instead of balancing the social and the psychological, postmodern educators like Lester Faigley posit that the contemporary subject is defined as being multiple, and identity is seen as a process.[19] In turn, this postmodern notion of subjectivity is contrasted with the Enlightenment ideology of subjective unity, coherency, objectivity, individuality, and universal scientific reason.[20] Moreover, for Faigley, postmodern culture and new media technologies challenge these modern ideologies by emphasizing the contingent and social nature of all acts of writing and knowledge construction.[21] It is also important to note that from Faigley's perspective, there is a growing divide between postmodern students and modern teachers in the ways students and teachers tend to understand the functions and roles of writing, technology, and literacy in culture and education. While I do agree with Faigley that new technologies help to build a growing divide between teachers and students in terms of how they conceive knowledge, identity, and media, my conception of automodernity argues that the simple replacement of modern individual unity with postmodern discontinuity fails to see how digital youth are merging the two sides of the modern divide: unified individuality and universal science. For example, in a prize-winning essay from the Global Kids contest on Digital Literacy, we find a digital youth making the following argument: "Today, almost all the information that humans have gathered over thousands of years is at the tips of my fingers . . . or those of anyone who cares to use this incredible technology" ("From Gutenberg to Gateway").[22] On the one hand, this statement points to a heightened sense of individual control and access, and on the other hand, it highlights a universal notion of information and technology. By stating that "anyone" can get almost "any" information from the Web, this writer universalizes both the subject and object of global information distribution. The internet is positioned here as using automation and modern science to enhance the ability of individuals to access all information. Of course, this common conception of universal access of the World Wide Web represses many real digital divides as it presents a universalized notion of individuality, and it is important to note that one possible reason for this rhetorical neglect of differences is that the power of automation tends to render social and material factors invisible.

The same essay indicates a possible source for this common contemporary rhetoric of universal access:

Of all the media that I use, I have only touched a spoonful of the ocean that is digital media. There are still thousands upon thousands of other sites, games, songs, and other things that I have never used and probably never will use. Every day, though, I find that I need some obscure piece of information, and this new technology allows me to find it. I play games and listen to music, and this helps define what I like and don't like.

This digital youth feels that since there is too much information available on the Web for one person to encounter, then all information must be available: here, information excess leads to a sense of universal access. Furthermore, it is often the automated nature of new media that functions to hide social disparities behind a veil of easy, global access. In turn, this automation and autonomy of access heightens a sense of individual control. Thus, what postmodern critics like Faigley might be missing in their accounts of contemporary digital youth is the power of new technologies to reinforce the imaginary and real experiences of individual autonomy through automated systems. In other terms, even in situations where information on the Web is determined by social mediation, digital youth are able to absorb cultural material into the frames of their individual point of view. As I will argue below, the PC often gives people the sense that they are in control of the information that appears on their screen, just as they are in control of the perceptions that they let into their own consciousness.

Another important clarification to make is the connection between universal science and automation. In the common understanding of modern science and culture, academics and philosophers often claim that science is universal because it does not rely on social or personal beliefs. In fact, a key to Descartes' development of the scientific method is his call to employ universal doubt to undermine all prejudices and approach every object of study with a shared transparent method open to all. Of course, Descartes developed his method as a counter to the dominant religious beliefs of his time, and central to his understanding of science was his investment in the idea of universal reason. While we may want to applaud the democratic and rational foundations of Descartes' universal approach, it is important to also note that this universalizing model of science, which posits the importance of a "value-free" method, can actually free scientists from ethical and social responsibilities. Furthermore, in the application of modern science through the development of new technologies, we see how automated devices may create a responsibility-free zone where it is hard to locate any responsible ethical subject.

What then often accounts for the connection between universal science and new automated technologies is the shared process of downplaying the role of social contexts in the shaping of science and technology. Within the context of education, science and math are usually taught as if these subjects were purely objective and neutral, and therefore void of any individual or social influences. For example, even when teachers are discussing such issues as genetic manipulation, pharmaceutical intervention, and technological innovation, the knowledge is delivered without concern for ethical and social issues. Here, we see a division between the postmodern stress on social mediation and the modern rhetoric of science as being objective, neutral, universal, and ultimately inevitable.

We can further understand the presence of modern universality in contemporary education by looking at how literacy is defined in many higher education institutions. Thus, in *Reinventing the University: Literacies and Legitimacy in the Postmodern University*, Christopher Schroeder posits that most textbooks and governmental policies present, "a universalized definition of literacy, as if what it means to be literate can be separated from the contexts in which literate practices are meaningful."[23] In this critique of the common use of the term literacy, Schroeder affirms the distinction between a functional and a critical understanding of literacy by distinguishing the modern stress on universal neutrality from the postmodern stress on social context. From Schroeder's postmodern perspective, the myth of a universal model of literacy is derived from the ability of powerful vested interests to hide their own particular values behind false claims of universal objectivity. Moreover, Schroeder posits that this rhetoric of universality still dominates the ways our educational systems are structured and the types of literacy that are affirmed in schooling.[24] It is also important to note how this universalizing rhetoric has been adopted by digital youth in their common claims of global access, and therefore a key task of critical literacy studies is to explore with students these rhetorical constructions that function to hide important differences and discrepancies. For instance, when students claim that, "Anyone can access any information from any place at any time," we need to engage them in a conversation about the role of the word "any" in falsely universalizing and globalizing a rhetoric of unquestioned equality. In other words, we need to counter a functional model of technological literacy with a critical model of rhetorical understanding.

In fact, essential to Schroeder's analysis of the conflict between functional and critical models of literacy is his claim that the more school literacies are based on de-contextualized, universal models of information delivery, the more individual aspects of culture become the sole purview of experts.[25] Thus, central to the modern organization of education is the dual process of universalizing educational access to school *and* segmenting individual subject areas into separate areas of expertise. Furthermore, from Schroeder's perspective, functional literacy is dominated by the modern ideological interests of white, middle-class America, and these modern values, which are presented as being universal, no longer fit with the majority of contemporary students.[26]

In opposition to the modern stress on universal reason and neutral functional models of literacy, Schroeder affirms that students bring multiple literacies to universities, and these diverse models of social knowledge and learning are most often neglected by our traditional institutions.[27] As many other scholars have argued, postmodern student literacies are shaped by the cultural realms of television, movies, the Internet, and advertising, and not by the modern emphasis on books and reading as the central source of literacy.[28] While I do feel that Schroeder and other postmodern critics are correct in seeing this conflict between older and newer models of literacy, the stress on the modern universality of school-based literacies versus postmodern diversity of student literacies does not account for the spread of globalized media in automodernity. In other terms, new media technologies have absorbed modern universality into the globalized structures of automated systems, which in turn act to hide social mediation and to highlight individual control. Therefore, as I will argue below, automodern literacies based on television, advertising, movies and the Internet do not typically function to undermine people's belief in modern universal reason and unified subjectivity; instead, automodern technologies help to provide a greater sense of technological neutrality, universalized information, and individual power, even if this sense may be illusory.

Automodernity

To clarify what I mean by automodernism, I will examine several common technologies that are used heavily by digital youth in the early twenty-first-century globalized Western world: personal computers, word processors, cell phones, iPods, blogs, remote-controlled televisions, and first-person shooter computer games. These technological objects share a common emphasis on combining a high level of mechanical automation with a heightened sense of personal autonomy.[29] In fact, this unexpected and innovative combination of autonomy and automation can be read as the defining contradictions of contemporary life in general and digital youth in particular. Importantly, while automation traditionally represents a loss of personal control, autonomy has been defined by an increase in individual freedom; however, automodernity constantly combines these two opposing forces in an unexpected way.[30]

We can begin our analysis of this strange combination of autonomy and automation in automodernity by analyzing the automobile as the precursor to this new way of being. In fact, the very name of the automobile indicates a technological push for both the autonomy and automation of movement. Moreover, cars represent a truly nonsocial mode of movement that conflicts with the more social modes of public transportation. Thus, in the contemporary car, the driver not only has the feeling that he or she can go where he or she intends, but there is also the development of a heightened sense of personal control and autonomy. After all, in American popular culture, the automobile is one of the central symbols for freedom, mobility, and independence: it is the car that allows the teenager and the angry adult to escape personal alienation and set out for individual autonomy.

The automobile also creates the sense of a personal environment where technology enables a controlled world full of processed air, artificial sounds, and windowed vision. The car may even be experienced as a second body, and even though many people spend so much of their time stuck in traffic, the car retains the virtual and psychological sense of automated autonomy. In fact, by analyzing the cultural and psychological import of the car, we can begin to see some of the limits of the postmodern notion that contemporary society is founded on the social construction of reality, the overcoming of individual unity, and the critique of universal science. For the car, as an early sign of automodernity, is a vehicle for a nonsocial mode of personal freedom combined with a strong belief in the naturalness of scientific technology: Cars are experienced as artificial bodies that combine automation with autonomy and seem to render invisible most forms of social and cultural mediation.

While the automobile appears to be a prime technology of modernity, I would like to posit that it embodies the seeds to automodernity through its integration of privacy and automation and its downplaying of social mediation. In fact, Raymond Williams coined the term "Mobile Privatization" to indicate how this type of technology, unlike the telegraph, the radio, and the subway, allows for mobility in a personalized and privatized milieu.[31] We can thus posit that the automobile has helped to lay the cultural groundwork for the new stress on autonomy through mechanical automation.

Like automobiles, personal computers indicate a paradoxical combination of individual autonomy and automated mechanics. While some of the postmodern theorists discussed above argue that computers and other modes of new media allow for a high level of social and cultural interaction, and thus these new communication technologies help digital youth to see how the world is based on social mediation and intersubjective communication, we can also understand these machines as central sources for an antisocial sense of personal control and autonomy. Therefore, in the PC, the world comes to me: not only can I bring my office to my home, but electronic commerce and e-mail allow me to escape from the need to engage with people in a public space. This privatization of public interaction echoes the larger political movement to undermine the notion of a modern public realm protected by a centralized government (The Welfare State). In short, the PC has unexpectedly enabled digital youth the freedom to avoid the public and to appropriate public information and space for unpredictable personal reasons. Furthermore, even when students are engaged in collaborative writing online, the power of the PC to personalize culture can turn this social interaction into a privatized experience. Thus, while it may appear that new communication technologies are actually broadening the social realm of digital youths, I am arguing that the ability of the individual user of new media to control the flow and intake of information provides a strong antisocial and self-reinforcing sense of subjectivity. For example, it is clear that students who are participating in an online discussion or chat room are free to read and respond to only the conversations that interest them or cater to their own individual points of view; however, in a classroom discussion, it is much harder for students to only respond to one person or to just respond to their own ideas over and over again.

It is important to point out here that my argument is not that new technologies are replacing the social realm with the private realm; rather, I want to stress that the power of new media to cater to real and imagined feelings of self-direction threatens to hide and render invisible important social and public forces. Therefore, although it is essential to consider the social construction of new technologies and their usages, we need to start off with a heightened attention to and analysis of the subjective and embodied nature of electronic culture in order to understand how new media is being lived and experienced by digital youth. In fact, one way of rereading the initials PC is to think of Personal Culture as a new mode of privatized social subjectivity. The feelings of personal choice and power that digital technologies so powerfully proffer are at least as important objects of investigation and critical reflection as the social networks they may enable. Perhaps the ultimate technology of personal culture is the laptop computer, which functions as the logical extension of the PC, as demonstrated by the way that it gives the individual user the freedom to perform private activities in public. Thus, the laptop may turn any public or commercial space into a private workplace or play space. Since people can take their work and their games with them wherever they go, the whole traditional opposition between workspace and private space breaks down. For example, when one goes to a café, one sees people working with their laptops as if these customers are sitting at home: they have their food, their phone, their newspaper, and other personal items displayed in public. The reverse of the public being absorbed into the private is therefore the private being displayed in public.[32]

Of course, both the privatization of the public and the publicizing of the private are fueled by the twin engines of autonomy and automation. In this context, subjective freedom is tied to the mechanical reproduction of a set system of technological functions. For instance, one of the central uses for the PC is the employment of various word and image processing programs. These technologies center on the preprogramming of "universal" templates and systems of scientific order, thus, programs like spell-checker function by automating tasks that individuals traditionally controlled. However, instead of seeing this transfer of responsibility from the individual writer to the machine, most digital youth that I have interviewed feel that this automation gives them more autonomy to concentrate on what really matters. Moreover, as we saw in my initial example of Benjamin exchanging texts with his friends, the automation of the copy and paste functions increases the freedom of the individual writer to move text around and to engage in acts of constant revision. Automation therefore adds to textual fluidity, which in turn, feeds a sense of personal autonomy.

Powering the PC revolution of automodernity are the Internet and the World Wide Web. At first glance, these technological systems appear to represent the epitome of the postmodern stress on multiculturalism, social interaction, and the movement away from the individuated modern self; however, we can read these technologies as actually undermining the social and the multicultural worlds by giving the individual consumer of information the illusion of automated autonomy. In many ways, the digital youth's experience of the Web challenges the postmodern idea that we are constrained by time and space and that our relationships with others are defined by our cultural and social differences and relations. From the perspective of digital youth, all information from any culture and any person is immediately available to any user at any time and from any place. Thus, in cyberspace, temporal and spatial restraints do not seem to matter.

In fact, by reviewing several of the Global Kids essay winners, we find a reoccurring theme concerning this loss of spatial and temporal differences and a growing sense that cultural differences no longer pose a barrier to understanding. For example, in the essay entitled "From Gutenberg to Gateway," mentioned earlier, the digital youth writes, "My generation is more understanding of other cultures, simply because we are better informed than our parents were. We play games that prepare us for the world by heightening our awareness and teaching us to solve problems." According to this writer, new media digital youth are not only more informed about cultural differences than previous generations, but new communication and gaming technologies are training youth for a globalized world. Another essay reiterates this same point about the growing multicultural awareness of globalized digital youth; however, in this writing, intercultural understanding is founded on a denial of differences, "Since there is no way to tell who people are when they're online, people have to be accepted for who they are. We learn to think about what a person says often times without knowing who said it, thus eliminating any possible bias" ("Digital Media in My Life"). This statement reflects on the fundamental conflict of modern universalism: on one level, universality promotes equal rights and a rejection of prejudices, but on another level, universality can indicate a lack of sensitivity regarding cultural and ethnic differences. Thus, if we are all treated equally, then none of our differences count.

In automodernity, the conflicted nature of modern universals is often repressed below a hyper-modern sense of globalized access and information exchange. Furthermore, as the following quote from the same digital youth essay implies, modern and automodern universality is haunted by the conflicted double legacy of individualism and social conformity:

Self-reliance and assertiveness are other important qualities gained from the Net. There are Web sites for all sorts of purposes, from fantasy football to free speech. Internet-based self-reliance comes from the independent nature of the computer because it is designed for use by one person. When on the Internet, people decide where to go and what to do entirely on their own, and that idea has been firmly engrained in the minds of this new generation. These thinking characteristics acquired through frequent use of the Internet can be valuable in society, whether taking a stand for a belief, accepting a person's opinion, or setting a goal, are all positive attributes of the way we think, which makes me optimistic about the new generation.

This digital youth rightly proclaims the power of autonomy afforded by the personal computer, and I do not think that we should posit that he is simply being duped by a lure of false individualism. However, what we do need to examine are the possible consequences of this universal model of libertarian self-reliance. One important issue that this same essay brings up is the common connection between individual autonomy and consumerism: "The way kids are going to function in the world is amazing, particularly as consumers. The Internet provides nearly unlimited options and choices. The vast 'information superhighway' gives so many options that it will become necessary to offer customization for every product." This statement does seem to reflect the notion that while the internet can increase our sense of individual control, it can also function to steer our autonomy into spaces that are controlled by economic interests. Furthermore, this version of autonomy appears to be predicated on the marketing rhetoric of free choice in a frictionless economy, and what we often see in this type of belief is a libertarian equation of free markets, free speech, and personal freedoms.

It is important to examine how this new media mode of libertarian autonomy often calls for a privatization of the public sphere and a use of automation in the pursuit of personal liberty and controlled social interaction. For instance, in the following statement from this essay, the young writer combines together a celebration of the social aspects of multiple-user video games with a denial of cultural and ethnic differences.

Online multiplayer video games are, contrary to common belief, very social atmospheres where players get to know one another personally. Gamers often group together in clans or guilds to play alongside each other on a regular basis. I've spoken to forty-year-olds with wives and children who still cut out a half-hour each day to play a World War II-based shooting game. One of the greatest aspects of these groups is that no one sees what the other people look like, but they respect each other nonetheless. These guys could have completely different backgrounds, different ethnicities, and totally different religions, but all of these variables dissolve when you are shooting virtual enemies as a team. Clans and guilds are microcosms of the business world in that people must learn to work together to achieve goals systematically.

In reading this passage, I believe that is necessary to not fall into a simple pro versus con conception of video games and virtual violence; rather, I want to stress that this new model of social interactivity transforms the public realm into a shared space populated by highly autonomous users/consumers. Instead of the public realm being a place of ethnic and cultural conflict and difference, the privatized public realm becomes a space to ignore differences and to focus on commonalities: once again this is both a positive and a negative universalizing gesture.

On one level, we are seeing a growing tolerance of cultural differences, and on another level, these differences are simply being denied. Moreover, as these digital youth essays reveal, this repression of cultural differences is linked to the veiling of temporal and spatial differences. From a critical perspective, we may want to affirm that without the limits of time and space, many modes of otherness begin to disappear and fade beneath a veil of global access. Therefore, while the Web may enable digital youth to encounter multiple cultures and various social relationships, they often experience those interactions through the window and frame of their PC, and in this technological context, all encounters with others become visually boxed into the confines of the screen: here, the frame of the screen serves as a mental container for Otherness.[33] Like a cage at a zoo or a picture frame at a museum, the structure of the framed screen provides a strong sense of limits and borders. Moreover, it is important to stress that it is the individual who decides what to put up on the screen, and this sense of individual control reinforces the feeling of autonomy for the PC user.

Another location of automated autonomy on the internet are search engines, which allow individuals to perform quickly and easily the complicated tasks of locating, sorting, and accessing diverse information. Through automation, search engines, like Google.com, render invisible the multiple methods and technologies employed to scan, for personal reasons, the globalized Web. Furthermore, instead of relying on experts or modern sorting systems, like library card catalogues, automated search engines appear to put the power of cultural filtering into the hands of the autonomous user. Of course, these technological systems have their own inner logic and preprogrammed priorities, but these systemic issues are most often hidden from view.

In fact, one could argue that PCs and the Web work together to hide social and technological determination behind the appearance of autonomous user control. For example, many blogging programs offer highly controlled and limited templates, but these technological restrictions are buried beneath the power of the individual to create his or her own media. Therefore, even though most MySpace sites look the same and have similar content, digital youth often feel that these automated templates provide for a great deal of personal freedom, self-expression, and personal identity. Furthermore, as in the case of other social networking technologies, personal blogs are a great example of the breakdown between the traditional division between the private and public realms: For blogs give every individual user the possibility of distributing private thoughts in a public space. Like personal homepages, these internet sites trace the movement of media control from large social organizations to the fingertips of individual users and producers. Thus, one of the most exciting aspects of these new media modes of information distribution is that instead of people having to rely on large, corporate media outlets for their news and information, private individuals can become their own public media reporters. In fact, this absorption of the public media into the private realm has also resulted in the use of these private blogging sources in traditional journalistic media. Furthermore, in an unexpected twist, broadcast journalists are now searching blogs for news and personal reporting.

While some may say that the use of blogs exemplifies the postmodern emphasis on the social foundations of knowledge production and exchange, I would argue that the PC world of personalized culture absorbs the social construction of information into the autonomous echo chambers of individuated media. In other words, when every user also becomes a producer of media, the multiplication and diversification of potential sources for information increases to such an extent that individual consumers are motivated to seek out only the sources and blogs that reinforce their own personal views and ideologies. Here, the screen truly becomes an automated mirror of self-reflection.

One way to summarize the effects of many of these automodern technologies that I have related to the PC is to look at the iPod. On one level, the iPod is the perfect example of the use of automation to give individuals the autonomy to select and filter information and to absorb a previously public domain into the control of the private individual. We often forget that at one time, music was heard mainly in public settings; however, with the advent of recording technologies, music was freed from its live expression and was allowed to enter into the homes of individuals through shared distribution systems. It is also important to point out that the radio, like the television, is still a public medium, which is most often absorbed into private homes and now automobiles. Yet, on the radio, the selection of songs belongs to someone else, and therefore it caters to a more public and shared reception of music. Likewise, albums combined songs in a particular order that pre-package a predetermined collection of music. However, with the iPod, these public and industry-related restraints are eliminated, and the user is free through automation to create his or her own selection of songs.

Most importantly, the iPod allows people to take music anywhere and to use headphones as a way of cutting off the social world around them. For example, I often see students in public spaces listening to their iPods and moving and singing to the music as if they were alone in their private bedrooms. Here, we rediscover the loss of the distinction between the private and the public realms. Also, the fact that so many digital youth take their songs from illegal peer-to-peer internet sites shows how the loss of the public realm is coupled with an undermining of certain commercial interests. In a way, individual users are privatizing the music industry by illegally downloading music and creating their own systems of distribution and consumption. Yet, the success of Apple and iTunes points to the ways that the anticorporate mentality of some peer-to-peer file sharers has been quickly absorbed back into a corporate and consumerist structure. The libertarian impulses of the autonomous new media user are thus quite compatible with the production of a new consumer economy. In fact, in many of my students' essays about their uses of new media, they often equate individual freedom with the free market. Of course, what is usually left out of this equation is the idea of a public realm of protected and enacted citizenship.

Automodern Convergences

Many people feel that the next stage of technology development will be the combination of the iPod, the PC, the internet, and the cell phone. In this synergistic approach to automodern technology, we see the desire for total mobility and individual autonomy through the use of highly automated systems. One fear is that once all of these new media and technologies are absorbed into the cell phone, individuals will lose all ability to differentiate how to act in public from how to act in private. Already, cell phones make it easy for people to have private conversations in public, and this ignoring of the public often results in a situation where people in a public setting are all having their own private interactions with people who are not in the same physical space.

Another danger is that cell phones tend to make people forget where they actually are physically. For instance, it has been shown that when people drive cars and talk on the cell phone at the same time, they are more prone to accidents because they literally forget that they are driving.[34] Like so many other automodern technologies, cell phones allow people to enter into a technological flow where the difference between the individual and the machine breaks down. In other terms, due to the fluid and immersive nature of these technologies, people forget that they are using them, and in many ways, they become one with their machines.

With the immersive fluidity of cell phones, digital youth often claim that they are addicted to the use of this technology and that they suffer from withdrawals when they are forced to not use these machines. In fact, I often see my students approach my classes while talking on the phone, and then when class ends, they immediately, compulsively get back on the cell. Sometimes, I overhear the conversations these students have between classes, and these communications seem to have no other content than "checking in" or stating the students' present location. It is as if they do not feel that they exist unless someone else hears about their current presence. Here, autonomy is shown to be dependent on the recognition of others. Furthermore, it is interesting that students often detail the location and the time of their calls as if to show that time and space are still relevant. Thus, as new automodern technologies break with past conceptions of time and space, they also call for a continuous unconscious return to temporal and spatial coordinates.[35]

This need for digital youth to have their autonomy registered by others can also be seen in blogs, Web cams, and online diaries. All of these new technologies point to the desire for people to be heard and seen by people they may not even know. Like public confessional booths, these automodern processes allow for an externalization of interior feelings and ideas. However, unlike past uses of confession by religious orders, psychologists, and police, these types of self-disclosure do not seem to serve any higher public purpose other than the desire for recognition. Moreover, the fact that the audience of the confession is often absent shows how this type of communication reduces the social other to the role of simply verifying the individual's presence. One could argue that the more mass society makes us feel that we are just a number and that our voices do not count, the more we need to simply use technology to have our autonomy registered through automation. For example, one of the appealing aspects of popular television shows like *American Idol* is that they allow for the individual viewer to call in and register his or her own preference and presence. Likewise, CNN news programs often read viewers' e-mail on air and hold constant polls where viewers can voice their own immediate opinions. In this new combination of autonomy and automation, we have to wonder if this is what direct democracy really looks like, or are these uses of personal opinions just a lure to make people feel like they have some control over situations where they really have very little power? From an automodern perspective, this question of whether these new modes of participatory technology produce false or real autonomy and democracy can be seen as irrelevant because automodern digital youth usually do not distinguish between real and virtual identity.

The production of false autonomy in highly automated systems can also be understood through the example of the elevator button, which is supposed to control the closing of the door, but in reality is not usually attached to any real function. When elevator designers were asked why they include this nonfunctioning button, they responded that many people feel out of control and anxious in elevators, and so this button gives them a sense of control and eases their worries. According to Slavoj Zizek:

It is a well-known fact that the close-the-door button in most elevators is a totally dysfunctional placebo which is placed there just to give individuals the impression that they are somehow participating, contributing to the speed of the elevator journey. When we push this button the door closes in exactly the same time as when we just press the floor button without speeding up the process by pressing also the close-the-door button. This extreme and clear case of fake participation is, I claim, an appropriate metaphor [for] the participation of individuals in our post-modern political process.[36]

For Zizek, automation often allows for a high level of false autonomy and therefore represents a fake mode of social participation. Here, we refind the short-circuiting of the public realm by the automodern combination of autonomy and automation. Therefore, like pushing a nonfunctioning elevator button, instant television polls may only be giving people the feeling that they are participating in direct democracy, while their actual individual power is being diminished.

This high reliance on automation to prove autonomy is connected to an interesting reversal of the modern opposition between the roles of active subjects and passive objects. For example, in modern science, the scientist is supposed to be active and mobile, while the object of study is fixed in time and space.[37] This same opposition can be seen in modern art where the natural object stays rigid on the canvas, as the painter is free to move around. Furthermore, modernity sees technology as a tool or object that is controlled by the active subject. However, in automodernity, all of these relationships are reversed. For instance, in video games, the player's activity is often reduced to the movement of a finger or fingers, while the object on the screen moves around.[38] Likewise, in contemporary physics, the object of study is in constant movement or chaos, while the scientist remains an immobile watcher. Therefore, through automation, autonomy has been projected onto the external object, while the subject remains passive (Zizek calls this "interpassivity").

Of course, television is really the technological object that first introduced us to this curious reversal between the subject and the object. In fact, when the television was first reviewed at the World's Fair by *The New York Times*, the reporter wrote that this invention would fail because no one would want to just sit in their homes and stare into a box for hours at a time. Yet, this type of autonomous passivity is precisely what the automodern culture is willing to do, and the fact that the television became the first real object of the global village shows that there is almost a universal desire for people to be inactive as they watch activity appear in the realm of their objects.

Not only do televisions and computer games share this reversal of the subject and object relationship, but both technologies represent a global spread of popular culture that denies its own value and meaning. For example, whenever I try to get students to analyze critically the shows they watch or the computer games they play, they insist that these activities are escapes and sources for meaningless enjoyment. From this perspective, culture is a way of escaping society and the burden of thinking. What then has helped this type of technology and culture to spread around the world is that it is essentially self-consuming, and by this term I mean it denies its own import and value.

Connected to the television and the computer game is the remote control, whose very name points to the idea of autonomous, automated control from a distance. As Christine Rosen argues in her essay "Egocasting," the clicker allows for a sense of total personal freedom:

The creation and near-universal adoption of the remote control arguably marks the beginning of the era of the personalization of technology. The remote control shifted power to the individual, and the technologies that have embraced this principle in its wake—the Walkman, the Video Cassette

Recorder, Digital Video Recorders such as TiVo, and portable music devices like the iPod—have created a world where the individual's control over the content, style, and timing of what he consumes is nearly absolute.[39]

For Rosen, the ability to just turn people off or go to the next channel represents a strong combination of automation and autonomy, which can be seen as being highly antisocial:

By giving us the illusion of perfect control, these technologies risk making us incapable of ever being surprised. They encourage not the cultivation of taste, but the numbing repetition of fetish. And they contribute to what might be called "egocasting," the thoroughly personalized and extremely narrow pursuit of one's personal taste. In thrall to our own little technologically constructed worlds, we are, ironically, finding it increasingly difficult to appreciate genuine individuality.[40]

From Rosen's perspective, these new technologies not only do not increase unexpected and innovative activities, but they work to get rid of new and unexpected encounters. While I will discuss below different ways that digital youth are now challenging this thesis of ego-centrism in new media, I often think that one reason why students seem to turn off so quickly in class is that they are so used to having so much control over what they see and hear, and yet, like video games, television still provides a highly limited set of possible interactions and activities. While it is common to point to the use of interactivity as the key driving force behind the popularity of computer games for the automodern generation, we often find that the type of interactivity allowed by automated games is highly restricted. Therefore, not only does most of the activity reside on the machine's side, but the activities the machine can perform are all prescripted and form a limited range of actions. In many ways, we are seeing a usage of new media technologies to simultaneously erase and produce individual freedom, while individual freedom is being equated with the free market.[41]

For instance, in order to allow for a high level of preprogrammed interactivity, first-person shooter computer games must replace human interaction with restrictive social stereotypes. However, people still enjoy playing these games and repeating the same scenarios and choices over and over again. While at first glance, this high level of automation and repetition would seem to preclude a sense of personal autonomy, we must see that individual freedom in automodernity often represents a freedom not to do something. Thus, the freedom not to think or not to interact in a social relationship is a highly valued freedom in this cultural order. Likewise, the automodern celebration of free speech is in part derived from the desire to be free from social, political, relational, and traditional restrictions. What is then loved about computer games and contemporary media is that they are often so politically incorrect, and therefore they celebrate the autonomy of the individual no matter how repetitive and reductive the media representation.

Future Uses of Automodern Technologies in Education and Politics

The challenge for educators and public policy makers in the period of automodernity is to first recognize the dominant combination of autonomy and automation and then employ this new cultural order in a more self-critical and social way. For example, educators can create learning spaces where students engage in creative file-sharing activities; however, these same students need to be given critical thinking tools to reflect on the social and public aspects of their activities. This process will require the development of critical technology studies as a central core to automodern educational systems, and essential to this new form of education will be a constant effort of forming a dialogue between "old" school and "new" home models of media and technology. Therefore, instead of simply ignoring how the digital youth are using new media and technologies in unexpected and innovative ways, it is important to first understand these usages, to theorize and analyze their appeal, and then to find ways to employ them in a productive social manner. Ethnographies like those found elsewhere in this volume offer one method of exploring usage; however, traditions in critical theory, rhetoric, and philosophy offer other modes of thinking about the age we inhabit. And, as I've suggested throughout this essay, careful attention to the subject positions crafted by new technologies will also help us refine the theories humanities scholars deploy when explaining the world around them. If, as scholars, our theories help us to discern the world around us, the new relations of self to power emerging in our networked age suggest we need more supple, nuanced theoretical tools. Whether automodernity represents an extension of postmodernity or a break from it, this chapter argues that we are certainly in a moment of shifting relations of self to other that we need to theorize and understand.

One place where new automodern technologies are being reconnected to the public realm is in the development of social networking Web sites and software dedicated to getting people to organize online and meet offline. For instance, Meetup.com provides templates and strategies for creating social networks that engage in particular group activities. According to their Web site, this electronic social network is involved in combining new media technologies with more traditional social and public activities: "Meetup.com helps people find others who share their interest or cause, and form lasting, influential, local community groups that regularly meet face to face. We believe that the world will be a better place when everyone has access to a people-powered local Meetup Group." Like Moveon.org, this site uses technology and media as a facilitator to connect people online and motivate them to meet in person. In fact, I would argue that this structure employs automodern media for postmodern purposes, and therefore these sites show that the privatization of the public realm is not the only possible result of the combination of autonomy and automation. Furthermore, these new social collective sites may point to the future of both democratic education and politics. In starting off with how people are already using new media technologies, these forums for digital connection offer a new hope for a more democratic public realm.

While I have found that most of my digitally minded students tend to use new media social networking sites as another mode of ego-casting popular culture and personal communication, it is possible to help work from students' own interests while also moving them toward more publicly minded online activities. For example, as an experiment in grassroots online social involvement, teachers can have students create social networks dedicated to a particular social intervention. In using their Viewbook or Facebook personal pages, students can transform their social networks into ad hoc, grassroots collectives directed to whatever causes they want to pursue. One place to look at possible projects for digital youth is the book *MoveOn's 50 Ways to Love Your Country*.[42] This text discusses ways new media technologies can be used to enact a wide variety of public action activities, including letter writing campaigns, product boycotts, social petitions, election activism, voting drives, media criticism, political house parties, and community service projects.

Another way of incorporating the unexpected activities of digital youth is to take advantage of the automodern fascination with viral videos. These short digital movies can be used to collect evidence of consumer fraud and political abuse. In fact, throughout the world, young people are using new technologies to document human rights abuses and other social issues. These social activities display the possible roles new media and digital youth can play in the global democratization and social justice movements. If we still believe that teaching is meant to broaden our students' horizons, challenge them to think and behave ethically, and expose them to ideas and worlds they might not otherwise encounter, we must take seriously the ways in which new technologies address and engage them and then use their interests as a platform for ethical engagement with the world.

Returning to my opening example of Benjamin as a multimedia, multitasking student, it is important to begin to reimagine how our institutions can both hold onto past effective modes of teaching and cater to new media methods of learning and new forms of the self. The first step in this process will be to develop a more critical and tolerant view of how new technologies affect all aspects of digital youth. My hope is that this chapter will begin a conversation that steers between the extremes of naïve celebration and pessimistic dismissal of radically ambivalent automodern media. In developing a critical model of new media literacy, we can work to integrate new modes of learning and living into older forms of social interaction. Furthermore, by defending the public realm against the constant threats of privatization, we can open up a new automodern public space.

Notes

1. Lester Faigley, *Fragments of Rationality: Postmodernity and the Subject of Composition* (Pittsburgh, PA: University of Pittsburgh Press, 1992).

2. Robert Samuels, *Integrating Hypertextual Subjects* (Cresskill, NJ: Hampton Press, 2006).

3. James Gee, *What Video Games Have to Teach Us about Learning and Literacy* (New York: Palgrave Macmillian, 2004), 169–198.

4. One of the most popular criticisms of postmodernism can be found in Alan Bloom's The Closing of the American Mind; see Alan Bloom, *The Closing of the American Mind* (New York: Simon, 1987).

5. The work of Homi Bhabha has shown a strong recognition of the role of multiple cultures and social movements in the postmodern challenging of modern universalism and European ethnocentrism; see Homi Bhabha, *The Location of Culture* (London: Rutledge, 1994).

6. It is hard to cite sources for the extreme form of postmodern relativism since it is often the critics of postmodernism who have defined this extremist position. A strong example of a critic who has insisted on an extreme version of postmodern relativism is Dinesh D'Souza's Illiberal Education; see Dinesh D'Souza, *Illiberal Education* (New York: Vintage Books, 1991).

7. Many of the first strong theories of social construction can be derived from Saussure's work in linguistics and Claude Levi-Strauss's work in anthropology. These social science works were imported into the humanities in Jacques Derrida's early work; see Ferdinand de Saussure, *Course in General Linguistics*, eds. Charles Balley and Albert Sechehaye, trans. Wade Baskin (New York: McGraw-Hill, 1966); Claude Levi-Strauss, *The Savage Mind* (Chicago: University of Chicago Press, 1970); Jacques Derrida, *Margins of Philosophy* (Chicago: University of Chicago Press, 1982).

8. One of the earliest theorists to connect collage and cultural re-mixing to postmodernity was Frederick Jameson.

9. While the work of Jacques Derrida has been blamed for ushering the extreme cultural relativism into Western philosophy and literary studies, I would argue that it has often been his followers and imitators who have offered a less nuanced and more generalized mode of postmodern extremism.

10. Zygmunt Bauman, *Modernity and the Holocaust* (Ithaca, NY: Cornell University Press, 1989); Ulrich Beck, *Risk Society: Towards a New Modernity* (London and Newbury Park, CA: Sage Publications, 1992); Jean Baudrillard, *The Transparency of Evil* (New York: Verso, 1993); Frederic Jameson, *Postmodernism: Or,*

the Cultural Logic of Late Capitalism (Durham, NC: Duke University Press, 1991); Jeremy Rifkin, *The Age of Access* (New York: Putnam, 2000).

11. Marilyn Cooper, Postmodern Pedagogy in Electronic Conversations, in *Passions, Pedagogy, and 21st Century Technologies*, eds. Gail E. Hawisher and Cynthia L. Selfe (Logan: Utah State University Press, 1999), 142.

12. While it may seem that Cooper's stress on the connection of diverse voices helps to explain my example above of the unexpected use by students of technology for collaboration, I argue here that automodern collaboration should not be confused with the postmodern stress on public and social mediation.

13. Marilyn Cooper, Postmodern Pedagogy in Electronic Conversations, 143.

14. Ibid., 143.

15. George Howard, Culture Tales, *American Psychologist* 46, no. 3 (1990): 187–197.

16. I have found that many students reject this type of argument because they believe that science is neutral and objective and not subject to cultural and historical influences. Students, and many academics, also tend to confuse social constructivism with subjectivism.

17. Alan Ryan, cited in Lawrence W. Sherman in Postmodern Constructivist Pedagogy for Teaching and Learning Cooperatively on the Web, *CyberPsychology & Behavior* 3, no. 1 (Feb. 2000): 51–57.

18. A central reason why students do not feel that their sense of self is being undermined by postmodern society is that the self is a psychological and virtual entity that is not strictly determined by social forces.

19. Lester Faigley, *Fragments of Rationality: Postmodernity and the Subject of Composition* (Pittsburgh, PA: University of Pittsburgh Press, 1992).

20. Ibid., 4–7.

21. Ibid., 8.

22. Essays from the 2006 Global Kids Digital Media Essay Contest can be accessed at http://www.community.macfound.org/crossvolume. This contest asked students from all over the world to write about their diverse experiences using new media (accessed November 12, 2006).

23. Christopher Schroeder, *Re-inventing the University* (Logan, Utah: Utah State University Press, 2001), 2.

24. Ibid., 3.

25. Ibid., 5.

26. Ibid., 6.

27. Ibid., 7.

28. Ibid., 10; Kenneth Gergen, *The Saturated Self: Dilemmas of Identity in Contemporary Life* (New York: Basic Books, 1991); Neil Postman, *Technopoly: The Surrender of Culture to Technology* (New York: Vintage, 1992); Henry A. Giroux, Slacking Off: Border Youth and Postmodern Education, *Journal of Advanced Composition* 14, no. 2 (1994). http://www.henryagiroux.com/online_articles/slacking_off.htm.

29. A major problem with my analysis is that it tends to hide the real economic divisions in our culture that prevent many young people from having access to the same technologies. However, I still feel that the technologies I will be discussing are used by a majority of students who end up going to college.

30. Throughout the 19th and 20th centuries, the mechanized assembly line is often seen as the ultimate example of how automation alienates people and takes away their sense of personal autonomy.

31. Raymond Williams, *Television: Technology and Cultural Form* (London: Fontana, 1974).

32. Behind this discussion of the privatization of the public realm through technology is an acknowledgment of the political movement to undermine the public realm and the welfare state.

33. I am drawing here from Heidegger's work on the enframing power of technology; Martin Heidegger, *The Question Concerning Technology and Other Essays* (New York: Harper Colophon Books, 1977).

34. In fact, some studies equate the effect of using a cell phone while driving to driving under the influence of alcohol.

35. I stress the unconscious nature of the retention of spatial and temporal concerns because students claim that they are not aware that they often have conversations about their locations in space and time.

36. Slavoj Zizek, Human Rights and Its Discontents, 2005, http://www.lacan.com/zizek-human.htm.

37. Jean Baudrillard's work is the major source for explaining this reversal of the subject and the object in contemporary science.

38. While it may be true that new game designers are trying to make the movements of the player a larger part of games, this movement is still highly restricted.

39. Christine Rosen, Egocasting, *The New Atlantis*, 2005. http://www.thenewatlantis.com/archive/7/rosen.htm.

40. Ibid.

41. All of these trends feed into the neo-conservative and neo-liberal movements to justify the cutting of taxes through the downgrading of public programs and the deregulation of the free market. Since the public realm has been absorbed into the automated activities of the machine, and the private realm has been equated with the free subject of the free market, there is no longer any need to fund public welfare projects.

42. MoveOn, *MoveOn's 50 Ways to Love Your Country* (San Francisco: Inner Ocean, 2006).

A Pedagogy for Original Synners

Steve Anderson and Anne Balsamo

University of Southern California School of Cinematic Arts, Division of Interactive Media

How can we gain perspective on the contemporary scene of digital learning? In the global era commonly known as the early twenty-first century, this cultural landscape is far from flat—it is marked by spikes of intense technological engagement and valleys of cultural impoverishment and illiteracy. Accounts of technological innovations dominate the headlines, while the stories of the illiterate and the technologically disenfranchised are relegated to back pages. This is the doubled reality of the dynamic educational scene of contemporary global culture: it has been transformed and is being continually transformed by the wide-scale use of new digital technologies. At the same time, it is a place where timeworn inequities stubbornly persist despite the concerted efforts of educational reformers. We agree with cyberpunk science fiction author William Gibson, when he writes: "the future is already here, it's just distributed unevenly."

In an effort to create a vantage point from which to gain a perspective on this dynamically shifting scene, we begin with a speculative scenario of a future-that-does-not-yet-exist assembled from science fictional narrative fragments of the present. We deploy this speculative narrative as a critical technique that enables us to probe the changes in a generation's disposition.[1] For the purposes of this essay, we call the members of this generation "students." We identify ourselves as the "teachers." There are many questions to consider in tracing the contours of the dispositional change of this generation born in a digital age, any of which could serve as the organizing topic for a robust investigation and analysis. For example: How do students of this generation assess information that comes to them in different media forms (in print, text, images, animation, simulation, personal experience, augmented experience, virtual experience, displaced experience)? How do they learn to form new ideas and new insights, both on their own and as part of collaborative groups? What is the tenor of their informal social learning networks? How do they interact with formal institutions that reify the values of the parent culture? How should these institutions change to address this generational disposition? How will these students be taught to be the stewards of culture for the future? How do we teach them the importance of history, of remembering? How do we prepare them and ourselves for the changes that will inevitably come next?

These questions offer a hint at what might be considered the "unintended consequences" of the deployment of digital technologies for the purposes of education and learning. In investigating the nature of digital learning—the topic of this MacArthur series—the danger lies in assuming either an overly critical or overly celebratory stance regarding the educational potential of digital technologies. Discussions about the relationship between technology and education have a long history. These discussions often devolve into well-worn debates: technology is either the source of salvation or of damnation. The reality is, of course, much more convoluted. We know that all technologies reconfigure culture, just as culture serves as the enabling condition for the creation of new technologies. The production of unintended consequences is inevitable; accommodating them is not. Anticipating them is an act of conscious engagement; designing against them is an ethical investment in the future.

The aims of this chapter are both more modest and more ambitious: we begin in the future and end with a manifesto for the present. Rather than rehearse the familiar structure of discussions about the essential nature of technological innovations in education, we begin with a set of fictional observations about the classroom of the future based on trends already emerging in 2007. This is an exercise in the narrative reconstruction of reality for the purposes of creating a cognitive map that not only helps us make sense of the shifting landscape of the present, but also guides our travels in the future. This speculative and *ironic* fictional scenario allows us to elaborate key elements of the generational disposition of those who inhabit this landscape as their native milieu. The pragmatic objective of this exercise is to draw out the implications of this sensibility for the purposes of developing appropriate and inspiring educational practices that take advantage of new technological innovations, but remain steadfastly attendant to the opportunities to reconfigure the educational/learning/schooling landscape in empowering ways. In the process of formulating suggestions for new pedagogical practices comes the opportunity, and indeed the responsibility, to seriously reexamine current institutional structures for learning.

2020 Vision[2]

It's 2016, and I'm meeting the first group of students from the class of 2020. I log on and see them for the first time—forty of them floating in front of me in null-zero gravity. I quickly scan the space and I'm pleasantly surprised to see the first (as far as I know) Human-Onkali mutant. I heard that the kids refer to them as "HuMonk-a-Li." Not surprisingly, I also see a retro Lara Croft, a couple of Akiras, the predictable slew of Ender Wiggens and a smattering of glyphs I don't yet recognize.

My IM-patch starts to heat up; one of them has already hacked my earring. I take a deep breath and think, "Let the Games Begin!"

The challenge of course is to get them to play the game that I want them to play, rather than the one they want to impose on me. Here's how their game works: They trick me into wearing a 1980s style head bobber with a sign that says: "Stump the teacher." Their head bobbers say things like: "Why should I care?" "Make me" and "Who R U?"

I turn on my left side to get their attention. They're going to do the game grid assessment exercise, the by-now best practice for evaluating gamers' learning potential. I give them the instructions: Enter your persona data—name, race, species, gender, special skills, goals, and connections/friends.

Then I tell them: Pick your Medium: Physical, Mental, Chance, or Arts. According to our assessment protocol, students are always limited to the same choices: those on the vertical axis of the game matrix.

Simultaneously my evaluation bots randomly select from the characteristics along the horizontal axis: (1) naked, (2) tool, (3) machine, (4) animal. These identify the modes of

The Assessment Grid
(Balsamo, 2008)

	[A] Naked	[B] Tool	[C] Machine	[D] Animal
[1] Physical				
[2] Mental				
[3] Chance				
[4] Arts				

Assessment Grid id#: 01102016.balsamo.mda140

Figure 1

assistance that determine the game play. *Naked* means without anything, just what you walk in with; *tool-assisted* means simple tools such as markers, dice, picks, hammers, and pens. *Machine* means the full range of digital devices and applications, as well as engines, robots, biolution devices, flickercladding and other nano manufacturing gadgets. *Animal* includes assistance from typical companion species such as dogs, horses, and dolphins, but also bush robots, gmos, tracer-birds and micromice.

The combination of the student selection and the bot selection determines the game they will play from the matrix of possibilities that are generated randomly each time the game grid is activated. I remind the students that the assessment game gives them a chance to test themselves against my evaluation bots that have been programmed to perform my minimal expectations for the achievement of a "B" in the course. If they can't beat my bots, then they should rethink the settings on their persona profiles. I suggest, for example, that they may want to increase their "IQ Point" setting that establishes the average amount of brainspace (and time) they want to allot to learning course material. I remind them that a simple recalibration of their "Attention Intensity" setting can do wonders for their grades, but it remains their decision about how they will calibrate their persona for their performance in the game known as this class.

I also remind them that after each game round concludes, they will have the opportunity to reset their profile preferences for the next set of interactivities. We limit their profile changes to in-between interactivities, because we learned early on that students could outsmart game bots by changing their profiles on the fly. The bots are programmed to "learn,"—which means that they can't change profile characteristics unless they have acquired experience through repeated encounters with course materials and exercises. Pedagogically, we believe that it is important for students to be constrained by the same rule. Thus, students have to play their profile preferences through the duration of a single interactivity. This guards against the temptation to acquire extrafactual memories. Students are actually encouraged to *reflect* on their interactivity performance in-between sessions, and to change their profiles and calibrations. We call this part of the *learning process*.

As I watch them play their games, I wonder which ones have signed up to participate in the make space practicum. I know that only the wealthiest students can afford to enroll in the reality-based course work, where we will meet face to face and work side by side on hand-made projects: paper writing, multimedia presentations, geo-caching exercises, and digital prototyping. Their socioeconomic class status will become evident at some point, no doubt, so that by the time they show up in LA, I'll know where they are coming from geographically, economically, and cosmically. This course is the first to enroll ship-schooled students, the children of the first colonists en route to UBIK4. These students won't be in LA in the flesh, obviously, but will send tele-controlled ditto blanks that they've imprinted themselves onto. Only the really wealthy and the military can afford them: the colonists are neither; it was one of the perks used as an enlistment incentive. I take a moment to contemplate the educational scene unfolding across diverse planes of reality to ask myself: what role can and should I play in their educational process?

Remarks on the Disposition of the Born Digital Generation

Born and raised in a digital, networked age, these students-of-a-future—who are already showing up in U.S. university classrooms—are as much shaped by the dominant cultural logic of the early twenty-first century as they reproduce it through their creative practices and social interactions: they are members of the *born digital* generation. Their beliefs and assumptions about the way "learning" occurs have been shaped by their early encounters with pervasive digital worlds and network technologies, and the ubiquity of "smart" and responsive environments. They present themselves as just-in-time learners, confident that when they need to know something, they'll know where to find it. By the time they are ready to enter the university, these students have amassed significant experience in mining their networks (both digital and social) for their information needs. They treat their affiliation networks as informal Delphi groups.[3] As the statistical phenomenon of Delphi groups demonstrates, even when a "factual" piece of information is not known to each and every person, the aggregate mapping of responses from group members tends to cluster around the correct answer. For these students, the process of "thinking" now routinely (and in some cases, exclusively) relies on social network navigation. Data = information = knowledge is their taken-for-granted epistemology, and for many of them, every world is a game, and all the people merely players. Their imaginations are structured and shaped through encounters in different kinds of mediated worlds: RL and online games, institutional and familial, peer-based and anonymous. They move easily through different kinds of networks: social, technological, material, and virtual. Consequently, their identities are a hybrid of multiple personae performed and shaped through their participation in dispersed (mixed reality) social networks as well as within simulated virtual (gaming) worlds. In this they are the quintessential decentered postmodern subjects marked by differing intensity flows and shifting affinities. Remix is their cultural vernacular.

Retooling our sense of students not as younger versions of ourselves, but as members of a generation with its own unique disposition, provides a starting point for the creation of pedagogical protocols that acknowledge and embrace their essential mutability. At base, this requires the reexamination of the notion of *education*—as the term for the institutionalized process of knowledge creation—and the role of professional teachers and academics in the cultural practices (and institutions) of knowledge production. For good reason, we abandoned the notion of education as the dutiful replication of received knowledge claims (at least at the university level, perhaps not so at the K-12 levels in the United States) in favor of an emphasis on learning. But, we need to push even further in augmenting our understanding of learning as a complex process of human identity formation that is shaped by cultural, cognitive, biological, and social forces. One step is to refine our understanding of "critical thinking" to focus more specifically on the skills of creative and critical *synthesis*. To assist us in these efforts, we might think of these students as "Original Synners," a title borrowed from science fiction author Pat Cadigan's cosmology, which identifies them as "original synthesizers" whose most important literacy will be the ability to create knowledge by harvesting information from diverse sources.

At a basic level, Original Synners must develop strong abilities to critically evaluate the veracity and reliability of information sources. Then, they need to learn how to integrate information that comes from different sources, critical frameworks, and academic disciplines. They will need to understand the structural function of "disciplinarity" as an institutionalized practice of knowledge verification. In this, the *born digital* generation has a daunting learning agenda: they must acquire appreciation for the depths of disciplinary knowledge, but not get mired in the merely academic, so that they can forge connections across disciplinary divides in the service of creating new understandings and formulating new questions to pursue. While they might understand intuitively that innovation is a multidisciplinary creative endeavor, they also need to understand how knowledge is produced in the *dialogue* among disciplines, through the process of social negotiation, and in creative collaboration with peers and experts. In short, they must learn how to engage in conversations with those who do not hold the same cultural values or intellectual commitments.

But equally importantly, this notion also suggests other considerations that they do not yet have the perspective to fully appreciate and embrace. For example, although they are already global citizens by virtue of their consumption habits and residence in particular nation states, they need to understand how the global flows of information and capital affect people in other geographic and cultural contexts. They need to become deeply multilingual, not only in the use of languages but also in their understanding of different cultural logics and global politics. Learning is a practice; knowledge is content. They will have to learn the value of both. In short, Original Synners require new literacies: cultural, technological, social, and epistemological. As professional educators, we have the responsibility to design learning environments and institutional practices that foster the acquisition of foundational skills that students will need for a lifetime of network navigation, information synthesis, social participation, and creative knowledge production.

Educational Institutions in Transition

As we suggest in the opening account of an imaginary meeting with the first group of students from the class of 2020, the classroom will serve as another stage for the performance of their generational disposition. When this happens, the teachers will have as much to learn as the students. These students do not consider their teachers the sole experts in knowledge certification and production, nor do they see the academy as the primary site for the production of knowledge claims. For members of the *born digital* generation, the process of knowledge creation happens across diverse settings, in formal institutions as well as through informal social and technological practices. For them, teaching and learning already occur in different kinds of informational spaces—distributed communities linked by wireless networks and mobile devices as well as on remote campuses, in "smart" classrooms, and in the virtual spaces of online environments. The multiplication of learning spaces is enabled in part by increased access to high-speed data networks, but perhaps more important is the increasing familiarity and ubiquity of collaborative online activities as a part of many people's daily lives. Tools such as blogs, wikis, social bookmarking, file-sharing, and tagging are information management applications that once were the domain of computer scientists and professional information architects, but are now in common usage among those with regular access to computers and broadband networks.

As educators reevaluate their role in the emergent knowledge economy, other issues must be addressed as well: the role of universities in the knowledge production industry, the waning cultural authority of the professoriate, the notion of education versus credentialing, and the professionalization of junior faculty and graduate students. For just as the development of new digital technologies and networking applications serve as the stage for reconfiguring learning practices of students, so too do these technological innovations provide an opportunity to reengineer common practices within institutions of higher education. For example, for the past decade, many universities have invested significant resources in the development of "distance learning" courses in an attempt to produce new channels for tuition revenue. These courses rely extensively on digital networks and course management software in the service of producing new "markets" for a university's product. There is an opportunity to productively reimagine these efforts as protocols of "technologically enhanced learning" that may enable the university to serve its core constituents better as well.

The idea of using emerging digital technologies for the purposes of educational innovation has been embraced by many faculties. This is simultaneously an exciting and a sobering turn of events: exciting because the experimentation requires teachers to consciously reflect on the nature of learning in a digital age, sobering because the types of learning to emerge from such innovations may not be entirely predictable, and in some cases, perhaps not even desirable. For example, the extent to which computer and video games have captured young people's attention makes games seem like a particularly promising learning platform. Game worlds not only provide dynamic visual, auditory, and sometimes bodily stimulation, they also offer opportunities for players to express emotion, to engage in structured play, and to gain a sense of accomplishment and social belonging. For many students (although not all), the bounded nature of a game world holds their attention in a way that traditional classroom educational activities may not. They are simultaneously capable of highly focused attention when they participate in a gaming world, and incapable (or perhaps unwilling) to pay attention to single-channel communication in the body-based world. Many games require participants to move between multiple planes of reality: the world of the game, of the strategy, of the goal, of other players, and of the real world. These types of games teach and condition a sensibility of rapid partial attending. Gamers learn by cycling through information spaces; they learn to iteratively scan multiple spaces and to adjust their activities in line with new information. In the process, the performance and temporality of "attending" is transformed. This type of "attending" is not easily accommodated by traditional classroom practices, and it remains the case that among university-age students across the United States, and indeed throughout the world, familiarity and access to gaming platforms and gaming literacy remain stubbornly uneven, with disparities that articulate along predictable axes of racial, economic, and geographic differences. As promising as it may appear, adopting online gaming as the primary digital learning paradigm may not serve all our students equally well.

In order to think concretely about the kind of institutional practices that will augment the literacies of Original Synners, we offer the following discussion of a sample of contemporary innovations that share a particular philosophical stance about the role of technology in digital learning. None of these efforts advocates the development of expensive new technologies per se; rather, they each use existing applications, information networks, and emergent social practices as the basis for the creation of new pedagogical models. They approach these technological practices and resources by asking what they already do best, in order to develop innovative and responsive pedagogical practices. These efforts illustrate three characteristics required for the creation of new pedagogies and institutional structures that appropriately address the learning needs of the *born digital* generation.

1   *Open*: extensible, participatory, non-proprietary, collaborative, distributed, many-to-many, multi-institutional, global

2   *Hybrid*: combining networked and physical spaces, blurring lines between academic and everyday social, creative and expressive practices; crossing traditional generational and cultural boundaries

3   *Media rich*: making sophisticated use of audio, video, and interactivity; multi-sensorial, expressive, affective.

The profiles that follow highlight exemplary projects, programs, classes and institutions that work with some or all of these characteristics in interesting ways. None of them proposes a transcendental model of digital learning; their innovations are context-specific, mutable, and recombinant. This is as it should be, for in a digital age, it is unimaginable to think that any single model of learning is going to provide the program of action to address the literacy needs of all members of the *born digital* generation. Our pedagogical task is a remix project in its own right, where we strategically select and combine elements from a range of theoretically grounded innovations for the purposes of developing a robust pedagogy for Original Synners.

Open: Open CourseWare at MIT

The Open CourseWare (OCW) consortium originated at MIT in the late 1990s as an effort to explore the potentials of distance education. Rather than pursue a revenue-driven model of one-to-many online teaching, MIT's Open CourseWare initiative sought to take seriously the institution's mandate to "advance knowledge and educate students in science, technology, and other areas of scholarship that will best serve the nation and the world in the twenty-first century," and so devised a *many-to-many* educational model that effectively expands the horizons of MIT's curriculum. Faculty participation remains voluntary, but the long-term goal of the initiative is to make available the complete MIT curriculum of over 1800 classes. The OCW administration assists with publishing course materials online and dealing with copyright clearances for course readings and materials; this institutional support is a crucial part of the success of this initiative. If individual faculty were left to navigate the Byzantine structures of information ownership and reproduction rights, few would have the time or resources to participate.

To encourage the collaboration of other institutions around the world, the OCW sets a deliberately low threshold for participation. An institution wishing to participate in the OCW consortium must agree to publish a minimum of ten courses under its own University's name.[4] The consortium provides resources and experience on how to make these course materials available and emphasizes the use of open source tools and software to support these efforts. OCW seeks to create a vast archive of freely accessible course content, including syllabi and a portfolio of readings and supplemental materials. At the very moment when many universities are focusing on branding and tightening controls over intellectual property, the MIT's OCW blueprint defies conventional wisdom in important ways. The key to this program's success lies not in chasing tuition revenue streams outside the university, but in creating learning paths that extend beyond the campus itself. A principal benefit of this program has been to enhance the institution's reputation for progressive thinking among a broad community of education professionals.

MIT is not the only institution to initiate an open source approach to the sharing of educational materials; a number of similar efforts have appeared in recent years, including Carnegie Mellon University's Open Learning Initiative,[5] Rice University's Connexions project,[6] and the Open University's OpenLearn project,[7] all of which share ideals of openness and ease of access. What is remarkable about these organizations and initiatives is the speed with which they have appeared and taken hold across a broad spectrum of university contexts. During the first seven years of its existence, the MIT initiative published more than 1,400 graduate and undergraduate classes from the MIT curriculum. Perhaps more importantly, the reach of the OCW is worldwide, with exceptionally active participation by institutions in France, Japan, and China. The many-to-many aspect of this rapidly expanding global network is of particular importance here. Rather than simply exporting cultural capital from American universities to the rest of the world, the OCW model encourages the multi-directional exchange and cross pollination of ideas, resources, and pedagogies.

One factor that contributed to the rapid rate of adoption of the Open CourseWare model is the broad success (in both commercial and noncommercial realms) of open source software development over the past two decades.[8] Although few forms of creative production lend themselves as readily to open source production as software programming, a number of similar undertakings have emerged from within other spheres of artistic, scholarly, and technical endeavor. These range from the *open source cinema* movements centered in the U.K. and the Netherlands to various open content organizations in the San Francisco bay area, such as Creative Commons,[9] the Internet Archive,[10] Electronic Frontier Foundation,[11] Open Source Initiative,[12] and Prelinger Library,[13] all of which take as their point of departure the value of peer-to-peer information sharing and the support of participatory culture.

Given the rising costs of tuition at both public and private universities and the resulting divisions of access along economic lines, it is likely that informal peer-to-peer networks and "viral education" will continue to increase in popularity.[14] To this end, a number of research efforts and organizations are examining these emerging forms of learning. Groups and research efforts including the Open Educational Resources Commons,[15] the Monterey Institute for Technology and Education (MITE), the New Media Consortium (NMC), and the Institute for the Studies of Knowledge Management in Education (ISKME) have all begun to explore the potentials of extrainstitutional learning. An evolving role for educators in this type of distributed, multiple, shared learning landscape is to orchestrate the conditions of possibility within which individuals may participate most productively, and to develop methodologies that fluidly cross traditional institutional boundaries. In this sense, teachers begin to resemble *educational designers*, whose expertise may include deep disciplinary knowledge, but whose practice involves mobilizing the efforts of communities and individuals in relation to institutional resources.

The proliferation of Application Programming Interfaces (APIs) accessible to ordinary Web users, has led to a similar reconfiguration of many users' approach to networked media. No longer considered mere consumers and navigators of networked content created by others, Web users are now designing their own tools, performing *mashups* of materials that are available through existing databases and online archives, and creating multiple user-interfaces that transform the nature of information access.[16] Perhaps more importantly, the nature of information that is made available in networks is itself being transformed. Data may no longer be simply understood as static nodes of information to be accessed with speed and efficiency. Databases are dynamic, reconfigurable systems. In interacting with these systems, users become *producers* as well as consumers of structured information systems. Other practices, such as DIY and "prosumer" cultural productions, including file sharing, writing in public, and social bookmarking, are also being investigated as possible new learning protocols for use not only by amateurs (those without the formal credentials to produce knowledge claims), but also by professional educators who recognize the power of these easily accessed information-sharing tools.

Two recent books, Henry Jenkins' *Convergence Culture* and Yochai Benkler's *The Wealth of Networks*, have discussed the potential social and economic benefits of participatory networks in the culture at large. Educators are poised to deploy the use of peer-to-peer information sharing as strategies for teaching and learning. For example, Linda Stone argues that the new disposition of "attending" common among gamers—a disposition she refers to as "continuous partial attention"—can be an extremely powerful mode of engagement.[17] As Stone points out, when individuals participate in multiple information streams, they learn to reinvent themselves as nodes within networks who are capable of contributing to information flows, as well as receiving them. Through the interactions in a backchannel, an individual's agency in the classroom expands in interesting ways. Simultaneously acting as "listener," "audience member," and "peer," the student oscillates between technologically mediated subject positions. None of these positions is "purer" than the other; in oscillating among them the opportunity emerges for the creation of new insights as one set of cognitive skills (of the listener, for example) interferes and collides with another set of cognitive practices (of texting).

Recent experiments in using a text messaging "backchannel" in the classroom suggest that the multiplication of information flows can productively stimulate conversation among students-as-peers in a classroom space.[18] But, as Howard Rheingold has argued, although they are extremely promising, the existing cultural vernaculars that emerge in these peer-to-peer social networking practices are not always applicable to academic contexts. Emergent practices such as "backchanneling," for example, can be either extremely distracting (e.g., when backchannel conversations digress from the topic at hand or become a forum for unconstructive criticism) or else highly productive as a conduit for otherwise overlooked channels of discourse. To use these tools effectively, faculties must not only understand the technological potential, but also the kinds of structures needed to focus the energies these tools unleash. This is the work of the techno pedagogical designer.

Hybrid: CyberOne: Law in the Court of Public Opinion

The concept of hybridity is one of digital culture's most venerable touchstones, a term with a history ranging from Homi Bhabha's "empowering condition of hybridity"[19] to the liminal minds and bodies of science fiction cyborgs, symbionts, and mutants. In digitally mediated learning environments—everything from classrooms that are WiFi-enabled to virtual meeting spaces—students are increasingly comfortable occupying more than one physical or mental space at a time. On one level, the type of hybridity described here is simply a literal descriptor for the combination of in-person and networked communication that characterizes many recent experiments with digital pedagogy. On another level, though, hybridity signifies an ontological status increasingly common among today's youth that should be neither ignored nor feared. It is perhaps no accident that some of the most interesting forays into digital education achieve success not through wholesale adoption of any one "new" technology, but through creatively combining, juxtaposing, or crosspollinating new with traditional practices.

"CyberOne: Law in the Court of Public Opinion" is a hybrid physical/virtual class offered through the Berkman Center for Internet and Society at Harvard Law School. The class was conceived and developed by the father–daughter team of Charles and Rebecca Nesson as an experiment in making the content of Harvard's prestigious Law School accessible to a broader public. The course is structured around a series of concentric tiers of participation, with a traditional law school class taught by Charles Nesson in physical space, an extension class led by Rebecca Nesson with paid enrollment, and a third tier composed of an at-large constituency who participate in the course free of charge within the online virtual world of *Second Life*. Although it is far from the first of its kind, this course has drawn a great deal of attention in part because of its association with Harvard's Berkman Center, which has been a leader in progressive thinking around issues of law, policy, and culture with regard to the internet.

In addition, this class may indicate that a critical mass of interest has formed around exploring the potentials of virtual learning environments. Many of the participants in the extension class and at-large communities are themselves educators seeking experience with distributed learning. Thus, in addition to the course's focus on visual argumentation in legal contexts, CyberOne functions for many participants on a meta-pedagogical level, modeling a number of extremely effective practices, particularly with regard to creating a vibrant sense of community among participants. CyberOne's emphasis on community answers the call issued by John Seeley Brown and Paul Duguid in 2003 when they argued that universities in the digital age should pursue a "community view" as opposed to a "delivery view" of education.[20] The open social environment of *Second Life* and minimal barriers to participation for students in the at-large community create opportunities for students to contribute their own expertise, to guide classroom activities in directions they are most interested in, and to decenter the authority of the instructors in favor of learning and activity that takes place along multiple axes. As a result, the community of CyberOne has both grown and flourished into an extraordinarily dynamic, engaged community that extends beyond the immediate boundaries of the class.

According to Rebecca Nesson, part of the key to CyberOne's success lies in informal interactions that take place before and after regularly scheduled course events. Course lectures and discussions are carefully crafted for accessibility by various tiers of course participants. In-world exercises and projects are conceived to facilitate participation across these virtual communities. CyberOne additionally benefits from highly accessible subject matter and stimulating, real-world relevance in a field that might otherwise seem arcane and specialized. The focus on visual argumentation in a courtroom context has clear resonances with visual expression in everyday life as well, and *Second Life* provides a rich, 3D platform for students to explore theories of communication as well as practical examples. An additionally effective strategy has been to have students undertake group projects—everything from simple exercises and assignments (e.g., leading other students on tours of Berkman Island, CyberOne's home in *Second Life*) to full scale collaborative work on video projects and experiments with synchronous, in-world voice communication. In addition, the CyberOne class hosted numerous supplementary events including an ethnomusicology lecture and concert, a panel discussion on the future of digital education, and the collective architecting and construction of virtual buildings to be used by future classes. But, as powerful as the *Second Life* learning environment is, its day-to-day functioning depends on a range of 2D Web-based resources including course Web logs and wikis, a course listserve, and online video and audio recordings of course lectures and events.

The effectiveness of the CyberOne class may be significantly attributed to this combination of elements that permit various points of entry and modes of participation for different groups of participants. The class is both multiply synchronous, with the law school class and *Second Life* discussions and events, and also asynchronous, allowing students to work with course materials in their own time, reading transcripts and watching videos online, as well as contributing their own reflections to various online resources. By refusing to privilege any one mode of student participation, CyberOne implicitly recognizes a key aspect of learning within the born digital generation: that different students learn best when allowed to process information and experience through various forms of engagement, at differing paces and via a multitude of technologies. It is no accident that the conception of this class originated with the multigenerational team of Charles and Rececca Nesson, who were perhaps uniquely situated to exploit the advantages of more traditional and experimental modes of pedagogy.

For all its benefits and possibilities, concerns about intellectual property, technology management, and branding within *Second Life* must be addressed. One student project that originated in the CyberOne class was an attempt to organize a movement among *Second Life* residents to pressure Linden Lab to change their terms of service agreement to exert less restrictive control over the intellectual property created by users. Questions of technical infrastructure and IP seem likely to persist with evolving generations of technology-enhanced learning, and universities will have to decide on the extent to which they are willing to depend on for-profit businesses for the kinds of experiences offered by *Second Life* and its competitors, such as *There* or *ActiveWorlds*. Alternative, open-source educational platforms, such as *Croquet,* have also appeared in recent years. High development and maintenance costs that sustain these fast-moving technologies will pose ongoing challenges for commercial as well as nonprofit developers. A key factor in the evolution and adoption of these platforms will depend upon universities' dispositions toward questions of intellectual property and control over the "content" of university education.

Importantly, in courses such as CyberOne, the design and development of the course curriculum is not driven by the affordances of any one technological platform. Instead, the course has been designed as an "information space" that crosses multiple platforms, from the physical classroom at the law school to the virtual spaces in *Second Life* and 2D Web tools. In this case, strategies of curriculum design closely resemble information architecture, with significant challenges posed by the mapping of potential paths through dynamic pools of course content. The lesson, drawn most clearly from the experience of CyberOne, is that no one platform alone is sufficient to create a full range of learning opportunities for a generation of digital learners. Flexibility, hybridity, and multiplicity are of crucial importance.

Media Rich: The Institute for Multimedia Literacy

The pedagogical experiments and research conducted at USC's Institute for Multimedia Literacy (IML) over the past decade are illuminating with regard to the creative uses of media rich authoring.[21] Initially funded by a grant from Atlantic Philanthropies in 1998, the IML was housed within the Annenberg Center for Communication at the University of Southern California until 2005. It has since been incorporated into the School of Cinematic Arts, from which it administers two undergraduate programs across the curriculum at USC. The Honors in Multimedia Scholarship Program is a four-year, undergraduate program open to students across the university, while the Multimedia in the Core program introduces multimedia authoring into the University's General Education program via single-semester classes designed to reach as broad a sector of the undergraduate population as possible. Although these two programs are very different in conception, support, and implementation, they represent viable approaches to thinking about the future of digital education.

The IML is devoted to the idea that, in order to be fully literate in today's world, students should be able to read and write using the languages of multimedia as readily as they read and write using text. Critical focus at the IML has emphasized developing analytical skills related to culture, media, and technology across a range of traditional academic disciplines. Because it is housed within the USC School of Cinematic Arts, the IML draws deeply on traditions of visual expression, narrative, and sound, which are often underrepresented in conventional academic production. Additional emphasis is placed on the emerging use of interactive media, ranging from games to immersive and mobile experience design. The goal of the IML programs is to explore the full range of expressive potentials offered by moving images, sound, and interactive media, with a continuing emphasis on the integration of text as part of the expressive palette of multimedia.

However, equally importantly, the IML seeks to address an urgent need within academia to keep pace with the "real-world" knowledge and experience of incoming college students. The IML believes that if the academy wants to retain its relevance in a shifting cultural landscape, it must actively identify and engage with emerging practices in these areas. At the same time, the IML programs are explicitly designed to be transformative. They seek to educate a new generation of students and faculty in strategies to enhance traditional academic practices through the use of multimedia modes of expression. In the end, students at the IML are expected not only to be multimedia literate, but also to be critically aware of the embedded social, political, and cultural values surrounding the uses of media, and ultimately to use this set of new communication tools in both creative and scholarly ways. The long-term goals of the Institute are to define and expand emerging scholarly vernaculars at the levels of undergraduate, graduate, and faculty publication and pedagogy.

Participants in IML programs learn to "write" multimedia by first learning to critically read it. Students develop proficiency with the modes of formal analysis required for the critical evaluation of a wide range of multimedia artifacts—including images, video, sound design, information visualization, typography, interface design, and interactivity. In addition, students become familiar with the major theoretical frameworks guiding the development of contemporary multimedia applications and interactive experiences. One of the key concerns of multimedia pedagogy is ensuring that students avoid the uncritical adoption of conventions of commercial or entertainment media. The IML curriculum addresses this concern by exposing students to a broad range of multimedia genres—such as argumentative, documentary, essayistic, experiential, game-based, narrative, and archival forms—and by teaching the relative strengths and weaknesses of each. In their own projects, students are required to justify their authoring and design decisions to demonstrate that their use of media and techniques are appropriate to their overall communicative goal.

As students become critical readers of multimedia, they also learn to produce it in a scholarly way. Students gain experience in both individual and collaborative forms of multimedia authorship. Rather than positioning "multimedia literacy" or "scholarly multimedia" as an emerging field, the IML focuses on developing strategies of integration with existing disciplines and academic practices. The strength of the IML methodology is its modeling of pedagogical practices that are highly mutable, scalable, and flexible in implementation. Thus, IML classes are routinely taught within disciplines as diverse as history, philosophy, religious studies, geography, linguistics, and anthropology, as well as more traditionally visually-oriented fields, such as cinema, communications, visual arts, and art history. The IML methodology, which is drawn significantly from the fields of cinema studies and communication, is readily adaptable to fields within the humanities and social sciences, many of which are in the process of adapting to accommodate or experiment with audio/visual expression and different forms of electronic publication and technologically enhanced teaching. "Multimedia," in these contexts, functions essentially to catalyze, refine, and promote innovations in research and pedagogy that are already emerging organically within various fields.

In consultation with faculty, teaching assistants, and IML staff members, students learn to choose appropriate media platforms for their projects, including video and audio productions, interactive DVDs, Web sites, games, exhibitions, and installations. This wide range of authoring modes necessitates a highly skilled and diverse support structure, which includes teaching assistants, technical support staff, and student mentors, in addition to full time faculty. This is clearly one of the limitations to the portability of IML's media-rich learning approach. During the first eight years of its existence while the IML enjoyed the generous support of Atlantic Philanthropies, the Institute employed a wide range of teachers, researchers, and media production specialists to facilitate and support the production of students' multimedia projects. The challenge facing the IML in its next phase is to create a new structure for the support and delivery of its pedagogical activities. As large-scale funding opportunities, such as those provided by Atlantic, become increasingly difficult to obtain, the lessons learned by IML must be disseminated and adapted to the shifting landscapes of higher education.

The first step that is already in place is to create a pipeline program that employs undergraduate students who have successfully completed an IML course as peer mentors who coach other students in the use of various media applications. As is true with other peer-to-peer systems, both sets of students learn something valuable: in mentoring a peer, the mentor's intellectual and technical understandings are reinforced and refined. The one who is being mentored learns how to respect peers for the knowledge they offer. A second step is to create the conditions for the development of a "crew culture." This is the process whereby less advanced students (sophomores and juniors, for example) serve as members of production teams for more advanced students (graduating seniors or graduate students). Again, the peer-to-peer structure not only supports informal learning activities, but also contributes to a vibrant creative environment. Students across grade levels not only learn from each other, but also they learn that they are part of a community-of-practice. This is an important part of social literacy that all students need to learn: how to interact with people who have different skill sets, different levels of expertise, and different intellectual and cultural profiles.

As university culture gradually shifts toward greater acceptance of technologically-enabled scholarly practice, numerous questions remain. Expensive, centralized technical infrastructures that have inhibited the development of programs such as the IML at many institutions are likely to become increasingly irrelevant. The ability to capture, process, store, and disseminate data intensive media projects is becoming increasingly accessible to both students and faculty as part of consumer grade computer hardware and software. Likewise, the emergence of peer networks and viral culture promises to radically decenter the hardware infrastructures (e.g., computer labs and media centers) traditionally provided by universities. A more important and viable legacy of programs, such as the IML, is the development of protocols for conceiving, implementing, and evaluating emerging forms of scholarship. In an evolving educational landscape where every computer user is a potential media producer, critical paradigms, reflective practices, and effective assessment protocols may prove to be the key to a successful learning environment.

A Manifesto for Original Synners

By way of conclusion, we offer the following assertions in the style of a manifesto that takes seriously the challenge to address the disposition of the *born digital* generation of Original Synners.

Teachers Should Also Be Synners

The need to learn practices of creative synthesis cuts across all levels of digital learning. Technologically enhanced teaching strategies too easily go astray when they are driven by the affordances of technology rather than proceeding from a clearly articulated set of philosophical and pedagogical commitments. This is particularly true of new technologies that promise utopian visions of the future and appear to provide easy answers to perennial challenges. The persistent difficulties of education in both traditional and technologically enhanced environments are not going away any time soon, and we should assume that any electronically enabled learning strategies will bring with them new problems, as well as opportunities for productive experimentation. We must therefore proceed from a set of flexible commitments that find resonances in the technologies we elect to use and develop. We understand that literacies develop within a rapidly evolving matrix of social practices, technologies, and communicative conventions. In order to participate actively in the most dynamic spheres of learning, educators must assume responsibility for developing their own technical skills and pedagogical vocabulary. Although an admittedly daunting prospect for many, we believe that this is a crucial aspect of developing an effective pedagogy for the future. In this sense, the teachers too are synners of another order.

Mobilize Existing Dynamic Vernaculars

Foremost among our polemical commitments is the need to speak to students using languages and technologies they understand and value. This means that educators must develop the ability to speak, write, and—equally important—read in an evolving, dynamic vernacular that takes account of emerging social practices as well as technological capabilities. We should avoid approaches that involve grafting technologies onto existing teaching methodologies and vice versa. Many decades of experiments have shown that new methods of "teaching with technology" offer as many pitfalls as advantages. The uneasy hybridization seen in Web cast lectures and audience-response clickers demonstrates what is, in our view, a limited approach to integrating technology into education. Even some of the most promising contemporary technologies that merge the advantages of networked communities with social software, such as blogs and wikis, may in some cases simply function as high-tech updates of timeworn practices, such as classroom journaling and shared notetaking. Instead, we advocate a model that is genuinely organic in conception, centered on the development of pedagogical strategies that are inextricably fused with the technologies and social practices familiar to students of the *born digital* generation. But while such collective social practices may come naturally to members of this generation, we believe that there is value in theorizing and developing self-awareness about the functioning of an evolving literacy that is both participatory and collaborative.[22]

Critique the Tools

In practical terms, classroom technologies must be critically evaluated, analyzed self-reflexively, and understood as part of broader cultural, economic, and political contexts. Inviting students to think critically about both the tools of technology and the uses to which they may be deployed is an empowering gesture that resonates at every level of educational exchange. This helps to position the tools of electronically enhanced learning in a zone that is resistant to the extremes of utopian techno-fetishism and technological determinism. As many cultural critics have argued, these technologies are neither good nor bad, they are both/and. This makes the process of technology assessment more difficult, but it is the necessary foundation for robust creativity.[23]

The nearly century-old strategy of defamiliarization offers a useful approach to contemporary technologies whose uses are increasingly conventionalized and naturalized. While cultural facility with and acceptance of these technologies is extremely effective for the purposes of market penetration, the transparency of media and technology may serve to obscure their ideological and historical embeddedness. Principles of "good" design that dictate the clear presentation of information, a navigational scheme that is readily discernible and an interface that facilitates access to the full range of content in a given project may all be strategies that are deliberately avoided, resisted, or problematized.

So, for example, a project seeking to critique public discourse surrounding video games and violence might begin by inviting users into a game space, where the user must answer a series of questions in order to move through multiple levels of information on the topic. The use of interface metaphors that echo the content of a project is common practice and can effectively convey a cohesive relationship between form and content. The pleasures of game play could likewise be mobilized in service of the project's goals, encouraging users/players to explore, think critically about the subject, and perhaps test their own reactions to relevant examples. On the other hand, an interface that resisted or drew attention to the conventions of game design or navigation might prove to be equally effective, encouraging the user to be aware of the apparatus of the computer, his or her own expectations, and perhaps mobilize the equally powerful effects of strategic frustration, uncooperative technology, and recalcitrant design. Thus, perhaps a user would experience a simulated "crash" at a strategic moment or attempts to navigate through the project would be deliberately frustrated and the user would be invited to reflect on the intensity and emotional quality of their reaction in relation to the debate over game violence.[24]

Against the Grain of Technology

We believe that a creative relationship to educational technology proceeds from the assumption that tools are made to be broken, misused, disassembled, reverse-engineered, hybridized, and brushed against the grain. We must be willing to invest a certain amount of effort in the sometimes difficult process of engaging with the way technology functions, both at the level of hardware and of code. Databases and object-oriented programming, for example, offer both powerful technical capabilities and rich metaphors for describing emerging configurations of intellectual thought and practice. The goal is not necessarily to become professional technologists, but to develop greater sophistication in our own technologized practices so that we may continue to play an important role in the education of these students-of-the-future. They need us as guides, as coaches, and as voices of support and challenge. In the end, we must be willing to adapt, evolve, and productively fail. We must consciously decide which aspects of the teaching/learning process we are unwilling to compromise and develop boundaries that are firm but moveable. And finally, we must proceed from an ethics not only of education, but of technology as well.

Try Nonstandard Tools
An ethical approach to technology will maintain a degree of skepticism about the consumerist frenzy surrounding the hardware and software industries. Work created with low-tech alternatives and underutilized tools may help resist the allure of high-tech commercial production values. Indeed, deliberately low-tech, DIY or handmade esthetics may well prove to be more interesting and creativity-inducing than the conventions that commercial media production and "industry standard" tools tend to offer. Put bluntly, we believe that the technologies and authoring strategies we use in the classroom should reflect and reinforce the values we hold in the realms of culture and pedagogy. To this end, we see great potential in making use of the rapidly expanding range of free and open-source software tools that are currently available and in creating awareness about the ideological and historical embeddedness of any technology.

Among the numerous, powerful commercial software applications that are widely used in educational contexts, Adobe's Flash and Director offer students the ability to develop skills with "industry-standard" development platforms. Likewise, video editing and handling programs such as Apple's Final Cut Pro and DVD Studio Pro, Adobe's Premiere and Encore DVD, and Avid Xpress familiarize students with tools and conventions that are analogous to those used in commercial film and television postproduction. And, while there is value in providing students with "real-world" technical skills that may assist them with obtaining internships or entry-level jobs upon graduation, an equally convincing case may be made for an approach that emphasizes *teaching students how to teach themselves software*. We believe that this will produce students who are able to move more fluidly from one platform to another, to adapt to new applications or revisions of existing programs, and most importantly, to develop their own conceptual literacy about how software functions and the uses to which it may be put.

Thus, in conjunction with introducing commercial software, we advocate exposing students to authoring tools that function outside of a commercial economy. Examples include a free, downloadable program called the Korsakow System, an interactive media-handling program developed by Florian Thalhofer at the University of the Arts in Berlin.[25] Korsakow allows users to create sophisticated interactive experiences without the need for specialized programming knowledge or database support. Principles of interface design and interactive structures may be fruitfully experimented with by using a number of low-cost authoring tools based on Apple's QTVR format. Dating back to the early 1990s, the often-overlooked QTVR format allows designers to embed hotspots and links to external media objects or Web pages within a dynamic, panoramic interface format. The QTVR format has often been regarded as a novelty in spite of its surprisingly versatile range of interface possibilities and crossplatform Web deliverability. Another free, open-source alternative to electronic book publishing and mainstream programs, such as Adobe Acrobat, may be found in *Sophie*, a product of Voyager founder Bob Stein's Institute for the Future of the Book.[26] Building on the success in educational circles of its predecessor, *TK3*, *Sophie* promises to deliver a rich text- and media-based authoring environment for nontechnical users without the need for design or programming experience. Finally, basic principles of code may be taught using free software programs, such as Ben Fry and Casey Reas' *Processing*,[27] or the coding language designed at the MIT Media Lab to introduce children to graphical programming, *Scratch*.[28] The limited range and noncommercial aspirations of such programs places emphasis on developing conceptual sophistication rather than final polish. We believe that this emphasis on process over product may allow students to pursue more experimental, concept-driven creative and critical production.

Our challenge as educators, once students learn how to critically synthesize knowledge from the information that comes to them from multiple sources, in multimediated forms, and through multiple social networks, is to teach them a value proposition: How will they create culture differently? This shifts the discussion about the purposes of education into a different register: one that focuses not on the act of critical consumption, but rather on the act of creative production. The real digital divide may be more about the differences among those who consume what others produce, and those with access to the tools and the intellectual frameworks to create the stuff that circulates via these mixed reality networks. Our challenge is to help Original Synners understand not only their creative potential as cultural prosumers, but also their role as cultural mediators of the futures we all will inhabit.

Back to the Future

Let us return once more to the fictional future scenario to consider one more possibility inherent in the wide-scale adoption of digital learning as a new educational paradigm. In our enthusiasm to explore the possibilities of distributed online digital learning spaces, we may set in motion a movement that radically evacuates the communal rituals of learning and teaching. Another possible *unintended* consequence of the turn to digital learning as an educational platform is the creation of a class system that institutionalized differential access to embodied, communal ritualized learning experiences. In this version of the digital divide, those without resources are consigned to virtual worlds and online courses, where they never meet face-to-face with teachers, coaches, or peers. In this scenario, only the wealthiest of students will be able to afford to engage the personal attention of a teacher or professor, to be in-residence in specially equipped learning environments, and to learn the hands-on skills that require individualized instruction and coaching. The new digital learning spaces may indeed foster the development of new social rituals and logics of sociality, but they will be dramatically impoverished by virtue of the radical disembodiment of all participants. This suggests yet another commitment that must be addressed in creating a pedagogy for Original Synners: the need to remember the importance of embodied learning, teaching, and making, which is to say that the deployment of new digital tools and learning spaces must involve embodied social interactions for the purposes of community building and material world building. Our futures depend on it.

Notes

1. Raymond Williams might have called this sensibility the generation's dominant "structure-of-feeling." We use the term "disposition" to make connections with the work of John Seely Brown and

Douglas Thomas who analyze the contours of gaming disposition for the purposes of elaborating the educational potential of gaming paradigms.

2. Science fiction readers will recognize references to the following: Octavia Butler's *Xenogensis* Trilogy; Orson Scott Card's *Ender's Game* series; and the Akira manga series. The game assessment grid is inspired by the Piers Anthony *Apprentice Adept* series. Ditto blanks are mentioned in David Brin's novel, *Kiln People* (2002). Biolution devices are biological manufacturing systems/devices from Paul Black's novel, *The Tels* (2003). Rudy Rucker developed the concept of Flickercladding in his novel *Wetware* (1988). Bush robots—branching "ultra-dexterous" robots—were first envisioned by Hans Moravec in 1997, but also show up in numerous science fiction works. Tracer birds—a mechanical surveillance drone—are mentioned in Roger Zelazny's novel *Changeling* (1980). Extra-factual memories were central to the Philip K. Dick novel, *We Can Remember It for You Wholesale* (1966). Schooling ship-bound children of the crew of off-world exploration missions was referred to in various *Star Trek* episodes. Serious gamers will understand the references to the *Tomb Raider* games; board game historians will recognize the TDK classic called *The Stupid Game*.

3. A Delphi group is a large group of people used as a statistical sampling resource.

4. As of early 2007, MIT's Open CourseWare consortium includes universities on five continents. http://ocwconsortium.org (accessed June 2007).

5. http://www.cmu.edu/oli.

6. http://cnx.org (accessed June 2007).

7. http://openlearn.open.ac.uk (accessed June 2007).

8. Open source software is one mode of nonhierarchical, communal programming in which a loosely affiliated network of programmers contribute their efforts to a code base without direct compensation. With some exceptions, the resulting software may be used in commercial applications as long as the code remains openly available and changeable by members of the community at large. At present, the commercial impact of open source programming on internet-based technologies is incalculable, with the majority of network servers, databases, and operating systems utilizing some form of open source software.

9. http://creativecommons.org (accessed June 2007).

10. http://archive.org (accessed June 2007).

11. http://eff.org (accessed June 2007).

12. http://www.opensource.org (accessed June 2007).

13. http://www.prelingerlibrary.org (accessed June 2007).

14. As open source movements proliferate throughout global technological cultures, we anticipate an increased interest in the development of open (educational) content. Although a bit off topic for this essay, this cultural movement will also be helped by an increase in public animosity in response to lawsuits over copyright infringement from the entertainment industries.

15. http://www.oercommons.org (accessed June 2007).

16. A "mashup" may be defined as a combination of two or more data sets or information processing tools that create access to new constellations of meaning. For example, a tool that combines the Google maps API with the geographic tags deployed by users of the Flickr photo sharing service results in a mashup in which photos are displayed on a map in proximity to the locations where they were taken (see Stamen Design's Mappr at http://www.mappr.com) (accessed June 2007).

17. http://radar.oreilly.com/archives/2006/03/etech_linda_stone_1.html (accessed June 2007).

18. See, for example, Justin Hall and Scott Fisher's "Experiments in Backchannel: Collaborative Presentations Using Social Software, Google Jockeys and Immersive Environments" presented at the CHI conference in April 2006. http://nvac.pnl.gov/ivitcmd_chi06 (accessed June 2007).

19. Homi Bhabha, *Nation and Narration* (New York: Routledge, 1990), 227.

20. According to Brown and Duguid, conversation among peers is what transforms copresent groups of students into interpretive communities, capable of analyzing and reaching consensus about matters of significance in their lives. "The University in the Digital Age" (2003). http://www.johnseelybrown.com/DigitalU.pdf (accessed June 2007).

21. Anne Balsamo is the Director of Academic Programs and Research at the Institute for Multimedia Literacy; Steve Anderson is the Director of the Honors in Multimedia Scholarship program at the Institute for Multimedia Literacy.

22. A particularly promising attempt to synthesize these practices in terms of "literacy" is Howard Rheingold's collectively authored "Participatory Media Literacy" wiki: http://www.socialtext.net/medialiteracy (accessed June 2007).

23. See Anne Balsamo's forthcoming book, *Designing Culture: A Work of the Technological Imagination* (Durham, NC: Duke University Press), for a discussion of the philosophical foundation of robust technological imagination.

24. This example is based on an undergraduate multimedia project titled "Videogame Subjectivity," created at the Institute for Multimedia Literacy in Fall 2004 by Erik Gieszelmann and Grant Toeppen.

25. The Korsakow System is distributed free of charge for non-commercial uses by the Korsakow Foundation, a non-profit organization supported by Mediamatic Amsterdam http://www.korsakow.com.

26. See http://www.futureofthebook.org.

27. http://processing.org.

28. http://scratch.mit.edu (accessed June 2007).